Autism

Teaching DOES Make a Difference

Autism

Teaching DOES Make a Difference

Brenda Scheuermann
Southwest Texas State University

Jo Webber
Southwest Texas State University

WADSWORTH
CENGAGE Learning

Australia • Brazil • Japan • Korea • Mexico • Singapore • Spain • United Kingdom • United States

WADSWORTH
CENGAGE Learning

Autism: Teaching DOES Make a Difference
Brenda Scheuermann, Jo Webber

Education Editor: Dan Alpert

Associate Development Editor:
Tangelique Williams

Editorial Assistant: Alex Orr

Marketing Manager: Becky Tollerson

Marketing Assistant: Adam Hofmann

Project Manager, Editorial Production:
Trudy Brown

Print/Media Buyer: Karen Hunt

Permissions Editor: Joohee Lee

Production Service: Carlisle Publishers
Services

Copy Editor: Lorretta Palagi

Cover Designer: Lisa Buckley

Cover Image: © Knauer/Johnston/Photonica

Compositor: Carlisle Communications, Ltd.

For product information and technology assistance, contact us at
Cengage Learning Customer & Sales Support, 1-800-354-9706
For permission to use material from this text or product,
submit all requests online at **www.cengage.com/permissions**
Further permissions questions can be emailed to
permission request@cengage.com

Library of Congress Control Number: 2001026929

ISBN-13: 978-1-56593-894-6

ISBN-10: 1-56593-894-1

Wadsworth Cengage Learning
20 Davis Drive
Belmont, CA 94002-3098
USA

Cengage Learning is a leading provider of customized learning solutions with office locations around the globe, including Singapore, the United Kingdom, Australia, Mexico, Brazil, and Japan. Locate your local office at:
www.cengage.com/global

Cengage Learning products are represented in Canada by
Nelson Education, Ltd.

To learn more about Wadsworth, visit **www.cengage.com/wadsworth**

Purchase any of our products at your local college store or at our preferred online store **www.cengagebrain.com**

Printed in the United States of America
7 8 9 10 11   20 19 18 17 16

Contents

5   Teaching: General Strategies   123

6   Remediating Deficits in Speech and Language   165

7   Remediating Deficits in Socialization   201

8   Remediating Deficits in Life Skills   223

9   Understanding Intervention Controversies   248

Index   279

Preface

This is a book for practitioners who work with children and youth with low-functioning autism and related disorders, a difficult job under the best of circumstances. The syndrome of autism is an intriguing disorder, often characterized by disturbing behaviors such as self-stimulation or self-abuse, a lack of interest in social interaction, and absent or unusual communication. It is a condition that generates the full spectrum of intense emotions in educators, parents, and other caregivers: determination, frustration, commitment, discouragement. Perhaps more than any other disability area, the field of autism is characterized by a continual search for "what works." What methods will produce a shift from social isolation to social interest? What are the most effective strategies for increasing meaningful communication? And perhaps the question of greatest concern: What can we do about the challenging behaviors so commonly exhibited by students with autism?

Our experiences with teachers of students with autism lead us to conclude that too often, educators and other caregivers are charged with providing educational programs for these students without the background, training, or resources necessary to guide their efforts effectively. This book is part of our effort to remediate that problem. We have designed the book to provide critical information for educational planning for teachers, parents, and other caregivers. Throughout the book, we have tried to present state-of-the-art information in a step-by-step, user-friendly format.

The field of autism is inundated with an incredible range of treatments, philosophical approaches, and intervention recommendations. It seems that we are constantly learning about "new, highly effective" programs that provide "the answer" for the behavioral, communication, or so-cialization problems associated with autism. Television, magazines, the Internet, books, and even word-of-mouth are all sources for spreading the word about new programs. Unfortunately, too often, intervention programs are touted without any scientific evidence of effectiveness. Too often, intervention approaches are adopted on the basis of testimonials, convincing advertising slogans, or simply what is popular at the moment. We believe that implementing interventions without first demanding rigorous evidence of effectiveness is, at best, a waste of valuable time and, at worst, reduces the likelihood of positive long-term outcomes.

The good news is that among the proliferation of questionable and unproven approaches are techniques that have extensive scientific support. This means that these techniques have been tested under a variety of conditions and, more often than not, have been shown to produce positive changes in one or more aspects of behavior. These techniques are part of a field known as "applied behavior analysis," a robust set of principles and procedures for generating behavioral change.

Like most disabilities, there is no quick or easy answer—there is no cure for autism. This is not to say that children with autism cannot be helped. The "answer," we believe, lies in the approaches described in this book. That is, careful, systematic application of the strategies and methods of applied behavior analysis. Correct use of these techniques will improve the prognosis for most students with autism. We believe autism is a lifelong disorder, meaning that aspects of the condition will probably always be present. However, well-planned and accurately implemented applied behavior analytical interventions will increase the potential for more independent and mainstream functioning.

This book includes several unique features. First, throughout this book, we describe the evidence behind the techniques presented, plus we have attempted to show why these techniques are effective with individuals with autism. We are not bound to any particular program or philosophy; rather, we believe that elements of many of these programs can be combined to more effectively meet the needs of students with autism. In addition, we have tried to explain how to use the techniques in clear, step-by-step fashion, with many examples illustrating use of the techniques under a variety of conditions. Because these strategies are seldom applied in isolation, we have made an effort to show the relationship between various areas throughout the book. For example, we discuss socialization interventions with reference to communication and managing challenging behavior. Also, throughout the book, we have addressed the curricular needs of school-aged children, from early childhood to adolescence. Finally, we are fortunate to have the contributions of Cheryl Archer, whose son, Jamie, has autism. Cheryl shares her family's experiences in dealing with the realization of Jamie's autism and the search for interventions that would at least buffer the devastating effects of his autism, if not cure him. Concepts and issues presented in the book are mirrored in an intensely personal and powerful way throughout Cheryl's story.

In each of the methodology chapters, we describe general information about the area addressed (e.g., communication, socialization). Next, we present assessment guidelines, always with regard to identifying socially valid skills to teach. Finally, we describe strategies that have been proven effective for the curricular area in question. We present these strategies within the context of how they are applied in school settings.

Chapter 1 presents an overview of autism, including a history of the condition, etiology, characteristics, and diagnosis and definition of autism and autism spectrum disorders. Family needs are also addressed here, and the first part of Cheryl's story is introduced. Chapter 2 describes the basic principles of applied behavior analysis with respect to application of ABA methods in classroom settings. Strategies for reducing challenging behavior are described in Chapter 3, with careful attention to using functional assessment to determine *why* those behaviors are exhibited, then designing interventions based on those hypotheses. A unique feature of Chapter 3 is that we describe possible interventions based on various functions of behavior. For example, we present different interventions for self-injurious behavior based on perceived functions of positive reinforcement, negative reinforcement, communication, and so forth. Chapter 4 describes how to develop curriculum for students with autism, and Chapter 5 presents a wide array of instructional strategies that are effective with students with autism. Chapters 6, 7, and 8 describe assessment and intervention strategies for communication, socialization, and life skills, respectively. Chapter 9, written by L. Juane Heflin and Richard L. Simpson, discusses a few of the intervention programs available for children and youth with autism, and presents guidelines for making program decisions. Finally, the rest of Cheryl's story is presented in Chapter 9.

We hope that this book helps teachers, parents, or other caregivers more effectively manage the challenges presented by children and youth with autism. Educational technology has much to offer this population. Without high-quality, long-term educational interventions, students with autism will probably make little progress toward more normalized and independent functioning. These students deserve better. The good news for educators and parents is that, as our title conveys, good teaching does indeed make a difference.

Acknowledgments

As with most books, this book has been enhanced by the efforts of many people. First and foremost, we wish to thank Cheryl Archer. We are well aware that writing her story stirred up many painful memories. Nevertheless, she was willing to share her experiences because she realized that school personnel could benefit from a parent's perspective. She also hopes that her experiences might help other parents. Thank you, Cheryl. You have added much to our book, and we are extremely grateful.

We wish to thank Juane Heflin and Rich Simpson for their work in Chapter 9. During the past few years, Juane and Rich have carefully analyzed many of the available programs for students with autism. We are indebted to them for their contributions to the field, and we believe our readers will benefit from their work.

Our students at Southwest Texas State University provided invaluable feedback about content and format. In particular, we wish to thank Jennifer Haines and Cara Weidman. They read the manuscript from a teacher's perspective. Much of their feedback, editing, and summaries are found in the finished product. We would also like to thank the following reviewers for their helpful suggestions during the preparation of this manuscript: J. Keith Chapman, University of Alabama; Linda Hickson, Columbia University; and Louise Keisker, Central Missouri State University. Many of our figures were developed through the skillful artwork of Amy Wilson and Lisa Adams on a short timeline. We thank them for their work and gracious, good humor.

We are grateful to our editors, Dan Alpert and Tangelique Williams, for their guidance, feedback, and assistance. They were quick to answer questions or provide needed information, and were patient with our queries.

We would be extremely remiss if we did not thank our husbands, Billy and Tom, and other family members who were forced to the "back burner" as the book progressed. To a person, they understood our distraction, and were untiring in their encouragement. Without their support, this project would not have been possible.

Finally, we would like to thank the students with autism and related disorders with whom we worked and their families. What appears in this book is a direct result of their teaching and sharing. We hope our work reflects positively on them.

1

✳

Overview of Autism

Did you know that:

- Special education for individuals with autism may have begun as early as the late 1700s?

- Autistic disorder is only one of many in an autism spectrum?

- Tantrums might be a way of asking for something?

- Teacher characteristics and beliefs may facilitate effective educational programming?

- Parents and families also need individualized support?

Autism is an intriguing disorder. Made popular by Dustin Hoffman's portrayal of a young adult with autism in *Rain Man,* this population has attracted the interest of many people. In fact, a sharp rise has been seen in the incidence of school-age students identified as autistic (approximately 34,000 in 1996–1997) (Sack, 1999), probably due to public awareness and better diagnostic procedures. However, the autistic syndrome is not new, and since the 1975 inception of P.L. 94-142, the Education for all Handicapped Children Act (renamed the Individuals with Disabilities Education Act [IDEA] in 1990), public school personnel have been developing educational programs for students with autism. Various educational approaches have been utilized with these individuals for more than 20 years with varying degrees of

success. We intend to share what we consider to be the most effective approaches.

This book is written primarily for practitioners, particularly for those who are concerned with educating young people with autism and related disorders. However, much of the content will also appeal to parents and family members who want to know more about the syndrome, and about ways to enhance growth and development in light of the associated characteristics. Although the terms *autism* and *autism spectrum disorder* pertain to individuals manifesting various combinations of characteristics, this book targets those individuals who also manifest mental retardation and relatively severe symptoms. For information pertaining to individuals at the mild end of the autism spectrum (e.g., with Asperger's syndrome) who require different curricula and instructional considerations we refer the reader to Myles and Simpson (1998) and Fullerton, Stratton, Coyne, and Gray (1996).

The content of this book will follow a logical progression from describing typical educational needs to delineating methods for addressing those needs. Thus, chapters will cover the topics of behavior management, curriculum development, instructional strategies, and special issues. After reading this book, practitioners should be able to develop an appropriate educational program for individual students with low functioning autism and related disorders.

HISTORY OF AUTISM

Researchers believe that individuals with autistic characteristics were living well before the 20th century. One of the most interesting accounts of such a child is described by Itard in 1803 (Itard, 1972). He wrote of a boy found living in the wilds of France who appeared to be about 11 years old. At the time he was found, the boy could not speak, did not try to communicate, preferred objects to human contact, displayed few adaptive behaviors, appeared to have perceptual difficulties, and often engaged in bizarre and inappropriate behaviors. Itard and his colleagues set out to socialize Victor, as he was named. The account of that process could be a lesson for special educators today. Victor was taught communication skills, self-help skills, attending, discrimination and imitation skills, and was often integrated into the community for dining and other functional activities. Certainly, Itard's careful account of Victor's progress in very specific skill areas and his constant questioning of his own expectations challenge us all to evaluate our intentions and our teaching techniques, and to document progress toward students' long term goals.

Despite Itard's early account of Victor, the syndrome of autism was not named and described as such until 1943 when Leo Kanner published his case material (Kanner, 1985). Kanner, a psychiatrist, described 11 children "whose condition differs so markedly and uniquely from anything reported so far, that each case merits . . . a detailed consideration of its fascinating peculiarities" (p. 11). The characteristics that these children had in common which set them apart from others included the following:

1. An inability to relate to others in an ordinary manner

2. An extreme autistic aloneness that seemingly isolated the child from the outside world

3. An apparent resistance to being picked up or held by the parents

4. Deficits in language including mutism and echolalia

5. In some cases, an excellent rote memory

6. Early specific food preferences

7. Extreme fear reactions to loud noises

8. Obsessive desire for repetition and maintenance of sameness

9. Few spontaneous activities such as typical play behavior

10. Bizarre and repetitive physical movement such as spinning or perpetual rocking

11. Normal physical appearance

Children who display these characteristics are often described as having classic Kanner syndrome. Despite the fact that Kanner (1985) surmised that these children came into the world *biologically* unable to form "affective contact" (p. 50), the comments that most define his work have to do with his observation that within this "autistic" group, "there were very few really warmhearted fathers and mothers" (p. 50). These observations set the stage for speculation that the condition was actually caused by cold, nonresponsive parents. Although a preponderance of current research has refuted that assumption, pointing directly toward organic causes such as genetic predisposition, abnormal brain structure, and abnormal brain chemistry (e.g., Harvard Medical School, 1997), many parents are still trying to overcome the guilt and the professional bullying associated with that initial blame.

Currently, several organizations serve parents and families of individuals with autism, their teachers, and other practitioners. Table 1.1 lists some organizations that provide resources, research findings, advocacy services, and training. It is highly recommended that parents and practitioners join appropriate organizations in order to keep abreast of current trends and issues in the field.

NATURE OF AUTISM

Current research supports the assumptions that autism is caused by neurological impairment affecting brain chemistry and/or brain structure (Harvard Medical School, 1997). The exact cause

Table 1.1 Parent and Professional Organizations Serving Individuals with Autism

Organization	Function
American Speech-Language-Hearing Association (ASHA) 10801 Rockville Pike Rockville, MD 20852 http://www.asha.org	Speech/communication resources
Association for Behavior Analysis (ABA) 258 Wood Hall, Western Michigan University Kalamazoo, MI 49008-5052 http://www.wmich.edu/aba/index.html	Behavior management research/resources
The Association for Severe Handicaps (TASH) 29 West Susquehanna Ave Suite 210 Baltimore, MD 21204 http://web.syr.edu/-thechp/subtash.htm	Professional training, advocacy, resources
Autism Research Institute 4182 Adams Avenue San Diego, CA 92116 http://www.autism.com/ari/	Parent/family advocacy, resources
Autism Society of America 7910 Woodmont Avenue, Suite 650 Bethesda, MD 20814-3015 Fax on-demand: 800-329-0899 http://www.autism-society.org	Parent/family resources, advocacy, training
Council for Exceptional Children 1110 North Glebe Rd. Suite 300 Arlington, VA 22201-5704 http://www.cec.sped.org	Special education resources, advocacy, training
Families for Early Autism Treatment (FEAT) P.O. Box 255722 Sacramento, CA 95865-5722 916-843-1536 http://www.feat.org	Parent support, newsletter/publications
MAAP Services, Inc. P.O. Box 524 Crown Point, IN 46307 219-662-1311 http://www.stepstn.com/nord/org	Newsletter/publications (high-functioning autism)
National Alliance for Autism Research (NAAR) 414 Wall Street, Research Park Princeton, NJ 08540 888-777-NAAR http://babydoc.home.pipeline.com/naar/naar.htm	Research publications

of the neurological impairment is not yet known, although many genetic links have been found (Autism Research Institute, 1998). Even though the exact etiology of the disorder is unknown, the symptoms are well defined, thus providing essential information for educational treatment.

Understanding how best to educate students with autism should be based on an understanding of autistic symptomology. Currently, treatment approaches are based on three main theories explaining the presence of common symptoms. The first theory, a **perceptual/cognitive theory,** posits that, due to brain malfunction, these children may have specific differences in their thinking ability and the way they receive external input (Schuler, 1995; Tager-Flusberg & Cohen, 1993). Researchers believe that they may be overly stimulated by auditory, visual, and tactile stimuli thus they need to withdraw, and have a very difficult time making sense of, or processing, physical phenomena.

Treatment of the disorder, given this perceptual/cognitive view, includes teaching students to attend to and communicate with people in socially appropriate ways. It also implies that a classroom needs to be highly structured and predictable (e.g., following the same schedule and routines every day), that methods should include primarily visual materials, and that external stimuli be kept to a minimum (e.g., no mobiles hanging from the ceiling, no wall decorations). Additionally, given the cognitive processing problems, it is recommended that information should be presented in ways that take those cognitive deficits into account, such as giving instructions one step at a time with no extraneous verbalizations (Grandin, 1995).

A second theory from a **developmental** explanation holds that brain malfunctions have caused individuals with autism to fail to meet typical developmental milestones in language, cognition, social, and motor domains. Because they are developmentally delayed, it is assumed that the student needs to progress through developmentally sequenced experiences in order to master necessary skills just as children without disabilities might progress (Twachtman, 1995). Developmental techniques might include environmental arrangements that encourage communication. For example, the teacher might have favorite items or foods present so that the student is motivated to make requests. This model might also include facilitating children's presumably natural desire to communicate by, for example, repeating the sounds/words they might emit. It might also include providing motor and sensory stimulation tasks to encourage language and cognitive development, such as having the child crawl or be pulled in a wagon, or providing colorful toys, music, and water play.

A third theory, the **behavioral** explanation, holds that the neurological impairment has prevented normal learning and resulted in severe **behavioral deficits** (i.e., most social, communicative, and imitative behaviors are not present) and some **behavioral excesses** (i.e., bizarre, aggressive, and noncompliant behaviors occur too frequently). Intervention within this view is based in **applied behavioral analysis (ABA),** and assumes that faulty learning can be corrected through an analysis of behavioral deficits and excesses and direct skill training. Appropriate behavior can be taught through the use of behavioral techniques such as direct instruction, antecedent control, reinforcement strategies, and reductive techniques. Instead of waiting for natural development to occur, many feel that the direct training of desired behavior is the best way to educate individuals with autism and related disorders (Heflin & Simpson, 1998; Simpson & Regan, 1988). To better illustrate these theories with regard to educational programs, Table 1.2 provides a list of educational techniques matched to each of the three theories.

The techniques presented in this book come primarily from the last theory described above, behavioral theory, for several reasons. First, the vast majority of current research regarding the effectiveness of instruction with students with autism has been conducted within a behavioral framework (Heflin & Simpson, 1998; Lovaas & Smith, 1989). Second, behavioral techniques have been used successfully with this population for more than 35 years, not including Itard's case analysis (e.g., Ferster, 1985). Third, special education teachers are typically taught to approach instruction utilizing behavioral principles. Thus, these techniques are compatible with most teacher training programs. Fourth, the behavioral approach provides for the best accountability system in terms of student progress.

Note that stressing this particular viewpoint of treatment does not preclude strategies that involve the provision of cognitive organizers such as color-coded materials, visual presentations such as picture-guided activities, and high-interest, func-

Table 1.2 Instructional Components by Theory

Perceptual/Cognitive Theory	Use visual cues such as pictures and color. Teach left/right and up/down orientation. Prevent loud noises and avoid excessive verbalizations. Establish and follow routines. Prepare child ahead of time for changes. Rehearse for new situations. Teach attending and imitating. Arrange the classroom using visual cues (e.g., carpet = leisure time activities) and avoid changing arrangement.
Developmental Theory	Provide many stimulating toys, objects, and people. Follow the child's interests. Take advantage of the teachable moment. When child appears interested, interact only as much as necessary for child to achieve independence. Refrain from direct guidance/commands/punishment. Repeat sounds/words as child spontaneously makes them. Encourage play and exploration. Provide gross motor opportunities and sensory stimulation.
Behavioral Theory	Teach compliance, attending, and imitating. Use one-to-one, trial-by-trial, and milieu training. Reinforce correct responding. Use prompting techniques. Provide intensive teacher-directed instruction. Train functional skills. Train to generalization. Use data-based instruction.

tional tasks such as making a sandwich. It does, however, assume a direct approach to teaching as opposed to an indirect, developmental one. This means, for example, that to teach a student to ask for a desired object, the teacher would show the student how to request the object, prompt the student to ask for the object, and reinforce the student for asking appropriately, rather than waiting for that skill to "unfold."

CHARACTERISTICS

Despite the various ways of explaining the syndrome of autism and related disorders, certain similar characteristics are usually present to some degree in all children with these diagnoses. In this book we will use the term **autism** to refer to individuals meeting criteria for autistic disorder or those with similar symptoms who also have mental retardation. Often these individuals are described as having **low functioning autism.**

Autism is believed to develop before a child is 3 years old and will last throughout a lifetime (American Psychiatric Association [APA], 1994). In most cases, symptoms might be noticed in early infancy, and even though the severity of symptoms might be alleviated, the syndrome is almost always recognizable in adulthood because of associated social judgment and empathy deficits. The incidence of autistic disorder is four to five times higher in boys, and most children with this disorder also have mental retardation (Wing, 1996). Those who use language to communicate and those with higher IQs have the best prognosis. A high percentage (approximately 25 percent) of these young people will probably develop seizure disorders in adolescence.

As previously mentioned, the characteristics of autism can be categorized as either behavioral excesses or behavioral deficits. For example, these children show many behaviors that are disturbing to those around them and sometimes dangerous to the child and others (e.g., aggression, self-abuse, and tantrums). We call these behaviors that happen too often *behavioral excesses.* These behaviors may get in the way of productive learning, cause the child to be punished, and make it very difficult to tolerate the child in normalized situations such as the community or general education activities. For this reason, it is very important to reduce or eliminate behavioral excesses. Chapters 2 and 3 will provide some effective techniques for alleviating these challenging behaviors.

Directly related to behavioral excesses are what we call *behavioral deficits.* That is, children with autism do not display adequate essential behaviors such as talking, dressing, reading, complying, and playing. Without essential functional behaviors, an individual is extremely handicapped. He cannot ask for what he wants. In this case, the communication deficit may lead to excessive tantruming as a method for getting his favorite food. A student who is not toilet trained must continue to wear diapers even when it is age-inappropriate to do so. He cannot make friends without appropriate socialization skills. She may not be able to live and work independently if she fails to develop essential life skills. It is believed that the more skills and abilities an individual lacks, the more that particular individual is forced to rely on inappropriate behavioral excesses for communicative and functional purposes. For example, a child who cannot ask someone to leave him alone may have to curl up in the corner and engage in self-stimulation to get the person to go away. A child who cannot ask to leave the cafeteria may resort to hitting in order to have the teacher remove her. A child who cannot communicate fright may scream instead. In Chapter 3 we will provide ways to determine how a student's excessive challenging behavior can be related to skill deficits, particularly communication deficits.

If behavioral excesses are linked to behavioral deficits, then it follows that teaching appropriate communicative and functional behavior is a primary goal. Chapters 4, 6, 7, and 8 will give information about assessing deficits and how to ameliorate them. Teaching appropriate behavior must also be part of the intervention package to reduce behavioral excesses. Educating individuals with autism

Table 1.3 Common Behavioral Deficits and Excesses

Deficits	Excesses
Receptive language	Tantrums
Expressive language	Screaming
Communicative intent	Self-stimulation
Social skills	Self-abuse
Self-care skills	Aggression
Compliance	Bizarre behaviors
Attending	Echolalia
Imitating	Perseveration
Auditory/visual discrimination	Refusing to follow directions
Work skills	
Leisure time skills/play skills	
Academic skills	
Eye contact	

and related disorders requires a balance of reductive techniques and good skill training strategies. As the individual masters communicative and functional skills, difficult behavior should diminish. Table 1.3 provides a list of common behavioral deficits and excesses present with the autistic syndrome.

Behavioral Deficits

An Inability to Relate. Common to nearly all individuals with autism, an inability to relate to others may be demonstrated in many ways:

- These children may exhibit a total absence of smiling in response to social situations. On the other hand, smiling and laughing may occur when there is no apparent reason to do so.

- These children often refuse to make direct eye contact, preferring instead to turn their heads and look out of the corner of their eyes.

- They almost all show an apparent preference for interaction with objects rather than people and may spend hours alone manipulating favorite articles, although usually not in the way the object was meant to be used. For example, a child may twirl a piece of string with one hand or flap objects against his palm. This preference for being alone is what prompted Kanner to choose the name *autism,* which is from the prefix "auto," meaning "self."

- Individuals with autism may have an aversion to physical contact. They typically do not like to be hugged, for example, even by parents. In fact, they may show distress, or no response whatsoever, when a family member attempts to show physical affection.

- Appropriate play behavior may be absent. A child with autism may repeatedly stack blocks in the same configuration and knock them down. Or he may turn a toy car over and spin the wheels rather than push it along the floor with accompanying "car noises." One student we knew had a favorite doll, but she didn't play with the doll in a typical fashion. Instead she dressed and undressed the doll over and over, always in the same sequence. Any type of play behavior will probably be stereotypic manipulation of toys or other objects. Individuals with autism do not typically share toys, nor display pretend, cooperative, or competitive play behaviors. Although they may be in proximity to other children, their play tends to remains isolated and object dominant (Schuler, 1995). This subsequent social isolation precludes the natural development of play behavior and further lowers the chance of natural reinforcement and age-appropriate peer models. Generally, children with autism have very restricted patterns of behavior, interests, and activities, and the activities that draw their interest are often nonfunctional.

- Children with autism often show no special recognition of parents, family members, or familiar people such as teachers. For example, a child with autism may show no response when a parent enters or leaves the room.

- These children usually show no desire to make friends. Typically they seem to be happiest when left alone. If other children are playing nearby, a child with autism will usually not show interest in interacting with them.

Lack of Functional Language. Language problems typically define autism. Many individuals with autism have no language at all and those who do normally do not appropriately integrate their language abilities into social interaction or emotional attachment (Frith, 1996). This inability to communicate in a functional manner may be the most handicapping of any of the symptoms of this disorder. Following are some specific language characteristics related to autism:

- Generally, most children with autism lack **communicative intent.** That is, they do not seem to want to communicate for social purposes, to get others to behave certain ways, nor to get others' attention (APA, 1994). These children seem to have few reasons to communicate because they have such restricted interests, so their motivation to learn language is generally lacking.

- It is thought that about 50 percent of these children are **mute**—possessing few or no verbal skills. They simply do not talk.

- Even when verbal language is present, frequent **echolalia** and **perseveration** may be observed. Echolalia means that the individual repeats words and phrases that have been uttered by someone else, even with the exact same intonation, with no appreciation of the conventional meaning. In other words, their utterances seem to be from rote memory rather than reflecting spontaneous speech. Nevertheless, echolalic speech can be communicative, serving to indicate turn taking, yes answers, requests, or declarations (Prizant, 1983). For example, a child may repeat a TV advertisement for a particular store when he wants to go for a ride in the car. Echolalia may be **immediate, delayed, or mitigated.** Immediate echolalia is a verbatim repetition of something someone just said, either the entire sentence or just a few words. Delayed echolalia is repetition of something heard at an earlier time, maybe on TV. Mitigated echolalia is repetition of something with some unique variation, usually in pronouns. For example, a child might say

"You like cookies" when another child said, "I like cookies." Perseveration means that the individual repeats the same words or phrases over and over, almost like verbal hyper-activity. Often the perseveration increases in times of high demand or anxiety such as when the child is frightened. Often, echolalic and perseverative speech is noncommunica-tive and not of much use to the individual.

- Those children with autism who have speech may show abnormal use of **prosody.** Prosody refers to voice tone and inflection. Individuals with autism typically speak in a monotone with little inflection. For example, a child requesting help when he is hurt may use the same tone and inflection as he does when requesting a cookie after dinner.

- Another interesting language characteristic is the preference for **pronoun reversals.** In other words, the child may use his name or the pronoun "you" when referring to "I." For example, "Do you want to go to the store?" means "I want to go to the store."

- Individuals with autism appear to show very little variety in their language. For example, they will use the phrase "You want out" to communicate wanting to have free time, go to the store, go for a ride, and other desired activities.

- Individuals with autism tend to be very **literal** in both expressive and receptive language. For example, Raymond, in *Rain Man,* waited at the crosswalk for the sign to flash "Walk." He then began to cross the street. The sign then changed to "Don't walk" before he reached the other side. Raymond stopped in the middle of the street even though cars were honking and people were yelling because he literally interpreted the crosswalk sign and refused to walk until it said so.

- Individuals with autism use **immature** grammar. For example, they will use only short sentences in a simple noun–verb format or often talk only in phrases (e.g., "Want the car?").

- Children with autism also tend to use limited **speech functions,** meaning they typically don't use language to converse, declare, or explore ideas (Schuler, 1995). Most often language is used only for requesting or protesting purposes.

- Language **comprehension** is generally limited although they seem to understand more language than they speak (Bondy & Frost, 1994). As mentioned before, these children tend to memorize only the literal meaning for words so that subtle meanings are not learned. An example is that of Raymond in *Rain Man,* who could repeat verbatim the comic bit about "Who's on first, what's on second," but had no idea that it was funny.

Sensory Processing Deficits. One rather fasci-nating characteristic of individuals with autism has to do with sensory processing (how auditory, visual, tactile, and other stimuli are perceived). Many individuals with autism underrespond to noise, touch, and sights. Originally, it was thought that they might be deaf or visually impaired. On the other hand, for some children, sensory percep-tion may be characterized by overresponding. Things that most of us would not notice draw this individual's attention. For example, a child may not react at all to very loud noises such as a fire alarm but notice immediately when a candy wrapper is crumpled a hundred feet away. Or an individual may not pay attention to a word on a card, but may focus intently on a small black dot on one corner of that card. The general belief is that the visual mode of input is preferred by most individ-uals with autism. Thus, it is often recommended that visual stimuli rather than verbal cues be used for instructional purposes and to help communi-cate environmental expectations. For example, as you will learn in Chapter 5, it may be helpful to use pictures for teaching a student to make a bed, rather than verbally explaining each step.

Cognitive Deficits. Much speculation surrounds the cognitive abilities and disabilities of individuals with autism. Although many children with autism have functional retardation and are unable to cope independently in the world, some show what is known as **islands of precocity** or **splinter skills.** That is, a child may be quite gifted in math computation but not be able to tell time or determine whether he has enough money to make a purchase. Common splinter skills include (1) calendar abilities, such as being able to give the day of the week for any date you might provide (e.g., May 12, 1896); (2) the ability to count visual things quickly, such as telling how many toothpicks are on the floor when a box is dropped; (3) artistic ability, such as the ability to design machinery; and (4) musical ability, such as playing the piano.

Due to language and perceptual problems, assessing cognitive functioning through intelligence tests becomes quite a challenge and may not be indicative of specific forms of intelligence. Children with autism are thought to display difficulty in coding and categorization of information, again relying on literal translations, and they seem to remember things by their location in space rather than through concept comprehension (Schuler, 1995). For example, "shopping" means going to a particular store on a particular street, rather than the concept of visiting any type of store, browsing around, perhaps buying something, looking through a catalog, or various other aspects of the concept of "shopping." In fact, it has been speculated that individuals with autism employ an "echo box-like memory store" (Grandin, 1995; Hermelin, 1976). This would explain why autistic children may excel at putting puzzles together and building things out of blocks, matching tasks, or drawing replicas. However, they tend to perform poorly on tasks requiring verbal comprehension and expressive language.

Behavioral Excesses

Not only do individuals with autism show many behavioral deficits, but many also possess a repertoire of behavioral excesses. Some of these excesses are thought to be a function of the nature of the disorder; that is, neurological differences. On the other hand, some excesses are believed to develop because of cognitive and language deficits. That is, when individuals cannot make their needs and wants known through functional communication, they must resort to a nonverbal means of communication, such as tantrums.

Self-Stimulation. One of the most noticeable characteristics of this population is a propensity to engage in **self-stimulation.** Self-stimulation is behavior that is repetitive and stereotypical in nature. For example, children with autism might engage in these activities:

- Spinning themselves and objects
- Repetitive hand movements
- Rocking
- Humming in a monotone
- Arranging and rearranging objects
- Twirling strings or ribbon
- Moving their hand between their eyes and a light to achieve a strobe effect
- Hand gazing
- Jumping up and down
- Gazing up at the ceiling or lights
- Smiling or laughing, not in response to social cues
- Compulsive eating

Self-stimulatory behaviors seem to occur for the purpose of obtaining sensory input. The high frequency of these stereotypical behaviors is what often sets this population apart. Many of us engage in some self-sensory input such as leg bouncing or nail biting when we watch TV or read. However, for people with autism, self-stimulation seems to be a highly preferred activity. Nothing, not even eating, seems to hold the same reinforcing value. Given the opportunity, a child with autism typically will engage in self-stimulation for very long periods of time and become very upset if interrupted. There is good news and bad news concerning this propensity to self-stimulate. The bad news is that, given the extremely high motivation to engage in self-stimulation, motivation to engage in more productive behaviors is diminished. The good news is that allowing students to earn self-stimulation time by completing learning tasks may provide the necessary motivation for the student to respond appropriately to instruction. Please note, however, that using self-stimulation as a reinforcer is controversial because it may be difficult to control its administration, because some forms of self-stimulation may be unhealthy (e.g., compulsive eating), and because of the unusual nature of many common self-stimulatory behaviors.

Resistance to Change. Because children with autism have a very narrow activity focus, they tend to show an extreme resistance to change in environment, food, room arrangements, familiar routes, and other established routines (Koegle, Rincover, & Egel, 1987). Presumably, this aversion to change has to do with cognitive processing characteristics. If external stimuli, as a rule, are difficult to comprehend, and individuals rely primarily on rote memory to create understanding, then change would only cause confusion and, in some cases, anxiety. For anyone with cognitive processing problems, a clear, predictable environment is indicated. If change needs to occur, then resistance can be alleviated through prior cognitive preparation. For example, if there is to be a family trip, begin talking about the trip a week or more before it is to occur. Describe exactly what will happen in regard to eating, sleeping, and so on, preferably in visual terms (e.g., what the motel room will look like). Also, it might be good to have a calendar hanging in the child's room with pictures of the car or the destination (e.g., grandmother's house) pasted on the days of the trip. Then have the child mark each day of the month with an "X" as it passes so that the impending trip will not be a surprise. At school, for example, if there is to be an assembly on Friday, the teacher could tell the student on Monday and each day thereafter about the assembly, where it is to be, what time it will be, how long it will last, what the behavioral expectations might be (e.g., sit on the floor with quiet

hands), and what will happen after it is over. Again, a calendar might be used to indicate each day's activity, and a destination card with a picture of the gym or auditorium given to the child on Friday morning with another verbal rehearsal before departing for the assembly.

Bizarre and Challenging Behaviors. Finally, individuals with autism often show bizarre and challenging behaviors. In some instances, they may display extreme fear reactions as Raymond, in *Rain Man,* did when the fire alarm went off. He screamed, held his hands over his ears, and slammed his head against the wall. In other cases they may not show typical fear reactions, such as with strangers or loud noises. Sometimes individuals with autism display many eating and sleeping disorders. For example, some may have **pica,** where individuals eat inappropriate objects like dirt and glass. Others may display problem behaviors, such as hyperactivity, short attention span, impulsivity, tantrums, aggression, and self-injurious behavior (SIB) (APA, 1994).

  Self-injurious behaviors certainly set this population apart. For example, individuals with autism may smash their heads on the ground or on a wall, pull their hair or bite their hands, gouge their eyes or hit themselves repeatedly, or hold their breath until they faint. Current thinking is that SIB and other challenging behaviors may have a communicative function (Durand & Berotti, 1991). This means that the child may be asking for something or asking to get out of something with these behaviors. One of the teacher's major instructional tasks is to teach these children an appropriate way to ask for what they want; providing other avenues for getting needs met usually reduces challenging behavior. This strategy and other reductive techniques will be discussed further in Chapter 3.

DIAGNOSES AND DEFINITIONS

Currently, children with autistic characteristics may be classified as having autism spectrum disorder, also known as **pervasive developmental**

disorder (PDD). Pervasive developmental disorder includes several differentiated disorders, including autistic disorder, but all are characterized by "severe and pervasive impairment in several areas of development: reciprocal social interaction skills, communication skills, or the presence of stereotyped behavior, interests, and activities" (APA, 1994, p. 65). Children with PDD display mild to severe neurobehavioral disorders and varying degrees of the characteristics described in the last section. Subtypes of PDD include autistic disorder, Asperger's syndrome, Rett's disorder, childhood disintegrative disorder, and pervasive developmental disorder not otherwise specified (PDD-NOS). Related disorders are differentiated from autistic disorder primarily by age of onset and the severity of other symptoms. Table 1.4 lists differential diagnostic indicators for these disorders.

At the mild end of the spectrum, students with **high-functioning autism** or **Asperger's syndrome** may have an average or above-average IQ and highly developed verbal skills. Nevertheless, they may communicate poorly, display poor social skills, have few friends, become upset if routines or expectations are violated, have learning difficulties

Table 1.4 Differential Diagnosis of Autism

Asperger's disorder is characterized by social deficits and restricted patterns of activities and interests; however, these individuals show few or no cognitive or language delays. They may possess motor clumsiness in early childhood.

Rett's disorder is diagnosed only in females, whereas autism is most common in males, and is characterized by physical and motor differences. Although these individuals show some difficulties in social interaction, they do not show the entire diagnostic pattern of autistic disorder.

Childhood disintegrative disorder shows a persistent decline in social, motor, and/or language skills after a few years of normal development.

Pervasive developmental disorder not otherwise specified (PDD-NOS) pertains to individuals who show patterns of the autistic syndrome but have a later age of onset than 3 years old, and/or only some of or less severe symptoms. Sometimes this is referred to as *atypical autism.*

From APA, 1994.

manifested in poor auditory processing, have poor motor skills including handwriting, and may show stereotypical behaviors (What is Asperger's disorder?, 1999). These children need interventions not unlike students with attention-deficit hyperactivity disorder (ADHD) and learning disabilities. These interventions include structured routines, tutoring, speech and occupational therapy, social skills training, cognitive behavioral interventions, contingency management, and individualized educational programs. In some cases, medication may be prescribed to relieve anxiety, psychotic responses, attentional deficits, and obsessive/compulsive behaviors (What is Asperger's disorder?, 1999). Most will have a good chance of functioning well as adults. However, children with more severe forms of PDD, particularly autistic disorder with mental retardation, need the instructional strategies described in this book.

Although autism is a disorder with relatively obvious and uniform characteristics, some variance is seen in the definitions used most often to describe the population. Definitions are developed for the purpose of identifying a distinctive group. If someone falls within a defined group, then it is assumed that services and treatment provided to others in that group might benefit this individual and that things that have failed to help others in the group will not help this individual. More importantly, funding, services, and advocacy are dispersed to populations who meet a particular definition. Table 1.5 provides the three most common definitions used to describe the autistic syndrome.

The Autism Society of America definition was originally developed in 1977 and recently revised (Autism Society of America, 2000). Note the emphasis on neurological dysfunction and the similarity to Kanner's original description. The IDEA or public school definition of autism was not added until 1990 as part of the amendments to P.L. 94-142, which created autism as a distinct category within special education. The *Diagnostic and Statistical Manual of Mental Disorders,* fourth edition (DSM-IV) (APA, 1994) provides the diagnostic guidelines developed by the American Psychiatric Association for the purpose of diagnosing psychological disorders. The DSM-IV description

Table 1.5 Autism Definitions

Autism Society of America (2000)

"Autism is a complex developmental disability that typically appears during the first three years of life. The result of a neurological disorder that affects the functioning of the brain, autism and its associated behaviors have been estimated to occur in as many as 1 in 500 individuals. Autism is four times more prevalent in boys than girls and knows no racial, ethnic, or social boundaries. Family income, life-style, and educational levels do not affect the chance of autism's occurrence.

Autism interferes with the normal development of the brain in the areas of social interaction and communication skills. Children and adults with autism typically have difficulties in verbal and non-verbal communication, social interactions, and leisure or play activities. The disorder makes it hard for them to communicate with others and relate to the outside world. They may exhibit repeated body movements (hand flapping, rocking), unusual responses to people or attachments to objects, and they may resist changes in routines.

Over one half million people in the U.S. today have some form of autism. Its prevalence rate now places it as the third most common developmental disability—more common than Down syndrome. Yet most of the public, including many professionals in the medical, educational, and vocational fields, are still unaware of how autism affects people and how to effectively work with individuals with autism" (p. 3).

Individuals with Disabilities Education Act (Martin, 1996)

. . . a developmental disability significantly affecting verbal and non-verbal communication and social interaction, generally evidenced before age 3 (34 C.F.R. ss300.7(b)(1)).

Diagnostic and Statistical Manual IV (APA, 2000. Reprinted with permission.)

A. A total of at least six items from (1), and (2), and (3), with at least two from (1), and one each from (2) and (3):
    (1) Qualitative impairment in social interaction, as manifested by at least two of the following:
        (a) Marked impairment in the use of multiple non-verbal behaviors such as eye-to-eye gaze, facial expression, body postures, and gestures to regulate social interaction
        (b) Failure to develop peer relationships appropriate to developmental level
        (c) Markedly impaired expression of pleasure in other people's happiness
        (d) Lack of social or emotional reciprocity
    (2) Qualitative impairments in communication as manifested by at least one of the following:
        (a) Delay in, or total lack of, the development of spoken language (not accompanied by an attempt to compensate through alternative modes of communication such as gesture or mime)
        (b) In individuals with adequate speech, marked impairment in the ability to initiate or sustain a conversation with others
        (c) Stereotyped and repetitive use of language or idiosyncratic language
        (d) Lack of varied spontaneous make-believe play or social imitative play appropriate to developmental level.
    (3) Restrictive repetitive and *stereotyped patterns of behavior, interests, and activities,* as manifested by at least one of the following:
        (a) Encompassing preoccupation with one or more stereotyped and restricted patterns of interest that is abnormal either in intensity or focus
        (b) Apparently compulsive adherence to specific, nonfunctional routines or rituals
        (c) Stereotyped and repetitive motor mannerisms (e.g., hand or finger flapping or twisting, or complex whole body movements)
        (d) Persistent preoccupation with parts of objects
B. Delays or abnormal functioning in at least one of the following areas, with onset prior to age three:
    (1) Social interaction
    (2) Language as used in social communication
    (3) Symbolic or imaginative play
C. Not better accounted for by Rett's Disorder or Childhood Disintegrative Disorder.

of autistic disorder also closely resembles Kanner's original definition. Unlike definitions of other special education categories such as emotional disturbance, definitions of autism do not significantly differ, so diagnosis of autism is fairly reliable. The important thing to remember is that educational programming for children and youth with any of these diagnoses will most likely be similar. However, school personnel should develop instructional programs based on individual assessments, rather than simply matching educational plans to diagnoses.

DIAGNOSTIC INSTRUMENTS

The diagnosis of autism is usually conducted by either psychologists, psychological associates, or psychiatrists who are trained to use the DSM-IV for that purpose (APA, 1994). However, many other assessment instruments are used for the diagnosis of autism, some of which can be completed by teachers and other school personnel. Many of the instruments are in the form of check-

lists and include subsections that address communication and interaction behaviors. Some of these instruments provide not only diagnostic information (e.g., whether or not the child is autistic) but information useful for educational programming (e.g., current level of language functioning). Table 1.6 presents a description of several instruments used for the purpose of diagnosing autism and for obtaining initial screening information regarding educational programming. More than one instrument should be used for these purposes to ensure reliability and a well-rounded view of the child. For more in-depth information regarding the diagnosis of autism, the reader is referred to an

Table 1.6 Sample Diagnostic Instruments

Autism Screening Instrument for Educational Planning (ASIEP), Krug, D. A., Arick, J. R., & Almond, P. J., 1980

This instrument can be used with preschool and school-age children suspected of having autism. It consists of five subtests (behavior checklist, sample of vocal behavior, interaction assessment, educational or functional skills, and prognosis of learning rate). The instrument can be used to differentially diagnose those with autism from those with other severe disabilities while giving useful information for placement, planning educational programs, and analyzing progress. The ASIEP requires some training, but can be administered by special education personnel.

Childhood Autism Rating Scale (CARS), Schopler, E., Reichler, R. J., & Renner, B. R., 1988

The CARS was developed to identify children with autism and distinguish them from those developmentally delayed children without autism. It can be used for ages 2 and above. It has 16 rating scores that result in a single score that indicates not only a differential diagnosis of autism, but also the severity of the disorder. It is an observational instrument that can be used in a variety of settings and may be used with information from the child's school and/or medical records. It takes minimal training to be able to use. It is recommended that it be used with other instruments to enhance reliability of diagnosis.

Psychoeducational Profile Revised (PEP-R), Schopler, E., Reichler, R. J., Bashford, A., Lansing, M. D., & Marcus, L. M., 1990

The PEP-R was designed more as an educational planning tool than a diagnostic instrument and is primarily used to identify the strengths, weaknesses, and learning needs for children with autism and related disorders ages 6 months to 12 years. It is not appropriately used for children who function above a first-grade level in most areas. The PEP-R has four subscores and a total score that in combination with other diagnostic instruments can indicate behaviors and learning patterns common to children with autism. It is best used for designing effective teaching techniques and educational programs for young children with autism.

Behavior Rating Instrument for Autistic and Other Atypical Children (BRIAAC), Ruttenberg, B. A., Kalish, B. I, Wenar, C., & Wolf, E. G., 1977

The BRIAAC was designed to measure the current functioning level of children with autism and other developmental delays. It is appropriate for children ages 3–12 years whose developmental level is below 5 years. It involves a 2-hour observation and rating of the child's social, motivational, and emotional behavior on eight subscales. It also provides a composite score, which provides a level of functioning and comparison to a typical 3- to 4-year-old child. Observers require intensive training (40–80 hours). The information can be used to assess the general level of autism, developmental status, and changes in the child over time.

Gilliam Autism Rating Scale (GARS), Gilliam, 1995

Another example of a rating scale, the GARS consists of four subtests listing typical characteristics of children and youth with autism. The subtests include stereotypical behaviors, communication, social interaction, and developmental disturbances manifested in the first 36 months of life. The rated characteristics closely match those described in the DSM-IV. The GARS can be completed by family members and special education personnel.

excellent issue of the *Journal of Autism and Developmental Disorders,* Volume 29 (Filipek et al., 1999). Keep in mind that a diagnosis gives only some of the necessary information needed for educational planning. Teachers will need to more fully assess specific educational need using the assessment methods described throughout this book.

PROGRAM CONSIDERATIONS

The presenting symptomology of individuals with autism can lead to impressive obstacles to learning. Not only do these students have language and behavioral disorders, but they also display perceptual deficits, limited comprehension abilities, social limitations, and interfering self-stimulatory responses. As a result they tend to develop few academic and functional skills when left to their own devices. Add to this list that these students are very seldom motivated to explore new environments, communicate their wants and needs, or participate in learning activities.

Another challenge is that students with autism may only attend to unimportant environmental cues and, thus, will struggle to learn discrimination tasks, the foundation for subsequent cognitive development. For example, a teacher may use two or three shirts to teach a student to sort white clothes from colored clothes for washing purposes. The student may notice that the shirt the teacher calls white has a tear on the sleeve and may separate that shirt each time from the other two, not on the basis of color, but on the basis of the sleeve tear. In this case, color discrimination was not learned, so that given different clothes, she probably will not be able to sort whites from colors. Additionally, individuals with autism tend to display idiosyncratic responses to typical reinforcers and punishers. That is, they do not prefer things that most other children enjoy, such as adult attention, but may enjoy things others do not like, such as social isolation. This challenging picture sounds discouraging in terms of educational potential. However, by utilizing techniques that result in direct skills training, that

bring clarity to a student's environment, and that accommodate the child's multifaceted needs, much can be done to alleviate the handicapping barriers common to this condition (Maurice, Green, & Luce, 1996). The critical task is to develop and implement a comprehensive, practical educational program.

A Practical Program

The first consideration for programming for this population is to establish a practical approach to education, one that is well founded in applied behavioral analysis. This approach should include clearly sequenced goals and objectives in the areas of communication, social competence, and functional life skills. It should also include direct instruction, probably in the form of trial-by-trial training, in an organized, predictable environment. Behavior management, including functional assessment, positive reductive techniques, and aversive consequences when necessary, should be an integral part of the program. Finally, a practical program will include ongoing data collection and evaluation in order to ensure that progress toward the goals continues in a consistent manner.

Clearly Sequenced Goals. Establishing educational goals depends not only on targets for current functioning but also consideration of the level at which students will need to function in the next few years and what skills they may need as adults. Assessment for educational programming calls for school personnel and parents to collaborate in pinpointing specific functional tasks that will serve the student well at home, in the community, and at school each year. It also requires speculation about and analysis of future placements. For example, if a student is to be transferred to a middle school in the next few years, it would be best to teach those skills that will be necessary for a successful transition. Additionally, goals should include consideration of the ultimate objective of preparation for independent functioning in normalized settings (Brown, Nietupski, &

Hamre-Nietupski, 1976). Later chapters explain how to conduct assessments to determine educational goals in all areas of functioning.

Direct Instruction of Skills. Functional goals are one aspect of a practical program; direct systematic instruction is another. Direct instruction implies that the teacher purposefully moves a student toward the designated goals utilizing a stimulus–response format. Direct instruction models usually include a multistep approach. First the teacher gains the student's attention, sometimes indicating what is to be learned (e.g., "Dana, look at me. It's time to work on your words"). Second, the teacher presents a stimulus, usually in the form of a command although it could also be a visual stimulus such as written directions. For example, the teacher may say "Dana, point to the word 'stop'." Third, the teacher may prompt the correct response by guiding the student's hand or by offering visual or verbal cues. Fourth, the teacher waits for the clearly defined student response (e.g., the student will point to the correct word card with the index finger within 10 seconds). Depending on the student's response, the teacher will now give a consequence or feedback as step 5. If the response was correct, the teacher may say "Good." If the response was incorrect, the teacher may not say anything, repeat the stimulus command, and provide more effective prompting. This drill-and-practice format has been found to be an effective instructional strategy for students with autism who need to learn new skills or to become fluent in skills already learned (Green, 1996).

Direct instruction allows for training skills in incremental steps (e.g., teaching each step for brushing teeth) or for teaching skills as whole tasks (e.g., teaching how to go through the cafeteria line as an entire process). In both cases, the teacher presents a cue, assists the student to respond correctly, identifies a correct response, and gives feedback to the student. Direct instruction can be used one on one or with groups of students. Direct instruction can be used to teach someone to talk, to read, or to compose a research paper. The point is that direct instruction provides clear expectations, assistance, and feedback, making the student's environment predictable and success more likely. Chapter 5 will provide more specific information about direct instruction strategies.

Direct instruction models also include ongoing assessment. Teachers will need to keep a record of correct and incorrect student responses. This type of assessment provides information as to whether the student is learning what the teacher intends to teach. Often these data are transferred to graphs, providing a visual presentation of the student's progress. This type of assessment forms the basis for revising goals, moving to new goals, or adapting instructional strategies. Without systematic program evaluation, the teacher may waste valuable instructional time either teaching things the student has already mastered or failing to teach things that the student needs to learn. Chapters 2 and 5 will provide more information on this type of assessment and evaluation.

Behavior Management. A third important component of a practical program involves behavior management. Because most students with autism display behavioral excesses, which will interfere with learning appropriate skills, teachers may find it necessary to apply strategies for reducing these excesses. It is generally recommended that an **instructional approach** to behavior management be utilized (Dunlap, Ferro, & Deperczel, 1994). An instructional approach to behavior management includes a **functional assessment** that will determine the relationship of the excessive behavior to environmental variables such as time of day or certain people. A functional assessment also provides information regarding the purpose of the student's excessive behavior (e.g., he gets out of the task when he tantrums).

After determining what might be cueing and maintaining an excessive behavior, an intervention plan is developed. This plan should include ways to change or eliminate environmental contributions to inappropriate behavior and ways to change things that might be happening apart from the school that might exacerbate inappropriate behavior (e.g., a new bus driver who yells). Additionally, the plan should include alternate appropriate, or replacement, behavior that the student needs to learn that will be functional for the student. In most cases, these replacement behaviors will be communicative. For example, if a student is thought to tantrum in order to get out of work, it would be best to teach him to say "out please" for that purpose. The plan should include strategies for teaching these replacement behaviors and for reinforcing their use. **Differential reinforcement** is an important component of this instructional approach. Sometimes additional reductive techniques, such as timeout or response cost, are needed so that the student can learn to respond in ways that will enhance learning. Chapters 2 and 3 provide specific information about reductive strategies and behavior management in general.

Ecological Assessment. One program component that almost guarantees an individualized, thus effective, educational plan is **ecological assessment**. Ecological assessment results in a list of skills that a particular student needs in order to function in settings in which she currently participates and those in which she will participate in the future (Browder & King, 1987).

First, an inventory of skills is constructed using checklists and/or direct observation. The subsequent inventory of necessary skills then becomes an assessment tool for determining the student's current functioning. Through further observations and interviews, the teacher can determine which of the skills listed on the inventory the student has already mastered, partially mastered, or still needs to learn. After delineating which specific skills remain to be learned, school personnel can work with parents to prioritize exactly what needs to be taught that will best meet the student's needs now and in the future. Chapter 4 will offer more specific information regarding ecological assessment.

Functional Skills. The ecological assessment process results in an emphasis on **functional skills** (those that an individual needs to perform

to avoid dependence on others) and on **age-appropriate** tasks. This means that educators must constantly evaluate curriculum for the purpose of weeding out those tasks that are not directly relevant to a particular individual in light of current and future performance. It also means choosing learning activities that meet a student's developmental and educational needs while reflecting activities in which other children of the same age participate. For example, a 17-year-old student who needs to practice fine motor skills would best be given a coffeepot to assemble rather than stacking colored blocks.

Attention to Generalization. Not only should functional age-appropriate skills be taught, but they need to be taught in a way that will allow the student to perform those skills in natural settings (e.g., settings where those skills are actually used). Thus, educators must plan and teach these students to use their language, social, and functional skills with different people, different materials, and in different settings. This will increase the likelihood that the student will eventually be able to use those skills independently in all settings. We call this transfer of skills **generalization.** Students with autism typically do not generalize their skills because of their dependence on rote memorization and their tendency to attend to unimportant environmental cues. If a student can only perform tasks with specific materials, then the task loses some of its functional qualities. For example, if a student can only sort whites from colors using the shirt with the torn sleeve, then he will not be able to appropriately wash any clothes except those three shirts. Or if a student can only read from one textbook, then she will not be able to read labels in the grocery store, signs on doors, or the newspaper. Or if a student learns to use a specific toaster in the classroom, he may not be able to use the toaster in his home simply because it is a different type of toaster.

Students may not only need to learn to use various types of materials, but they also need to learn to perform in various settings even with the same materials. Because students with autism overattend to environmental cues, they often become dependent on those very cues in order to respond. Thus, a student may read his book only when sitting in his bedroom because a specific chair by the window cues him. This is one reason why change typically bothers individuals with autism—because the external cues that they have come to rely on may no longer be available. It is, therefore, imperative that students with autism be taught to perform in a variety of settings and under various conditions.

One way to ensure generalization across settings is to teach skills in the environment in which they will be used. Referred to as **community-based instruction,** students are taken to various places, such as their home, a laundromat, a recreational center, restaurants, and/or a shopping mall and taught skills required to operate in that specific environment. For example, a student is taught to order hamburgers during lunchtime at the local hamburger restaurant instead of during a drill-and-practice session in the special education classroom. Other methods of ensuring generalization across people, materials, and settings will be discussed further in Chapter 5.

Integration and Placement. Attention to generalization across settings also means that teachers, in keeping with the least restrictive environment clause of IDEA, may teach students to perform successfully in general education classrooms if the student's individual education plan (IEP) committee determines such a placement is appropriate. Integration and independent functioning in normalized settings are always long-term goals. Thus, we encourage consideration of placement into specific integrated settings based on individual needs. General education classrooms do not typically simulate out-of-school environments, so that teaching particular students in settings outside of school altogether may be more effective than concentrating on inclusion in general education. Placement, which should be age appropriate, is determined by deciding where particular functional goals can best be taught. A practical program emphasizes that curricular,

strategy, and placement decisions are dictated by individualized assessment. Not only is this practical, but it is required by law.

Teacher Characteristics

A final point regarding educational programming for students with autism concerns teacher competency. Given that the best program will require individualized assessment, an organized classroom, specific and detailed curriculum development, collaboration skills, and the relentless application of behavioral principles, successful teachers are those with certain attributes. Table 1.7 lists those attributes thought to enhance successful instruction for students with autism. These attributes probably do not predict success, nor does the absence of these attributes prohibit success; however, given the requirements for personnel who will be teaching these challenging students, discussion of facilitating characteristics seems helpful.

Consistent. Because individuals with autism have difficulty with discrimination and social interactions, they respond best within consistent environments. In fact, they often insist on routine and sameness. Teachers who are consistent in terms

Table 1.7 Characteristics of Successful Teachers

Consistent

Persistent

Flexible

Creative

Organized

Intuitively sensitive

Energetic

Likes children

Well-developed sense of humor

Mastery of applied behavioral analysis and developmental theories

Mastery of data-based instruction

Commitment to the right to the most effective treatment

of their commands, prompts, routines, body language, and consequences will elicit the best responses from students with autism.

Persistent. Teachers need to be persistent in their effort to teach, in the sense that they should try over and over to find effective instructional strategies.

Flexible. A teacher of these students must be flexible and be willing to try new things when others do not work. They need to refrain from insisting on "the way they've always done it." In this book we will provide a toolbox of options from which teachers can choose. The important thing is to work with an expansive toolbox.

Creative. Creativity is called for because of this population's idiosyncratic responses to common stimuli and their bizarre behavior. For example, an adolescent who insists on carrying bags of trash might be taught to put his trash in a briefcase and limit himself to only 10 trash items. A teacher's creative idea to redefine the way trash is carried rather than eliminating the behavior altogether would probably result in socially appropriate behavior without causing undo anxiety or aggression.

Organized. Teachers also need to be extremely organized in several ways. First, the classroom and the instructional process need to be predictable. Second, goals and objectives must be specified, sequenced, and clearly communicated to anyone who works with the student. Third, the teacher needs to monitor interventions conducted by related service personnel (i.e., speech therapist, occupational therapist, teacher assistants) and ensure that consistency is established. Finally, the teacher needs to document progress in a fashion that is understandable to everyone. For example, Project TEACCH (Schopler, Reichler, & Lansing, 1980) trains teachers to create a sheltered environment with predictable workstations and picture schedules. In this case, the primary emphasis of the educational program is on an organized classroom.

Intuitively Sensitive. Due to the fact that students with autism do not communicate well, it is important for teachers to be intuitively sensitive. By this, we mean that teachers need to be able to understand what a child is trying to communicate even though he cannot say it. This sensitivity depends on astute observations of body language and contextual variables. Chapter 3 provides instruction on functional assessment that will facilitate this skill. Low communication ability also dictates that teachers be able to view the world from the student's point of view or "walk in his shoes."

Energetic. Relentless intrusion requires enormous energy. Teachers who are tired and lethargic are not likely to be able to elicit responses from students who are unmotivated themselves and cannot easily decipher subtle social cues. Monotone voices and apathetic facial expressions do little to facilitate responses from these children.

Likes Children. Furthermore, a teacher needs to *like children*. Teaching is a strenuous profession requiring long hours of planning and coordination. Students with autism need teachers who genuinely care for them and enjoy spending time with young people. Although these students may need assistance attending to social cues, they seldom have trouble determining who likes or dislikes them.

Well-Developed Sense of Humor. One attribute that will do much to prevent burnout among professionals working with challenging students is a sense of humor (Webber, 1994). Humor provides a successful outlet for stress and prevents teachers from taking failures or themselves too seriously. A good sense of humor also facilitates the flexibility factor previously mentioned.

Belief in Efficacious Programs. Effective teachers of students with autism also hold certain beliefs. These essential beliefs for teachers of students with autism have to do with program efficacy. We have found that the most effective professionals believe in the efficacy of *applied be-*

havioral analysis and *data-based instruction*. This mindset results in their mastery and implementation of behavioral programming and formative assessment. Clearly, these effective instructional techniques will be adequately applied if personnel believe they will work. If they do not believe these techniques will work, then there is a good chance they will not.

Commitment. Finally, a key attribute for school personnel is the *commitment to the right to the most effective treatment*. Programs should be chosen based on what we know, through research, will work, as opposed to what is easy to apply (Green, 1996); based on what the student needs to learn rather than what the teacher wants to teach; and based on the student's best interest rather than the teacher's disposition. It is important to scrutinize fad cures and refuse to apply techniques that have no efficacy basis in research. It is also important to be willing to apply techniques that are known to be effective with this population, even though they may require a great deal of work. Chapter 9 will offer further discussion of efficacious programs. Furthermore, these techniques must be applied correctly. Time-out, for example, is a widely used, but often misused, technique.

Teacher competence can be one of the deciding prognostic influences for students with autism, especially for young children (Maurice et al., 1996). It is extremely important that teachers be well trained, possess essential attributes, and implement the most effective program possible. Without this, most students with autism will not only fail to progress, but may actually regress.

FAMILY ISSUES

Given the characteristic behavioral excesses and deficits associated with autism, it should come as no surprise that parenting these children is a difficult task—one for which most parents are ill prepared (Moes, Koegel, Schreibman, & Loos, 1992). It is important that educators understand the continuous and pervasive challenges faced by these parents. A healthy awareness of parents' experiences will better prepare the teacher to establish a collaborative relationship with parents and family members and to provide necessary support (Webber, Simpson, & Bentley, 2000). It will also hopefully reduce the tendency of some educators to blame parents for their children's disability, for not taking an active enough role in the child's education, for not accepting "reality" when it comes to their child's needs, for not being willing to look ahead and plan for the future, and so forth. As the saying goes, "walking a mile in their shoes" will build empathy and should make for a better parent–teacher relationship. Perhaps most importantly, good collaborative relationships with parents can benefit all parties. Our experiences have been that parents are invaluable sources of information—sometimes significantly more informed about current research, legislation, and issues than teachers!

We are honored to have contributions to this chapter and to Chapter 9 from a parent of a child with autism. Cheryl and Rick Archer are the parents of Jamie, age 8, and Katy, age 11. Jamie was born with autism. From the moment Cheryl and Rick learned of their son's disability, they worked diligently to provide him with the very best services. This commitment to quality services has not been easy, as you will see. The Archers have devoted hours and hours of their time to research the various services and intervention approaches, find people to work with Jamie, and train caregivers and teachers, while trying to maintain a semblance of normal family life. Cheryl's story provides a valuable view of family issues, a view that educators should seriously consider as part of the educational process.

Cheryl's Story

I worried about Jamie from the very beginning. When my husband, Rick, and I learned that I was expecting a baby, I was 42, and we had an already busy life with our bright, lovable, lively 4-year-old daughter, Katy, whom we classified as a high-maintenance child. Katy came into our lives as a newborn, through adoption. The anxiety began the very first moment I suspected that I was pregnant. Much of the pervasive worry concerned this baby's impact on Katy. I had a closely monitored pregnancy, receiving chorionic villi sampling (CVS) at around the twelfth week. CVS was the earliest possible prenatal testing for genetic abnormalities available. The 10-day wait between the procedure and receiving the results was agonizing. I knew that I couldn't end any pregnancy, but I had to know if this baby was all right. When we learned that our baby had the "right" number of chromosomes, we were elated.

Finally, James Campbell Archer was born by C-section, an 8-pound 10-ounce boy with red hair and a nice, high Apgar score. I was amazed, thankful, and exhausted, both from the months of worry and from the actual pregnancy and surgical delivery.

Jamie had his first behavioral intervention when he was less than 1 week old. Jamie was having difficulty with "latching on" for nursing, so we visited a lactation consultant. She pronounced him beautiful, healthy, and in need of some special training in sucking. His oral muscle tone seemed somewhat low. Teaching Jamie how to suck was the answer. Our consultant was a bit puzzled that Jamie, obviously healthy and normal, didn't fit the usual profile of newborns who had difficulty sucking, since they were often babies with special needs such as Down syndrome. I allowed myself to put thoughts of low muscle tone and developmental problems out of my consciousness. Jamie was fine. But worry still nagged me: Why was it *so* difficult for Jamie to go to sleep? Why, unlike Katy, did riding in the car upset, rather than calm, him?

Katy started kindergarten when Jamie was 2 months old, and the 20-minute-long afternoon waits in the carpool pickup line were pure torture. Jamie's inconsolable crying would go up a notch after Katy and her carpool buddy got on board, hungry, cranky, and needing attention themselves. I learned to drive with one hand, while reaching behind my seat with the other to jiggle Jamie's car seat or to let him suck on my finger. On trips of 10 miles or more, I often pulled over, stopped the car, and nursed him, buying a few moments of peace. Jamie disliked all of the standard baby-soothing techniques. We purchased or borrowed three different snuggly carriers, tried every orthodontic pacifier on the market, and checked out every available library book on colicky, "difficult" babies.

It wasn't until Jamie was around 3 months old that I wondered if his development might be lagging. He disliked being placed on his stomach, and we couldn't interest him in pushing his head and shoulders up with his arms. He was content to lie on his back on the floor and look up at the lights or the turning ceiling fan. He was fascinated with his own hands as well, and turned them over and over to see them at every possible angle. Such a keen interest in observing things in great detail must be a sign of extra sensitivity and awareness. Didn't I remember my own mother proudly recalling how I did the very same thing? Yet, whenever I saw Jamie with other babies close to his age, my anxiety returned, and I became more anxious as his first birthday approached. We were in a babysitting co-op, where Jamie was always a welcome guest. We often exchanged visits with Caleb, who was a couple of months younger than Jamie, but the two were close in size. I remember one particular visit, when

Jamie was around 11 months old. Caleb was crawling everywhere, exploring everything. He found his way into the VCR cabinet in a flash, checked every corner of the living room, and fussed by the back window because he wanted to explore some more outside. Jamie, who wasn't even crawling yet, would stay pretty much where we put him. Caleb pointed at everything, saying "Dat?" Jamie had never done that. I was seized by a pang of fear. What was wrong?

We were thrilled when Jamie began crawling with gusto right before his first birthday. However, by the time Jamie had his 15-month checkup, our concern was returning because he showed little interest in walking. He was also awfully quiet. He had babbled frequently, playing with a wide variety of sounds right on schedule until he was between 9 and 10 months old. At that time, he began an endless series of ear infections and sinusitis. I knew that temporary hearing loss could delay language development and attributed the slowdown in producing sounds to that.

Our pediatrician was concerned, too. She referred us to an audiologist for a hearing evaluation and to Home Spun, our Early Childhood Intervention (ECI) agency for children from birth to age 3. We were fortunate that the pediatrician suspected a problem and referred Jamie so early, but, at the time, I just felt frightened and angry. I wasn't ready to face the very real possibility that I had a child with special needs. My favorite scenario was that the audiologist would find a hearing loss caused by Jamie's frequent ear infections. That wouldn't be too serious, and we could correct the problem with tubes in his ears, speech therapy, and a "language-rich environment." Yet, I wrote in my journal, "I'm afraid he has autism."

Autism had fascinated me for a long time. When I taught first grade in the early 1980s, one little boy was successfully "mainstreamed" (the term we used then) into my class for music, P.E., and recess. At the other end of the spectrum was Danny, a 5-year-old I encountered during a graduate practicum in early childhood special education. Danny careened wildly about, muttering his only word, an obscenity. My reading had included *A Child Called Noah* and *A Place for Noah,* Josh Greenfeld's personal journals about life for his family with his son with severe autism. It was unthinkable that Jamie could be like Noah.

Jamie's hearing evaluation was normal. We were to return in 3 months for a second evaluation. Home Spun sent a family consultant to our home for an intake interview. The consultant was friendly and positive, and I felt that she liked Jamie immediately. Still, I just wanted her to disappear and leave Jamie and me alone. She invited our family to the upcoming Halloween party for Home Spun families, and I accepted with all of the graciousness I could muster. I really wanted nothing more than to run away with Jamie and forget about parties, Halloween, Home Spun, and everything that had happened to us since that checkup in the pediatrician's office a week ago. The consultant scheduled Jamie for an extensive developmental evaluation to be done by an interdisciplinary ECI team. The 5-week wait seemed to last forever. During that time, I experienced an irrational, powerful desire to go back in time. If I could still be pregnant with Jamie, maybe I could keep him safe and whole. I must have made a mistake before. I would do anything to repair it.

The day of the evaluation, the Home Spun team, including people with backgrounds in special education, social work, nursing, occupational therapy, and speech therapy, came to our home. The positive, energetic tone set by this group stood in stark contrast to my feelings of apprehension and despair. I felt only the tiniest bit of hope. They worked with Jamie in the familiar, secure setting of his home and encouraged our input, so I knew they were seeing a reliable cross-section of his behavior. My spirits sank even further as we all witnessed Jamie's relentless interest in pushing the handle of a carrying case up and down, over and over. Rick and I received a good deal of feedback immediately. Jamie's development was significantly delayed in communication, social, and cognitive skills, while motor development was slow, but still within the normal range. Jamie had begun walking 10 days after the intake interview. We tried to joke that just having contact with Home Spun had already taught Jamie to walk. Now all they needed to do was get him to talk! Jamie would be able to receive an array of services. These would include a weekly home visit from our family consultant, weekly visits to our local gym's preschool parent–child play program, therapeutic horseback riding, a visit with the physical therapist every month, and regular consultation with a speech therapist, an occupational therapist, and a nutritionist. He would also be included in the Mother's Day Out program where he was already a regular, but everything would be different now. He would no longer be just Jamie, but Jamie with special needs, who got to be included with typically developing kids. I would be different, too. I was the mom of a special needs child, like the ones I read about in *Exceptional Parent* magazine. (I had often chosen to read their stories in the pediatrician's waiting room, wondering what it must be like to live their lives.) Jamie's problems

were severe enough to warrant all of these services. This must be serious. But what was it?

We didn't finish our afternoon with Home Spun with a diagnosis. We knew something about Jamie's development in different areas, and that he (and we) needed help. I was more frightened than ever that Jamie had autism, and I was soon sure. The speech therapist had suggested that we inquire at the University of Texas about a communication class for parents and young children with communication difficulties called the Hanen course. When I called, I immediately asked the director what kinds of disorders children who had taken the course in the past typically had. She answered that the Hanen course was helpful for children with a variety of issues, but that last semester's group had consisted completely of children with autism. She then added, "Well, some had PDD." I had never heard the term PDD before, and asked her to explain what it was. The gist of her answer was that PDD (pervasive developmental disorder) was basically synonymous with autism. That was all I needed to hear. I was certain that Jamie had autism. Rick, on the other hand, was not convinced. He couldn't have autism because he loved being hugged and tickled and engaged in all kinds of vigorous, physical play. He looked at us, and responded to us, especially to Daddy. Rick was afraid that my anxiety was causing a lot of the problem. He urged me to stop obsessing about autism, to stop haunting the library, and to get on with life. I wanted him to understand, but I was crushed when he finally did. About a month later, I gave him a simple checklist of the symptoms of autism. As he read it over, his face visibly fell. He agreed with me. As long as Rick believed that Jamie's problems might not be serious, I could still hope I was wrong. Now denial was no longer an option.

At this point, I was seriously depressed. I recognized that the grieving process had crossed over into something more serious, but I could not gain control over my feelings of hopelessness. I could only think of the once-imagined Jamie who was lost. The feeling washed over me when I went by the preschool our daughter had attended, when I saw a new baby or an expectant mother in the grocery store, when a baby was being baptized in church—even when I saw television commercials for diapers or baby formula. I felt that I had lost Jamie. I had experienced the loss of both my parents, and had known grief before, but this loss was unlike any other. I understood what it meant to have a heart that was breaking. During this period, I lost a little yellow sweatshirt that Jamie had been wearing. I frantically retraced every step we had taken that day. I somehow believed that if I could find that sweatshirt, I could recover some sense of hope for Jamie. I never found it and failed even in my attempt to find a duplicate.

Although it is widely accepted that parents cannot cause autism and that evidence strongly points to neurological dysfunction as the cause of autism, parents of an autistic child still have to deal with many practical and emotional problems, as Cheryl Archer conveys. Emotionally, many parents must deal with the shame and guilt that accompanies the birth of a damaged child. Even with evidence to the contrary, they may still believe that somehow they are responsible for their child's disorder. As the child grows older, thwarted expectations continually arise as parents see normal children reach childhood and adolescent milestones, while their own child lags behind. The child's lifelong dependency on his or her parents causes anxiety about what will happen after their death. Will their autistic child be able to live and work independently? Will siblings have to assume responsibility for their autistic brother or sister?

Due to possible cognitive and functional retardation, the child may linger in infant and toddler stages. This creates the practical problems of teaching self-help skills that other children seem to learn effortlessly, dealing with general health factors, and managing difficult behavior. Additionally, few services (e.g., day care, respite services, health care, leisure-time options) might be available to the family due to their autistic child's language and behavioral disorders. Social activities for the family might be severely curtailed and financial burdens may increase as additional services are purchased.

Because children with autism appear physically normal, the general public may not realize the child has a disability when the child displays aggressive or bizarre behavior in public places. Onlookers may blame parents for inadequate parenting. Furthermore, the parents, seeing some precocity in memory, artistic tendencies, or mathematical skills, may have unrealistic expectations for the child and continue to be disappointed or blame themselves if the child does not progress. Children with autism show little affection and, in fact, appear very aloof; therefore, overwhelmed, disappointed parents may receive little reinforcement from the children themselves.

Because autism is a fairly rare disorder (2–5 incidences per 10,000 children; APA, 1994), parents cannot easily be in contact with others who have children with autism. Support systems of people who understand the disorder are often not readily available and parents may be forced to deal with their difficult child virtually alone. Naturally, the family most likely experiences stress and strain. This means that educators must attempt to understand the extreme emotional turmoil experienced by families with exceptional children and assist in supporting them while including them in their individualized planning process.

Most parents have much to offer in terms of effective programming. Parents are the keys to continued advocacy and consistent progress. Family members, not teachers, will follow a child's progress throughout her school career. Parents usually know best about which things might be effective reinforcers or punishers and might best be able to pinpoint essential skills and set long-term goals. When dealing with parents and other family members, school personnel would do well to determine what each can contribute to a child's educational program and do whatever is necessary to facilitate that contribution.

Parents, like students, have unique abilities, needs, and limitations. Because of these unique needs and abilities, parent involvement may take place at one of five levels: (1) awareness, (2) open communication, (3) advocacy and participation, (4) problem solving and procedural application, and (5) partnership (Kroth, 1985). Awareness refers to sharing crucial information with parents regarding the disorder, educational procedures, and resources. Open communication implies consistent interaction among family members and all appropriate school personnel. Advocacy and participatory involvement characterizes parents and family members who desire to be involved actively in promoting services and programs for their children. This may include volunteer service, active participation in advocacy organizations, and participation in training programs. Problem solving and procedural application is an option for parents and families who are able and motivated to implement programs and procedures for their children in natural environments. Finally, partnership refers to parent/family involvement wherein families participate on an equal basis with professionals in identifying, implementing, and evaluating programs for their children. This level demands technical knowledge and commitment.

Remember that the prognosis for a student with autism is much better if that child remains living at home as opposed to being placed in a residential facility. School support toward that end is crucial. Support for families often comes in the form of information sharing (information about prognosis, characteristics, etiology, and the nature of the disorder), advocacy training (information regarding resources, workshops, IDEA training), skill training (training in applied behavioral analysis, curriculum development), counseling (crisis intervention services), and therapeutic support programs (group counseling and support) (Simpson & Webber, 1991). Table 1.8 lists some sample

Table 1.8 Sample Parent Training Programs

Program Title	Components	Reference
Winning!	■ For parents of 3- to 12-year-olds ■ Basic behavioral techniques ■ Training modules include written material and videotapes ■ Uses role-plays and homework	Dangel & Polster (1984)
RETEACH	■ 10-week, data-based training ■ Behavior modification and language development ■ Specific lesson design format ■ Homework, pretest, post-test ■ Ongoing consultation	Handlemann & Harris (1986)
UCLA Early Intervention Model	■ Initial intensive behavioral training ■ Regular follow-up training ■ Written notes for continual programming ■ Videotape consultation ■ Group problem solving	Lovaas (1996)
Project TEACCH	■ In-home training in workstations, picture schedules ■ Training in language development ■ Training in picture communication ■ Ongoing consultation ■ Provides teaching manuals	Schopler, Reichler, & Lansing (1980)

parent involvement programs with corresponding components. These components include family training, problem-solving sessions, home intervention programs, and ongoing consultation. Advocacy organizations such as the Autism Society of America or the Association for Retarded Citizens also provide parent/family programs and resources. Parents who receive training in the techniques outlined in this book and who provide a rich, consistent home environment will do much to improve outcomes for their children with autism (Lovaas & Koegel, 1973). Well-trained energetic parents plus good teachers are the essential ingredients for effective education.

SUMMARY

Although we can read about historical characters appearing to have autism, only relatively recently have we specifically described the disorder and researched its etiology. Currently, it is believed that the distinguishing social, language, and cognitive characteristics are a function of neurological impairment. Unfortunately, the exact nature of this impairment and possible causes for it remain elusive. Despite this, we have learned much in the past 35 years about how to educate children and youth with autism.

The most convincing findings regarding effective education pertain to behavioral interventions. This means that curriculum is clearly and specifically delineated, that the teacher directs instruction, often in a one-to-one format, and that the teacher keeps data to ensure that learning is occurring. Furthermore, it means that behavior management of excessive behavior includes an analysis of contextual contributors, manipulation of environmental predictors, and the application of positive reductive techniques whenever possible.

The best curriculum for a student with autism is that which is age appropriate, functional, and taught in natural environments. It should also be determined individually. Best practices dictates that parents and family members be included in their child's program to the greatest extent possible.

Keeping in mind the extreme emotional, physical, and economic toll a child with autism can place on a family, parents should be encouraged to participate at their own pace. Because these students have such multifaceted needs, their education and treatment require teachers to master applied behavioral analysis and functional curriculum development and to believe that this type of programming will work. It also demands that fad cures be viewed warily until research substantiates them.

KEY POINTS

1. The syndrome of *autism* was first named and described by Leo Kanner in 1943.

2. Current research supports the hypothesis that autism is a neurological disorder characterized by impairment in cognitive, communication, and social ability. Exactly what causes the neurological impairment has not yet been determined.

3. Autistic characteristics may be mild or severe; thus, we refer to an autistic spectrum called pervasive developmental disorder (PDD) in the DSM-IV. PDD includes several related disorders. Autistic disorder most closely resembles those characteristics first put forth by Leo Kanner.

4. Autistic characteristics can be divided into behavioral deficits and behavioral excesses.

5. Due to the nature of autism, techniques based in behavioral learning theory or applied behavioral analysis (ABA) are generally recommended. These techniques include direct instruction, reinforcement, and data-based instruction.

6. Cognitive theory also provides a basis for recommended techniques, such as adding structure to the classroom environment and providing cognitive organizers.

7. Families with children with autism have unique issues and perspectives. Teachers should include family members as integral participants in educational program planning.

REFERENCES

American Psychiatric Association. (1994). *Diagnostic and statistical manual of mental disorders* (4th ed.). Washington, DC: Author.

Autism Research Institute. (1998). Another genetic defect linked to autistic behavior, retardation. *Autism Research Review International, 12*(1), 4.

Autism Society of America. (1997). What is autism? *Advocate: The newsletter of the Autism Society of America, 29*(6), 3.

Autism Society of America. (2000). *Advocate, 33*(1), 3.

Bondy, A. A., & Frost, L. A. (1994). The picture exchange communication system. *Focus on Autistic Behavior, 9*(3), 1–18.

Browder, D. M., & King, D. (1987). Comprehensive assessment for longitudinal curriculum development. In D. M. Browder (Ed.), *Assessment of individuals with severe handicaps* (p. 14). Baltimore, MD: Paul H. Brookes.

Brown, L., Nietupski, J., & Hamre-Nietupski, S. (1976). The criterion of ultimate functioning and public school services for the severely handicapped student. In A. Thomas (Ed.), *Hey don't forget about me: Education's investment in the severely, profoundly and multiply handicapped.* Reston, VA: Council for Exceptional Children.

Dangel, R. F., & Polster, R. A. (1984). Winning! A systematic, empirical approach to parenting training. In R. F. Dangel & R. A. Polster (Eds.), *Parent training: Foundations of research and practice* (pp. 166–174). New York: Guilford Press.

Dunlap, G., Ferro, J., & Deperczel, M. (1994). Nonaversive behavioral intervention in the community. In E. C. Cipani & F. Spooner (Eds.), *Curricular and instructional approaches for persons with severe disabilities* (pp. 117–146). Needham Heights, MA: Allyn & Bacon.

Durand, V. M., & Berotti, D. (1991). Treating behavior problems with communication. *American Speech and Hearing Association, 11,* 37–39.

Ferster, C. B. (1985). Positive reinforcement and behavioral deficits of autistic children. In A. M. Donnellan (Ed.), *Classic readings in autism* (pp. 53–73). New York: Teachers College Press.

Filipek, P. A., Accardo, P. J., Baranek, G. T., Cook, E. H., Dawson, G., Gordon, B., Gravel, J. S., Johnson, C. P., Kallen, R. J., Levy, S. E., Minshew, N. J., Prizant, B. M., Rapin, I., Rogers, S. J., Stone, W. L., Teplin, S., Tuchman, R. F., & Volkmar, F. R. (1999). The screening and diagnosis of autistic spectrum disorders. *Journal of Autism and Developmental Disorders, 29*(6), 439–484.

Frith, U. (1996). Social communication and its disorder in autism and Asperger's syndrome. *Journal of Psychopharmacology, 10,* 48–53.

Fullerton, A., Stratton, J., Coyne, P., & Gray, C. (1996). Higher functioning adolescents and young adults with autism. Austin, TX: Pro-Ed.

Gilliam, J. E. (1995). *Gilliam Autism Rating Scale (GARS).* Austin, TX: Pro-Ed.

Grandin, T. (1995). The learning style of people with autism: An autobiography. In K. A. Quill (Ed.), *Teaching children with autism: Strategies to enhance communication and socialization.* New York: Delmar Publishers.

Green, G. (1996). Early behavioral intervention for autism: What does research tell us? In C. Maurice (Ed.), *Behavioral intervention for young children with autism: A manual for parents and professionals* (pp. 29–44). Austin, TX: Pro-Ed.

Handlemann, J. S., & Harris, S. L. (1986). *Educating the developmentally disabled: Meeting the needs of children and families.* San Diego: College-Hill Press.

Harvard Medical School. (1997). Autism—Part I. *The Harvard Mental Health Letter, 13*(9), 1–4.

Heflin, L. J., & Simpson, R. L. (1998). Interventions for children and youth with autism: Prudent choices in a world of exaggerated claim and empty promises. Part I: Intervention and treatment option review. *Focus on Autism and Other Developmental Disabilities, 13*(4), 194–211.

Hermelin, B. (1976). Coding and the sense modalities. In L. Wing (Ed.), *Early childhood autism.* London: Pergamon.

Itard, J. (1972). *The wild boy of Aveyron* (E. Fawcett, P. Ayrton, & J. White, Trans.). London: NLB, 7 Carlisle St. (Original work published 1801.)

Kanner, L. (1985). Autistic disturbances of affective contact. In A. M. Donnellan (Ed.), *Classic readings in autism* (pp. 11–53). New York: Teachers College Press.

Koegle, R. L., Rincover, A., & Egel, A. L. (1987). *Educating and understanding autistic children.* San Diego: College-Hill Press.

Kroth, R. L. (1985). *Communicating with parents of exceptional children.* Denver, CO: Love.

Krug, D. A., Arick, J. R., & Almond, P. J. (1980). *Autism screening instrument for educational planning (ASIEP).* Austin, TX: Pro-Ed.

Lovaas, O. I. (1996). The UCLA young autism model of service delivery. In C. Maurice (Ed.), *Behavioral intervention for young children with autism: A manual for parents and professionals* (pp. 241–250). Austin, TX: Pro-Ed.

Lovaas, O. I., & Koegel, R. L. (1973). *Behavior modification in education, NSSE Yearbook.* Chicago: University of Chicago Press.

Lovaas, O.I., & Smith, T. (1989). A comprehensive behavioral theory of autistic children: Paradigm for research and treatment. *Journal of Behavior Therapy and Experimental Psychiatry, 20,* 17–29.

Martin, J. L. (1996). *Overview of legal issues involved in educating students with autism and PDD under IDEA.* Corpus Christi, TX: Region II ESC.

Maurice, C., Green, G., & Luce, S. C. (1996). *Behavioral intervention for young children with autism.* Austin, TX: Pro-Ed.

Moes, D., Koegel, R.L., Schreibman, L., & Loos, L.M. (1992). Stress profiles for mothers and fathers of children with autism. *Psychological Reports, 71,* 1272–1274.

Myles, B. S., & Simpson, R. L. (1998). *Asperger syndrome: A guide for educators and parents.* Austin, TX: Pro-Ed.

Prizant, B. (1983). Language acquisition and communicative behavior in autism: Toward an understanding of the "whole" of it. *Journal of Speech and Hearing Disorders, 48,* 296–307.

Ruttenberg, B. A., Kalish, B. I., Wenar, C., & Wolf, E. G. (1977). *Behavior rating instrument for autistic and other atypical children (BRIAAC).* Chicago: Stoelting Company.

Sack, J. L. (1999). Sharp rise seen in identification of autistic pupils. *Education Week, 19*(8), 1, 14–15.

Schopler, E., Reichler, R. J., Bashford, A., Lansing, M. D., & Marcus, L. M. (1990). *Psychoeducational profile revised.* Austin, TX: Pro-Ed.

Schopler, E., Reichler, R. J., & Lansing, M. (1980). *Individualized assessment and treatment for autistic and developmentally disabled children, Vol. 2: Teaching strategies for parents and professionals.* Austin, TX: Pro-Ed.

Schopler, E., Reichler, R. J., & Renner, B. R. (1988). *The childhood autism rating scale.* Los Angeles: Western Psychological Services.

Schuler, A. L. (1995). Thinking in autism: Differences in learning and development. In K. A. Quill (Ed.), *Teaching children with autism: Strategies to enhance communication and socialization* (pp. 11–32). New York: Delmar Publishers.

Simpson, R. L., & Regan, M. (1988). *Management of autistic behavior.* Austin, TX: Pro-Ed.

Simpson, R. L., & Webber, J. (1991). Parents and families of children with autism. In M. J. Fine (Ed.), *Collaboration with parents of exceptional children.* Brandon, VT: Clinical Psychology.

Tager-Flusberg, H., & Cohen, D. (1993). An introduction to the debate. In S. Baron-Cohen, H. Tager-Flusberg, & D. J. Cohen (Eds.), *Understanding other minds: Perspectives from autism* (pp. 3–9). New York: Oxford University.

Twachtman, D. D. (1995). Methods to enhance communication in verbal children. In K. A. Quill (Ed.), *Teaching children with autism: Strategies to enhance communication and socialization.* New York: Delmar Publishers.

Webber, J. (1994). Psychological immunization. Resisting depression, neurosis, and physical illness in a strenuous profession. *Preventing School Failure, 38*(4), 21–26.

Webber, J., Simpson, R. L., & Bentley, J. K. C. (2000). Parents and families of children with autism. In M. J. Fine and R. L. Simpson (Eds.), *Collaboration with parents and families with children and youth with exceptionalities* (2nd ed.). Austin, TX: Pro-Ed.

What Is Asperger's disorder? (1999). *The Harvard Mental Health Letter, 16*(4), 8.

Wing, L. (1996). *The autistic syndromes.* London: Constable.

2

✳

Basic Behavioral Principles and Strategies for Changing Behavior

Did you know that:

- Sometimes, students with autism communicate their wants and needs through their behavior?

- Many of the inappropriate behaviors exhibited by students with autism are learned behaviors that serve a purpose for the student?

- It is possible—and desirable—to use positive reinforcement to *reduce* inappropriate behaviors?

- If you want a student's behavior to change, you must change something that *you* are doing?

As you learned in Chapter 1, children and youth with autism exhibit many behavioral characteristics that make this population challenging to teach. An effective educational program must be well designed to address the excesses (e.g., tantrums) and deficits (e.g., language) characteristic of autism. Instructional approaches that work well with students with other types of disabilities may not produce desired outcomes for children with autism. However, procedures are available that are effective for most students with autism, regardless of the types or severity of their behavioral excesses or deficits. These procedures are known informally as behavior modification techniques; however, we prefer the more precise term of **applied behavior analysis (ABA).**

ABA procedures can be used to increase desired behaviors, decrease inappropriate behaviors, and teach new behaviors to students of all functioning levels. Although ABA procedures are most often associated with behavior management, they are powerful tools for teaching as well. Based on the available research, we believe that ABA procedures are essential components of effective programs for students with autism. This chapter will describe the assumptions of applied behavior analysis and will explain basic behavior change procedures, including antecedent interventions, measuring target behavior, and consequence interventions.

ASSUMPTIONS OF APPLIED BEHAVIOR ANALYSIS

ABA interventions are based on the following assumptions:

An individual's past learning and biological make-up contribute to present behavior (Ross & Nelson, 1979). For a student with autism this might mean that he or she has learned to communicate wants by screaming, crying, or hitting. It also means that some of the student's self-abusive behavior, self-stimulatory behavior, or lack of learning might be related to inadequate levels of neurotransmitters in the student's neurological system. However, even when a biological explanation exists for the behavior, research indicates that ABA procedures can help change it. For example, behavioral procedures have been successfully applied as part of comprehensive intervention plans for depression, seizures, and attention deficit hyperactivity disorder.

All voluntary behavior, both appropriate and inappropriate, is governed by the same principles (Morgan & Jenson, 1988). Generally, a student's inappropriate behavior can be explained in terms of one or more of the basic behavioral principles described in this chapter. For example, it may be that a child screams when asked to do something he doesn't like to do, and that when he screams, the request is usually withdrawn. Thus, the student is negatively reinforced for screaming (he avoids a disliked task as a result of screaming). Knowing that all voluntary behavior is governed by the same principles, teachers can attempt to identify the behavioral principles that may explain a student's inappropriate behavior, then use these same principles to teach or increase desired behaviors and reduce inappropriate behaviors.

Behavior is functional and communicative (Foster-Johnson & Dunlap, 1993). This means that behaviors, even inappropriate behaviors, serve a purpose for the child. For example, a child's misbehavior may function to get the child something she wants or help the child avoid something she doesn't like, and is often used as a way for the child to communicate these purposes. The goal of effective interventions is not only to reduce inappropriate behaviors, but to teach appropriate alternative behaviors that address the same function as the inappropriate behavior. For individuals with autism these are most often communication skills. Unless the function of an inappropriate behavior is correctly identified and an intervention is designed based on that function, the intervention is likely to be ineffective. Therefore, functional assessment is a critical step in designing behavioral interventions. In Chapter 3, we explain how to conduct a functional assessment.

Behavior is contextual (Foster-Johnson & Dunlap, 1993). Behavior is related to the environment in which it occurs. Attempts to change a behavior without first identifying contextual elements that may be contributing to the problem behavior are nonproductive. Contextual elements may be external, such as the way instructions are given, a difficult or disliked task, or a distracting environment (excessive noise in the classroom, a crowded cafeteria, large open spaces in the gym, etc.). Contextual elements may also be internal. For example, when children are hungry, sleepy, bored, or excited, they find it much more difficult to concentrate and follow directions. An important part of assessment of behavior is identification of relevant contextual elements. Intervention might be as simple as changing how instructions are given, or reducing the time the student is required to work on certain tasks, or teaching the student a better way to deal with the environment. For example, careful analysis of noncompliance may reveal the noncompliance to be a result of vague, ambiguous directions that are given without having the student's full attention. Rather than punishing the student for noncompliance, a more effective intervention would be to change the manner in which directions are given.

BEHAVIORAL APPROACH TO TEACHING STUDENTS WITH AUTISM

When a student with autism joins your class, you may not know where to begin. However, the steps described below will guide you in designing an effective instructional program for the student. These steps are simply a brief summary of each procedure; the procedures mentioned will be explained in detail later in this chapter or in other chapters.

1. *Identify the student's behavioral excesses and deficits.* Usually the excesses are inappropriate behaviors that need to be reduced (e.g., self-stimulatory behavior, refusal) or eliminated (e.g., aggression, self-abusive behaviors). The deficits indicate skills that need to be taught and/or reinforced (e.g., using appropriate communication, playing with toys, completing assigned tasks, following directions). Excesses and deficits are identified through a variety of assessment methods, such as ecological assessment, direct observation, or checklists. Later chapters will describe assessment approaches for purposes of determing what skills to address in your instructional and behavior management interventions.

2. *Conduct a functional assessment.* The purpose of this step is to determine why a student is misbehaving. In a **functional assessment,** you gather information about the student's inappropriate behaviors, the contexts in which they occur, and the antecedents and consequences associated with each. Next, you formulate hypotheses about the purpose(s) an inappropriate behavior may be serving for the student (e.g., to get something, to avoid something, to communicate something). Then an intervention is developed based on your hypotheses. This process, an essential part of effective behavior change programs, is explained in Chapter 3.

3. *Select target behaviors.* Target behaviors are specific behaviors for which intervention will be developed: behaviors to be taught, increased, or decreased. The information gathered in steps 1 and 2 will help you determine and prioritize target behaviors.

4. *Begin measuring target behaviors.* You should measure target behaviors before you begin intervention. This measure is called a **baseline** and it serves much the same purpose as a pretest: It lets you know where the student is

functioning prior to intervention so you can determine if intervention is effective.

5. *Design and implement intervention.* Your intervention should be designed based on your hypotheses from the functional assessment. Generally speaking, interventions are designed to increase behaviors (e.g., desired behaviors such as compliance, task completion), decrease behaviors (e.g., inappropriate behaviors such as self-stimulatory behaviors, screaming, self-injury), and/or teach new behaviors (e.g., communicative behaviors). Furthermore, intervention may target antecedents, consequences, or both. This chapter will describe the role of antecedents in teaching and behavior management and the basic approaches to increasing, decreasing, and teaching new behaviors. More advanced strategies are described in later chapters.

6. *Continue to measure target behaviors.* The data you collect will help you determine if the interventions are working. If they are, data should indicate an improvement in the target behaviors. If the data do not indicate such improvement, the intervention needs to be reevaluated.

THE A–B–C MODEL

Behavior does not occur in isolation. Most of the behaviors exhibited by students with autism—appropriate and inappropriate behaviors alike—are related to events in the environment that occur either before the behavior is exhibited (these are called **antecedents**) or after the behavior is exhibited (**consequences**). This theory is called the **A-B-C model** and is illustrated in Table 2.1.

The A-B-C model plays an important role in developing effective intervention strategies for students with autism. Too often in programs for these students the focus is on consequences, with too little attention given to antecedents. As we will show you, however, any intervention for students with autism should pay as much attention to antecedents as to consequences.

Table 2.1 The A-B-C Model

	Antecedent	→	Behavior	←	Consequence
External	Verbal commands People Tasks Materials Time of day Physical environment Activities		Appropriate Inappropriate		Positive reinforcement Negative reinforcement Extinction Punishment Determines whether or not a behavior will be repeated
Internal	Physical state (e.g., hungry, tired, too hot) Emotional state (e.g., angry, excited)				

Antecedents

Antecedents are events that occur before a behavior is exhibited. Antecedents play an important role in the nature of the subsequent behavior: Some antecedents serve as cues for appropriate behavior, others are cues for inappropriate behavior. Before you implement a consequence for a particular behavior, you should first identify the relevant antecedents that precede the behavior and examine whether those antecedents should be changed. In addition, when teaching new behaviors, you should identify antecedents that you want to cue those behaviors. For example, if you are teaching a student to say or sign desired food items, you might teach the student to exhibit that behavior in response to the cue "What do you want?" Or perhaps you teach the student to shake hands in response to someone extending a hand in greeting. Using specific antecedents to cue specific behaviors is called *stimulus control* and is explained below.

Antecedents can be internal or external, and usually occur in proximity to the behavior in question (see Table 2.1). For example, if you give a student a task that involves mechanical noise (e.g., vacuuming or starting the dishwasher), and he dislikes this type of noise, that task may serve as an antecedent for aggression, refusal, or self-abuse. Likewise, a student who is hungry or tired is less likely to be compliant and complete tasks satisfactorily. On the other hand, music time is likely to be an antecedent for paying attention and following directions for a student who loves music.

You need to understand the relationship between antecedents and behavior and use this information when planning instruction or behavior management. If you know a particular antecedent is likely to result in challenging behavior, you may be able to either eliminate or modify the antecedent. The following examples illustrate how modifying antecedents can produce desirable changes in behavior:

- In the example of your student who dislikes mechanical noises, you could modify the task to make it more agreeable (e.g., let the student vacuum while listening to music on headphones).
- Consider a student who tantrums in the hallway each time the class goes to lunch. You speculate that her tantrums are due to the loud and crowded conditions of the hallway. Because there is no other route to the lunchroom, you arrange to go to lunch at another time, when the hallways are not filled with students.
- You have a student who has severe tantrums unless he is allowed to have a favorite object. You first allow the student to keep the object on his desk during work times. Gradually, you move the object further and further away, and then you begin covering parts of it until it is out of sight.
- Another student is noncompliant to verbal instructions. However, when you begin simpli-

fying instructions (e.g., giving only one direction at a time, with no unnecessary explanations), the student's compliance improves.

Sometimes antecedents are used in a more precise form of behavior and instructional management called stimulus control. Alberto and Troutman (1999) define stimulus control as "the relationship in which an antecedent causes behavior or serves as a cue for the behavior to occur" (p. 502). In stimulus control, antecedents are called **discriminitive stimuli (S^Ds)**. These are specific antecedents that predictably cue specific behaviors, and the behaviors tend to occur somewhat automatically. Schools, even most aspects of our society, are filled with stimulus control applications. For example, the telephone rings (S^D) and you pick up the receiver and say "hello" (behavior). The ring serves as a cue for you to pick up the receiver—you typically do not pick up the receiver and say "hello" unless you hear the ring. Or,

when a new acquaintance extends his hand and says "Hi, my name is John" (S^D), you grasp his hand and reply "Hi, John. I'm glad to meet you" (behavior). Again, this particular behavior only occurs—and predictably occurs—in the presence of that antecedent.

Stimulus control is a valuable teaching tool, with the potential to increase desired behaviors and reduce behavior problems. In fact it is a primary component of Discrete Trial Teaching, which we will present in Chapter 5. Many types of discriminitive stimuli are available that can be established to cue desired behaviors: verbal signals, nonverbal signals, mechanical signals, schedules, environments, or situations. Table 2.2 lists examples of the variety of S^Ds that can be used in the classroom, and specific behaviors that could be taught in response to those S^Ds.

Stimulus control is a learned process. While students learn to respond to some S^Ds without

Table 2.2 Examples of Discriminitive Stimuli and Possible Responses

Discriminitive Stimulus	Response
Verbal S^Ds	
■ "Hands quiet!"	Student stops self-stimulatory behavior and puts hands in lap.
■ "Time to work."	Student sits in assigned seat and waits for task.
■ "Stop!"	Student who is running from teacher stops immediately.
■ "Play time!"	Student goes to toy shelf, selects a toy, and sits on play rug.
Nonverbal S^Ds	
■ Teacher raises her arm, with two fingers extended in a "V."	Students stop talking and look at the teacher.
Mechanical S^Ds	
■ Timer runs during independent work time.	Student remains on-task.
■ Bell rings following recess.	Student lines up in front of teacher.
■ "Cricket" clicker is used.	Student stops biting himself.
Schedule as an S^D	
■ A regularly scheduled activity ends.	Student stands up and moves to the area of the room where the next regular activity is held.
■ Student finishes toileting.	Student approaches sink and washes hands.
Routine as an S^D	
■ Student approaches the lunchroom worker waiting at the end of the lunch line.	Student hands the worker her lunch card.
■ Student gets in car.	Student fastens seat belt.
■ A peer approaches student on playground and asks if he wants to play ball.	Student responds verbally, and joins the game.
■ Student approaches fast-food counter.	Student places order.
■ Student enters checkout lane at grocery store.	Student unloads cart.
■ Bus pulls up to bus stop and door opens.	Student enters bus.

special instruction (e.g., students typically learn that the end of one activity within the daily schedule signals the beginning of another familiar activity), other S^Ds and the expected responses must be taught using the following steps:

1. *Determine the desired target behavior.* What is it you want the student to do, or stop doing, in the presence of the S^D? Some examples of target behaviors include begin work, continue working (remain on-task), respond to a greeting, look at the teacher, stop self-stimulatory or self-abusive behavior, or stop running (for a student who runs away from the teacher).

2. *Determine what you will use as the S^D.* Virtually any word, phrase, sound, gesture, and so on can be established as an S^D. However, the S^D that you select should be easy to use and unique in some way—that is, it should be something that the student sees or hears only when the target behavior is called for; something that will get the student's attention—that is, it must be noticeable by the student, even when accompanied by many distractions.

3. *Present the S^D and prompt the desired response (see Chapter 5 for help in using prompts).* Remember, the student does not yet know what he is supposed to do, so immediately after you present the S^D, either instruct the student about what to do or help the student perform the desired response. For example, if you are teaching Andy to stop when he hears the clicker, use the discrete trial teaching method described in Chapter 5 to teach this response: Ask another adult to help you and explain her role (which will be to use the clicker). You walk with Andy (e.g., down the hall). After a few steps say "Andy, listen," as the other adult clicks the clicker (the S^D). Immediately tell Andy to stop, and hold his arm or shoulders to illustrate if necessary. When he stops, reinforce, then repeat these steps, saying "Let's walk again."

4. *Teach the student to discriminate between the S^D and other stimuli.* Because you want the

student to respond predictably to specific stimuli, the next step is to introduce other stimuli. Once the behavior occurs predictably and without prompting in the presence of the S^D, use other stimuli as part of the instructional process. Of course, the target response is reinforced only when it occurs in the presence of the S^D. For example, Andy is reinforced when he stops after hearing the clicker, but not if he stops when a bell is rung.

5. *Once the desired response is established (that is, the student consistently exhibits the response, with no prompts, when the S^D is presented), fade the reinforcement.* Once the response is established, reinforce intermittently (that is, reinforce regularly, yet not for every response).

Thus, antecedents play an important role in behavior management. Modifying antecedents and teaching stimulus control are usually simpler and often more effective approaches to behavior management than relying on consequences alone. But sometimes, antecedent modification alone is insufficient. The second part of the A-B-C model is *behavior*, which refers to behaviors or skills targeted for change. Special considerations regarding behavior are described next.

Behavior

Behavior refers to specific observable behaviors exhibited by students. These might be academic behaviors (reading sight words, solving math problems, writing names), language behaviors (answering yes/no questions, initiating social greetings, using sign language to make requests), motor behaviors (hitting a ball, hopping on one foot, climbing stairs, riding a bike), play or leisure behaviors (stacking blocks, playing a video game), work/daily living behaviors (folding towels, stocking shelves), or self-help behaviors (combing hair, tying shoes). In terms of teaching students with autism, some behaviors must be increased, some must be decreased, and some must be newly taught.

We have said that data-based teaching is an important element of programs for students with autism. As you will see in the following sections, to accurately measure progress, you must describe

Table 2.3 Examples and Nonexamples of Pinpoint Behaviors

Examples of Pinpoint Behaviors:

- On-task: working on assigned task; listening to teacher while teacher is speaking
- Finger-flicking: holding or wiggling fingers in front of or to the sides of eyes
- Screaming
- Tantruming: hitting head with fist or open hand
- Rocking back and forth or side to side
- Playing: using a toy or other play material (e.g., clay, puzzle) in the manner in which it is intended to be used, with no spinning, smelling, or tasting of the object
- Face-touching: touching any part of the face to any part of the body or any other object
- Read aloud
- Point to
- Write answers to

Examples of Nonpinpoint Behaviors:

- Silly
- Rude
- Self-abusive
- Noncompliant
- Learn
- Understand
- Play nicely
- Work hard
- Be polite

target behaviors precisely, using observable, measurable terms. In behavioral terms, we refer to this as **pinpointing** a behavior. A good rule of thumb for determining if a behavior is adequately pinpointed is that two people should be able to look at the student and agree on whether the behavior, as defined, is occurring or not. Pinpoint descriptions of target behaviors will enable you and your staff to be consistent when measuring and consequating a behavior. Vague descriptions of behavior will result in ineffective interventions and inaccurate measures of progress. Table 2.3 lists examples and nonexamples of pinpoint behaviors.

As we said, some behaviors need to be newly taught, some behaviors need to be increased, and some behaviors need to be decreased. If a student has never exhibited a certain appropriate behavior, you might assume the student has not learned that behavior. In this case, you must teach the behavior using one or more of the procedures described in Chapter 5. If the student exhibits a

desired behavior too infrequently, that behavior must be increased using reinforcement procedures described later in this chapter. Finally, if the student exhibits an inappropriate behavior, that behavior must be reduced or eliminated using one or more of the techniques described later in this chapter and in Chapter 3.

Measuring Behaviors. Later in this chapter, you will meet Michael, a student who exhibited high rates of off-task behavior (touching his face) during individual work sessions with the teacher. Before intervention, Michael was touching his face an average of 139 times per 20-minute work session. In the first phase of intervention, Michael's face-touching dropped to 130 face touches per work session, and then 120 touches in the second phase. Without counting those face touches, it would have been very difficult for Michael's teacher to determine that intervention appeared to be reducing face touches. In fact, if she had not counted face touches, she may have abandoned her intervention, incorrectly assuming that it was not working. By measuring the target behavior, she was able to detect the subtle changes in the frequency of face-touching, and thus made a correct instructional decision to continue treatment. Sometimes, such as in Michael's case, target behaviors change in such small increments that it would be difficult to determine whether the intervention is working without data and a corresponding graph.

Behavior measurement allows you to determine pretreatment levels of behavior. Once intervention is initiated, continued measurement of target behaviors enables you to carefully oversee the effects of instructional and behavioral management interventions so that modifications can be made in a timely fashion if the intervention is not producing desired effects. The following sections explain these behavior measurement techniques.

Behavior Measurement Techniques. Behavior measurement systems are used to monitor all types of behavior, including both excesses and deficits. Data collected using these systems are usually graphed on a simple line graph for easy interpretation. Graphs allow teachers or parents to

Table 2.4 Measurement Systems for Specific Target Behaviors

Following are measurement systems that can be used to monitor each of the target behaviors listed. Keep in mind that sometimes more than one measurement system might be used. In these cases, we have listed the most appropriate system first.

Desired Behaviors	Most Appropriate Measurement System
Responding to a greeting	Event recording (restricted event)
Number of words read correctly from a passage	Event recording (restricted event)
Number of math problems solved	Event recording (restricted event)
Following directions	Event recording (restricted event)
Number of dishes washed before refusing	Event recording (restricted event)
Making a request	Event recording (nonrestricted event)
Initiating verbal greeting to peers	Event recording (nonrestricted event)
Number of envelopes stuffed	Event recording (nonrestricted event)
Amount of time spent vacuuming before refusing	Duration recording
How long it takes student to put on jacket	Duration recording
Working on-task	Duration recording
Sitting next to peers without hitting	Duration recording
Stacking blocks with a peer	Duration recording or nonrestricted event (the number of blocks stacked per play period)
Keeping glasses on face	Duration recording
Participating in group game	Duration recording
Brushing teeth	Duration recording
Amount of time spent climbing on playground equipment	Duration recording

Inappropriate Behaviors	Most Appropriate Measurement System
Biting self or others	Nonrestricted event recording
Grabbing materials	Nonrestricted event recording
Screaming	Nonrestricted event recording
Noncompliance	Restricted event recording
Hitting teacher in response to a direction	Restricted event recording
Finger-flicking	Nonrestricted event recording or duration recording
Rocking	Nonrestricted event recording or duration recording
Posturing	Nonrestricted event recording or duration recording
Tantrums	Event recording (restricted or nonrestricted, depending on the situation) or duration recording

determine objectively whether target behaviors are changing in the desired direction and to check progress of target behaviors over time.

Behavior measurement is not difficult. The steps in measuring any behavior are as follows: First, pinpoint the target behavior. Remember to use observable descriptions of behaviors. Second, determine which measurement system you will use. The most commonly used measurement systems are described in the next section. The system you use is determined by the nature of the target behavior being measured (see Table 2.4). Third, determine a specific measurement period. Depending on the target behavior, this may be anywhere from a few minutes to the entire day. Keep this measurement period consistent each time you collect data

on that particular behavior. Remember, you do not need to collect data all day every day; a sample collected at the time the behavior is most likely to occur (e.g., just before lunch) or is most problematic (e.g., during vocational time) is sufficient.

The next step is to measure the behavior for three to five observation periods before you begin intervention. The observations collected are called **baseline data** and allow you to examine the effects of the intervention on the level of the target behavior as compared to the level of the behavior before intervention began. For example, in Michael's case, his teacher counted how many times Michael touched his face to any part of his body or any object (a behavioral excess) during three work sessions before implementing the intervention. These baseline data were graphed (see Figure 2.2 later in this chapter), and the intervention was implemented. The teacher continued collecting data during work sessions and charting those data on the graph. These data, compared to baseline data, indicated improvement in the target behavior.

Baselines should also be established when the target behavior is a deficit. For example, Jason is a student who uses simple signs to communicate wants; he screams and bites his hand to tell his teacher he does not want to do something. To reduce the screams and hand-biting, his teacher decided to teach Jason to sign "no" to say he does not want to do something. Before teaching him to sign "no" for refusal and reinforcing him for using the sign, his teacher collected baseline data by counting how many times Jason currently signed "no" to refuse. Jason displayed no instances of appropriate refusal (e.g., signing "no") during each of the 3 days she counted this behavior. During intervention (which consisted of showing him how to sign "no," reminding him to use the sign, and reinforcing him for using the sign), Jason's teacher continued to count his instances of signing "no." If this number gradually increases, she can assume the intervention is successful; if not, the intervention should be modified.

The exception to the baseline rule is that if the target behavior is dangerous to the child or others, you should *not* collect baseline data! Skip this, begin intervention immediately, and continue to measure to determine that the behavior is decreasing.

The final step in measuring behavior is to convert raw data if necessary, and regularly graph the data for ease of use. Generally, data are graphed using a simple line graph. This gives you a picture of how the behavior is changing: if it is increasing or decreasing as desired, and if it is changing significantly as a result of intervention. Graphs are helpful for making instructional decisions and for communicating with parents and other professionals about a student's progress. Sometimes it is appropriate to have students participate in graphing data collected on their target behaviors. For example, using data collected by the teacher, a stu-

dent who is able to do so might graph how many times he initiated social interactions with peers during the day, how many math problems he completed correctly, or how long it took her to vacuum the carpet in the teacher's lounge. Participating in graphing such data or observing daily improvements in target behaviors depicted on the graph may be reinforcing to some students.

In the following sections we describe two behavior measurement systems, give general examples for application, and explain how to graph data. Note that although many behavior measurement techniques exist, we believe that the two presented in this chapter will provide teachers with sufficient information to make informed instructional decisions.

Event Recording. This method is used when the goal is to increase or decrease the *number of times* a student exhibits a target behavior. Event recording is used for behaviors that:

- Have a clearly observable beginning and end (e.g., pointing to named coins, following directions, saying words).

- Do not occur over long periods of time. Sleeping, staring out the window, vacuuming, playing with a toy, or staying in a seat would not be appropriate for event recording because these are likely to occur for extended periods of time.

- Do not occur at extremely high frequencies. Hand-flapping or finger-flicking may not be appropriate for event recording because the motions would probably occur too quickly to count.

Event recording is easy to use: Simply record a tally mark each time the target behavior occurs during the measurement period. Golf stroke counters are easy to obtain and may be useful for situations in which it is inconvenient to carry a pencil and recording sheet (e.g., on the playground, on field trips).

Some behaviors occur in response to a specific stimulus (e.g., number of times student follows a verbal direction, number of sight words read correctly, or number of puzzle pieces correctly placed). These behaviors are called **restricted events,** which simply means they occur (or should occur) in response to a specific external stimulus. For example, in Jason's case, signing "no" appropriately occurs only in response to a direction or when a task is presented the specific stimulus. In measuring these behaviors, you should record the number of stimuli (that is, the number of opportunities to respond, such as the number of directions given) as well as the number of times

the desired behavior occurred (Figure 2.1). Data should then be converted to a percentage for graphing purposes.

If the behavior is not in response to a specific stimulus, simply graph the number of times the behavior occurred. (Remember to keep the measurement period the same length of time each day.) These behaviors are called **nonrestricted events,** which means they can occur at any time—they do not occur only in response to external stimuli. Examples of nonrestricted events

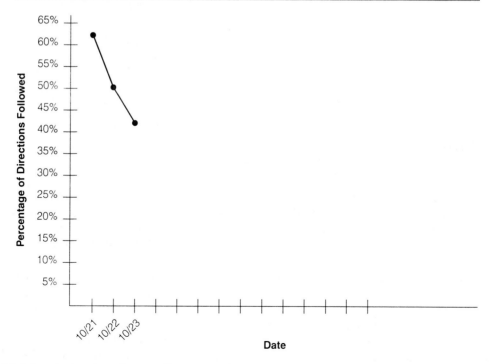

TARGET BEHAVIOR   Compliance with verbal directions

OBSERVATION PERIOD   9:15–9:30 (morning group)

DATE	DIRECTIONS GIVEN	DIRECTIONS FOLLOWED	CALCULATION	PERCENTAGE
10/21/01	✝✝✝ ✝✝✝ |||	✝✝✝ |||	8/13 x 100	62%
10/22/01	✝✝✝ ✝✝✝ ||||	✝✝✝ ||	7/14 x 100	50%
10/23/01	✝✝✝ ✝✝✝ ||	✝✝✝	5/12 x 100	42%

FIGURE 2.1 Sample data form for recording restricted event data, and corresponding graph.

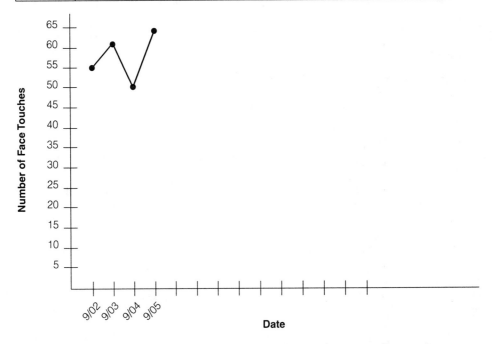

TARGET BEHAVIOR _Number of face touches (face touching any surface for any length of time)_

OBSERVATION PERIOD _____ 2:00–2:20 (working 1:1 with teacher or assistant) _____

DATE	OCCURRENCES	TOTAL FOR DAY
9/02/01	卌 卌 卌 卌 卌 卌 卌 卌 卌 卌 卌	55
9/03/01	卌 卌 卌 卌 卌 卌 卌 卌 卌 卌 卌 卌 |	61
9/04/01	卌 卌 卌 卌 卌 卌 卌 卌 卌 卌	50
9/05/01	卌 卌 卌 卌 卌 卌 卌 卌 卌 卌 卌 卌 ||||	64

FIGURE 2.2 Sample data form for recording nonrestricted event data, and corresponding graph.

include screaming, initiating a verbal interaction, biting, or asking a question. See Figure 2.2 for a sample form for recording nonstimulus–specific event data.

Duration Recording. This technique is used to measure how long a behavior occurs, and it is the technique of choice when the goal is to increase or decrease the amount of time a behavior is exhibited. It is used for behaviors that have a clear beginning and end, such as how long it takes a student to use the restroom, how long it takes a student to complete an assigned task, or how long a student sits next to a peer without grabbing. A stopwatch is a convenient way to measure the duration of behaviors, or you may simply record the start and stop times of the target behavior, as shown in Figure 2.3. Duration data should be graphed as minutes and/or seconds. Remember to observe the same amount of time each session.

Measuring the behaviors you are trying to change increases the likelihood of desired outcomes. Without precise monitoring of these be-

TARGET BEHAVIOR Amount of time student keeps Walkman headphones correctly placed on his head

OBSERVATION PERIOD _____ Free time (in classroom), 3:00–3:20

DATE	START	STOP	DURATION
1/07	3:04	3:05	1 minute
1/08	3:05	3:05:30	30 seconds
1/12	3:07	3:07:30	30 seconds
1/13	3:00	3:03	3 minutes
1/14	3:06	3:08:30	2 min., 30 sec.
1/15	3:05	3:10	5 minutes
1/16	3:08	3:14	6 minutes

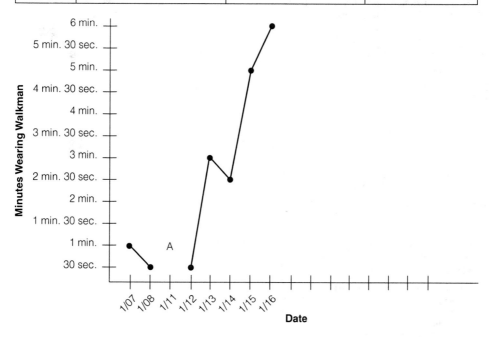

FIGURE 2.3 Sample data form for recording duration data.

haviors, it is unlikely that you will know in a timely manner if an intervention is working or that you will be able to detect subtle changes in target behaviors. Once you have gathered data on target behaviors, the next step is to graph the data. A graph allows for quick and easy visual inspection of data. The following section explains how to graph data and provides guidelines for making instructional decisions based on your graphs.

Graphing Data. Graphing data is easy, takes very little time, and is usually fun for teachers and students! Table 2.5 explains the steps in graphing data. Figures 2.1, 2.2, and 2.3 each show graphs of the raw data depicted in each figure.

Table 2.5 How to Graph and Interpret Data

Graphing Data

1. *Convert the data if necessary.* This ensures consistency within data for each target behavior. Guidelines for deciding if you need to convert are as follows:

   a. Is the target behavior a restricted event? If so, convert data to a percentage (number of correct responses ÷ number of opportunities to respond × 100).

   b. Is the target behavior a nonrestricted event? If so, observe for the same amount of time every observation period. Do not convert; simply graph the number of times the behavior occurred.

   c. Did you use duration recording? If so, observe for the same amount of time every observation period and graph the *total* number of minutes and/or seconds the behavior occurred.

2. *Set up a graph for each target behavior.* To set up a graph, use commercially available graph paper.

   a. Draw the vertical line and label it to reflect the target behavior that was measured. For example, "number of head hits during play group," "number of responses to social questions," "time spent brushing teeth," or "time between being told to put on jacket and when task actually began."

   b. Draw the horizontal line and label it to reflect each observation period. For example, your label might be "daily language sessions" or "daily play periods."

   c. Divide the vertical line into *equal* increments (it is usually easiest to simply use the squares of the graph paper as increments) and number each increment to show number or percentage, or minutes and/or seconds. The intersection of the vertical and horizontal lines is always "0," and numbering begins from there. For example, to set up a graph for restricted event data you might number the increments "10%, 20%, 30%, 40%," and so on. For a graph to depict duration data, the increments may be numbered "15 sec.; 30 sec.; 45 sec.; 1 min.; 1 min. 15 sec.; 1 min. 30 sec.;" and so on.

   d. Divide the horizontal line into equal increments to reflect the observation periods when data were collected. For example, "2–19, 2–20, 2–21," or "10–4, a.m.; 10–4, p.m.; 10–5, a.m.; 10–5, p.m."

3. *Plot baseline data.*

   a. Data from each observation session is plotted on a consecutive vertical line. These points are called **data points**.

   b. *Connect data points using straight lines.*

4. *Once you are finished gathering baseline data, draw a vertical dotted line next to the last baseline data point.* This line separates baseline data from intervention data. It makes the graph easier to read.

5. *Begin intervention and continue the same methods of collecting and graphing data.*

6. *Do not connect the last baseline data point and the first intervention data point.* That is, do not draw a line across the dotted vertical line to connect data points.

7. *If student is absent for a day, or if data are not collected during an observation session, skip that vertical line. Do not connect data points across this space.* Figure 2.3 shows an example of a student's absence and how this is handled on the graph.

8. *If you change anything about the intervention, again draw a dotted vertical line next to the last data point of the last intervention. Begin plotting data from the new intervention on the other side of the dotted line.*

Interpreting Data

1. *If data line shows steady progress in the desired direction (up for behaviors you are trying to increase, down for behaviors you wish to decrease), continue the intervention or instruction until student reaches criterion.* After that, you no longer need to regularly collect data on the behavior. However, it is good practice to measure the behavior once in awhile (e.g., once per week, once per month, once every other month) to be sure it is maintained at desired levels.

2. *If data line is erratic or inconsistent, you should do one or more of the following:*

   a. Examine the intervention to be sure it is being done consistently and correctly.

   b. Modify the intervention slightly. For example, you may wish to reinforce more frequently, use a different reinforcer, use a different form of time-out, or break a target skill down into small steps for instruction.

   c. If the target behavior is a challenging behavior, you may need to develop a new hypothesis regarding the contributing factors and/or function of the behavior (see Chapter 3).

   d. Change interventions entirely. This may mean using a different instructional technique. For a challenging behavior, the new intervention should reflect your new hypothesis.

3. *If data line is flat for more than three data points (thus indicating no progress), you should take one of the actions listed in step 2.*

Consequences

The last part of the A-B-C model is *consequences.* The type of consequence that a student experiences following a behavior determines whether or not the behavior will be repeated. If the consequence is pleasing to and desired by the student, the behavior will probably be repeated. If the consequence is disliked by the student, chances are that the behavior will not be repeated. In general, consequences are divided into two main categories: reinforcement, which increases the likelihood that a behavior will be repeated, and reductive techniques or punishment, which reduces the likelihood that a behavior will be repeated. These consequences are described in the following sections.

Reinforcement. The behavioral deficits of autistic children often reflect behaviors or skills that are either nonexistent or occur too infrequently to be functional. The frequency of these behaviors can be increased using the behavioral principles of positive reinforcement and negative reinforcement. In addition, some inappropriate behaviors exhibited by students with autism are maintained by these principles. This section will explain these principles and how to use them effectively.

Positive reinforcement is the process in which a consequence is presented following a response, and as a result, that same response is likely to be exhibited again in the future, particularly under the same conditions. This is a functional definition; that is, positive reinforcement has occurred only if the response is repeated in the future as a result of that particular presentation. The consequence is called a **positive reinforcer,** or **reinforcer.** For example, each time a student responds correctly during individual teaching time, you clap your hands and praise her. If she continues responding correctly, you could assume that you have positively reinforced her. Or, periodically as a student plays appropriately with blocks, with no self-stimulation, you give him a piece of cereal and praise him. If the student continues playing appropriately, positive reinforcement has occurred.

Positive reinforcement is an important tool that will help increase students' repertoires of appropriate behaviors. However, like any tool it must be used correctly in order to be effective, and if used incorrectly it can create problems. Correct use of positive reinforcement means applying it systematically and contingently (e.g., the reinforcer is *only* given when the student exhibits the desired behavior) as a consequence for desired behaviors, following the guidelines listed below. If reinforcement is used incorrectly, it may not increase desired behaviors. Worse, it may even increase undesired behaviors. Recall that earlier you learned that *all* behavior is governed by the same principles. This means that the principle of positive reinforcement can also serve to maintain or increase *inappropriate behavior,* even inadvertently. For example, perhaps a student works quietly but gets little teacher attention until she pushes her work away and stands up. Because she is given attention only when she stops working, this student may be learning that the way to get the teacher's attention is by *not working!*

Reinforcers can take many forms. The following section will introduce you to the different types of reinforcers, and will describe recommendations for which type of reinforcer to use under certain conditions.

Types of Reinforcers. When teaching students with autism, teachers sometimes face a challenge when trying to identify effective reinforcers that they can control. The reason for this is that many things that are powerful reinforcers for other children and adolescents are either disliked by students with autism (e.g., praise, attention, playing with friends, hugs) or not useful because they haven't learned to value the items as reinforcers (e.g., games, stickers, toys, stars, happy faces, watching videos). In fact, these students often have noncontingent access to reinforcers that are far more powerful than anything we have to offer (e.g., self-stimulatory behaviors, social withdrawal). This doesn't mean that positive reinforcement cannot be used with these students. It does mean that teachers must look more carefully to identify potential reinforcers or that they may have to *teach* students to like certain reinforcers. Procedures for identifying reinforcers and teaching students to like reinforcers are described below.

There are two categories of reinforcers: **primary reinforcers** and **secondary reinforcers.** Specific examples of each type of reinforcer are listed in Table 2.6. Remember that the teacher may need to teach students to value many of these reinforcers.

Primary Reinforcers. Primary reinforcers are things that are biological necessities: food, water, warmth, and so on. Children do not have to learn to like these reinforcers; they are intrinsically reinforcing. Because many children with autism, especially young children, have not learned to like other types of reinforcers, primary reinforcers are valuable teaching tools. For example, you may teach a student with autism to look at you by holding a small piece of cracker close to your face,

Table 2.6 Examples of Reinforcers

Primary Reinforcers

- Sips of juice or water
- Small bites of apples, crackers, carrots, cheese, pretzels, chips, etc.
- Pieces of cereal
- Peanuts
- Popcorn

Secondary Reinforcers

Social Reinforcers

- Praise statements—be sure to be enthusiastic and use lots of variety when giving praise statements!
- "Way to go!"
- "Excellent!"
- "What a great job!"
- "You're such a hard worker!"
- "Good job sitting quietly!"
- "ALL RIGHT!"
- High five
- Thumbs up
- Clap hands
- Shake hands
- A quick tickle
- Hug

Material Reinforcers

- Stickers: regular or scratch-and-sniff
- Pictures of favorite objects or people
- Small trinkets
- Posters
- Personalized pencil
- "Good Work" certificate
- Cologne
- Hand cream
- Bubbles
- Silly Putty, Slime, or other toys with interesting texture
- Balloons
- Nail polish
- Bracelets, necklaces, or other inexpensive jewelry
- Noise makers
- Slinky toy
- Kaleidoscope

Activity Reinforcers

- Play a game
- Listen to music with headphones
- Play a computer game
- Use a special toy or material
- Do classroom jobs: water plants, feed animals, erase board, take attendance form to office, empty pencil sharpener, pass out snack items, etc.
- Take a walk with a teacher
- Make toast or sandwich, popcorn, lemonade, pudding, etc.
- Jump on trampoline
- Play in water or sand
- Watch a video
- Choose a favorite chair or place to sit (e.g., beanbag chair)
- Use roller skates or inline skates
- Assemble models
- Do arts and crafts activities
- Watch and/or feed fish in the class aquarium
- Use visual entertainment activities (e.g., Lava Lamp, Perpetual Motion balls, Wave Machine)

Token Reinforcers

- Points
- Play money
- Stickers
- Self-inking stamps
- Plastic counting chips
- Legos

giving the command "Look at me," then giving the child the cracker as soon as he looks at you. Primary reinforcers are also helpful for teaching communication skills: at snack time or lunch time, it is natural to ask a student "What do you want?" and then require the student to verbalize (or sign or point to a picture) the name of the food or liquid being offered before receiving it.

Some professionals believe that the self-stimulatory behaviors exhibited by so many children and youth with autism function much like a primary reinforcer: that the behavior satisfies a physical need, or "feels good," much like a big yawn or stretch feels good. The question of whether students should be allowed to earn time to engage in self-stimulatory behavior is controversial. Some professionals feel that this is inappropriate, that self-stimulatory behavior should never be allowed. Others believe that it is acceptable as long as the student produces desired behaviors first, and as long as there is only limited time allowed for self-stimulatory behaviors. We believe it depends somewhat on the student: If this is the only known reinforcer for the student, if the teacher can control access to it, and if the student will work to be allowed to engage in self-stimulation, we feel it is acceptable. However, in this case, we strongly advise concentrating on identifying and/or teaching other reinforcers, then gradually limiting access to self-stimulation as a reinforcer (in favor of other reinforcers).

Secondary Reinforcers. Secondary reinforcers are things or events that we learn to like, but do not need biologically. The four types of secondary reinforcers are social reinforcers, material reinforcers, activity reinforcers, and token reinforcers.

- **Social reinforcers** include praise, smiles, gestures (e.g., a high five or thumbs up), physical contact (e.g., a hug or pat), attention, and even physical proximity. Because social reinforcers are available in virtually any environment, children with autism need to learn to value this type of reinforcer. However, the nature of their disability means that children with autism often do not automatically learn

to appreciate social reinforcers; they must be taught. The guidelines for using reinforcement, described later, explain how to do this.

- **Material reinforcers** are objects: stickers, toys, posters, pictures, magazines, and pencils.

- **Activity reinforcers** include playing a game, singing a song, doing a special job, drawing a picture, or listening to music. Although both material and activity reinforcers are found in other environments (e.g., children in general education classrooms often get to do special activities when they finish their work, and they earn stickers for good work), teachers should not rely on them exclusively.

- **Token reinforcers** (or tokens) are not intended to be reinforcers per se. Because it is often impractical to deliver activity or material reinforcers after each correct response, tokens serve as an indication that the student has exhibited a desired behavior and is on the way to earning an actual reinforcer. Tokens may be happy faces, plastic chips, points, stars, stickers, marbles, check marks, and so on. The student accumulates tokens during a predetermined period of time, then exchanges the tokens for a **back-up reinforcer:** a material, activity, or primary reinforcer. Because token reinforcers are more abstract than other forms of reinforcers, they should be introduced gradually, with back-up reinforcers earned quickly in the beginning of the program. As the student learns the connection between the token reinforcer and the back-up reinforcer, he or she may be able to work for longer periods of time before earning the back-up reinforcer.

One interesting study evaluated the use of the Autism Reinforcer Checklist (ARC, shown in Table 2.7) with autistic preschoolers, elementary-aged children, and adolescents to determine their most and least preferred reinforcers (Atkinson, Jenson, Rovner, Cameron, Van Wagenen, & Petersen, 1984). The results of this study indicated that the ARC is a reliable and valid instrument for

Table 2.7 Autism Reinforcer Checklist

Name: _____   Rater: _____

Age: _____   Date: _____

Edible Reinforcers		Yes	No
Candy:	1. M&Ms	____	____
	2. Jelly Beans	____	____
	3. Licorice	____	____
	4. Candy Canes	____	____
	5. Gum	____	____
	6. Smarties	____	____
	7. Lollipops	____	____
	8. Candy Kisses	____	____
	9. Chocolate	____	____
	10. ____	____	____
Cereals:	11. Cheerios	____	____
	12. Fruit Loops	____	____
	13. Trix	____	____
	14. ____	____	____
Fruit:	15. Raisins	____	____
	16. Apples	____	____
	17. Oranges	____	____
	18. Bananas	____	____
	19. ____	____	____
Liquids:	20. Milk	____	____
	21. Chocolate Milk	____	____
	22. Juice	____	____
	23. Soda Pop	____	____
	24. Lemonade	____	____
	25. ____	____	____
Frozen:	26. Popsicle	____	____
	27. Ice Cream	____	____
	28. ____	____	____
Soft:	29. Pudding	____	____
	30. Jello	____	____
	31. Yogurt	____	____
	32. Marshmallows	____	____
	33. Cheese	____	____
	34. Cottage Cheese	____	____
	35. Peanut Butter	____	____
	36. Jam/Jelly	____	____
	37. ____	____	____

		Yes	No
Others:	38. Cake	____	____
	39. Cupcakes	____	____
	40. Doughnuts	____	____
	41. Crackers	____	____
	42. Frosting	____	____
	43. Pretzels	____	____
	44. Corn Chips	____	____
	45. Cheez Balls	____	____
	46. Doritos	____	____
	47. Cookies	____	____
	48. Popcorn	____	____
	49. Vegetables	____	____
	50. ____	____	____

Material Reinforcers:		Yes	No
	1. Stopwatch	____	____
	2. Hand Cream	____	____
	3. Bubbles	____	____
	4. Combs	____	____
	5. Stickers	____	____
	6. Play Dough	____	____
	7. Perfume	____	____
	8. Toy Instruments	____	____
	9. Puzzles	____	____
	10. Beads	____	____
	11. Stamps	____	____
	12. Masks	____	____
	13. Crayons	____	____
	14. Fans	____	____
	15. Balloons	____	____
	16. Bean Bags	____	____
	17. Hats	____	____
	18. Mirrors	____	____
	19. Books	____	____
	20. Coloring Books	____	____
	21. Whistles	____	____
	22. Blocks	____	____
	23. Paints	____	____
	24. Colored Chalk	____	____
	25. _____	____	____

Activity Reinforcers	Yes	No			Yes	No
1. Rocking	___	___	47. Looking at Pictures		___	___
2. Brushing Hair	___	___	48. Basketball		___	___
3. Clapping Hands	___	___	49. Finger Paint			
4. Airplane Rides	___	___	with Pudding		___	___
5. Drawing Pictures	___	___	with Whipped Cream		___	___
6. Run Outside	___	___	with Soap		___	___
7. Hide and Seek	___	___	with Paint		___	___
8. Piggyback Rides	___	___	50. Racing		___	___
9. Chase	___	___	51. Wagon Rides		___	___
10. Peek-A-Boo	___	___	52. Thrown in Air		___	___
11. Sing Songs	___	___	53. Make Copies		___	___
12. Sprinkle Glitter	___	___	54. Water Plants		___	___
13. Tickles	___	___	55. Going for Walks		___	___
14. Water Play	___	___	56. Making Treats		___	___
15. Puppets	___	___	57. Icing Cupcakes		___	___
16. Sand Play	___	___	58. Making Popcorn		___	___
17. Trampoline	___	___	59. Playing Ball		___	___
18. Dancing	___	___	60. Playing with Tools		___	___
19. Bring Toy From Home	___	___	61. Birthday Parties		___	___
20. Turn Lights On/Off	___	___	62. Playing with Zippers		___	___
21. Pour Liquids Back & Forth	___	___	63. Blowing Bubbles		___	___
22. Video Tapes	___	___	64. Swimming		___	___
23. Stories	___	___	65. Listen to Music		___	___
24. Being the Teacher	___	___	66. Play with Typewriter		___	___
25. Talking on Phone	___	___	67. Stringing Beads		___	___
26. Drink in Office	___	___	68. Turning Water On/Off		___	___
27. Drawing	___	___	69. Smelling Spices		___	___
28. Draw on Chalkboard	___	___	70. Fishing Game		___	___
29. Lunch/Snack Helper	___	___	71. Dart Board		___	___
30. Field Trips	___	___	72. Grab Bag		___	___
31. Twirling in Air	___	___	73. Surprise Box		___	___
32. Blankets over Head	___	___	74. Spinner		___	___
33. Taking Pictures	___	___	75. _____		___	___
34. Going to Trash	___	___				
35. Roll Down Hill	___	___	**Social Reinforcers**		**Yes**	**No**
36. Teacher's Helper	___	___	1. Hugs		___	___
37. Making Pictures:			2. Shaking Hands		___	___
with Popcorn	___	___	3. Kisses		___	___
with Noodles	___	___	4. Tickling		___	___
with String	___	___	5. Winking		___	___
38. Running Errands	___	___	6. Give Me Five		___	___
39. Playing in Boxes	___	___	7. Rubbing Noses		___	___
40. Dressing Up	___	___	8. Smiling		___	___
41. Climbing	___	___	9. Whistling		___	___
42. Stim Time	___	___	10. Patting		___	___
43. Rocking in Boat	___	___	11. Praising		___	___
44. Cutting Pictures	___	___	12. Back Scratch/Rub		___	___
45. Playing with Glue	___	___	13. Praise		___	___
46. Treasure Hunt	___	___	14. _____		___	___

SOURCE: Atkinson, R.P., Jenson, W.R., Rovner, L., Cameron, S., Van Wagenen, L., & Petersen, B.P. (1984). Brief report: Validation of the Autism Reinforcer Checklist for Children. *Journal of Autism and Developmental Disorders, 14*(4), 429–433. Reprinted by permission.

determining reinforcers for students with autism. In addition, results indicated the reinforcers that were most preferred versus least preferred by the students in the study (Table 2.8). Students seemed to like "junk foods" (e.g., crackers, chips, cookies) more than cereal, raisins, fruits, vegetables, and so on. In terms of material and activity reinforcers, they opted for objects that reflected light or moving objects (e.g., bubbles, mirrors, climbing, wagon rides). Least liked reinforcers in these categories were activities that involved using special materials (e.g., Play-Doh, painting). Interestingly, the students liked social reinforcers that involved social interaction (e.g., tickling, hugging, patting) more so than more aggressive social activities (e.g., pinching cheeks, whistling). The ARC could be a useful tool for determining effective reinforcers for your students (see the Selecting Reinforcers section on page 48).

Guidelines for Using Positive Reinforcement. Like any procedure, certain rules must be followed if reinforcement is to work. The following sections describe rules for using reinforcement. If the target behavior does not increase when a reinforcement contingency is implemented, it doesn't

Table 2.8 Most and Least Popular Reinforcers as Ranked Using the Autism Reinforcer Checklist

Category	Most	Least
Edible reinforcers	Crackers	Licorice
	Cookies	Raisins
	Marshmallows	Cheerios
	Cupcakes	Apples
	Ice cream	Jello
	Juice	Raw vegetables
	Soda pop	Candy canes
	Doughnuts	Oranges
	Popcorn	Milk
	Corn chips	Frosting
Material reinforcers	Toy instruments	Paper and crayons
	Bubbles	Play-Doh
	Balloons	Hats
	Mirrors	Coloring books
	Blocks	Beads
Social reinforcers	Tickling	Blowing
	Smiling	Pinching cheeks
	Praising	Twitching noses
	Hugging	Back scratching
	Patting	Whistling
Activity reinforcers	Going for walks	Having mom leave class
	Watching popcorn pop	Cutting pictures from magazines
	Rocking	Making pictures with popcorn, noodles, or string
	Musical instruments	Stringing beads
	Time alone	Taping and tearing paper
	Water play	Playing with paper
	Clapping hands	Crayons
	Playing in front of mirror	Drawing pictures
	Field trips	Stories in teacher's lap
	Running outside	Finger painting with paint, pudding, or whipping cream
	Drinking out of pop bottles	
	Climbing	
	Wagon rides	
	Flushing toilet	

SOURCE: Atkinson, R.P., Jenson, W.R., Rovner, L., Cameron, S., Van Wagenen, L., & Petersen, B.P. (1984). Brief report: Validation of the Autism Reinforcer Checklist for Children. *Journal of Autism and Developmental Disorders, 14*(4), 429–433. Reprinted by permission.

mean reinforcement "doesn't work." It usually means either you are using something the child does not like or value, the procedures have not been applied correctly, or that other principles are at work and therefore the intervention needs to be adjusted accordingly.

Deliver reinforcement immediately after the desired behavior. This is how the student learns to associate that behavior with reinforcement. The longer the delay between the behavior and reinforcement, the less likely the student is to make that association.

Always use social reinforcers, even when you are using primary, material, or token reinforcers. Some students with autism have not learned to value social reinforcers. However, you can teach students to like praise, smiles, and so on by using social reinforcers each time you give the student another type of reinforcer. Eventually, you should be able to reduce the use of primary or material reinforcers and depend more on social and token reinforcers to maintain behavior. This is important for generalization, because other types of reinforcers, such as social reinforcers, are more common than primary reinforcers in settings outside of the classroom.

Be sure that desired reinforcers are contingent on appropriate behavior. Contingent means that the student does not get the reinforcer until the behavior is displayed. This is also how students learn to associate the behavior with the reinforcer. If students have access to reinforcers without exhibiting desired target behaviors, they have less motivation to engage in the target behaviors.

Use small amounts of reinforcers. For primary reinforcers, give the student only small amounts after each response: a single piece of cereal, a small bite of cracker or fruit, a small sip of juice. If the child has too much to eat or drink, the primary reinforcers may cease to serve as a reinforcer for a period of time. If you are using activity reinforcers, limit the amount of time allowed for the

activity; usually a few minutes is sufficient. With material reinforcers, use smaller, less valued material reinforcers more frequently; save larger, more prized reinforcers for when the student has exhibited desired behaviors over an extended period of time.

Fade primary reinforcers as soon as possible. Primary reinforcers are valuable for teaching a new behavior, or for students for whom other reinforcers have not been identified. However, you should fade these as soon as new, desired behaviors are being exhibited regularly and frequently, and gradually move to other types of reinforcers.

Fade the frequency of reinforcement. When you are teaching a new behavior, you should reinforce the student each time that behavior is exhibited to the desired criterion level (**continuous reinforcement**). However, once the behavior is established (e.g., the student is exhibiting the behavior regularly), you should gradually reinforce less frequently—only after several behaviors or several minutes of the behavior (**intermittent reinforcement**). Be careful, though, not to move too abruptly from continual reinforcement to intermittent reinforcement, or the student may not maintain the skill through the transition. For example, if you have been giving a student a small cracker and praise each time she initiates a greeting to a teacher, you should fade the reinforcement by giving her the cracker and praise for every two greetings, then every four greetings, then once a day, and so on.

Rely on natural reinforcers as much as possible. Natural reinforcers are reinforcers that normally exist in students' environments. For example, a natural consequence for saying "Milk, please" is that the student gets a drink of milk. A natural consequence of learning to operate the VCR is that the student is able to view a videotape. Teachers must rely on natural reinforcers as much as possible because these will maintain desired behaviors even in the absence of other reinforcers. In the above example of teaching a student to initiate greetings, eventually you could stop using the cracker and praise altogether: The natural consequence of the teacher's response to the greeting should maintain the behavior.

Selecting Reinforcers. How do you decide what will be an effective reinforcer? Several approaches are described in Table 2.9. Generally, however, you should select the reinforcer that is most similar to what might be found in other environments, or used with children of similar age to your students. The more you can teach your students to respond to naturally occurring reinforcers, the more likely the student is to generalize skills to other environments. However, particularly for very young children or children who exhibit severe behavior problems, you may need to first use primary reinforcers. If so, you should soon introduce other types of reinforcers, as described in the rules for using reinforcement above, and eventually rely on

those exclusively. In the vignette titled *Colin Learns to Sit Next to His Friends,* you will see how Colin's teacher applies many of the rules for using reinforcement.

It is also important to remember that students with autism often respond to what are called **idiosyncratic reinforcers,** which means that an activity, object, type of interaction, and so on that would be neutral for most students may function as a reinforcer for a student with autism. By definition, idiosyncratic reinforcers are unique to the child. For example, one student of ours would quickly complete his structured teaching tasks to obtain the reinforcer of sitting in the teacher's car for a few minutes! Another student would comply with tasks so that she could use a spray bottle of water to clean the counters in the classroom. Still another student worked hard to get his preferred reinforcer: a bite of lemon! The point here is observe your students carefully to identify potential reinforcers that might not be discovered through more traditional channels.

Table 2.9 How to Select Reinforcers

1. *Observe the child.*
   - What activities, objects, foods, and so on does the child choose when allowed free choice?
   - Are there certain phrases, gestures, and so on that seem to produce a pleasant response from the child?
   - What self-stimulatory behaviors does the student exhibit?
2. *Use a reinforcer menu to let the child choose reinforcers.*
   - Create a menu of possible reinforcers listed either by name, if the child can read, or by picture (photographs are best).
   - When the child earns a reinforcer, allow him to select a desired object, food, activity, and so on from the menu. You may have to teach the child how to make choices.
3. *Ask the student.*
   - Ask the student, if he has sufficient language skills, what he would like to earn for good work.
4. *Ask others.*
   - Ask the child's parents what the child likes to do, likes to play with, or likes to eat at home.
   - Ask other teachers who have worked with the child.
5. *Conduct a reinforcer sampling.*
   - Arrange several possible reinforcers on a table.
   - Allow the child to noncontingently choose the objects, foods, and so on that she likes.
6. *Use the Autism Reinforcer Checklist.*
   - Have parents complete a copy of the checklist.
   - Use the checklist to generate ideas for new or novel reinforcers.
   - Have students who can read check off the items they like and dislike.

Colin Learns to Sit Next to His Friends

Ms. Preston had a new student in her room, Colin, who hit or pinched any student who sat next to him. To teach Colin to sit next to other students without hurting them, Ms. Preston determined that one target behavior for Colin would be for him to sit next to another student during morning group, with no hitting. She gave Colin a piece of cookie and praised him every 30 seconds he remained seated and did not hit. Realizing that she needed to teach Colin to respond to other types of reinforcers for appropriate sitting, Ms. Preston followed this sequence:

- When Colin could sit for 30 seconds with no hitting or pinching attempts, Ms. Preston began giving him the cookie after sitting appropriately for 1 minute.

- When he was successful at this level, she began giving Colin a happy face stamp on a card at the same time she gave him the piece of cookie. At the end of the group, Ms. Preston helped Colin count the stamps. If he had 10 stamps, he earned a small cup of juice.

- Next, she gave him the happy face stamp at the end of each minute of sitting appropriately, but she gradually eliminated the cookie by giving him the cookie only every few times he earned a stamp. Of course, she continued to praise him each time he earned a happy face stamp, and he still earned juice if he had ten happy faces at the end of group.

- When Ms. Preston had eliminated the cookie reinforcer and was using only the happy face stamps, she began increasing the length of time he was required to sit appropriately before earning a happy face stamp.

Eventually, Colin learned to sit next to other students without hitting or pinching, and with only verbal praise as his reinforcer.

Negative Reinforcement. Another form of reinforcement, negative reinforcement, means that an aversive condition is avoided or ends by exhibiting a particular behavior. It is "negative" because of the aversive condition that is removed or avoided, and "reinforcement" because it results in a behavior being repeated under similar circumstances. Negative reinforcement can be used to increase desired behaviors, particularly task-related behaviors, for students with autism. Remember that children with autism often do not like close physical contact—they prefer to be left alone. You may find that a child who prefers to be left alone will comply with your request to work when he learns that compliance means you will "back off" for a moment. For example, let's say you have a student who does not like you to be close to him, and you want this student to collate and staple two papers. You stay close to the student (aversive condition), guiding him through the task as needed. As soon as he completes the task, you move away from him for a few seconds (removal of the aversive condition). Once he learns that collating and stapling will earn him a few moments of not being "bothered," he is likely to complete the task with little resistance.

Because of the difficulty in finding effective positive reinforcers for students with autism, and because of their characteristic desire to be left alone, negative reinforcement is often more effective than positive reinforcement. However, despite its potential effectiveness, we recommend that negative reinforcement be used only if you are unable to identify positive reinforcers. Furthermore, if you use negative reinforcement, the aversive condition should not look aversive to anyone except the child with autism. That is, we are *not* advocating any action that involves physical pain or discomfort for the student, or any extremely negative conditions such as yelling or a harsh tone of voice. A good rule of thumb is that the aversive condition should not be anything that you would not use with any other student. It is only aversive because of the unique nature of autism.

Negative reinforcement sometimes explains students' inappropriate behavior. Some students tantrum, scream, or hit or bite themselves when asked to do certain tasks or engage in certain activities. If the student's behavior results in his avoiding the task or activity (the aversive condition), he may be more likely to exhibit that behavior under similar circumstances in the future (negative reinforcement). For example, perhaps a student hits himself when asked to work on a disliked task—folding clothes—and as a result that task is removed; he is not required to fold the clothes. The student escapes an aversive situation (folding clothes) by hitting himself; therefore, each time a disliked task is presented in the future, we can expect the student to hit himself.

Positive reinforcement and negative reinforcement are the procedures used to increase desired behaviors. However, children and youth with autism exhibit many inappropriate behaviors that must be decreased or eliminated. For this you need another type of consequence: behavior reductive procedures or punishment.

Behavior Reductive Procedures. Students with autism exhibit numerous behavioral excesses that interfere with their ability to function successfully in school and other environments. Reducing or eliminating these excesses is an important goal of educational programs for students with autism. However, as you will see, reducing inappropriate behaviors is only one component of a quality program; it is also essential to implement well-designed programs for teaching and increasing desired behaviors and to provide appropriate curriculum and instruction.

The two general categories of behavior reductive techniques (Cooper, Heron, & Heward, 1987), listed here in order of aversiveness and in-trusiveness, are nonpunishment procedures, which include differential reinforcement techniques and extinction; and punishment procedures, including response cost, time-out, presentation of an aversive stimulus, and overcorrection. As a general rule we recommend that teachers use less aversive reductive procedures, such as differential reinforcement, for reducing problem behaviors. If undesired behaviors are not reduced using those procedures, you can move to more aversive procedures such as response cost or time-out. One exception to this rule may be if the student exhibits a behavior that is dangerous to herself or others; in this case, you should use the procedure that is most likely to have an immediate effect.

The following sections describe nonpunishment and punishment procedures for reducing inappropriate behaviors. Nonpunishment procedures rely on either positive reinforcement or withholding positive reinforcement to reduce behaviors. Punishment procedures involve removal of a previously earned reinforcer, blocking the opportunity to earn positive reinforcement, or the presentation of an unpleasant stimulus as a consequence for misbehavior.

Nonpunishment Procedures. The nonpunishment procedures include differential reinforcement and extinction. We strongly recommend you consider one or more of the differential reinforcement procedures as your first intervention for problem behaviors. They are an effective way of reducing inappropriate behavior while increasing desired, functional behavior at the same time.

Differential Reinforcement. Differential reinforcement is a set of unique procedures that relies on positive approaches to *reduce* behaviors. In differential reinforcement, you determine what the student needs to do instead of the problem behavior, and then you teach and systematically reinforce that desired behavior. The desired behavior is given direct, positive attention, while the undesired behavior either receives no attention or is consequated with a mild punisher. As a result, the desired behavior increases and the undesired behavior diminishes. Differential reinforcement is an effective procedure for reducing problem behaviors without worrying about the negative aspects sometimes associated with punishment. The four general types of differential reinforcement are described below, some of which can be used in combination. The procedure you should use depends largely on the nature of the problem behavior, as you will see.

Differential Reinforcement of Lower Levels of Behavior (DRL). This strategy is used when the target inappropriate behavior does not need to be reduced immediately or completely. For example, it is acceptable, even desirable, for a student to ask a few questions about a task or to ask once or twice when it is time for a snack. It is unacceptable to ask dozens of questions about a task or to ask about a snack repeatedly throughout the morning. To use this strategy, you determine how many of the target inappropriate behaviors the student is allowed to exhibit during a certain time period and still earn a reinforcer. This initial criterion is based on how many behaviors the student is currently exhibiting; you should choose a criterion that is achievable. Once the student meets this criterion (perhaps for 2 or 3 days), you slightly reduce the number of target behaviors allowed. When the student is successful at this level, the number of inappropriate behaviors allowed is reduced still further. This pattern continues until the behavior is either eliminated or reduced to acceptable levels. Earlier we mentioned Michael, who had problems with high levels of face touching. In the vignette titled *Michael Learns Not to Touch His Face,* we see how Michael's teacher used DRL to reduce this behavior.

Michael Learns Not to Touch His Face

Michael was a 10-year-old boy with the bad habit of touching his face to various places during individual work time with the teacher. He covered his eyes with his hands, covered his face with his shirt, put his forehead down on the table or on his knees, turned his face to his shoulder, and so on. Obviously, this significantly interfered with his compliance to tasks. For 3 days, his teacher used a handheld counting device to count how many times Michael's face touched anything during the 20-minute work time. During those 3 days, he averaged 139 face touches per session! The teacher then told Michael if he wanted to earn his reinforcer (a spider drawn on his hand at the end of the session), he could face-touch no more than 130 times. While Michael did not truly understand the concept of "130," he quickly learned that each "click" meant he was closer to not getting his spider. The teacher required the 130-touches criterion to be met for 3 consecutive days, then she lowered the allowable number of face touches to 120 touches per session. When this criterion was met for 3 consecutive days, she lowered it again. This pattern continued until Michael was exhibiting less than 10 face touches per session, a level Michael's teacher felt did not interfere with tasks.

Differential Reinforcement of Incompatible Behaviors (DRI). This strategy allows the teacher to reinforce a behavior that is incompatible with the problem behavior. For example, a student who is appropriately working on a puzzle cannot be flicking his fingers in front of his face. Or a child who is sitting with her hands in her lap cannot be biting her hand. The student receives reinforcement for the target behavior, but nothing for the inappropriate behavior.

The target behaviors chosen for reinforcement should, as much as possible, be either incompatible (that is, the student cannot exhibit the problem behavior and the target behavior at the same time) or as close to incompatible as possible. For example, the behavior of pushing a toy truck along the floor would be a likely target for a student who spins the truck's wheels as a self-stimulatory activity, because both of those behaviors cannot occur simultaneously. However, reinforcing a student for being in-seat might not work if the problem is verbal self-stimulation, rocking, self-abuse, or even hitting. The student could exhibit any of those behaviors and still be in-seat. You should target a behavior for reinforcement that is more directly incompatible with the problem behavior.

Differential Reinforcement of Other Behavior (DRO). This differential reinforcement procedure is especially helpful when the target behavior must be eliminated, such as aggressive behaviors, self-abusive behaviors, or extremely disruptive self-stimulatory behaviors. DRO (sometimes called differential reinforcement of zero rates of behavior) means that the student is reinforced at the end of a period of time during which the target inappropriate behavior was not exhibited. The reinforcement periods are brief at first, then are gradually increased as the student learns to control the behavior. For example, a student receives a raisin at the end of each 30-second interval during which she does not hit her head. When she has been successful at controlling head-hitting for 80 percent of the 30-second intervals over several days, the reinforcement period is increased to 45 seconds, then later to 1 minute, then 1.5 minutes, and so on.

To implement DRO, you must decide how long the initial reinforcement interval should be. To do this, gather baseline data to determine how frequently the behavior occurs. The initial reinforcement interval should be slightly less than the baseline average. For example, if baseline data indicate that Stacey pokes her eyes approximately every 25 minutes, you might set 20 minutes as the initial reinforcement interval: If she doesn't poke her eyes for 20 minutes, she earns a reinforcer. The initial reinforcement interval must be short enough for the student to have a high probability of success. In addition, the length of the intervals should not be increased too rapidly.

One of the potential drawbacks of DRO is that the student receives reinforcement as long as

the target inappropriate behavior is not exhibited, no matter what else the student does or does not do during the interval. Obviously, under these circumstances you run the risk of reinforcing some behaviors that are not desirable. However, this is a trade-off that sometimes must be made in order to get a more serious behavior under control (see vignette titled *Ben Learns Not to Run Away*). Once the more serious behavior is eliminated, you can address other behaviors.

Ben Learns Not to Run Away

Ben was a 12-year-old who frequently ran away from teachers. When he ran, he darted out the door and out of the building so fast that it was difficult to catch him. Of course, this was a very dangerous behavior that had to be controlled quickly. Ben's teacher used a combination of DRI and DRO to reduce his runaway behavior. Baseline data indicated he ran away an average of six times per day, or about once every hour. During the first phase of intervention, for each 10-minute period that he remained within arms' length of a teacher or paraprofessional (DRI), he earned tokens that he could exchange at the end of the morning and afternoon for play in the gym. In addition, after each half-hour period that he did not run away (the teacher used a timer to mark these periods), he earned a primary reinforcer (DRO). It did not matter what else he did during that period, as long as he did not run away. If he ran away during a half-hour period, he was placed in time-out for 3 minutes, then a new half-hour interval would begin. Gradually, both the DRI and the DRO intervals were increased until Ben's runaway behavior had been reduced to zero.

Differential Reinforcement of Communicative Behavior (DRC). As you have learned, sometimes inappropriate behavior may be a form of communication, particularly if the child does not have other effective ways of communicating. For example, a child may bite himself when he is frustrated, or may attempt to pull your hair when he does not want to do the task you have assigned. If an inappropriate behavior has a communicative function, simply eliminating that behavior (using DRO, for example), will probably be ineffective because the child will have to find another way to communicate. How do you know if a behavior has a communicative function? A functional assessment will help you determine this (see Chapter 3). If your functional assessment indicates that a behavior may be for purposes of communication, DRC would be the intervention of choice.

DRC means that you identify what the student is trying to communicate, then determine a more appropriate way for the child to express that need, want, or wish (and teach the child how to use the more appropriate form of communication, if necessary). The student is then reinforced for using the appropriate form of communication. For example, if a student pulls your hair when she does not want to do something, you could teach her to say or sign "no" instead. Her reinforcer for saying or signing "no" at appropriate times might be a primary reinforcer *and* you might withdraw the task, at least temporarily. But you might wonder if it is appropriate to teach the student refusal skills! In our opinion, the student is already refusing—you are simply teaching her a more acceptable way to do it. Also, while you might withdraw tasks at first, eventually you will require the student to complete disliked tasks. However, in our experience, this is less of a problem once the more inappropriate (often aggressive) form of refusal is eliminated.

Extinction. Extinction means to withhold reinforcement (usually attention) for a behavior that previously was reinforced. When the target behavior occurs, you do not look at the child, you do not say anything to the child, and you might move away from the child—perhaps to give attention to another student who is behaving appropriately. Note that you withhold reinforcement for a specific target *behavior,* not the child; as soon as the target behavior ceases, you must again attend to the child.

Given the fact that most children and adolescents with autism prefer "no attention," extinction may have limited value as a reductive technique for this population. Extinction would only be useful for mildly inappropriate behaviors if your functional assessment leads you to hypothesize that the behavior is functioning as a means for the child to get your attention or that of other teachers or staff. Extinction will not be effective for behaviors serving other functions, such as avoiding a disliked task or self-stimulation; nor would it be appropriate to use extinction for extremely disruptive behaviors or behaviors that are dangerous to the student or others. Note that the attention the child is getting for the misbehavior does not necessarily have to be positive. For example, say a student screams briefly when left alone to work on a task. Each time he screams, a teacher approaches him to scold him for screaming and to admonish him to "Work quietly!" Because this is the only attention the child gets during independent work time, that negative attention may actually be maintaining (e.g., reinforcing) the screaming, despite the fact that the teacher intended the scolding to reduce the screaming.

A few cautions should be noted if you plan to use extinction. First, once you begin withholding attention for the target behavior, the behavior often worsens before it begins to diminish. For example, if a brief scream no longer produces attention, the child may scream louder and longer. If that does not produce a response, he may leave his seat to stand directly in front of the teacher to scream! You must be prepared to withhold attention for all forms of escalation of the behavior. This means extinction may not be an appropriate intervention for students who are aggressive because the escalation may likely include some form of aggression toward other students, toward the child himself, or toward teachers.

Also, sometimes a behavior that has been eliminated using extinction spontaneously reappears much later, sometimes weeks later. You must be ready to withhold attention for the behavior any time it is exhibited. Finally, extinction typically does not produce rapid reductions in the target behavior. This means that you must be prepared to apply the intervention for an extended period of time, even on days when the behavior does not particularly annoy you, or when you have visitors in the room, or when you are in other parts of the school or on field trips.

When faced with an inappropriate behavior, we strongly recommend you first apply one or more of the nonpunishment procedures. However, if these do not sufficiently reduce the behavior, you might need to implement one or more punishment procedures.

Punishment Procedures. **Punishment** is the contingent presentation of a stimulus immediately after a behavior that reduces the likelihood that behavior will be repeated (Azrin & Holz, 1966). Although punishment is usually associated with something aversive (e.g., spanking), the consequence does not have to be traditionally "aversive"; in fact, a consequence that most people would perceive as pleasant or desirable may actually function as a punisher for some students with autism. For example, a student who receives teacher praise for saying "Good morning" in response to her teacher's greeting may not respond the next time she is greeted if she dislikes teacher attention. Likewise, consequences that you might view as aversive (e.g., the taste of lemon juice, seeing a teacher get angry) might actually function as a reinforcer for some children. Thus, you can only determine whether a consequence is a punisher by monitoring whether or not the behavior decreases as a result of the consequence. A tool that is often helpful in identifying potentially punitive consequences is anecdotal recording, described in Chapter 3.

Perhaps more so than any other procedure, ethical concerns are associated with the misuse of punishment. Therefore, if you determine that it is necessary to use a punishment procedure, you

must take care to ensure that the procedure is applied correctly, that you monitor the effects of the procedure, and that the procedure is used in conjunction with positive reinforcement of desired behaviors. Table 2.10 lists guidelines for ethical and correct use of punishment.

Response Cost. Response cost is a procedure in which reinforcers are removed as a consequence for inappropriate behavior. Our society uses response cost as one way of punishing undesired behaviors. For example, if you are caught speeding, you may have to give up some of your reinforcers (money). If you fail to make your car payments, you may lose your car. In the classroom, response cost involves removing tokens, material reinforcers, or activity reinforcers. These are the steps involved in developing and implementing a response cost program:

1. *Determine the target inappropriate behaviors.* Remember to describe these behaviors in observable terms.

2. *Determine the reinforcer to be removed.* This might be tokens (e.g., chips, points), a reinforcement activity (e.g., earned minutes to play a computer game), or a material reinforcer (e.g., a favorite toy). We do not advise using response cost with primary reinforcers; students are likely to eat the reinforcers before they can be removed!

3. *Determine how much of the reinforcer, or how long the reinforcer, will be removed for each instance of the behavior.* This is a matter of trial and error. You should remove enough of the reinforcer to be meaningful, but you do not want to overpunish by removing too much of the reinforcer. For example, you might take one token away each time the student screams. Or perhaps each time a student completes a task during vocational instruction, a "1" is recorded on a chart, which means he has earned 1 minute of time to play a computer game. However, each head-hitting instance during vocational time results in a "1" being crossed off the chart, meaning he has lost a minute of computer time.

Table 2.10 Rules for Using Punishment

1. *Punishment should only be used if necessary, preferably after other, more positive interventions have been implemented.* Antecedent strategies, positive reinforcement, and differential reinforcement are all strategies that can help reduce or avoid problem behavior; effective use of these may mean you do not need to use punishment. Only implement a punishment procedure if the problem behavior is still present after these strategies have been applied or if the target behavior is dangerous.

2. *Determine the target behavior.* Remember, the punishment procedure must be tied to one or two specific inappropriate behaviors, not everything the student does that is mildly annoying!

3. *Use the least aversive procedure necessary to control the behavior.* Do not overpunish! Time-out, for example, is preferable to an aversive stimulus. The most aversive punishment procedures (overcorrection and aversive stimuli) should seldom be required if you have a well-planned instructional program that relies on positive procedures to teach desired behaviors.

4. *Deliver the punishment consequence immediately after the target behavior.* If you delay, you run the risk of punishing appropriate behaviors that occur during the delay interval.

5. *Be calm and unemotional when you deliver the punishment consequence.* It is hard not to respond emotionally in some situations, such as when you have been hit or bitten by a student. However, if you are angry or frustrated, you are likely to overpunish. Better to cool down first (this is the one exception to the "punish quickly" rule described in rule 4) or let another teacher or paraprofessional administer the punishment.

6. *Be consistent!* One of the most difficult aspects of using punishment correctly is that you must administer the consequence *every time the target behavior occurs!* If you fail to do this, you have probably *reinforced* the behavior (avoiding punishment is often a reinforcer). For example, if you received a ticket every time you exceeded the speed limit, you would probably soon learn not to speed. However, because most people frequently escape this punisher, they are more likely to drive faster than the speed limit.

7. *Monitor the effects of the procedure on the target behavior.* Remember, the procedure is not working if the target behavior does not decrease. You must measure the target behavior to determine if it is, in fact, decreasing.

4. *Be sure that the student has access to earning the reinforcer, as well as losing the reinforcer.* Otherwise, you run the risk of the student losing all of her reinforcers with no hope of recovering them. You do *not* want to be in this position because then the student has little motivation to continue exhibiting appropriate behavior.

5. *Briefly describe the inappropriate behavior and the consequence.* A simple statement will suffice: "No spitting. You lose a token."

6. *Remove the token or other reinforcer quickly, with no more discussion or explanation.* If removing the token becomes difficult (e.g., each time you remove a token the student tantrums), response cost may not be the best behavior reductive approach.

Response cost is a fairly easy procedure to apply, provided the reinforcer is easily removed. Removing the reinforcer can usually be done quickly, with virtually no interruption in instruction. However, it is not appropriate as a consequence for all behaviors. For example, taking away a disliked task as a consequence for self-stimulation during the task may actually be reinforcing to the student. Rely on your data to inform you of the effectiveness of the procedure.

Time-Out. Time-out is the procedure in which an individual is denied access to reinforcement for a specific period of time. If time-out is to be effective, the difference between the "time-in" situation and the time-out situation must be obvious (Alberto & Troutman, 1999). That is, the time-in environment must be reinforcing to the child; the child must *want* to avoid time-out.

Time-out is not a punishment technique that we typically recommend for students with autism. Remember that these individuals have a propensity to withdraw from people and stimulating environments. Thus, it would make no sense to have them withdraw as a form of punishment; in fact, such a procedure might very well be a reinforcer for the student. However, some forms of time-out such as refusing the student access to a favorite stim-toy for a certain amount of time might be an effective punisher. If students appear to like being in the classroom, around other peers and adults, then typical time-out procedures might work as punishers. If this is the case, time-out offers several potential advantages over other types of punishment:

- Time-out, especially the nonexclusionary forms, is an easy procedure to implement both in and out of the classroom (e.g., hallway, field trips).

- Research indicates that time-out is a fairly acceptable type of punishment, particularly in comparison to overcorrection or presentation of an aversive stimulus (Kazdin, 1980). This may be an important consideration when proposing the intervention to parents or other teachers.

- When applied correctly, time-out usually reduces behavior quicker than other reductive procedures (Cooper, Heron, & Heward, 1987), sometimes after only a few applications. Therefore, time-out may be the preferred procedure for aggressive, extremely disruptive, or self-abusive behaviors (assuming the function of the self-abusive behavior is to get attention).

- For some children, time-out may be more concrete, and therefore more meaningful, than response cost.

The two basic approaches to time-out are nonexclusionary and exclusionary (Cooper, Heron, & Heward, 1987). In addition, there are several forms of time-out within each of these two approaches. Table 2.11 describes each of these forms of time-out, listed in order from the least

Table 2.11 Types of Time-Out

Nonexclusionary
- *Head down.* Student must put head down on desk for a brief time.
- *Removal.* Take away materials or toys for a period of time.
- *Teacher turnaway.* The teacher or staff working with the student at the time of the inappropriate behavior turns away from the student for a brief time.
- *Time-out card.* This is used in conjunction with a token system. Contingent on the inappropriate behavior, turn the student's point card over (no points can be given while the card is turned over). Hops and Walker (1988) recommend using a two-color card: green on the point side, red on the "time-out" side. An alternative, if you are using objects as tokens rather than points, is to briefly remove the container in which you are placing the tokens.
- *Contingent observation.* Move the student's chair slightly away from the group or activity.
- *Time-out chair.* Have the student sit in a specially designated time-out chair in another part of the room.
- *Time-out square.* Outline a square (approximately 2 feet by 2 feet) on the floor using masking tape or brightly colored tape. Students sit inside the square for time-out.
- *Time-out rug.* Have the student sit on a small rug (carpet samples work nicely) for time-out. This is a nicely "portable" time-out: You can take the rug or carpet on field trips, or use it in other parts of the school or playground.

Exclusionary
- *Screen.* Have the student sit behind a screen or partition.
- *Time-out room.* Move the student to an empty room that is used only for time-out. To avoid misuse of time-out rooms, Gast and Nelson (1977) recommend the following guidelines:
1. The room should be at least 6 feet by 6 feet in size.
2. The room should have proper ventilation and lighting (preferably recessed, with the switch outside the room).
3. The room should have no objects or fixtures with which children could harm themselves.
4. There should be a way for teachers or staff to monitor a child both visually and auditorially.
5. The room should not be locked.
Additionally, we recommend that you obtain parents' permission before using a time-out room.

exclusionary to the most exclusionary. Exclusionary time-out is usually not recommended for students with autism. Remember from Chapter 1 that these individuals typically shun people, learning tasks, and interpersonal interactions, wanting instead to be alone to engage in self-stimulation. If our goal is to teach them communication and social skills, excluding them from social situations seems counterproductive. On the other hand some students with autism may be frightened of small dark rooms and strange places and sounds. The premise of time-out is not that the individual will be frightened in the time-out situation and thus want to avoid it, but that they cannot access reinforcers during time-out periods. Social isolation works as a punisher for most children because they like people and classrooms and don't want to be removed from those things, not because they are frightened of the time-out place.

If exclusionary time-out is used with students with autism, there is a danger of causing the student undue anxiety, or conversely, of the child preferring the exclusionary situation because he can engage in self-stimulatory behaviors uninterrupted. In the first case, the student may develop an extreme dislike of school and school personnel, thwarting goals to educate him or her. In the second case, the student may continue to act badly in order to access the time-out room. We are not saying never use exclusionary time-out, but short non-exclusionary time-outs will probably serve you best.

The following are a few simple guidelines that will help ensure that time-out is used correctly.

Be sure that time-in is more reinforcing than time-out! Time-out will not work if students *like* the time-out situation. Remember that students with autism typically *like* being left alone.

Determine the specific target behavior(s) that will be consequated with time-out. Be sure that these are behaviors for which time-out would be appropriate. Time-out is usually not appropriate for self-stimulatory behavior or self-abusive behavior because the behaviors themselves may be reinforcing.

Establish a consistent time-out area and procedure. For the student to understand that the inappropriate behavior results in time-out, it is important that each time the target behavior occurs, the same time-out procedure is followed.

Determine the length of time-out. Use brief time-outs—time-out does not need to be long to be effective. The longer a student is in time-out, the more likely he is to forget why. We even argue that the old adage "1 minute per year of age" may be too long for some students. Five minutes feels like a very long time even for an adult who has a well-developed sense of time. To a 5-year-old, it may seem endless. For some students, a 30-second time-out may be sufficient.

Determine the criterion for ending time-out. The three basic approaches to ending time-out are as follows: (1) Time-out is for a predetermined period of time. When that time is up, the student again gains access to reinforcers. (2) Time-out is for a predetermined period of time. However, if the student is misbehaving at the end of that time, the student remains in time-out until she is behaving appropriately. (3) The student must spend the entire predetermined period of time in time-out. If he misbehaves, the timer is reset. For students with autism, we recommend the first approach. Above all, don't tell the student to "Come back when you're ready to behave!" Time-out is a teacher-managed procedure, and the teacher should decide when time-out is over.

Don't threaten the student with time-out. If time-out is the predetermined consequence, use it each time the target misbehavior occurs!

When the target inappropriate behavior occurs, simply describe the behavior and tell the student to take a time-out. Do not explain, remind, or argue. Simply say, "You hit Samantha. Time-out," or "No screaming. Put your head down."

Ignore mildly inappropriate behavior while the student is in time-out. Students may scream, cry, or exhibit other inappropriate behaviors in time-out situations. It is important, however, that you not give any reinforcement, especially attention, to a student in time-out.

As soon as possible after the time-out is over, reinforce the student for an appropriate behavior. Remember, you are trying to help the student differentiate appropriate from inappropriate behavior and learn the desirability of the time-in environment compared to the time-out situation.

Monitor the effects of time-out. If the target behavior does not begin to diminish within a few applications of time-out, you may need to use another procedure.

Presentation of an Aversive Stimulus. An aversive stimulus is something the child dislikes that is delivered as a consequence for an inappropriate behavior. Remember that individuals with autism tend to have idiosyncratic preferences. Just as typical reinforcers may not have reinforcing quality for these students, typical punishers may not have a punishing quality. These students may actually like things that we think are aversive. If we present such consequences it might result in an actual increase in inappropriate behavior. For example, if we physically restrain a student for scratching others and she likes the restraint (deep pressure is appealing to some individuals with autism), then scratching will probably continue and might actually increase. Thus, as a general rule, we recommend only one type of aversive stimulus: a stern reprimand. While other aversives (e.g., physical restraint) are sometimes used for severely challenging behaviors (e.g., voluntary vomiting, severe self-abuse), we feel that some teachers turn too quickly to this type of intervention without first conducting a functional assessment to guide the development of an appropriate intervention, and before trying other, less aversive procedures. We once consulted with a teacher of a high school student with autism who screamed and/or dropped to the floor when she wanted to stop working or when she did not want to leave the room. This teacher planned to use a spray mist of water in the student's face as a consequence for these behaviors. However, as we pointed out to the teacher, because the student was non-verbal, and because the teacher had not taught the student any other form of communication (e.g., sign language or a communication book), the student's behavior was the only way she could communicate her wants. We recommended teaching the student to use a picture/symbol card to communicate "I want to stop working," "I don't want to go," and so on, then strongly reinforcing the student for using the card. The inappropriate behaviors soon stopped without using any type of punishment.

A stern reprimand can be an effective response to inappropriate behavior, particularly when you need an effective way of returning the student's attention to you or to the task. To use reprimands, you must first define the target behavior to be reprimanded and determine the wording you will use for the reprimand (it should be short and simple). Then when the target behavior is exhibited, immediately deliver the reprimand in a loud voice. For example, if a student is absorbed in self-stimulation by flicking her fingers in front of her eyes, you say in a firm voice "*No stim!*" or simply "*No!*" Reprimands are more effective when you are close to the student, as opposed to delivering a reprimand from across the room. As soon as the inappropriate behavior stops, you should praise the student for an appropriate alternative behavior (e.g., "Good quiet hands!" or "Good working!").

Overcorrection. We discuss two types of overcorrection procedures. **Positive practice overcorrection** involves having the child engage in extensive practice in a behavior that is an appropriate alternative to the misbehavior. For example, if a student self-stimulates while walking in the hall, the student must walk 10 times up and down the hall with hands at his sides. **Restitutional overcorrection** requires the student to make up for the inappropriate behavior by extensively correcting anything in the environment that was damaged as a result of the misbehavior. An example of restitutional overcorrection would be to require a student to wipe off the table and all of the chairs, and sweep the floor, as a consequence for throwing food. In each of these examples, the key is that the desired behavior, or the restitutional behavior, is practiced long enough to make the practice aversive. That is, the student will not exhibit the inappropriate behavior in the future in order to avoid the overcorrection.

Overcorrection has been shown to be an effective intervention for reducing inappropriate behaviors, including rumination (Simpson & Sasso, 1978), tooth flicking, and out-of-seat (Sasso, 1977). Positive practice overcorrection, in particular, is considered by many to be an acceptable procedure, probably due to the focus on establishing a replacement behavior, as opposed to simply eliminating the inappropriate behavior (Simpson & Regan, 1986). Despite potential effectiveness, overcorrection has several disadvantages. First, it is extremely time consuming, usually requiring one staff member to remain with the student throughout the procedure. Therefore, we do not recommend overcorrection if your functional assessment indicates the misbehavior is for purposes of getting attention. Next, overcorrection sometimes requires that the student be manually guided through the procedure. This might be possible with young children, but probably would not be practical with older students. Furthermore, manually guiding even a young child through the procedure might result in the child's behavior escalating (fighting the manual guidance, going limp, etc.), making it extremely difficult to complete the procedure. In fact, this type of struggle might even be reinforcing to some children.

Because of these disadvantages, we only recommend overcorrection if other interventions have proven ineffective. Even then, overcorrection should be used only if the inappropriate behavior is not for purposes of getting attention, if the child is small enough to manually guide through the procedure if necessary, and if manual guidance will not result in other problems (aggression, fighting the guidance, etc.).

SUMMARY

As you have seen in this chapter, applied behavior analysis procedures are effective and efficient ways of achieving desirable outcomes for students with autism. Of course, a specific process must be followed, and behavior change procedures must be designed and implemented correctly in order to attain desired outcomes. In particular, you must consider information gathered through functional assessment, as explained in Chapter 3, and your students' unique characteristics, likes, and dislikes when choosing behavior change interventions. However, if you adhere to the guidelines we described throughout this chapter, and if you pay careful attention to other important aspects of the educational program, such as curriculum (as described in several later chapters), we predict you will see positive results.

KEY POINTS

1. Applied behavior analysis is a comprehensive approach that offers empirically based strategies for measuring behavior, increasing behavior, and reducing behavior.

2. Stimulus control is a powerful teaching tool in which students learn to respond in a particular way to specific antecedents.

3. Behaviors may be measured using restricted event recording, nonrestricted event recording, or duration recording.

4. Reinforcement may be positive or negative, and relies on primary or secondary reinforcers.

5. Secondary reinforcers include social reinforcers, material reinforcers, activity reinforcers, and token reinforcers.

6. The four differential reinforcement techniques can effectively reduce inappropriate behavior without using punishment.

7. Differential reinforcement procedures include differential reinforcement of lower levels of behavior, differential reinforcement of incompatible behavior, differential

reinforcement of other behavior, and differential reinforcement of communicative behavior.

8. Punishment procedures include response cost, time-out, and administration of aversive stimuli including overcorrection.

REFERENCES

Alberto, P., & Troutman, A. (1999). *Applied behavior analysis for teachers* (5th ed.). Englewood Cliffs, NJ: Merrill.

Atkinson, R. P., Jenson, W. R., Rovner, L., Cameron, S., Van Wagenen, L., & Petersen, B. P. (1984). Brief report: Validation of the Autism Reinforcer Checklist for Children. *Journal of Autism and Developmental Disorders, 14*(4), 429–433.

Azrin, N. H., & Holz, W. C. (1966). Punishment. In W. K. Honig (Ed.), *Operant behavior: Areas of research and application.* New York: Appleton-Century-Crofts.

Cooper, J. O., Heron, T. E., & Heward, W. L. (1987). *Applied behavior analysis.* Columbus, OH: Merrill.

Foster-Johnson, L., & Dunlap, G. (1993). Using functional assessment to develop effective, individualized interventions for challenging behaviors. *Teaching Exceptional Children, 25*(3), 44–50.

Gast, D. L., & Nelson, C. M. (1977). Legal and ethical considerations for the use of time-out in special education settings. *Journal of Special Education, 11,* 457–467.

Hops, H., & Walker, H. M. (1988). *CLASS: Contingencies for Learning Academic and Social Skills.* Seattle, WA: Educational Achievement Systems.

Kazdin, A. E. (1980). Acceptability of alternative treatments for deviant child behavior. *Journal of Applied Behavior Analysis, 13,* 259–273.

Morgan, D. P., & Jenson, W. R. (1988). *Teaching behaviorally disordered students.* Englewood Cliffs, NJ: Merrill.

Ross, A. O., & Nelson, R. O. (1979). Behavior therapy. In H. C. Quay & J. S. Werry (Eds.), *Psychopathological disorders of childhood* (3rd ed.). New York: John Wiley.

Sasso, G. (1977). The use of overcorrection procedures in a public school setting for the modification of self-stimulatory and disruptive behaviors in a severely emotionally disturbed child. Unpublished master's thesis, University of Kansas.

Simpson, R. L., & Regan, M., (1986) *Management of autistic behavior.* Austin, TX: Pro-Ed.

Simpson, R. L., & Sasso, G. (1978). The modification of rumination in a severely emotionally disturbed child through an overcorrection procedure. *AAESPH Review, 3,* 145–150.

3

Reducing Challenging Behavior

Did you know that:

- Challenging behavior is probably the easiest way for non-verbal students to communicate?

- Students may do similar behaviors for very different reasons?

- You should answer the question "Why does he do that?" with regard to a student's challenging behaviors?

- Challenging behavior probably serves a purpose for the student?

- Sometimes the easiest way to get students to follow a direction is to give several directions?

Students with autism characteristically exhibit challenging behaviors, referred to as behavioral excesses. For example, many students are non-compliant, either by simply ignoring directions or by exhibiting more overt negative behaviors such as screaming or crying when given a direction. Some students bite, pull hair, pinch, or exhibit other aggressive acts. Some students engage in self-stimulatory behaviors such as rocking, hand-flapping, finger-flicking, or spinning objects. Still others exhibit self-abusive behaviors such as biting their hands or arms or hitting or scratching themselves. And some students exhibit behaviors that place themselves at risk, such as running out of the classroom or away from the playground, eating inedible objects (a condition known as **pica**), or smearing feces. Of all the instructional concerns facing a teacher of students with autism, managing challenging behavior is perhaps the most pressing.

Challenging behaviors pose many of the following problems for teachers and parents:

- Challenging behavior interferes with learning (Koegel & Covert, 1972). For many students, challenging behavior is such an established part of their behavioral repertoire that attempts to teach the student are ineffective. In fact, attempts at teaching (e.g., giving directions) often produce an escalation in challenging behavior.

- Challenging behavior reduces the likelihood that the child will be able to participate in mainstream environments, and increases the likelihood that the student will need a more restrictive instructional arrangement (e.g., one-on-one instruction with little interaction with other students) (Danforth & Drabman, 1989).

- Challenging behavior reduces the likelihood that the child will be able to participate in community-based instructional activities (e.g., Dunlap, Ferro, & Deperczel, 1994). It may not be advisable to take a student to the grocery store to practice shopping skills if the student runs away from teachers or attacks others, and it may be nonproductive to take a student who tantrums every time she is given a direction to a restaurant.

- Challenging behavior increases the likelihood that parents may be forced to seek placement outside the home for their child with autism, particularly as he gets older. Parents may reach the point where they are unable to keep the child safe, or the child may be too great a disruptive influence on other children in the home. An adolescent may simply become physically dangerous or too difficult for parents to control.

Because of the negative impact of challenging behaviors, teachers must realize how critical it is to use effective behavior reductive strategies to quickly get these behaviors under control. However, teachers will probably find it nonproductive to apply traditional reductive strategies in isolation. That is, if a student screams when you ask her to vacuum, simply having her sit in time-out may not work. Likewise, taking points away for biting fingers probably will have little impact on the behavior. The reasons for this are that even the most difficult challenging behavior probably serves a purpose for the student (O'Neill, Horner, Albin, Sprague, Storey, & Newton, 1997), and challenging behavior is usually related to antecedents or consequences in the immediate environment (Koegel, Koegel, Frea, & Smith, 1995). Unless the purpose for the behavior is addressed as part of the behavior change process, or unless antecedents or consequences that are contributing to the behavior are identified and modified as appropriate, simply punishing the child probably will not produce desired results.

This chapter will describe how to determine what purpose a behavior may be serving for a student and how the challenging behavior is related to environmental conditions or events. This procedure is known as **functional assessment.** We will also describe how to develop intervention strategies based on the information gathered during functional assessment. Finally, we will present strategies for remediating some of the more common challenging behaviors exhibited by children and youth with autism, such as noncompliance, self-stimulation, and aggression.

FUNCTIONAL ASSESSMENT

Functional assessment, also called **functional behavioral assessment,** addresses the question of "Why does he do that?" when referring to challenging behavior. The answer to that question lies not in deep-seated psychological explanations, but in the child's environment. Functional assessment will help determine why a student is behaving inappropriately; that is, what purpose an inappropriate behavior is serving for the student and the environmental variables that may be maintaining the behavior.

Functional assessment is based on five assumptions (Foster-Johnson & Dunlap, 1993; O'Neill et al., 1997):

1. **Behavior is related to specific antecedents and consequences in the immediate environment.** This means that challenging behavior is often prompted by certain antecedent stimuli (e.g., nature of the task the student is asked to do, sitting close to another student, being asked to stop a preferred activity) and is maintained by attractive consequent stimuli (e.g., getting a desired object, escaping a disliked task or situation, experiencing a pleasurable sensation as the result of engaging in stereotypic behaviors). For example, a child who dislikes writing may scream and pull her hair when asked to work on writing tasks, because sometimes this results in the student avoiding the task. A student may engage in hand-flapping as a more pleasurable alternative to a boring or disliked task. If a child who cries when she wants a snack is given the snack as a result of the crying, she may cry whenever she's hungry. Identifying contributing antecedent and consequent stimuli is an important step in functional assessment and will contribute important information about effective interventions.

2. **Behavior may be affected by conditions other than immediate antecedents and consequences.** Sometimes, events or conditions beyond direct antecedents and conse-

quences may increase or decrease the likelihood of challenging behavior. These conditions, known as **setting events,** do not directly "cause" problem behavior; rather, they increase the likelihood of certain behavior. Setting events may take many forms. For example, setting events may be events or conditions internal to the student, such as pain, hunger, fatigue, illness, or boredom, or external to the child, such as a long bus ride or a noisy cafeteria. In addition, setting events may be present at the same time as an inappropriate behavior (e.g., a child screams because of a flickering light or an annoying hum from the ventilation system), or may occur temporally and contextually distant from the behavior (e.g., a student who is particularly noncompliant following a bus ride with a substitute bus driver) (Conroy & Fox, 1994; Gardner, Cole, Davidson, & Karan, 1986). These conditions set the stage for problematic behavior. For example, a student who is hungry or sleepy may refuse to do his janitorial duties, even though he typically enjoys these jobs. Or a student who is fearful of thunder may be off-task and noncompliant during storms. Identifying probable setting event contributions may lead to more effective interventions.

3. **Behavior may be related to biological causes.** Some behaviors have biological explanations. For example, in children with autism and PDD, some self-abusive behaviors may be related to insufficient levels of the neurotransmitter serotonin in the brain (Harvard Medical School, 1997). This is why some behaviors improve with medication. However, this does not mean that behavioral interventions are ineffective or should not be used. First, establishing a definitive biological explanation for challenging behaviors is usually difficult. Also, even if challenging behaviors have a clear biological foundation, behavioral explanations are often apparent as well (for example, the student has a history of reinforcement for the behavior). Finally, even if a clear explanation exists, medication may not be an option for many reasons (undesirable side effects, parental choice, etc.). Therefore, behavioral interventions should always be used, even if a student is taking medication.

4. **Challenging behavior may serve a function for the student.** Challenging behavior may be a way for the child to get what he wants, to avoid or escape unpleasant situations, or to communicate something. For example, a student who dislikes running may hit his head or bite his arm as a way of communicating his dislike for the activity when his P.E. teacher tells him to run around the track. If, as a result, this student is allowed to watch the activity from the bleachers instead, he may continue arm-biting under these circumstances as an effective way of getting out of that disliked task. A student who wants to stop washing dishes but has no way to communicate this may throw a dish as a way of saying "No more!" A student who dislikes sitting close to peers may pinch the person closest to him. This is a critical step in functional assessment: Before planning interventions for challenging behavior, you should first identify the possible function that behavior serves for the student. The intervention, then, should include teaching and reinforcing an appropriate alternative behavior that will serve the same function.

5. **Challenging behavior may be the result of a skill deficit.** Often, a student's challenging behavior reflects the fact that the student does not know a more appropriate way of getting needs met or communicating desires. For students with autism, this is especially important, because language deficits are a primary characteristic. Any child who is unable to use socially acceptable forms of communication undoubtedly must rely on more unacceptable ways of communicating, often through inappropriate behaviors. Therefore, when a child lacks appropriate functional communication skills, part of the intervention must be to teach the student more suitable and effective ways of communicating.

How to Conduct a Functional Assessment

Functional assessment has three basic steps. The first is to gather information about the student's behavior and related contextual variables. That is, you should identify setting events that set the stage for challenging behavior, antecedents that immediately precede the inappropriate behavior, consequences regularly associated with the target behavior, and possible functions the inappropriate behavior may be serving for the student. How regularly does the inappropriate behavior result in the student getting something he wants or avoiding something he dislikes? How strong are the consequences for inappropriate behavior as compared to consequences for appropriate behavior? Inappropriate behavior, for example, often produces a much stronger reaction from others than does appropriate behavior. The teacher must understand the efficiency of the inappropriate behavior so that equally efficient appropriate behaviors can be taught. For example, if a child's screams always result in her getting something to eat, and teachers decide to teach her to point to a picture when she wants food, then pointing to the picture must *always* produce the same result (while at the same time, screaming no longer does).

Identification of contextual variables and possible functions may be obtained using both indirect and direct methods. *Indirect assessment* means interviewing people who are familiar with the student to determine, in their opinion, (1) when appropriate and inappropriate behaviors are most likely to occur, or not occur, (2) what happens after these behaviors occur, (3) how regularly these consequences occur (e.g., the efficiency of the inappropriate behavior), and (4) possible functions of the inappropriate behaviors. The forms shown in Tables 3.1 and 3.2 address these questions. Persons familiar with the child's behavior—teachers, paraprofessionals, support personnel, parents—should complete the interview form, the Functional Assessment Report (FAR), shown in Table 3.1. To complete the FAR form, list four inappropriate behaviors and four appropriate behaviors. Then, for each behavior, answer the remaining questions. The response recorded next to "A" refers to the first behavior described in the first question, "B" responses refer to the second behavior from question 1, and so forth. Part II pertains only to the inappropriate behaviors "A," "B," "C," and "D" as described in the first question. The questions posed are the first step in identifying contextual events and possible functions associated with the inappropriate behaviors.

The Motivation Assessment Scale (Delaney & Durand, 1986) shown in Table 3.2 is a questionnaire designed to help identify possible functions of inappropriate behaviors and the efficiency of those behaviors in attaining those functions. Again, persons familiar with the child's behavior should complete the form by circling the number that best describes the frequency of the situation described in each item. Once the form is completed, record the number associated with each answer in the box on the second page that corresponds with the item number. For example, if "5" was circled for item 1, you would record "5" in box number 1 on the second page. Once all scores have been recorded, total each column. Next, find the mean (average) score for each column by dividing the total score for the column by 4. The column with the highest score strongly suggests motivation (function) for the inappropriate behavior. As you can see from Eddie's MAS (Table 3.3), escape appears to be the function associated with his inappropriate behavior.

Indirect assessment is helpful, but *direct assessment* (i.e., actually observing the student in various contexts) is also necessary to accurately identify antecedents and consequences associated with the behavior and likely functions of the behavior (Calloway & Simpson, 1998). The two techniques discussed next are used for direct assessment.

Scatter Plots. As shown in Figure 3.1, scatter plots can help isolate specific times of day or other antecedent conditions (e.g., certain activities or environments) under which the behavior is likely to occur. Although a scatter plot does not help you identify specific antecedents and consequences associated with the behavior, it

Table 3.1 Functional Assessment Report (FAR)

Part I

Inappropriate Behavior

1. Describe inappropriate behavior(s). Be specific.
   A.
   B.
   C.
   D.

2. When are these most likely to occur? Describe specific situations.
   A.
   B.
   C.
   D.

3. When are these *least* likely to occur? Describe specific situations.
   A.
   B.
   C.
   D.

4. Are there conditions under which the behavior is *more* likely to occur? (student is ill, problems at home, etc.)
   A.
   B.
   C.
   D.

5. What happens when the student exhibits this behavior (e.g., what do other students do? What does teacher do?)
   A.
   B.
   C.
   D.

Appropriate Behavior

1. Describe appropriate behavior(s). Be specific.
   A.
   B.
   C.
   D.

2. When are these most likely to occur? Describe specific situations.
   A.
   B.
   C.
   D.

3. When are these *least* likely to occur? Describe specific situations.
   A.
   B.
   C.
   D.

4. Are there conditions under which the behavior is *more* likely to occur? (certain days or times of day, etc.)
   A.
   B.
   C.
   D.

5. What happens when the student exhibits this behavior? (e.g., what do other students do? What does teacher do?)
   A.
   B.
   C.
   D.

Part II

Why do you think the student exhibits each inappropriate behavior?

	A	B	C	D
Attention from teacher				
Attention from peers				
Attention from other adults				
Gain power or control				
Gain status				
Self-entertainment				
Avoid work or other tasks				
Avoid situations				
Avoid failure, embarrassment				
Lack of self-control				
Lack of social skills for situation				
Insufficient structure				
Unsure				

Table 3.2 Motivation Assessment Scale

Name:_____ Rater:_____ Date:_____

Description of Behavior (be specific): _____

Setting Description: _____

Instructors: The MAS is a questionnaire designed to identify those situations where an individual is likely to behave in specific ways. From this information, more informed decisions can be made about the selections of appropriate replacement behaviors. To complete the MAS, select one behavior of specific interest. Be specific about the behavior. For example "is aggressive" is not as good a description as "hits other people." Once you have specified the behavior to be rated, read each question carefully and circle the one number that best describes your observations of this behavior.

QUESTIONS	Never	Almost Never	Seldom	Half the Time	Usually	Almost Always	Always
1. Would the behavior occur continuously if this person was left alone for long periods of time?	Never 0	Almost Never 1	Seldom 2	Half the Time 3	Usually 4	Almost Always 5	Always 6
2. Does the behavior occur following a request to perform a difficult task?	Never 0	Almost Never 1	Seldom 2	Half the Time 3	Usually 4	Almost Always 5	Always 6
3. Does the behavior seem to occur in response to your talking to other persons in the room/area?	Never 0	Almost Never 1	Seldom 2	Half the Time 3	Usually 4	Almost Always 5	Always 6
4. Does the behavior ever occur to get a toy, food, or an activity that this person has been told he/she can't have?	Never 0	Almost Never 1	Seldom 2	Half the Time 3	Usually 4	Almost Always 5	Always 6
5. Would the behavior occur repeatedly, in the same way, for long periods of time if the person was alone (e.g. rocking back & forth for over an hour)?	Never 0	Almost Never 1	Seldom 2	Half the Time 3	Usually 4	Almost Always 5	Always 6
6. Does the behavior occur when any request is made of this person?	Never 0	Almost Never 1	Seldom 2	Half the Time 3	Usually 4	Almost Always 5	Always 6
7. Does the behavior occur whenever you stop attending to this person?	Never 0	Almost Never 1	Seldom 2	Half the Time 3	Usually 4	Almost Always 5	Always 6
8. Does the behavior occur when you take away a favorite food, toy, or activity?	Never 0	Almost Never 1	Seldom 2	Half the Time 3	Usually 4	Almost Always 5	Always 6
9. Does it appear to you that the person enjoys doing the behavior (It feels, tastes, looks, smells, sounds pleasing)?	Never 0	Almost Never 1	Seldom 2	Half the Time 3	Usually 4	Almost Always 5	Always 6
10. Does this person seem to do the behavior to upset or annoy you when you are trying to get him/her to do what you ask?	Never 0	Almost Never 1	Seldom 2	Half the Time 3	Usually 4	Almost Always 5	Always 6
11. Does this person seem to do the behavior to upset or annoy you when you are not paying attention to him/her (e.g. you are in another room, interacting with another person)?	Never 0	Almost Never 1	Seldom 2	Half the Time 3	Usually 4	Almost Always 5	Always 6
12. Does the behavior stop occurring shortly after you give the person a food, toy, or requested activity?	Never 0	Almost Never 1	Seldom 2	Half the Time 3	Usually 4	Almost Always 5	Always 6
13. When the behavior is occurring does this person seem calm and unaware of anything else going on around her/him?	Never 0	Almost Never 1	Seldom 2	Half the Time 3	Usually 4	Almost Always 5	Always 6
14. Does the behavior stop occurring shortly after one to five minutes after you stop working with or making demands of this person?	Never 0	Almost Never 1	Seldom 2	Half the Time 3	Usually 4	Almost Always 5	Always 6
15. Does this person seem to do the behavior to get you to spend some time with her/him?	Never 0	Almost Never 1	Seldom 2	Half the Time 3	Usually 4	Almost Always 5	Always 6
16. Does the behavior seem to occur when this person has been told that he/she can't do something he/she had wanted to do?	Never 0	Almost Never 1	Seldom 2	Half the Time 3	Usually 4	Almost Always 5	Always 6

	Sensory	Escape	Attention	Tangible
	1.	2.	3.	4.
	5.	6.	7.	8.
	9.	10.	11.	12.
	13.	14.	15.	16.
Total Score =				
Mean Score =				
Relative Ranking =				

Motivation Assessment Scale: Functions for usage
   Caveat: Person(s) filling out the form must be familiar with the individual who has the behavior challenge.
- To direct our understanding of the behavior challenge to the intent of the challenge versus the way it appears or makes us feel.
- To understand the correlation between the frequency of the challenging behavior and its potential for multiple intents.
- To identify those situations in which an individual is likely to behave in certain ways (e.g., requests for change in routine or environment lead to biting).

Outcomes:
- To assist in the identification of the motivation(s) of a specified behavior.
- To make more informed decisions concerning the selection of appropriate reinforcers and supports for a specified behavior.

Note well: Like any assessment tool, the MAS should be used in an ongoing continually developing mode.

may give you a general picture of the patterns of the behavior over time.

In the sample shown in Figure 3.1, you can see that Erica seems to pinch and scratch other students mostly during snack and play times or P.E. The next step would be to examine these times more closely using an anecdotal report (described on page 69). Also, these data suggest that Mondays are especially problematic for Erica. At this point we do not know why this is (perhaps she is responding to the change back to school from the weekend); therefore, we would need to more closely examine Mondays to see if something was occurring during the course of the day that might be contributing to her behavior (e.g., maybe there are people present on that day who are not present other days; perhaps that is the day she rides the bus to school as opposed to parents driving her). We may need to change something about her Monday schedule to make it less likely that pinching/scratching will occur on that day; for example, provide more structure or allow less play time.

Table 3.3 Motivation Assessment Scale

Name: _Eddie_   Rater: _Scheuermann_   Date: _3-10_

Description of Behavior (be specific): _Hits self, grabs teacher_

Setting Description: _Work time_

Instructors: The MAS is a questionnaire designed to identify those situations where an individual is likely to behave in specific ways. From this information, more informed decisions can be made about the selections of appropriate replacement behaviors. To complete the MAS, select one behavior of specific interest. Be specific about the behavior. For example "is aggressive" is not as good a description as "hits other people." Once you have specified the behavior to be rated, read each question carefully and circle the one number that best describes your observations of this behavior.

QUESTIONS	Never	Almost Never	Seldom	Half the Time	Usually	Almost Always	Always
1. Would the behavior occur continuously if this person was left alone for long periods of time?	0	①	2	3	4	5	6
2. Does the behavior occur following a request to perform a difficult task?	0	1	2	3	4	⑤	6
3. Does the behavior seem to occur in response to your talking to other persons in the room/area?	0	①	2	3	4	5	6
4. Does the behavior ever occur to get a toy, food, or an activity that this person has been told he/she can't have?	0	1	②	3	4	5	6
5. Would the behavior occur repeatedly, in the same way, for long periods of time if the person was alone (e.g. rocking back & forth for over an hour)?	0	①	2	3	4	5	6
6. Does the behavior occur when any request is made of this person?	0	1	2	3	4	5	⑥
7. Does the behavior occur whenever you stop attending to this person?	0	1	②	3	4	5	6
8. Does the behavior occur when you take away a favorite food, toy, or activity?	0	1	②	3	4	5	6
9. Does it appear to you that the person enjoys doing the behavior (It feels, tastes, looks, smells, sounds pleasing)?	0	①	2	3	4	5	6
10. Does this person seem to do the behavior to upset or annoy you when you are trying to get him/her to do what you ask?	0	1	2	③	4	5	6
11. Does this person seem to do the behavior to upset or annoy you when you are not paying attention to him/her (e.g. you are in another room, interacting with another person)?	⓪	1	2	3	4	5	6
12. Does the behavior stop occurring shortly after you give the person a food, toy, or requested activity?	0	1	②	3	4	5	6
13. When the behavior is occurring does this person seem calm and unaware of anything else going on around her/him?	0	①	2	3	4	5	6
14. Does the behavior stop occurring shortly after one to five minutes after you stop working with or making demands of this person?	0	1	2	3	4	⑤	6
15. Does this person seem to do the behavior to get you to spend some time with her/him?	0	①	2	3	4	5	6
16. Does the behavior seem to occur when this person has been told that he/she can't do something he/she had wanted to do?	0	1	②	3	4	5	6

	Sensory	Escape	Attention	Tangible
	1. *1*	2. *5*	3. *1*	4. *2*
	5. *1*	6. *6*	7. *2*	8. *2*
	9. *1*	10. *3*	11. *0*	12. *2*
	13. *1*	14. *5*	15. *1*	16. *2*
Total Score =	*4*	*19*	*4*	*8*
Mean Score =	*1*	*4.75*	*1*	*2*
Relative Ranking =	*1*	*4.75*	*1*	*2*

Motivation Assessment Scale: Functions for usage
   Caveat: Person(s) filling out the form must be familiar with the individual who has the behavior challenge.

- To direct our understanding of the behavior challenge to the intent of the challenge versus the way it appears or makes us feel.
- To understand the correlation between the frequency of the challenging behavior and its potential for multiple intents.
- To identify those situations in which an individual is likely to behave in certain ways (e.g., requests for change in routine or environment lead to biting).

Outcomes:

- To assist in the identification of the motivation(s) of a specified behavior.
- To make more informed decisions concerning the selection of appropriate reinforcers and supports for a specified behavior.

Note well: Like any assessment tool, the MAS should be used in an ongoing continually developing mode.

The Motivation Assessment Scale, copyright Monaco & Associates Incorporated, may be obtained from Monaco & Associates Incorporated, 4125 Gage Center Drive, Topeka, KS 66604. 1-785-272-5501, 1-800-798-1309, http://www.monacoassociates.com.

A-B-C Recording or Anecdotal Recording.
Once you know when a problem behavior is most likely to occur, you should do an A-B-C report during that time. An A-B-C report is a written description of everything that happens concerning the student during a specific observation period (Alberto & Troutman, 1999), arranged in a three-column format as antecedents, behaviors, and consequences. An A-B-C report can help you determine antecedents that may trigger the behavior (e.g., certain types of tasks, certain directions, being asked to end an enjoyable activity) and consequences that may be maintaining the behavior (e.g., getting out of a disliked task, gaining teacher attention, gaining access to desired objects). This information will help you formulate hypotheses about why the student exhibits the challenging behavior (e.g., to get something, to avoid something, or to communicate something).

Figure 3.2 shows an example of an A-B-C report. To conduct an anecdotal report, observe the

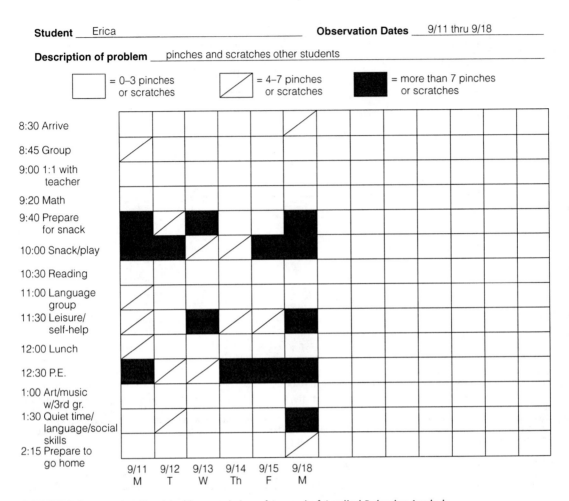

FIGURE 3.1 Scatter plot. Reprinted by permission of *Journal of Applied Behavior Analysis.*

student during the time when the problem behavior is most likely to occur. If you know that the behavior usually occurs just before lunch, for example, you might observe from 11:00 until 12:00 (lunchtime). If you are not sure about when the behavior occurs, it may be helpful to do several anecdotal reports during different times of the day. Use a form that allows you to record time along the left side of the page, and has three additional columns: one each for antecedent, behavior, and consequence. Figure 3.3 shows a sample anecdotal recording form set up in this way.

You should make a note of environmental conditions on the A-B-C report. For example,

make a note of what teachers and students are present, a brief description of the physical arrangement of the room, and any unusual circumstances (e.g., the room is next to the band hall and the band can be heard playing) that might help explain the behavior in question. Then, as you observe, write down everything that happens related to the student in question in the appropriate column (antecedent, behavior, or consequence). You should record everything the teacher says to the student, tasks the student is given, anything the student does, responses by the teacher or other students, and so forth. When you are writing, record fact only, not opinion. For example, al-

Note: Observation during vocational activity in classroom; 4 students and teacher present.

	Antecedent	Behavior	Consequence
9:03	1. T.:"Work time, Eddie. Come to the work area."	2. E. begins rocking and moaning, stays in seat.	3. T. busy preparing materials in work area.
9:05	4. T: "Eddie, time to work. Come now or you won't earn your money for today."	5. E. screams and hits his head with his fist.	6. T:"Eddie, no hitting. It's time to work and earn your money so you can go the store."
9:06		7. E. screams and hits his head repeatedly with both fists.	8. T. waits.
9:07	9. T:"Eddie, come now or I'll have to help you."	10. E. continues screaming and hitting his head with both fists.	
	11. T. appraoches Eddie and says, "I said it is time for work." T. places hands under Eddie's arms and lifts him to a standing position.	12. E. screams and grabs teacher's hair with both hands.	13. T. says loudly: "NO PULLING HAIR! Go to time-out."
	14. T. guides E. to time-out area.	15. E. sits in time-out chair and rocks.	
9:11	16. T:"Time-out is over, Eddie. Go to the work area."	17. E. screams and grabs teacher's hair.	18. T: "NO PULLING HAIR! BACK TO TIME-OUT!"
	19. T. points to time-out chair.	20. E. sits.	
9:15	21. T.:"Time-out is over, Eddie. I'm sorry. You've lost your work time for today. No work. Go back to your seat."	22. E. returns to seat quietly and sits down.	23. T. gathers materials.
9:16	24. T:"OK, Eddie. You need to practice writing your name in cursive. Here is your paper and pen."	25. E. writes quietly.	26. T. works with another student.

Summary: Eddie's inappropriate behavior escalates each time he is asked to go to the work area. However, he is compliant with requests that do not involve going to the work area (e.g., sitting in time-out, working on writing at his desk). This report suggests four possible conclusions:

1. Eddie does not like working in the work area.
2. Eddie prefers time-out to going to the work area.
3. The money earned at the work area is not a strong enough reinforcer for Eddie.
4. Eddie may not know an appropriate way to communicate his desire not to go to the work area.

FIGURE 3.2 A–B–C report.

though you might be tempted to say "Sonya is angry and throws her food," you should simply record "Sonya throws her French fries."

Once you are finished with the observation, review the report. According to Alberto and Troutman (1999) you should look for (1) what the student is doing that is inappropriate; (2) how frequently this inappropriate behavior occurs; (3) consistent patterns of reinforcement or punishment of that inappropriate behavior; (4) iden-

tifiable antecedents to the inappropriate behavior; (5) patterns to the antecedents; (6) recurring chains of specific antecedents, behaviors, and consequences; and (7) possibilities for intervention (e.g., change antecedents, change consequences, teach the student a more appropriate response). Note how the summary of the report shown in Figure 3.2 addresses these areas.

Once information has been gathered, the second step in functional assessment is to develop

Name _____ Date _____

Setting _____

Activity _____

Time	Antecedent	Behavior	Consequence

FIGURE 3.3 A–B–C form.

one or more hypotheses about why the student is exhibiting the problem behavior. Your hypotheses should address one or more of the following areas:

The purpose the behavior serves for the student. Based on the information you have gathered, do you think the student's problem behavior is serving as an effective way of getting teacher attention (*any* teacher attention—not just positive attention)? Is the student avoiding certain tasks or situations because of the behavior? Does the student appear to be communicating something through the behavior? Reviewing the anecdotal report shown in Figure 3.2, we might conclude that Eddie's behavior is serving as a way of communicating that he does not want to go to the work area, and that his hitting often results in his avoiding vocational work.

Possible skill deficits. Although we have no absolute way of determining skill deficits, we recommend the following rule of thumb: If you seldom see the child exhibit the desired behavior under similar circumstances, assume the child does not know how to do the behavior (i.e., assume a skill deficit). Students with autism frequently exhibit inappropriate behaviors that reflect skill deficits in language (both expressing wants/needs and understanding what others say), interpersonal social skills (e.g., responding to conversational initiations, sharing, taking turns), and self-control skills (e.g., handling anger or frustration in appropriate ways). For example, in Figure 3.2, we might assume Eddie lacks the skill to express his dislike for vocational work, particularly if we have never observed him using more appropriate ways to communicate that he does not want to go to work.

How the behavior is related to setting events, antecedents, and consequences. Do you see a pattern in terms of when or where appropriate and/or inappropriate behavior occurs? Does it typically occur in the presence of certain people? In response to particular demands? At about the same time

each day? Also, do you see a pattern in the consequences for the behavior—both positive and negative consequences? From the data shown in the scatter plot in Figure 3.1, we might assume that Erica is more likely to pinch or scratch during less structured times (snack/play and P.E.). In Eddie's case (Figure 3.2), it appears that hitting himself or acting aggressively against the teacher predictably occurs when he is told to go to the work area. We might also conclude that this behavior is reinforced by Eddie avoiding going to the work area. During this observation period, Eddie avoided going to the work area every time he was asked to do so. Therefore, his hitting behavior appears to be very efficient: It consistently produces desired results.

The last step is to develop an intervention plan based on the data you have collected and the hypotheses you have developed. Your intervention plan will include, as appropriate, modifying setting events (when possible) and antecedents, changing consequences, or teaching new behaviors, including interim **replacement behaviors.** Figure 3.4 provides a format for organizing the information you have gathered, and planning interventions based on your hypotheses about function and the contributing roles of setting events, antecedents, skill deficits, and consequences. The top portion of this form provides space for you to describe (in pinpoint terms) the problem behavior; hypothesized setting events and skill deficits that may be contributing to the behavior; and the function of the problem behavior.

The second section allows you to identify an interim replacement behavior—a more appropriate way for the student to attain the same outcomes as the original problem behavior. Sometimes, moving from the inappropriate behavior to the ultimate desired behavior may be too great a change. Identifying a replacement behavior enables the student to continue getting desired consequences without the undesired behavior, while you teach the student the more appropriate desired behavior. On the form, you should list setting

PLANNING FORM

Name _____ Date _____

Problem Behavior _____

Setting Events/Antecedents	Skill Deficit	Function

Replacement Behavior _____

Setting Events/Antecedents	Skills to Teach	Consequences

Desired Behavior _____

Setting Events/Antecedents	Skills to Teach	Consequences

FIGURE 3.4 Functional assessment intervention planning form.

events or associated antecedents that will typically precede the replacement behavior, what needs to be taught for the replacement behavior, and consequences that should follow display of the replacement behavior. For example, in Eddie's case, our hypothesis is that Eddie dislikes the work area but lacks an appropriate way to communicate this. Currently, Eddie's misbehavior often results in his avoiding work. Our ultimate goal is for Eddie to go quietly to the work area when told to do so; however, given the effectiveness of his inappropriate behavior in avoiding work, it is unlikely that this will be an easily acquired new behavior.

Therefore, in the meantime, we recommend teaching an interim replacement behavior. This behavior should produce the same results (avoiding work) for the time being. In Eddie's case, his teacher could teach him to say or sign "no" when told to go to work. We will discuss this more thoroughly later in this chapter, but the point here is to teach Eddie a more acceptable form of noncompliance. At first, each time Eddie signs "no," the teacher should respond, "Eddie, that's a good way to tell me you don't want to work," then allow him to do something else instead. Once Eddie is saying "no" consistently, the teacher should

PLANNING FORM

Name _Eddie_   Date _3-15_

Problem Behavior _Noncompliance: screaming, hitting head, grabbing teacher_

Setting Events/Antecedents	Skill Deficit	Function
– Work time, being asked to go to work area	– Communicating that he doesn't like work or that he doesn't want to go to work	– Escape "work"/avoid

Replacement Behavior _Sign "no" when asked to go to work_

Setting Events/Antecedents	Skills to Teach	Consequences
– Being asked to go to work	– Sign "no"	– Avoid work

Desired Behavior _Going to work and working on assigned tasks_

Setting Events/Antecedents	Skills to Teach	Consequences
– Being asked to go to work, given work tasks	N/A	– Money earned may be used to buy "break passes," to be used during work time

FIGURE 3.5 Completed planning form.

begin requiring a small amount of time in the work area before allowing him to leave (e.g., he must complete one brief task). Gradually, he should be required to work for longer periods of time before leaving the work area. However, once in awhile, he should be allowed to avoid work entirely when he signs "no." This type of intermittent reinforcement will help avoid the recurrence of the previous problem behavior.

The third section of the form helps you identify ultimate desired behaviors, and setting events/antecedents that may cue those behaviors, skills that need to be taught, and consequences

that should follow the desired behaviors. Figure 3.5 shows a sample planning form that was completed for Eddie. When using the planning form, a separate form should be used for each class of behaviors (behaviors associated with the same function). In Eddie's case, we would use one planning form for hitting, screaming, or any other behaviors associated with escape from a disliked task. However, for behaviors associated with getting something he desires (e.g., self-stimulatory behaviors), we would use a separate form.

Table 3.4 presents some sample hypotheses (categorized in terms of setting events, antecedents,

Table 3.4 Sample Hypothesis Statements and Related Interventions

Setting Events

Hypotheses

1. Tim is more likely to hit himself when he has a cold or allergies.

2. Jonathan's noncompliance increases toward lunchtime when he is getting hungry.

3. Tomas is noncompliant in the mornings because his morning bus ride is too long.

Setting Event Strategies

1a. Talk to Tim's parents about possible medications or other treatments to relieve symptoms of colds or allergies.

2a. Provide a midmorning snack for Jonathan.

3a. Talk to the transportation company about a new route or new schedule for Tomas.

3b. Talk to Tomas' parents about sending activities for him to do on the bus.

Antecedents

Hypotheses

1. Erica is more likely to pinch or scratch during unstructured times.

2. Colin is likely to hit or pinch other students when he sits next to them during group time.

Antecedent Strategies

1a. Provide more structure: clear expectations and instructions, frequent feedback, clearly defined activities, etc.

1b. Use differential reinforcement (DRO or DRI) during those times.

2a. Use DRO to reinforce Colin for gradually longer periods of time during which he sits next to peers without hitting or pinching.

2b. Allow Colin to hold a favorite object in his hands during group time (as long as this does not interfere with his participation in the group).

2c. Teach Colin to sit with his hands tucked under his legs. Reinforce him for increasingly longer periods of time in which his hands are tucked under his legs.

Skill Deficits

Hypotheses

1. Eddie hits because he doesn't know how to express his dislike for vocational tasks.

2. Aviv screams when required to use his spoon or fork for eating, as opposed to his hands.

Strategies for Teaching New Skills

1a. Teach Eddie to say or sign "no" rather than hitting.

1b. Give Eddie choices of vocational tasks.

1c. Use a shaping procedure to teach Eddie to work at disliked tasks. For example, at first, reinforce him just for moving toward the work area; after a few days, reinforce him for moving toward the work area, then sitting in his chair; a few days later, begin making reinforcement contingent on his beginning his task; and so forth until he is completing tasks with no hitting.

2a. Teach Aviv some way of communicating (e.g., sign, verbal statement, point to picture, etc.) that he wants to eat with his hands.

2b. Use DRI to shape utensil use: Allow Aviv to eat with his hands only after first picking up his utensil. After a few days, make eating with his hands contingent on holding his utensil for a few seconds. Later, require him to take one bite with the utensil before he is allowed to use his hands, then two bites, and so on until he eats all appropriate foods using utensils.

Consequences

Hypotheses

1. Eddie avoids going to the work area by hitting.

2. Ben runs away to get attention.

3. Travis engages in auditory self-stimulatory behaviors (e.g., cups his hand between his mouth and ear and makes noises) because he likes the echo-like sound quality.

Consequence Strategies

1a. Allow Eddie to earn "out" of work by using this as a reinforcer, at first for signing or saying "no" in response to the direction to go to the work area, or for moving in the direction of the work area with no hitting. Later, he will be required to complete a portion of his assigned task before being allowed to leave the work area. Eventually he must complete all of the task; at this point he would probably be on some type of simple token system where he can use earned tokens to "buy" a day off work.

2a. Provide Ben with high levels of attention for walking within arms' length of teacher. In addition, if he runs, place him in time-out and give no attention for a specific amount of time.

3a. Use DRA: Reinforce Travis for listening to seashells or for using a microphone/headphones combination to speak into and listen to his voice.

---

skill deficits, and consequences) and possible interventions for each hypothesis. Note how closely each intervention matches the perceived function of the behavior or the assumed relationship between the behavior and contextual circumstances. The intervention examples described in Table 3.4 are not meant to be definitive recommendations for interventions for the specific problem behaviors listed; they are intended only to illustrate the relationship between the nature of the hypothesis and the type of intervention that might be indicated. Interventions for your students should be designed based on the unique variables associated with each situation.

Once you have implemented your interventions, be sure to monitor the effects of the interventions on the target behaviors using one of the measurement techniques described in Chapter 2. If the behavior improves after a reasonable time of implementing the intervention, you can conclude that your hypothesis was valid. If not, you may need to adjust the intervention or develop a new intervention based on a different hypothesis.

Functional assessment is a critical step in designing effective interventions for the behavioral

excesses of students with autism. Because these children have limited repertoires of appropriate behaviors (e.g., they have significant skill deficits), their inappropriate behaviors are often the only way they have of getting needs met, thus they exhibit behavioral excesses. Failure to recognize this and act on it will probably mean that behavior management programs will do little to reduce challenging behaviors.

INTERVENTIONS FOR SPECIFIC CHALLENGING BEHAVIORS

As we have discussed so far, many children and youth with autism predictably exhibit certain types of challenging behavior: noncompliance, self-stimulatory behaviors, self-injurious behaviors, and aggression. Although the presenting behaviors may appear similar across children, there is often great variability in how children respond to treatment (Koegel et al., 1995). Because of this, a "one-size-fits-all" approach to choosing interventions is unsuitable. Interventions must be based on assessment of the function the challenging behavior may serve for the student, and the relationship between the challenging behavior and environmental variables. For example, one child may tantrum as a way of getting out of disliked tasks; another child's tantrums may be an attempt to communicate that she is hungry and wants to eat; still another child's tantrums may be an effective way for the child to get attention. Intervention would differ for each of these children. Therefore, the first step in dealing with challenging behavior is to conduct a functional assessment, as described earlier in this chapter. Using the information gathered, interventions are designed that reflect hypotheses about the function of the behavior and the contextual variables influencing the behavior.

In this section, we will describe interventions that research has shown may be effective in reducing specific challenging behaviors, based on their function. We wish to emphasize that our purpose in describing these interventions is not to provide a "cookbook" approach to responding to challenging behavior. This section is simply meant to serve as a model for the process of designing interventions based on functional assessment data.

Noncompliance

Noncompliance may take many forms, ranging from passive noncompliance (e.g., the student simply does not do what she is told) to tantrums to overt aggression in response to a demand. At the least, noncompliance can interfere with instruction. At worst, it can result in placement in more restrictive settings and can limit opportunities for meaningful interaction with peers and adults in a variety of contexts. Furthermore, noncompliance in young children can escalate into more serious behavior problems (Cipani, 1998).

Remember, before designing interventions for noncompliance, you must first conduct a functional assessment of noncompliant behavior. Once contributing variables and possible functions of the noncompliant behavior have been identified, intervention should be designed to address these factors. Several common functions for noncompliance and possible interventions for each function follow.

Attention as a Function for Noncompliance. Sometimes children get more attention for noncompliance than for compliance. For example, a student may work appropriately for several minutes with no teacher feedback, but as soon as the student stops working, the teacher approaches, talks to the student, examines work done so far, and encourages the student to continue working. Thus, the student gets more attention for noncompliance (not working) than compliance. If functional assessment data indicate that a student's noncompliance is for the purpose of getting attention (not typically found for students with autism), the recommended intervention is differential reinforcement of alternative behaviors. In this case, compliance would be immediately, consistently, and strongly reinforced while noncompliance would not get reinforcement. In the example given earlier, the student would be given frequent attention for on-task behavior, and no attention when he stops working before the task is finished. Likewise, a student would be given strong reinforcement (e.g., a piece of cookie) for following directions quickly, and no attention or other reinforcement for noncompliance.

Sometimes students' noncompliance results in attention from peers. Although this is also not a common explanation for noncompliance in students with autism, if data point to peer attention as a maintaining function, peers must be taught to differentially respond to compliance. That is, peers must be taught to ignore noncompliance. To do this, simply reinforce peers for ignoring target noncompliant behavior. A simple praise statement may be sufficient (e.g., "I like the way you're doing your work and not looking at Kristin right now"). In addition, peers should be instructed to attend to the target student when he or she is behaving appropriately.

Escape or Avoidance as a Function for Noncompliance. If assessment data suggest the noncompliance is to avoid a disliked task, situation, or person, which is often the case for students with autism, we recommend one or both of the following two approaches to intervention.

First, make the disliked situation more appealing, if possible. Depending on the situation, this might be done in several ways:

Change how a task is done. For example, a student who dislikes writing could be allowed to write with a colored marker instead of a pencil. A student who dislikes washing dishes because she does not like putting her hands in water could be allowed to wear rubber gloves. Or a student who dislikes using the vacuum cleaner because of the noise could be allowed to listen to music through headphones while vacuuming.

Increase the functionality of a task. Tasks should be functional for the student, which is to say that tasks should lead to independence in some aspect of daily living. Tasks that are not functional are not only a waste of time, but they may be boring for students as well. For example, rather than have students sort colored blocks, a more functional task would be to sort washclothes and towels by color. A nonfunctional approach to addressing the goal of strengthening pincher grasp would be to have the student place spring clothespins on a piece of cardboard. A functional way to develop pincher grasp is to have the student package items in plastic bags with zipper seals. Teaching a student to answer questions could be done by asking questions throughout the day (e.g., "Where is your coat?" "What toy do you want?" "What do you want to drink?").

Increase reinforcement during the disliked situation. Sometimes a task cannot be altered to make it more intrinsically appealing. If this is the case, stronger external reinforcement should be provided. For example, M'Kayla disliked sitting next to peers and resisted when requested to do so (e.g., during group). Her teacher designed an intervention to frequently reinforce M'Kayla (e.g., praise and primary reinforcers) for sitting appropriately next to peers. Or, if a student does not like shaving, the student could earn a token for each stroke of the razor. When he is finished, tokens could be exchanged for a desired item or activity. Or, the student could simply be allowed to choose a favorite cologne or aftershave to apply once he is finished!

Decrease the time the student is required to participate in the disliked situation. In the early stages of intervention, the student would be required to engage in the activity for brief periods of time. The student would then gradually be required to participate for longer and longer periods of time. For M'Kayla, who disliked sitting next to her peers, an alternate intervention would be for her to sit next to peers for 1 minute. At the end of 1 minute of appropriate sitting, she would be allowed to move away. After several days of successful 1-minute periods, she would next be required to sit appropriately for 2 minutes before being allowed to move away. Required "sitting time" would be gradually increased until M'Kayla is able to sit next to peers for an entire group activity. Likewise, if a student dislikes loading the dishwasher, the first step of intervention might be to have her place one dish in the dishwasher, then stop the activity. After several days of loading one dish with no inappropriate behavior, the student would be required to put two dishes in the dishwasher before stopping the activity. The number of dishes required to be loaded before the activity ends would gradually be increased until the student is loading all the dishes at one time. For another example of how noncompliance may be related to the nature of the task, see the vignette titled *Leah Learns More and Mr. Feldman Stops Being Frustrated!*

Leah Learns More and Mr. Feldman Stops Being Frustrated!

Mr. Feldman was frustrated. For the most part, his elementary class of students with autism was doing well. However, 11-year-old Leah was still exhibiting high levels of problem behavior. Mr. Feldman consulted with another, more experienced teacher, who reminded him not to forget what he knows: step-by-step functional assessment of the problem behavior, then interventions designed to address probable functions of the misbehavior. Mr. Feldman sheepishly admitted that, although he had tried various reinforcement programs, he had not conducted a functional assessment.

Realizing he had skipped an important step in designing behavioral interventions, Mr. Feldman, his paraprofessional, and the adaptive P. E. teacher each completed the form, Functional Assessment Report (FAR) (see Table 3.1). Mr. Feldman then compared the information on these forms. All three teachers agreed that noncompliance was a problem: At times, Leah refused to work, giggled uncontrollably, and sometimes threw materials. Everyone indicated that Leah typically started an activity with few problems, but became increasingly noncompliant about 20 minutes into an activity. Noncompliant behaviors were worse when Leah was asked to do repetitive tasks (e.g., sort shape blocks, collate papers, do calisthenics). All three teachers also agreed that Leah did some activities with no problems: preparing for lunch, all self-care tasks, and playing kickball.

Next, Mr. Feldman had a fellow teacher conduct an A–B–C observation during prevocational class. The assigned task was folding papers, inserting the papers in an envelope, and sealing the envelope. The A-B-C report indicated that Leah completed 15 envelopes with no noncompliance. On the next envelope, Leah began giggling and looking at the ceiling; Mr. Feldman redirected her. Leah did two more envelopes slowly, then began turning around in her chair and giggling. Attempts to redirect her back to task

resulted in her grabbing the stack of envelopes and throwing them. Mr. Feldman eventually placed Leah in time-out.

Based on the indirect and direct assessment results, Mr. Feldman formulated the following hypotheses:

- Leah tires of repetitive tasks after approximately 15 minutes.

- Leah dislikes repetitive tasks.

- Leah is most compliant during tasks that are functional.

With these hypotheses in mind, Mr. Feldman made a few changes in Leah's daily schedule. First, he made sure that Leah worked on tasks that had a high degree of functional value. Following are some of the tasks Leah had been working on (with the task objective in parentheses), and how Mr. Feldman changed them to make them more functional:

Old Task (Objective)	New Task
Sort coins (recognize like coins)	Pick out like coins to spend in school store
Collate papers (engage in a vocational activity)	Collate letters in the school office 10 minutes at a time
Name pictures (articulation, increasing vocabulary)	Name objects as the teacher asks her throughout the day
Cut on quarter-inch lines (improve fine motor skills)	Cut out coupons to use on class shopping trip.

In addition, Mr. Feldman developed a reinforcement system for use during less-liked tasks. During these activities, Leah earned stars for compliance (on-task behavior). When she accumulated 10 stars, she could "take a break." At first stars were given frequently; gradually, time between stars was increased.

These changes did not completely eliminate Leah's noncompliant behavior. However, Mr. Feldman believed that these interventions were responsible for the fact that noncompliant behavior greatly lessened in frequency and severity. The result was that Leah began making measurable progress on target skills. And Mr. Feldman learned an important lesson: Remember basic rules for assessing challenging behavior and using assessment data to design interventions any time you are dealing with challenging behavior!

Be sure the student has the skills necessary to complete the task. Research has shown that noncompliance as an escape function is often positively correlated with a lack of ability to perform the target task (Cipani, 1998). Therefore, it is critical that teachers present instructions and tasks that they know for a fact the student can do. The teacher should rely on recent formal or informal assessment information to determine a student's readiness for tasks, rather than assuming a student has the necessary skills.

For example, Brandon is noncompliant when he is asked to sort coins. His teacher, Ms. Hall, incorrectly assumes that, even though coin discrimination has not been taught, Brandon "should" be able to do this task. What Ms. Hall failed to realize is Brandon's inability to distinguish between subtle elements of coins (e.g., size). Or consider Tamara, a 14-year-old new to Mr. Lawson's class. Tamara resists when asked to put on her shoe. Mr. Lawson has been treating this as a motivation problem. However, during their first conference, Mr. Lawson learns from Tamara's mother that Tamara has never learned to put on her shoe; mother does it for her every day!

The second procedure is known as **behavioral momentum** (Cipani, 1998; Mace et al., 1988). The purpose of this technique is to increase the likelihood that a student will comply with a command for a disliked task by preceding it with several more appealing commands. That is, a stu-

dent is given two or three high-probability directions (directions to which the student is usually compliant and thus can be reinforced). Immediately after the student finishes complying with those directions, the low-probability direction (the command to which the student is typically noncompliant) is given. For example, if a student is predictably noncompliant to the request "Danny, you need to shave," you would first give two or three commands to do tasks that Danny likes. So, you might instruct him as follows: "Danny, turn on the radio" (and praise him when he complies), "Danny, get a drink of juice" (followed by praise), "Danny, give me 'five' " (followed by enthusiastic praise), then give him the shaving instruction.

Communication as a Function for Noncompliance. Some students may use noncompliance as a means to communicate that they do not want to do something, that they are tired of doing something, or that they do not know how to do something. Therefore, if functional assessment data indicate that noncompliance may be for communicative purposes, you would need a two-pronged intervention. First, you must attempt to make the disliked activities more appealing, as described earlier, or more appropriately suited to the child's abilities. Second, we recommend teaching the student a more appropriate way of communicating his dislike for the requested task or refusing the command. Sometimes teachers or parents are uncomfortable with teaching a student to say "no," or refusal. However, most of us use ways of saying "no" when we do not want to do something: We either directly refuse, or we try to negotiate the request (subtly, at times), or we simply do not do what was asked. Students with autism typically have not learned socially appropriate ways of saying they don't want to do something, so they communicate this through noncompliance or other challenging behavior. Therefore, teaching a student refusal skills should reduce the noncompliance or challenging behavior that is serving that function.

On the other hand, it is not acceptable for a student to always be able to avoid disliked tasks simply by saying "no." Eventually, students must learn to comply even with directions they do not wish to do. That, then, becomes the long-term goal, and the process of shaping (see Chapter 5) is used to accomplish this goal. For example, if a student is noncompliant when asked to complete a puzzle, you should teach the student how to say "no" or "No, I don't want to." This might be by using words, signs, or some other form of communication. (See Chapter 6 for various communication systems and how to teach students to use these systems.) Basically, the child should be prompted to use the words ("Say 'no' ") or other communication method ("Point to 'no' "). As soon as the child says "no," the puzzle is removed and a more desirable task is presented (thus the child is reinforced for saying "no").

Of course, this is not our ultimate goal, so once the student responds to the request to do a puzzle with "no" consistently and independently, we start having him place one puzzle piece, even after he says "no," then removing the puzzle. After several days of successful responding at this level, we have him place two puzzle pieces before removing the puzzle. This pattern slowly continues until the student is completing the entire puzzle. However, since he probably still does not like doing the puzzle, once in awhile throughout the intervention, when he says "no," you should remove the puzzle immediately, even after he is able to complete the puzzle. The reason for this is that removing the puzzle from time to time, contingent on his saying "no," will intermittently reinforce using "no" instead of other inappropriate behavior. As you remember from Chapter 2, intermittent reinforcement is the most powerful schedule of reinforcement available and will maintain a behavior indefinitely.

Noncompliance as a Skill Deficit. Two potential types of skill deficits may lead to noncompliance: a skill deficit in understanding verbal commands and a skill deficit in compliant behavior. Treatment may vary, depending on the nature of the skill deficit.

The first type of skill deficit is a receptive language deficit. Remember from Chapter 1 that one theory of autism posits that these children have difficulty organizing and understanding auditory stimuli. This characteristic has implications for how verbal directions are given. Research shows that, for some students, noncompliance is a function of the degree of clarity in instructions (Walker & Walker, 1991). Therefore, if functional assessment data lead you to no other hypotheses regarding the function of noncompliant behavior, you may want to consider poor understanding of verbal directions as an explanation. Intervention would consist of modifying how verbal commands are given. According to Forehand and McMahon (1981), verbal instructions should have these characteristics:

- **One or two steps only.** Don't give long, multistep directions. For example, instead of "Chandler, take off your coat, hang it up, then go choose a play station—don't forget to hang your name tag on the play station you choose," say "Chandler, take off your coat and hang it up." When Chandler finishes those tasks, give the next instruction.

- **Brief.** Do not make instructions confusing by adding explanations, cajoling, repeated reminders or warnings, or other discussion. Do not, for example, give an instruction like this: "Katie, I want you to set the table. Don't forget the placemats—yesterday you left them out. And remember where the napkins go. Are you going to fold the napkins? Remember—if you finish quickly you may watch TV until dinner, but if I have to keep reminding you, no TV."

- **Clear and specific.** For example, if you want a student to clean his desk area, you should say "Quentin, please put your books away and throw away the trash on the floor around your desk." This type of specificity is important; a clear direction such as this is more likely to be followed to the expected standard than a vague direction such as "Clean your desk area."

- **Stated in the form of a command, not a question.** If you want a student to do something, tell them, don't ask them. You can be polite without weakening the command. Don't ask a student, "Do you want to go to Ms. Gonzalez' room now?"; tell him "It is time to go to Ms. Gonzalez's room—you need to go now." Likewise, "Are you ready to work on writing?" has a lower probability of compliance than "It is time for writing. Get out your pencil, please."

- **Given in such a way that they are prominent and distinct.** One of the authors once consulted with a teacher of a secondary class for students with autism and developmental disabilities regarding a particular student who was described as highly noncompliant. On observation, the author saw that the student was quite compliant during class time when most students were quietly engaged in task-related behavior. However, during transition times, which were noisy and somewhat chaotic, the target student's noncompliance increased significantly. The author hypothesized that the noncompliance was primarily a function of the confusing environment: The student was not attending to instructions and seemed disturbed by the noise and activity level. The recommendation was to improve transitions, and to give this student individual instructions. Remembering the need for clarity in the environment for students with autism, you should first get the student's attention before giving an instruction. Prefacing the instruction with the student's name is one way of doing this. Be sure the student is not engaged in a distracting activity when you give instructions. And it may be necessary to bend down to eye level with the student before giving an instruction.

- **Given from no more than a few feet away from the student.** This helps increase the prominence of the direction for the student. Instructions that are given from across the room are less pronounced than instructions that are given in immediate proximity to the student. This is especially important when giving instructions to children with autism, who easily tune out external stimuli.

The second type of skill deficit related to noncompliance is seen in some children, particularly young children or students who have not been in highly structured, instructionally focused educational programs. These children simply may not yet have learned to comply. The intervention, then, is to teach compliance. This situation is analogous to the fact that parents of toddlers must teach their children to follow directions. They do this by giving their children many opportunities to practice, using reminders, giving feedback, and applying consequences for both compliance and noncompliance. As a result, young children eventually learn to follow instructions most of the time.

If assessment data reveal a likely skill deficit in compliance (e.g., the student seldom complies, particularly to commands for disliked activities), the recommended intervention is a procedure known as **compliance training** (Colvin & Engelmann, 1983; Simpson & Regan, 1986). In compliance training, the student is taught to comply. This is done by using a highly structured teaching format to present simple commands, prompt compliance if necessary, reinforce compliance, and consequate noncompliance. This instructional procedure is presented several times per day until the student is compliant during the instructional sessions at a predetermined target level, e.g., 90 percent of the time. A form such as the one shown in Figure 3.6 is used to record compliant and noncompliant responses. The next step is to conduct the same structured teaching sessions in a different environment, such as the playground or workshop, and/or with a different teacher (e.g., the teaching assistant). The steps in compliance training are described in the following section, and the teaching methods used in this procedure (known as trial teaching) are described more fully in Chapter 5.

Compliance Training. Conduct the training at scheduled times several times throughout the day. The length of the compliance training sessions should reflect the student's age, functioning level,

Name _____

	Date							
+ = correct response − = incorrect response								
Phase I								
Sit down								
Touch your nose								
Clap hands								
Stand up								
Do this (imitate movement)								
Phase II								
Go get the ball								
Go touch the door								
Put this on the table (give object)								
Go touch your desk								
Come here (when child is a few feet away from teacher)								
Phase III								
Take off your coat								
Stack the blocks								
Throw the ball								
Go to group								
Get your lunch								

FIGURE 3.6 Compliance training form.

and attention span. For some students, 3-minute sessions would be appropriate; other students could work for 10 or 15 minutes per session. During the compliance training sessions, the student should be seated in an appropriately sized chair with the teacher in a chair immediately in front of the child's. If you are working with a student who may try to leave the training area, the training area should be configured in such a way as to prevent this from happening. For example, the child's chair might be placed in a corner (facing the room), with the teacher's chair blocking the child's exit path.

Phase I: Beginning Training. Commands are given using three steps:

1. Give the child simple commands such as those listed in Figure 3.6. Commands should be simple tasks that the child can perform and should not involve the student leaving the immediate training area. The command should be stated succinctly, with no unnecessary verbiage: "Stacey, stand up," "Stevie, sit down," "Quentin, clap hands."

2. If the child does not comply within approximately 5 seconds, repeat the command while physically guiding the child to perform the task. For example, gently pull the child into a standing position or move the child's hands in a clapping motion.

3. Once you have helped the child perform the task, praise her. Praise should be descriptive and enthusiastic: "Stacey, good job standing up!" or "Stevie, I like the way you sat down!" No other reinforcement should be provided if you had to prompt the child to perform the task. If the child performs the task independently, give praise and a small amount of another reinforcer. Primary reinforcers are often appropriate for compliance training: small bites of cookie, a small sip of juice or milk, or a small bite of fruit. On the data recording form, record the appropriate code next to the command that was just given.

Repeat steps 1 through 3, giving the various commands in random order. Once the student is consistently complying to these commands 80 percent of the time or more, move on to Phase II.

Phase II: Advanced Training. In this phase of training, the student is given commands that require movement away from the training area (see Figure 3.6). Follow steps 1 through 3 as described in Phase I. In this phase of training, we recommend you thin the schedule of primary reinforcement (see Chapter 2). That is, rather than giving a primary reinforcer after every correct (unprompted) response, provide the primary reinforcer only after 5 or 10 correct responses. Once

the student is complying to these commands consistently 80 percent of the time or more, move on to Phase III.

Phase III: Generalized Training. In this phase of training, the student is given commands in natural contexts throughout the day. For example, the student might be told "Rolando, take off your jacket" or "Olivia, throw the ball." These are commands that are given as part of the daily routine. However, all incorrect or incomplete responses are prompted and correct responses are reinforced. In addition, data should be recorded so that the child's rate of compliance in generalized settings can be monitored. Once the student is complying with these commands consistently 80 percent of the time or more, formal data collection on compliance can be discontinued. You should, however, continue to reinforce compliance on an intermittent basis.

The goal of compliance training is to teach the student that compliance is expected and required when a command is given. This highly structured, instructional approach to noncompliance reflects requirements for an effective program (e.g., clarity, practicality) as discussed in Chapter 1. Compliance training is especially important if you are working with primary- or intermediate-age children. It is critical that students with autism learn compliance, and compliance training is often the most efficacious route to this goal.

However, because it requires physical prompting when a student does not comply, compliance training may not be appropriate for older students or students whose size precludes full physical prompting. For these students, educators are advised to rely on the other techniques described in this section, either alone or in combination.

Self-Stimulatory Behaviors

Self-stimulatory behavior is one form of challenging behavior commonly seen in children with autism and pervasive developmental disorders. Self-stimulatory behavior poses unique challenges for educators because it is usually so self-reinforcing for the child that it is difficult to find equally powerful alternative reinforcers. Self-stimulatory behavior is so pervasive in some children that without direct guidance to participate in other activities, these children would spend virtually all their waking hours engaged in self-stimulatory behavior (Schreibman, Koegel, & Koegel, 1989).

Self-stimulatory behaviors appear to serve no function other than to provide sensory stimulation for the child, and they often interfere with learning, relationships, and even neurological development (Koegel, Valdez-Menchaca, & Koegel, 1994). Addressing these behaviors is critical, as evidenced by research that has demonstrated an inverse relationship between stereotypic behaviors and more functional behaviors. A number of researchers have reported spontaneous increases in academic and play behaviors when self-stimulatory behaviors are suppressed, as well as spontaneous decreases in self-stimulatory behaviors as a result of teaching physical exercise skills (e.g., Kern, Koegel, & Dunlap, 1984; Kern, Koegel, Dyer, Blew, & Fenton, 1982; R.L. Koegel, Firestone, Kramme, & Dunlap, 1974). This research has important implications for teachers and parents: Interventions for stereotypic behaviors must include teaching and strengthening more appropriate alternative behaviors. If the child does not have more appropriate behaviors in his repertoire, he undoubtedly will continue to self-stimulate.

The concept of teaching more appropriate alternatives, however, presents an interesting problem for educators. Self-stimulatory behavior appears to diminish the child's responsiveness to external stimuli (Lovaas, 1981). The child is unlikely to respond to the teacher's efforts to teach more functional behaviors as long as she is engaging in self-stimulatory behavior. So the teacher must find a way to stop the self-stimulation long enough to get the child's attention to teach. We recommend several strategies for managing self-stimulatory behaviors, as described below.

Differential Reinforcement of Incompatible Behaviors (DRI). This differential reinforcement procedure is a logical choice for reducing self-stimulatory behavior. To use DRI, determine the type of sensory input provided by the child's self-stimulatory behavior, then select an acceptable alternative behavior that could provide similar sensory stimulation. Lovaas (1981) describes categories of sensory input:

- **Visual stimulation.** Flicking fingers in front of eyes; gazing at lights, objects, or hands.
- **Auditory stimulation.** Repetitive vocalizations, clicking tongue, tapping fingers.
- **Tactile stimulation.** Touching objects, clothing, or people; placing fingers in mouth.
- **Vestibular stimulation.** Refers to sensory input related to balance or equilibrium: rocking, bouncing, spinning.
- **Proprioceptive stimulation.** Refers to sensory input experienced through muscles and joints: assuming unusual positions; walking on toes, flapping hands, holding head to one side.

To this list we would add the following categories:

- **Olfactory stimulation.** Sniffing or smelling objects, people, or clothing.
- **Gustatory stimulation.** Tasting by licking or putting things in mouth: hands, objects, and so on.

Once the likely sensory system affected by the self-stimulatory behavior has been determined, the next step is to find more appropriate avenues for stimulating that system. Most of us engage in one or more self-stimulatory behaviors, but we typically choose socially acceptable forms of those behaviors. For example, some people shake their foot or bounce their leg while sitting; others whistle or hum or make other mouth noises. Table 3.5 lists possible alternative sources for the types of sensory consequences typically produced by self-stimulation. This list was compiled from recommendations from Hill and McMackin (as described in Lovaas, 1981), various procedures reported in research studies, and our own experiences in working with children with autism.

Table 3.5 Alternatives for Self-Stimulatory Behaviors

Sensory System	Replacement Behaviors
Visual	Prism, pinwheel, kaleidoscope, toys that make flashing lights, View Master, Lite-Brite, Slinky, lava lamp, wind-up toys, perpetual motion balls, string puppets, yo-yos
Auditory	Talking toys, music boxes, music through headphones, noise-makers, clickers, seashells, talking through a microphone (amplification), using headphones to listen to prerecorded tapes of the child's own voice, compact discs or audiotapes of animal noises (whales, dolphins), or white noise
Tactile	Pieces of cloth with a variety of textures (velvet, burlap, chenille, suede, satin, fur), Silly Putty, Slime, Koosh balls, vibrator, finger paints, bean bags, Beanie Babies, plastic bubble wrap, hand exercise balls, "worry" beads, or rocks
Vestibular	Rocking horse, rocking chair, hammock, swing, tire swing, trampoline, pogo stick, Sit-and-Spin, Ring-Around-the-Rosey, rolling on large therapy balls or in barrels, somersaults
Proprioceptive*	Wave handheld fan, wrist or ankle weights, isometric exercises, hanging on monkey bars or chin-up bars, hand weights, weight machines, gymnastic exercises (headstands, handstands, cartwheels, somersaults, etc.), grip-strengthening exercise tool
Olfactory	Cologne or aftershave, either worn on the student's body or offered in small vials; other fragrances offered in vials (e.g., scents used in making potpourri or dropped on light bulbs)
Gustatory	Gum, mints, hard candies

* Most of the activities listed as substitutes for proprioceptive self-stimulatory behaviors should be used with parent permission, with guidance from an occupational therapist, physical therapist, or physical education teacher.

Once an appropriate alternative behavior has been identified, this behavior is taught to the child using the discrete trial and prompting procedures described in Chapter 5. Initially, each time the child engages in the appropriate alternative behavior, she is reinforced using a powerful reinforcer, such as food. Remember, self-stimulatory behavior is naturally highly reinforcing. You must find an equally powerful competing reinforcer to motivate the child to engage in the alternative behavior. As the alternative behavior increases in frequency and/or intensity (e.g., as the child begins responding to the reinforcing properties of the new behavior) external reinforcement can be gradually faded and possibly eliminated eventually. Rincover (1981) reported that if you carefully select alternative activities that are more fun and provide a richer source of stimulation for the child, he probably will actually prefer the alternative activities over the self-stimulatory behavior, and may even give up the self-stimulatory behavior as a result.

Self-Stimulation as a Reinforcer. The powerful reinforcing qualities of self-stimulatory behavior make such behavior worthy for consideration as a reinforcer for other desired behaviors (Koegel, Rincover, & Egel, 1982; Lovaas, 1981). For example, Luis is allowed to spin his favorite blocks after 10 minutes of appropriate work behavior. Ashley's reinforcer for finishing her vocational tasks with no screaming is that she is allowed to jump on the small trampoline (a substitute for her self-stimulatiory behavior of bouncing on her toes). Isaac controls his auditory self-stimulations (making high-pitched noises into his hand cupped between his ear and mouth) during his job at the local grocery store because he knows he can listen to his whale-sounds tape as soon as he clocks out.

Some may express concerns about using an inappropriate behavior (self-stimulation) as a reinforcer (Devany & Rincover, as cited in Simpson & Regan, 1986). However, results of research suggest that self-stimulation as a reinforcer may be an effective teaching tool. Devaney and Rincover (1982) showed that self-stimulation as a reinforcer resulted in longer on-task periods and more learning than when food reinforcers were used. Furthermore, when used as a reinforcer in treatment, self-stimulation outside of the treatment session did not increase; in fact, one child stopped engaging in self-stimulatory behavior altogether outside of treatment.

Sensory Extinction. Another approach to reducing self-stimulatory behavior involves blocking the behavior's reinforcing effects (Rincover, 1978; Rincover, Newsom, & Carr, 1979). For example, Rincover (1978) describes several sensory extinction interventions that resulted in significant decreases in the target self-stimulatory behavior. In one case, auditory feedback from spinning a plate was blocked by covering the top of the table with carpet. The student was still allowed to spin (on the table), but the sound, which was reinforcing to the student, was eliminated. In a second case, finger flapping was virtually eliminated through the use of a small vibrator attached to the back of the child's hand, blocking the proprioceptive feedback of finger flapping. Finally, a third student's frequency of twirling objects diminished when a small vibrator was attached to her hand, again blocking the proprioceptive feedback of twirling. This last case is particularly interesting because it demonstrated the importance of accurately identifying the maintaining sensory reinforcement. In this case, because the student twirled objects in front of her eyes, a logical conclusion might have

been that she sought visual stimulation from the twirling. However, blocking the child's visual input from twirling objects (placing a blindfold over her eyes when she twirled objects) had little effect on twirling behavior, because the twirling was apparently maintained by proprioceptive consequences. Table 3.6 describes possible ways to mask the effects of certain self-stimulatory behaviors.

Sensory extinction as an intervention for self-stimulatory behavior may pose two problems. First, it is difficult to find effective ways to mask many self-stimulatory behaviors. For example, it may be difficult or impossible to block the sensory input from gazing, vocal self-stimulations, some proprioceptive self-stimulations, or some olfactory self-stimulations. Second, simply eliminating the self-stimulatory behavior may actually result in an increase in another, less frequently displayed form of self-stimulation (Lovaas, 1981). However, research on the use of this procedure is encouraging. We recommend it for consideration, but advise pairing sensory extinction procedures with reinforcement of more appropriate alternative (incompatible) behaviors (DRI).

Rincover (1981) points out that, because this technique is a form of extinction, you should expect that the self-stimulatory behavior may actually get worse before it gets better (remember the discussion of extinction from Chapter 2). This is a good sign: It means that you have successfully identified and blocked the maintaining sensory feedback. The child is now working harder (e.g., flapping harder, spinning more frequently) to get the sensory stimulation that he previously got from that behavior but no longer receives. If you keep the sensory extinction procedures in place, the behavior should begin to diminish and eventually disappear.

In addition, you should also try to gradually fade out use of the sensory extinction procedure (Rincover, 1981). For example, if you use an alternative substance to disguise smells for a student who sniffs objects, you might gradually apply less and less of the alternative substance. Or if ankle weights successfully reduced bouncing, you could gradually reduce the size or weight of the ankle weights.

Table 3.6 Sensory Extinction Techniques

Visual

Finger-flicking	Put mittens on the child's hands.
Turning lights on and off	Unplug the lights or disconnect the light switch.

Auditory

Spinning objects	Cover surfaces with carpet or cloth.
Multiple sources of auditory input	Have the student wear earplugs.

Tactile

Touching objects	Put gloves (cloth or rubber) on the child's hands.
Hitting self	Put soft gloves or mittens on the child's hands.
Hitting head against objects	Have child wear padded helmet; cover objects that he bangs on his head with foam padding or carpet.

Olfactory

Consistently smelling particular objects	Disguise the scent by putting some fragrance on the objects: cologne, flavor extracts, cleaning solution (e.g., pine), vinegar, etc.

Gustatory*

Consistently tasting or chewing on particular objects or substances	Disguise the taste by adding a flavor that the student would find unpleasant. For example, if a student chews on his shirt sleeve, put vinegar, flavor extracts, soy sauce, etc., on it—anything edible that the student would not like.
Chewing or sucking on fingers	Put gloves or mittens on the student's hands.

Proprioceptive

Flapping hands or arms	Put wrist weights on the child's arms.
Flicking fingers	Put gloves or mittens on the child's hands.
Bouncing on toes	Put ankle weights on the child's ankles.
Rocking	Have the child wear a weighted vest.

*Rincover (1981) reported a successful treatment for a student who regurgitated his food and then ate it, apparently because he liked the flavor. Because this student hated lima beans, treatment consisted of adding lima beans to the regurgitated food! The student made a few attempts to eat, but spit it out each time, then eventually gave up.

Use of a Mild Aversive. Use of a mild aversive may be necessary to teach the student that self-stimulation is not allowed during work time. Any time the student begins to display self-stimulatory behavior at an inappropriate time, the teacher (or whoever is working with the child at the time) might say "NO" or "NO ROCKING" in a firm, no-nonsense voice. If the child does not stop immediately, it may be necessary for the teacher to physically interrupt the self-stimulatory behavior, such as briefly holding the child's hands to stop flapping or finger-flicking, holding the child's arms to stop rocking. This restraint should be gentle and brief; the purpose is simply to prompt the child to stop the self-stimulatory behavior. As soon as the child is sitting appropriately, the teacher should reinforce her, with praise and possibly a primary or token reinforcer.

Restraint has two potential problems. First, some children may find the physical contact reinforcing (Lovaas, 1981). Thus, the child may continue to exhibit self-stimulatory behavior to get the teacher to hold his hands. The second problem is that the nature of some self-stimulatory behaviors make them difficult or impossible to restrain. For example, restraint would not be an appropriate response for gazing, sniffing objects, or vocal self-stimulations. The teacher's best tool in these situations is a firm reprimand. In the case of gazing, the teacher might clap her hands, cover the students eyes briefly with her hand, or snap her fingers close to the child and loudly say the child's name to more effectively interrupt the behavior.

As a final note on self-stimulatory behaviors, we should point out that certain procedures are probably inappropriate as interventions. Keeping in mind the highly intrinsically reinforcing nature of self-stimulation, ignoring and time-out may not be effective treatments (Devany & Rincover, 1982). In fact, those interventions may actually serve to increase self-stimulatory behavior: The child may *like* being ignored or placed in time-out because those conditions provide excellent opportunities to engage in self-stimulation!

Self-Injurious Behavior

Many children and youth with autism engage in behaviors that are hurtful or dangerous to themselves. **Self-injurious behavior (SIB)** sometimes occurs with such intensity that it results in physical damage: bruising, bleeding, tissue damage, vision loss, etc. (Dunlap et al., 1994). Because of the potential for causing permanent, even life-threatening, injury, and because of the highly stigmatizing nature of self-injurious behavior, it is critical to develop effective intervention plans to treat such behavior.

At one time, punishment was widely used to reduce these behaviors. Now, however, the recommended approach is to assess the function of those behaviors and then design interventions that reflect the function of the behavior and the relationship between the behavior and the environment (Koegel et al., 1995). In addition, there is growing support for nonaversive interventions to control challenging behavior (Dunlap et al., 1994). A large research base strongly supports the efficacy of interventions that rely on reinforcement of appropriate alternative behaviors, teaching new skills, and manipulating antecedents (Carr, Robinson, Taylor, & Carlson, 1990).

Some self-injurious behavior may have an organic basis (Carr, 1982). The two basic categories of organic explanations are genetic aberrations, such as Lesch-Nyhan and deLange syndromes, and nongenetic problems, such as otitis media

(middle ear infection). Carr proposed a screening sequence to identify the function of self-injurious behavior (Table 3.7). In this sequence, the first step is to rule out an organic explanation for the SIB, particularly if the SIB involves lip, finger, or tongue biting (Lesch-Nyhan and deLange syndromes) or head banging (otitis media). We would also encourage parents and educators to consider the recent onset of SIB, when the student has shown little or no history of this behavior, as a possible indicator of a nongenetic abnormality (e.g., sinus infection, headache, stomachache).

While organic explanations may account for some self-injurious behavior, a convincing body of empirical data points to challenging behavior as learned behavior, serving one or more of the following functions: getting something (e.g., positive reinforcement, sensory stimulation), avoiding something (e.g., negative reinforcement), or communicating something (Dunlap et al., 1994). The following sections describe intervention strategies based on each of these functions.

Positive Reinforcement as a Function for SIB. Sometimes, SIB occurs because the child gets attention—sometimes more attention or more intense attention for challenging behavior than for appropriate behavior (Iwata, Dorsey, Slifer, Bauman, & Richman, 1982) or desired objects or food (Bostow & Bailey, 1969; Day, Rea, Schussler, Larsen, & Johnson, 1988). Indicators for a positive reinforcement function for SIB might include these:

- SIB increases when the child is not directly interacting with a teacher.
- SIB increases when the teacher's attention is specifically focused on another student in the room.
- SIB occurs after a period of interaction with the teacher, as the teacher is moving away.
- SIB occurs when preferred objects or food are removed or denied.

Let's say Anthony's teacher, for example, determines that Anthony is most likely to hit himself when he is required to work for an extended period of time with no attention. We might rec-

Table 3.7 Carr's Screening Sequence

A Screening Sequence to Determine the Motivation of Self-Injurious Behavior

Step 1

Screen for genetic abnormalities (e.g., Lesch-Nyhan and deLange syndromes), particularly if lip, finger, or tongue biting is present.

Screen for nongenetic abnormalities (e.g., otitis media), particularly if head banging is present.

If screening is positive, motivation may be organic.

If screening is negative, proceed to step 2.

Step 2

Does self-injurious behavior increase under one or more of the following circumstances:

a. When the behavior is attended to?
b. When reinforcers are withdrawn for behaviors other than self-injurious behavior?
c. When the child is in the company of adults (rather than alone)?

If yes, motivation may be positive reinforcement.

If step 2 is negative, proceed to step 3.

Step 3

Does self-injurious behavior occur primarily when there are no activities available and/or the environment is barren?

If yes, motivation may be self-stimulation.

From Carr, E. G. (1977). The motivation of self-injurious behavior: A review of some hypotheses. *Psychological Bulletin, 84,* 800–816. Copyright 1977 by the American Psychological Association. Reprinted with permission.

ommend that Anthony's teacher implement a combined program of DRI and extinction: Anthony earns praise and a sticker if he is on-task, with no self-hitting, at the end of each 3-minute period. If he is hitting himself at the end of a 3-minute period, the teacher would simply say "You're hitting. No sticker." In addition, anytime Anthony hits himself during the work period, the teacher should turn away (extinction). Thus, the goal is to change the contingencies for attention: Anthony gets attention for appropriate behavior; he gets less attention when he is hitting himself.

Negative Reinforcement as a Function for SIB. More typically, students with autism may attempt to hurt themselves or others for the purpose of avoiding a task or a particular situation. Research has shown, for example, that such challenging behavior may be positively correlated with:

- The type of task presented (Carr & Durand, 1985)
- The type of instruction used (Iwata, 1987)

- Setting events such as the number of people present (McAfee, 1987) or extended periods of sitting (Bailey & Pyles, 1989)

If data indicate a relationship between external events and challenging behavior, we recommend one or more of the procedures described for noncompliance as an avoidance behavior. SIB as avoidance is essentially a compliance problem.

Communication as a Function for SIB. Current thinking regarding SIB in children with autism is that these behaviors may have communicative intent (Donnellan, Mirenda, Mesaros, & Fassbender, 1984; Dunlap et al., 1994). If assessment data point to communication as a function of self-injurious behavior, the first step is to determine what the student is attempting to communicate (e.g., Dunlap et al., 1994). Perhaps a student bites her hand when she is bored with a task. Another student might hit his head on the table when the teacher approaches to begin a work session. Or another student may dig her fingernails into her skin when she is excited. Whatever the case, once you identify the communicative purpose, the next step is to decide a more appropriate way for the student to communicate. For example, a student might be taught to point to a "Stop" sign to indicate he wants to stop working. The student who bangs his head when the teacher tries to begin working with him could be taught to say or sign "No work," much like we described in the section on noncompliance. Or the student who exhibits SIB when she is excited might be taught to clap her hands instead. Any form of communication that is appropriate for the student may be used: words, sign language, pictures, symbols, or electronic communication devices.

Sensory Stimulation as a Function for SIB.
Researchers have shown that sensory consequences may be the maintaining factor in some instances of self-injurious behavior (Koegel et al., 1982). Two lines of research support a sensory stimulation hypothesis for SIB. First, studies have shown that sensory extinction procedures can reduce SIB (Koegel et al., 1982). When sensory input from SIB was blocked, the self-injurious behavior diminished. Second, other studies have shown that SIB increases when children are placed in barren, stimulus-free environments (Iwata et al., 1982). That is, when no external activities were available, students' rates of SIB increased.

If sensory stimulation is the suspected function of the SIB, or if interventions based on other hypotheses have been implemented without success, we have two recommendations. First, the teacher should make sure sufficient external stimulation is always present. That is, the student should be engaged in meaningful activities at all times. SIB is more likely to occur when there is no alternative activity available, or when there is no teacher guidance to engage in the alternative activity. Second, it may be prudent to design a two-pronged intervention that combines controlling the sensory consequences of SIB with differential reinforcement of appropriate alternative behaviors. Suggestions follow for techniques that could be used to mask the reinforcing effects of SIB:

- A helmet to reduce head-banging
- Covering walls and floor with padded mats to reduce head-banging
- Heavy mittens to reduce finger-biting
- Removable plastic arm casts to reduce arm-biting or nail-gouging
- Goggles to reduce eye-gouging
- Rubber gloves to reduce scratching

An important point should be made here. We have discussed designing interventions based on hypothesized functions of challenging behavior. Our discussion has presented strategies that may effectively address several possible functions. However, in reality, a single form of challenging behavior may actually serve several functions that vary according to the immediate context (Dunlap et al., 1994). It may be too simplistic to develop an intervention strategy based on only one function. For example, DeShaun might hit his head when he dislikes a task, when he's bored, when he's hungry, and when he wants a toy that a peer is using. A single intervention that was based, for example, on his hitting himself during a disliked task would probably have little effect on his self-hitting when he is hungry or bored, or when he wants a toy from a peer. Therefore, educators must carefully evaluate all contexts in which challenging behavior occurs, then design interventions to target the specific functions of the challenging behavior within different contexts.

Aggression

Aggression may cause injury to other students, staff, or property. Aggression can take many forms, including hitting, kicking, pinching, throwing objects, pulling hair, spitting, biting, and grabbing clothing (Dunlap et al., 1994). Aggression, like most forms of challenging behavior, may also occur for a variety of reasons. Students may aggress as a form of communication, as a means of avoidance, or for attention.

Positive Reinforcement as a Function for Aggression. The indicators for a positive reinforcement function for aggression would be the same as those described for a positive reinforcement function for SIB. If the suspected function of aggressive behavior is to get attention or desired objects, the goal must be to change the rules for attaining those outcomes: The student must be taught more appropriate ways of getting desired consequences. Use of those appropriate alternative behaviors should consistently result in desired consequences (thus addressing the efficiency of the behavior), while aggression no longer does. For example, Nathan pinches peers who are playing with something he wants. Nathan should be taught to ask to use the toy. We do not recommend taking the toy away from the other student to give to Nathan, but Nathan's appropriate asking should be reinforced. Perhaps, at least in the beginning of the intervention, the teacher could have duplicates of Nathan's favorite objects so that when he asks correctly, he can be reinforced by giving him the desired object without taking it away from the peer.

In another example, consider Alex, who frequently spits on others when the teacher or peers are not attending to him during playtime on the playground or in the classroom. We would recommend a DRI intervention by first having the teacher provide Alex with structured play interactions with peers during play period (tossing the ball with a peer, building with blocks, playing with Mr. Potato Head, etc.). In addition, during each play period the teacher should set a timer to ring at brief, random intervals. If Alex has no instances of spitting and has been playing appropriately during the interval since the timer last rang, he would be praised and given a raisin (for example), which would be put in a bag for him to eat at the end of the play period or class activity.

Avoidance or Escape as a Function for Aggression. Some students learn that aggressive behavior serves as an efficient way to avoid or escape disliked situations. For example, if a student grabs handfuls of the teacher's hair every time the teacher asks him to write, a likely result would be that the teacher might stop asking him to write. When avoidance is the suspected function of ag-

gressive behavior, consider the following interventions:

- Make the associated antecedent more attractive or more suited to the student's skill level. For example, a student who predictably aggresses when it is time for her to vacuum because she does not like the sound of the vacuum cleaner could wear headphones and listen to music while vacuuming.

- Use behavioral momentum, as described in the noncompliance section.

- Teach the student a more appropriate way to avoid the situation, such as saying "no" or "I don't want to," then use differential reinforcement of this alternative behavior to strengthen this desired behavior.

Communication as a Function for Aggression. The most recent view of aggression is that it typically has communicative functions (Koegel et al., 1995). As was the case with SIB, educators must first determine the communicative purpose of the aggressive behavior. Perhaps a student hits peers when they try to play with him as a way of expressing his dislike for their overture. Or another student may try to grab a teacher's clothing because he wants her to move away from him. Still another student might throw items when he wants to do something other than the task he has been given. For each of these students, the appropriate intervention is to teach a more appropriate method of communication. As appropriate communication skills increase, aggression should diminish or even disappear, assuming communication was in fact the function of that behavior (Koegel et al., 1995).

Aggression as a Result of Disruption in Routine or Interruption of Ritual. As you remember from Chapter 1, many individuals with autism engage in repetitive rituals, such as lining objects up in a particular way, or they insist on sameness in routine or in the environment. For example, students may have a tantrum if desks are rearranged or may aggress toward the teacher if the child's milk is placed on the "wrong" side of the plate. We should point out that disruption in preferred routines or rituals does not always result in aggression. Although we are discussing aggression as a behavioral expression of this characteristic, the management techniques would be the same whether the behavioral manifestation of these characteristics is aggression, tantrums, SIB, or other inappropriate behavior (e.g., screaming, crying).

Koegel and colleagues (1995) note that this characteristic demand for sameness in routine or environment is often detected because the child shows great distress when a specific aspect of the environment or routine is changed in any way. If you have a student who aggresses, cries, self-injures, or tantrums under these circumstances we recommend one or more of three interventions:

1. **Differential reinforcement of other behavior (DRO),** which involves reinforcing the *absence* of inappropriate behavior when the environment is changed. To use this procedure successfully you would need to start with extremely short DRO periods. For example, if your student aggresses when milk is put on the left side of the plate instead of the right side, in the first stage of a DRO intervention you might reinforce the student for quiet sitting as you place the milk on the left side (use a powerful reinforcer). The next phase would entail reinforcing the student for sitting quietly for 10 seconds after the milk has been placed. Next, the student would be required to sit for 30 seconds, then 1 minute, and so forth.

2. **Response interruption procedures** are particularly appropriate for rituals. Some children engage in rituals over and over if they are not redirected to other activities. Response interruption procedures involve stopping the ritual, then reinforcing the student for not aggressing or tantrumming once the ritual is stopped (DRO). Jacob, for example, when asked to set the table, prefers to line the silverware up in a single line along the edge of the table: He insists on placing each piece exactly even with the table edge.

When Jacob first entered Mr. Kline's class, he would scream and pinch Mr. Kline if this routine was disrupted. However, through the use of response interruption and DRO, Jacob no longer screams and pinches. Mr. Kline began intervention by physically interrupting the ritual, then using a 3-second DRO period, meaning once the ritual was stopped, Mr. Kline reinforced Jacob 3 seconds later if he had not engaged in the ritual during that 3 seconds, then again 3 seconds later, and so forth. Later Mr. Kline extended the DRO to 10 seconds (reinforcement was given after every 10-second period of time during which no lining up occurred), then 15 seconds, then 30, then 1 minute. In addition, he now needs to give only a verbal reminder to Jacob (e.g., "Get back to work"). Jacob still displays distress—he whimpers and looks upset, but he continues his task with no further outbursts.

3. **In differential reinforcement of incompatible behaviors (DRI),** the student is reinforced for appropriate behaviors other than rituals or other than challenging behavior when the environment is disrupted. For example, if a student insists on putting crayons in the box in a particular order, reinforce him for putting them in a different order. Or if a student ritualistically dresses and undresses a baby doll with the same set of clothes, reinforce her for putting different clothes on the doll, in a different order. Likewise a student who aggresses when the furniture is moved should be taught to say or sign "I'm angry" or some other statement, and reinforced for using that instead of aggressing.

BEHAVIOR REDUCTIVE PROCEDURES FOR CHALLENGING BEHAVIORS

In addition to the hypothesis-based procedures described above, use of a behavior reductive procedure may be required, especially if the challenging behavior is so severe as to jeopardize the student's placement, the student's safety, or the safety of others. As a general rule, we recommend against using extinction as an intervention for these behaviors, even when the perceived function is to gain attention. However, other behavior reductive procedures could be appropriate, depending on the circumstances. These include non-seclusionary time-out, response cost, and overcorrection.

Time-out

Time-out may be an appropriate intervention for aggression and noncompliance, particularly when the function is attention getting. We would advise against time-out for self-stimulatory behavior and SIB because the child may continue to engage in the behavior during time-out. Remember that time-out should be applied immediately after the challenging behavior and should be brief. For example, a student who spits on the teacher may be told firmly "No spitting. Go to time-out," then guided to the time-out chair in the corner. The student must stay there for 3 minutes or whatever the predetermined length of time-out. If the student engages in high levels of self-stimulatory behavior during time-out, and if the target challenging behavior does not decrease, time-out should not be used.

Response Cost

Some children may respond to response cost as a reductive procedure for noncompliance, self-stimulatory behavior, SIB, or aggression. This would mean that one or more tokens or a desired object is removed, contingent on the inappropriate behavior. For example, each instance of self-stimulatory behavior during work time might result in the loss of one token. Of course, if response cost is used, the student should always have access to earning tokens as well as losing them.

Overcorrection

Overcorrection might be an appropriate intervention for noncompliance, SIB, or aggression. For example, a restitutional overcorrection proce-

dure for hitting might involve the student saying or signing "I'm sorry" to the person he hit, as well as to every other person in the room. Restitutional overcorrection for self-biting might mean that, when he bites himself, the student is required to rub lotion on his arms for 5 minutes.

The other form of overcorrection, positive practice, involves having the student practice an appropriate alternative to the problem behavior. A student who kicks the teacher when angry might be made to practice stomping her foot and saying "I'm mad at you" 25 times. Hitting the punching bag for 3 minutes might be the consequence for hitting a peer.

Given the potential drawbacks of overcorrection procedures (as discussed in Chapter 2), they should be used only when other less aversive forms of reduction have proven ineffective. Furthermore, punishment techniques, including overcorrection, should always be used in conjunction with frequent and strong reinforcement of desired behavior.

SUMMARY

Challenging behaviors may pose one of the most difficult aspects of teaching students with autism and developmental disabilities. These behaviors are often well-established components of students' behavioral repertoires, and without diligent application of the best practices for managing such behaviors, may be highly resistant to change. Challenging behaviors, perhaps more than any other characteristic of students with autism, pose significant threats to learning and functioning in normalized environments. It is critical that these behaviors be reduced or eliminated.

This chapter has described how to conduct functional assessment to determine purposes of challenging behavior for a particular student, and to identify contextual variables that may contribute to challenging behavior. Functional assessment is an essential step in designing effective interventions for behavioral excesses. In addition, we described recommended strategies for dealing with specific challenging behaviors that are commonly present in children and youth with autism. These strategies are not recipes for "fixing" these behaviors, but rather must be selected based on contextual contributors to the behavior.

KEY POINTS

1. Functional assessment is a process of identifying contextual variables that may be contributing to misbehavior, and potential functions for that misbehavior.

2. Functional assessment includes both indirect (interviews and checklists) and direct (scatter plots and A–B–C recording) assessment methods.

3. Intervention plans should be developed based on hypotheses resulting from functional assessment.

4. Interventions for challenging behaviors associated with autism (e.g., self-stimulatory behaviors, self-injurious behaviors) should take into consideration the perceived function(s) of those behaviors.

5. Possible functions for challenging behavior include gaining attention or sensory stimulation; avoiding situations, people, or tasks; or communication.

6. Sometimes, challenging behavior reflects a failure to learn other, more appropriate behavior.

REFERENCES

Alberto, P., & Troutman, A. (1999). *Applied behavior analysis for teachers* (5th ed.). Englewood Cliffs, NJ: Merrill.

Bailey, J. S., & Pyles, D. A. M. (1989). Behavioral diagnostics. In E. Cipani (Ed.), *The treatment of severe behavior problems* (pp. 85–106). Washington, DC: American Association on Mental Retardation.

Bostow, D. E., & Bailey, J. (1969). Modification of severe disruptive and aggressive behavior using brief timeout and reinforcement procedures. *Journal of Applied Behavior Analysis, 2,* 31–37.

Calloway, C. J., & Simpson, R. L. (1998). Decisions regarding functions of behavior: Scientific versus informal analyses. *Focus on Autism and Other Developmental Disabilities, 13*(3), 167–175.

Carr, E. G. (1982). The motivation of self-injurious behavior. In R. L. Koegel, A. Rincover, and A. L. Egel (Eds.), *Educating and understanding autistic children* (pp. 158–175). San Diego: College-Hill Press.

Carr, E. G., & Durand, V. M. (1985). The social–communicative basis of severe behavior problems in children. In S. Reiss and R. Bootzin (Eds.), *Theoretical issues in behavior therapy* (pp. 219–254). New York: Academic Press.

Carr, E. G., Robinson, S., Taylor, J. C., & Carlson, J. I. (1990). Positive approaches to the treatment of severe behavior problems in persons with developmental disabilities: A review and analysis of reinforcement and stimulus-based procedures. *Monograph of the Association for Persons with Severe Handicaps, Number 4.* Seattle, WA: The Association for Severe Handicaps.

Cipani, E. (1998). Three behavioral functions of classroom noncompliance: Diagnostic and treatment implications. *Focus on Autism and Other Developmental Disabilities, 13*(2), 66–72.

Colvin, G., & Engelmann, S. (1983). *Generalized compliance training.* Austin, TX: Pro-Ed.

Conroy, M. A., & Fox, J. J. (1994). Setting events and challenging behavior in the classroom: Incorporating contextual factors into effective intervention plans. *Preventing School Failure, 38,* 29–34.

Danforth, J. S., & Drabman, R. S. (1989). Aggressive and disruptive behavior. In E. Cipani (Ed.), The treatment of severe behavior disorders: Behavior analysis approaches. *Monographs of the American Association on Mental Retardation, 12,* 111–127.

Day, R. M., Rea, J. A., Schussler, N. G., Larsen, S. E., & Johnson, W. L. (1988). A functionally based approach to the treatment of self-injurious behavior. *Behavior Modification, 12,* 565–589.

Delaney, M. J., & Durand, M. V. (1986). *Motivation Assessment Scale.* Topeka, KS: Monaco & Associates.

Devany, J., & Rincover, A. (1982). Self-stimulatory behavior and sensory reinforcement. In R. L. Koegel, A. Rincover, & A. L. Egel (Eds.), *Educating and understanding autistic children* (pp. 127–141). San Diego: College-Hill Press.

Donnellan, A. M., Mirenda, P. L., Mesaros, R. A., & Fassbender, L. L. (1984). Analyzing the communicative functions of aberrant behavior. *Journal of the Association for the Severely Handicapped, 9*(3), 201–212.

Dunlap, G., Ferro, J., & Deperczel, M. (1994). Nonaversive behavioral intervention in the community. In E. C. Cipani & F. Spooner (Eds.), *Curricular and instructional approaches for persons with severe disabilities* (pp. 117–146). Needham Heights, MA: Allyn & Bacon.

Forehand, R., & McMahon, R. (1981). *Helping the noncompliant child.* New York: Guilford Press.

Foster-Johnson, L., & Dunlap, G. (1993). Using functional assessment to develop effective, individualized interventions for challenging behaviors. *Teaching Exceptional Children, 25*(3), 44–50.

Gardner, W. I., Cole, C. L., Davidson, D. P., & Karan, O. C. (1986). Reducing aggression in individuals with developmental disabilities: An expanded stimulus control, assessment, and intervention model. *Education and Training of the Mentally Retarded, 21,* 2–12.

Harvard Medical School. (1997). Autism—Part I. *Harvard Mental Health Letter, 13*(9), 1–4.

Iwata, B. A. (1987). Negative reinforcement in applied behavior analysis: An emerging technology. *Journal of Applied Behavior Analysis, 20,* 361–387.

Iwata, B. A., Dorsey, M. F., Slifer, K. J., Bauman, K. E., & Richman, G. S. (1982). Toward a functional analysis of self-injury. *Analysis and Intervention in Developmental Disabilities, 2,* 1–20.

Kern, L., Koegel, R. L., & Dunlap, G. (1984). The influence of vigorous versus mild exercise on autistic stereotyped behaviors. *Journal of Youth and Adolescence, 19,* 233–244.

Kern, L., Koegel, R. L., Dyer, K., Blew, P. A., & Fenton, L. R. (1982). The effects of physical exercise on self-stimulation and appropriate responding in autistic children. *Journal of Autism and Developmental Disorders, 4,* 399–419.

Koegel, L. K., Valdez-Menchaca, M. C., & Koegel, R. L. (1994). Autism: Social communication difficulties and related behaviors. In V. B. Van Hasselt & M. Hersen (Eds.), *Advanced abnormal psychology* (pp. 165–187). New York: Plenum Press.

Koegel, R. L., & Covert, A. (1972). The relationship of self-stimulation to learning in autistic children. *Journal of Applied Behavior Analysis, 5,* 381–387.

Koegel, R. L., Firestone, P. B., Kramme, K. W., & Dunlap, G. (1974). Increasing spontaneous play by

suppressing self-stimulation in autistic children. *Journal of Applied Behavior Analysis, 7,* 521–528.

Koegel, R. L., Koegel, L. K., Frea, W. D., & Smith, A. E. (1995). Emerging interventions for children with autism: Longitudinal and lifestyle implications. In R. L. Koegel & L. K. Koegel (Eds.), *Teaching children with autism: Strategies for initiating positive interactions and improving learning opportunities* (pp. 1–15). Baltimore, MD: Paul H. Brookes.

Koegel, R. L., Rincover, A., & Egel, A. L. (1982). *Educating and understanding autistic children.* San Diego: College-Hill Press.

Lovaas, I. (1981). *Teaching developmentally disabled children: The ME book.* Austin, TX: Pro-Ed.

Mace, F. C., Hock, M. L., Lalli, J. S., West, B. J., Belfiore, P., Pinter, E., & Brown, D. K. (1988). Behavioral momentum in the treatment of non-compliance. *Journal of Applied Behavior Analysis, 21,* 123–141.

McAfee, J. K. (1987). Classroom density and the aggressive behavior of handicapped children. *Education and Treatment of Children, 10,* 134–145.

O'Neill, R. E., Horner, R. H., Albin, R. W., Sprague, J. K., Storey, K., & Newton, J. S. (1997). *Functional assessment and program development for problem behavior: A practical handbook* (2nd. ed.). Pacific Grove, CA: Brooks/Cole.

Rincover, A. (1978). Sensory extinction: A procedure for eliminating self-stimulatory behavior in psychotic children. *Journal of Abnormal Child Psychology, 6,* 299–310.

Rincover, A. (1981). *How to use sensory extinction.* Austin, TX: Pro-Ed.

Rincover, A., Newsom, C., & Carr, E. (1979). Using sensory extinction procedures in the treatment of compulsive like behavior of developmentally delayed children. *Journal of Consulting and Clinical Psychology, 47,* 695–701.

Schreibman, L., Koegel, R. L., & Koegel, L. K. (1989). Autism. In M. Hersen (Ed.), *Innovations in child behavior therapy* (pp. 395–428). New York: Springer-Verlag.

Simpson, R. L., & Regan, M. (1986). *Management of autistic behavior.* Rockville, MD: Aspen Publishers.

Walker, H. M., & Walker, J. E. (1991). *Coping with noncompliance in the classroom.* Austin, TX: Pro-Ed.

4

✳

Deciding What to Teach: Curriculum Development

Did you know that:

- Curriculum development may be the most important educational function?

- The best curriculum cannot be purchased?

- Curriculum decisions must precede decisions about strategies and placement?

- More heads are better than one?

- Curriculum must "fit" the student?

Chapters 2 and 3 delineated various techniques for reducing unwanted excessive behavior. Chapters 4 to 8 will present various methodologies for teaching new behavior; that is, teaching to alleviate deficits. In regard to students with autism it is sometimes difficult to decide which should come first, reducing behavioral excesses or remediating deficits. It might be said that if teachers do a good job teaching these students what they need to learn, excessive behavior will decrease automatically or never occur in the first place. On the other hand if students are already displaying excessive challenging behavior, it will be difficult to teach anything new until that behavior is brought under control. The best course of action lies in a balance between effective instruction and behavior management. Establishing such a balance should begin with curriculum development.

For our purposes, we define curriculum as *what* you teach (i.e., skills, activities, strategies, concepts, content). Decisions about what to teach directly impact what the student will learn. What the student learns directly impacts what choices will ultimately be available for that individual in terms of independent living, working, and interpersonal relationships. Thus, teachers must make sure they choose what to teach based on individual needs, abilities, and long-term goals. Teachers must also participate in a curriculum development process that includes the child's family and other significant people interested in the child's welfare.

Curriculum development not only requires choosing what a student needs to learn, but it also includes a process for organizing the skills, activities, and/or content in ways that facilitate mastery. Choosing and organizing curriculum such that the result is a quality individualized education plan (IEP) is a complex process. Fortunately, this daunting task does not have to be performed by only one person. The IDEA mandates that IEPs be developed by a team consisting of various educational experts, the student's parents, and the student when appropriate. A team approach to curriculum development, it is thought, augments its validity (or effectiveness). This chapter will provide information regarding general procedures for choosing and organizing curriculum for students with autism and related disorders of various ages. Chapters 6 through 8 will present specific curricula in the areas of language/communication, socialization, and life skills. These chapters will also cover preferred methods for teaching these curricula.

CURRICULAR AREAS

When we consider educational curricula, we typically think of academic content. Public schools are generally charged with creating a literate, well-informed, self-sufficient citizenry. The curriculum designated toward that end consists of academic tool subjects (reading, writing, spelling, written expression, computer literacy), personal care subjects (e.g., health, physical education, home economics), fine arts (e.g., music, art, drama), and academic content (e.g., math, social studies, science, foreign language, literature). It is presumed that students enter school ready to learn the prescribed curriculum by having mastered basic social, behavioral, and oral language skills at home. The general education curriculum prepares students for further study at institutions of higher learning where they typically consolidate their liberal arts training into a marketable profession.

Those students who prefer to pursue a vocational trade may be placed into a vocational curriculum (e.g., industrial arts, distributive education, auto mechanics). Note that the general education academic and vocational curricula are standardized, not individualized. That is, they are developed and organized by grade level, based on students' ages, rather than on individual needs and goals. For example, students are placed into fourth-grade social studies curriculum when entering fourth grade whether or not they need to, or have the prerequisites to, learn it. For students with disabilities, particularly those with cognitive delays as is the case with most students with autism, the standardized curriculum is often not relevant, nor is it accessible because most often it has not been broken down into small chunks of learning and presented in ways that result in mastery.

The good news is that the above-mentioned curricula (found as curricular sequences of goals and objectives in textbooks or in school district-

and state-produced documents) are available to special education teachers and do not have to be developed. The bad news is that, due to the large number of deficits typically displayed by students with autism, academic content, and perhaps even general education vocational content, may not be appropriate. Instead, many of these students need to learn basic functional skills that are not included in the general education curriculum. For such students, appropriate curricular content may be quite different from that presented in general education classrooms.

It is important to realize that deciding *what* to teach a student should be the first decision—before deciding *how* to teach it or *where* to teach it. Too often, placement decisions precede any other decision. For example, due to the current emphasis on inclusion, a student may be placed in a sixth-grade general education classroom for the purpose of making friends. Unfortunately, this student's curriculum may be compromised with such a decision. Let's say that the student needs to learn to purchase something at a store. This skill might best be taught in a shopping mall; however, due to the initial placement decision, the curriculum must now more closely match what students are doing in the general education classroom. Instead, the student is instructed to place coins on corresponding number cards—a skill that everyone else in the classroom has mastered and one that may not transfer to the community. In this case, the placement decision drove the curriculum decision to the detriment of the student. Thus, it is imperative that all decision makers have a clear idea of what each student needs to learn and let that knowledge direct other educational decisions.

For students who need a functional education, curricular areas usually consist of communication, social skills, domestic skills, community living skills, leisure and recreational skills, motor skills, and vocational skills. Additionally, for many individuals with autism, basic prerequisite learning behaviors may need to be taught (i.e., compliance, attending, imitating, discrimination skills). Table 4.1 lists various curricular areas typically available in the public schools.

Table 4.1 Academic Areas and Functional Domains

Tool Subjects	Personal Care
Reading	Physical education
Handwriting	Health
Spelling	Home economics
Written expression	**Functional Domains**
Computer literacy	Communication
Academic Subjects	Social competence
Social studies	Community living (do-
Math	mestic skills, self-care
Science	skills, community skills)
Foreign language	Prevocational/vocational
Literature	Leisure/recreational
Fine Arts	Learning strategies
Art	Motor
Drama	
Music	
Vocational	
Industrial arts	
Cosmetology	
Auto mechanics	
Agriculture	
Horticulture	
Distributive education	
Building trades	

Note that curriculum development for students with autism is usually not just a matter of adapting what exists for all schoolchildren. Instead, for each particular student, curriculum development is a longitudinal planning process resulting in an integrated and community-referenced program (Falvey, Grenot-Scheyer, & Luddy, 1987). Several considerations must go into developing such an educational program and these assumptions should hold regardless of the specific curriculum development procedure utilized.

CURRICULAR CONSIDERATIONS

Whatever we decide to teach students should facilitate that student's ability to live a productive, fulfilling life. When we are dealing with students who learn at a slower rate, pinpointing an appropriate curriculum is even more important because we do not want to waste instructional time on superfluous content. School personnel and parents should consider the following assumptions while choosing and organizing what to teach in order to ensure the most effective and efficient educational program.

Curriculum Should Be Functional

We say that curriculum is functional if it results in the student being able to perform essential tasks independently (Brown, Branston, Hamre-Nietupski, Pumpian, Certo, & Gruenwald, 1979). For example, everyone needs to be able to dress and toilet themselves. If an individual cannot perform these tasks, someone else must assist her in doing so. Curriculum content that allows the student to independently (without assistance) live and work in integrated adult environments is said to be functional. Brown and his colleagues (1979) classified function curriculum into four domains: domestic, recreation/leisure, vocational, and general community. For students with autism, we would add the additional categories of appropriate behavior, communication, and socialization. Whether your curriculum matches these areas or not, everything taught to students with autism should be functional.

Curriculum Should Be Chronologically Age Appropriate

Not only should curriculum be functional, but it should also be age appropriate (Falvey et al., 1987; Neel & Billingsley, 1989). Consider what activities, materials, and places same-age peers perform, use, frequent, and desire, and provide similar content and conditions for the student with autism. In many cases environments are age appropriate, but the activities to be performed may be different. For example, children of various ages participate in grocery shopping. However, young children are usually accompanied by their parents and assisted in the various skills. So, teaching a young child with autism to grocery shop would require teaching him to participate with parent assistance. On the other hand, adolescents often shop independently. For a 16-year-old student with autism, the curriculum would contain skills necessary for independent shopping. Or, rather than have an 18-year-old student with autism listen to preschool sing-along records, he might be taught to listen to rock music just as his peers do.

Often, although the curriculum is age appropriate, the instructional placement is not. Students should be taught in environments in which same-age peers are taught. Even though a 12-year-old student may mentally function as a 6-year-old, placing him in a primary school would be inappropriate. His size will differentiate him and he will not be exposed to materials and activities performed by his same-age peers. Delineating age-appropriate skills, materials, and activities may present a challenge when mental retardation is a factor, but the benefits of applying the chronological age-appropriate criterion are worth the effort.

Curriculum Should Be Longitudinal

Curriculum should be vertically coordinated. This means that skills, activities, and content taught at one point in time should facilitate mastery of skills and activities that will be taught later. The way to ensure longitudinally integrated curriculum is to establish long-term, intermediate, and short-term goals toward which all instruction leads. Goal development will be discussed later in this chapter. Too often, curriculum is established on an annual basis with no view at long-term implications. For example, knowing that a student should walk through middle school hallways without assistance, the elementary schoolteacher would do well to instruct an 8-year-old student with autism to transition independently from room to room rather than walk holding the teacher's hand.

Curriculum Should Be Horizontally Integrated

We refer to a horizontally integrated curriculum when skills, activities, or content in one curricular area or domain connects to that taught in another area. For example, a history teacher delivering a unit on the Revolutionary War would coordinate (integrate) her content with the literature unit be-

ing taught in the English class so that European literature from the late 1700s would be discussed relative to the politics of the time and vice versa. For individuals who need a functional curriculum, communication, social, and motor skills should be integrated with life skills instruction. For example, a student who is learning to ride a bus to work will need to learn vocabulary and voice inflection in order to ask what time a bus arrives, determine the fare, and ask to be let off. He will also need to be taught the appropriate social skills for those interactions. He will need the fine motor skills to handle coins and manage the pay machine on the bus, and the gross motor skills to walk up the bus steps, ride a bus standing up if necessary, and climb down off the bus. In this case the student would not benefit from having the PE teacher address ball-throwing skills if bus riding is a priority.

Curriculum Should Be Community Referenced

Community-referenced curriculum refers to the notion that all curricula are developed for the purpose of teaching a student to function independently as an adult in his or her community. Thus, curricular content is chosen and organized in a way that reflects the individual's life space (Brown et al., 1979). Skills and activities are chosen with consideration for what is culturally appropriate, the types of environmental demands, the accessibility of the community environments, and those environments in which the individual will most likely function. Furthermore, researchers recommend that skills and activities be taught in those environments in which they will be used and at times when they would be used. For example, if a student lives in a small town, riding a bus would not be a relevant activity to teach. However, walking safely to and from school might be important. If a student lives in an apartment building, then manipulating an elevator may be a useful thing to learn. This would not be true for someone living in a trailer park where, instead, the use of appropriate social skills with neighbors is expected and would therefore be important to learn.

Curriculum Should Emphasize Communication and Socialization

Because individuals with autism always have language and socialization difficulties, choosing and organizing curriculum to enhance these areas is an important consideration. Appropriate communication and social skills should be interwoven into all skills and activities. Prognosis is better for children who have functional language and who can form and maintain personal relationships. Planning communication skills to be taught only in the presence of the speech therapist would be inappropriate. Everyone involved with a child with autism should be teaching a coordinated communication and social skills curriculum. For example, on the way to the cafeteria, the child is asked to say or sign "lunch" or "eat" or "I would like to eat a sandwich, please." During lunch he is required to ask someone for "more" using "please" and "thank you." At home, when the child desires a favorite toy, she is required to communicate in order to obtain it, and at dinner she is required to look at others and take turns commenting. Specific strategies for teaching communication and social skills will be discussed in Chapters 6 and 7. The point is that communication skills, particularly, should be incorporated into all curricular areas.

Developing an individualized curriculum is a dynamic process involving several decision points. Most of the decisions should be based on accurate and relevant assessment data. Some of the decisions may be based on personal preference. All of the decisions should be based on what serves the particular student's best interest. By applying the above criteria to any curriculum development procedure, an individualized, appropriate educational program is very likely to emerge.

A CURRICULUM DEVELOPMENT PROCEDURE

In addition to general curriculum considerations, a curriculum development process requires several steps: (1) delineating long- and short-term goals, (2) creating an inventory of what needs to be

Table 4.2 Curriculum Development Process Steps

1. Establish placement goals:
   Long-term adult goals
   Intermediate goals (within the next 5 years)
   Short-term goals (current environments)
2. Develop an activity/skill list for reaching goals.
3. Assess for current level of functioning.
4. Obtain social validity and prioritize.
5. Write annual goals and objectives.
6. Develop an IEP.

learned to reach those goals (Brown et al., 1979), (3) assessing what the student has already mastered, (4) prioritizing what to teach, (5) organizing it to achieve mastery, and (6) developing an IEP. Table 4.2 lists six steps of a curriculum development procedure similar in form to a discrepancy analysis. In a discrepancy analysis, you first decide where you want to go, then decide what steps it will take to get there. Next you determine at which step you currently stand. The discrepancy (in the form of steps) between where you are and where you want to go becomes your plan of action. In this case, it becomes an individualized curriculum.

Establish Placement Goals

Targeting where we want students to be functioning in the future is the first step of curriculum development. This look at the future includes setting long-term, intermediate, and short-term goals. This goal-setting process should include as many people as possible who are interested in the student's educational plan. It should also be a process that allows review and revision as progress and priorities are gauged.

Long-Term Goals. Ideally, parents and professionals should engage in discussion about a vision for the student on reaching adulthood. This would involve discussing possible living situations, work situations, relationships, and recreational situations for the student. It might be best to begin this discussion when the child is very young, but parents often find it difficult to look that far down the road. First, they may not be aware of various living and working possibilities from which to choose. Second, they may not be able to consider much beyond tomorrow, especially if their child is displaying very challenging behavior. Third, they may not be willing to engage in a long-term goal discussion because it means admitting that their child may differ significantly from other children, a fact that is difficult to accept. Fourth, parents and teachers may be reluctant to set goals early, fearing those decisions might affect the quality of intervention. For example, if a goal for preparing a student to function in a sheltered workshop is set when the student is young, then he might not be taught competitive employment skills, which he may have been able to master.

This notion of establishing long-term goals in order to guide current curriculum decisions is referred to as the **criterion of ultimate functioning** (Brown, Nietupski, & Hamre-Nietupski, 1976). Brown and his colleagues define this criterion as "an ever-changing, expanding, localized, and personalized cluster of factors that each person must possess in order to function as productively and independently as possible in socially, vocationally, and domestically integrated adult community environments" (p. 8). This criterion ensures that special education students would have IEPs that (1) are continuous rather than short term, (2) recommend "real" rather than artificial materials, (3) specify education in integrated settings, and (4) target age-appropriate and culturally appropriate skills (Spooner & Test, 1994).

Teachers also need to realize that the goal-setting process is not static. That is, goals can be adapted and altered as the child progresses. However, providing some long-term vision of the student as an adult will assist in keeping school personnel and parents on track in terms of what they choose to teach him. Generally, for children with autism, long-term goals target independent living and competitive employment. For students with higher cognitive functioning, long-term goals may include postsecondary education either at universities, community colleges, or trade schools. For a few, it might be reasonable to assume they will marry and have a family. However, the vast majority of adults with autistic disorders need regular supervision and assistance in order to work and live in the community. It might be wise for those involved in establishing individual long-term goals to visit supervised apartments, residential facilities, and group homes. Additionally, it might be helpful to visit some retail and/or manufacturing businesses in the community, speak with school-based job coaches, and visit a sheltered workshop so that the parents and educators of young children have a realistic view of future possibilities and environmental demands. This view will be what drives the curriculum development process.

Intermediate Goals. Once long-term goals have been articulated, then intermediate goals can be discussed. Intermediate goals should hinge around the student's school placements and/or living placements within the next 3 to 5 years. This concept is known as the **criterion of the next environment** (Vincent, Salisbury, Walter, Gruenwald, & Powers, 1980). For example, the long-term decision may have been made that a particular student would most likely remain at home as an adult and work in his father's hardware store assisting with various tasks. This student is now 7 years old. In 3 years, regardless of functioning level, the student will be moved to the middle school, because that is the age-appropriate placement. Thus, intermediate goals will also need to be established such that the student can function in the middle school where he will need to be able to negotiate chaotic hallways, a crowded cafeteria, and bell-cued periods while continuing to learn skills that will contribute to the ultimate vocational goal. Transitions from early childhood programs to elementary schools, from elementary schools to middle schools, and then to high schools are difficult for all students. For students with autism and related disorders, who do not deal with change easily, these transitions can be very traumatic. We need to target intermediate-range placements and prepare students for success in these various environments so that they can continue to make progress toward their long-term goals.

Short-Term Goals. Short-term goals are those goals that address placement demands for the current year. Known as the **criterion of the immediate environment** (Peterson, Trecker, Egan, Fredericks, & Bunse, 1983), these goals focus on skills necessary to function under current conditions. For example, the 7-year-old student previously mentioned may be spending some time in a general education music class because he likes music, be in the special education classroom as well, and be attending a day care center in the afternoons. In the music class, the student will need to learn to interact with his general education peers, independently find his seat, and function in a large-group instruction format. In the special education classroom, he will need to work in one-to-one drill formats, choose free-time activities, and use picture cards to guide his daily activities. At day care, he is expected to "play" with other children. In addition to curriculum that addresses these immediate goals, the student will need to be gradually exposed to large groups of peers, negotiate hallways and cafeterias, and express his needs, skills that will serve him well in middle school. Overall, in order to reach his long-term goals, the student will need to improve his receptive and expressive speech, master basic self-help and domestic skills, develop vocational skills relevant to a retail business, and build his leisure time repertoire. Essentially, curriculum should address skills and activities necessary to function in the immediate placements, those that will lead to a successful experience in the near future, and those that will facilitate success as an adult.

Develop a Curricular Inventory for Reaching the Goals

After short-term, intermediate, and long-term goals have been established, the curriculum team should examine existing curricular sequences or should develop its own for reaching the goals. From this examination, skills and activities that lead to the established goals can be chosen and organized. Many published curricula exist that provide information to teachers for assessing, organizing, and presenting instruction. Spooner and Test (1994) present a way of categorizing published curricula as **domain based, activities based,** or **non-domain based.**

In domain-based curricula, content is divided into a number of areas or domains where skills are listed in developmental sequences. For example, *Community-Based Curriculum* (Falvey, 1989) organizes curriculum into domains such as recreation, employment, motor, communication, domestic, community, and functional academic skills.

In an activities-based curriculum, the content is listed as activities. For example, Wilcox and Bellamy (1987) provide a catalog of activities compiled under the sections of leisure, personal management, and work. Rather than listing skills relative to these headings, activities such as planning a meal or using a vending machine are described. For each activity, the catalog provides suggestions for teaching the activities. Rather than providing skill or activity sequences, non-domain-based curricula describe methods of developing such a sequence particular to an individual. An example is the *IMPACT* curriculum (Neel & Billingsley, 1989), which provides information about curriculum development, some suggestions for choosing what to teach, and inventory forms for delineating skills and activities necessary for specific individual students to learn. Table 4.3 provides a list of sample published curricula that should be appropriate for students with autism and related disorders who also have mental retardation.

For individuals who manifest such differences in abilities and who need to learn so many basic skills, the notion of developing an individualized functional curricula, rather than purchasing a commercial curriculum, is widely recommended (e.g., Falvey et al., 1987). A curriculum developed solely based on individual needs is guaranteed to be functional, age appropriate, community referenced, integrated, and individualized. We recommend developing a curriculum with a team of people who know the student well. This curriculum development process should be based on an analysis of specific environments in which the student must function. The product of this type of analysis is known as an **ecological inventory** (Brown et al., 1979; Falvey, 1989).

The first component of the ecological inventory process requires delineation of current and future environments and subenvironments for a particular student. For example, a student may

Table 4.3 Sample Published Curricula for Use with Students with Autism

Functional Curricula

Life Centered Career Education: The Complete Curriculum and Assessment Package
Arlington, VA: The Council for Exceptional Children

Independent Living Skills Curriculum
University of Oregon, Eugene

The Syracuse Community Referenced Curriculum Guide for Students with Moderate and Severe Disabilities
Baltimore, MD: Paul H. Brookes

The Teaching Research Curriculum for Moderately and Severely Handicapped
Springfield, IL: Charles C. Thomas

The Activities Catalog: An Alternative Curriculum for Youth and Adults with Severe Disabilities
Baltimore, MD: Paul H. Brookes

IMPACT: A Functional Curriculum Handbook for Students with Moderate to Severe Disabilities
Baltimore, MD: Paul H. Brookes

Steps to Independence: A Skill Training Series for Children with Special Needs
Champaign, IL: Research Press

Behavioral Characteristics Progression
Palo Alto, CA: VORT Corporation

Community Places
Employment Signs
Home Cooking
Looking Good
Select-a-Meal
Shopping Smart
Stepping Out
Verona, WI: Attainment Company

Social Skills Curricula

ACCEPTS
Austin, TX: Pro-Ed Publishing

ACCESS
Austin, TX: Pro-Ed Publishing

ASSET: A Social Skills Program for Adolescents
Champaign, IL: Research Press

Skillstreaming Series
Champaign, IL: Research Press

Social Skills Strategies
Eau Claire, WI: Thinking Publications

Getting Along with Others: Teaching Social Effectiveness to Children
Champaign, IL: Research Press

Academic Curricula

Developmental 1 Reading Laboratory
Chicago, IL: Science Research Associates

Edmark Reading Program, Level 1
Birmingham, AL: EBSCO Curriculum Materials

Functional Reading Series
Bellevue, WA: Edmark Corporation

I Can Print
Portland, OR: ASIEP Education Company

Reading for Independence
Chicago, IL: Science Research Associates

SRA Corrective Reading Materials
SRA Reading Mastery Materials
SRA Spelling Mastery Materials
SRA Reasoning and Writing
DISTAR Arithmetic
DeSoto, TX: SRA

I can + and − Arithmetic Program
Portland, OR: ASIEP Education Company

Real-Life Math
Austin, TX: Pro-Ed Publishing

Programmed Reading: A Sullivan Program
New York: McGraw-Hill

Recreation Curricula

Community Recreation and Persons with Disabilities: Strategies for Integration
Baltimore, MD: Paul H. Brookes

Communication Curricula

Implementing Augmentative and Alternative Communication: Strategies for Learners with Severe Disabilities
Baltimore, MD: Paul H. Brookes

DISTAR Language
DeSoto, TX: SRA

Peabody Language Kit
Circle Pines, MN: American Guidance Service

Karnes Early Language Activities
Champaign, IL: Generators of Educational Materials

Fokes Sentence Builder
Boston, MA: NYT Teaching Resource Corporation

Multidomain Curricula

Portage Guide to Early Education
Portage, WI

RADEA Program (Specific Skills Development)
Dallas, TX: Melton Book Company

currently need to participate in her home, school, church, shopping mall, grandmother's house, and the park (environments). Within her home, she must function in the kitchen, dining room, den, bedroom, and bathroom (subenvironments). Note that students with lower cognitive functioning typically have access to a restricted set of environments. After the student's subenvironments are delineated, the team should list the activities that a particular student would be expected to perform in each of those settings. It might be best to obtain information about various environmental expectations from those who know the student best. For example, our student may be expected to make her breakfast, wash dishes, and obtain snacks in the kitchen, and take a shower, brush her teeth, and wash her face in the bathroom. The more comprehensive the list, the more useful a particular inventory will be.

The comprehensive list of activities now provides a working document for curriculum development (the curricular inventory). Each activity can be further analyzed for the necessary skills required for performing it. For example, taking a shower requires dressing, undressing, preparing the water, washing body and hair, drying, combing hair, and cleaning up. The skills can be further broken down into small chunks for instructional purposes (i.e., task analysis). For example, washing with soap requires several different steps. Remember to keep in mind the long- and short-term goals throughout the process. Table 4.4 provides the steps for developing an ecological inventory, and Table 4.5 contains

Table 4.4 Ecological Inventory Steps

1. **List all environments in which the individual must function presently and in the future.**
   For example, home, school, church, day care, grandma's house

2. **List the subenvironments for each environment.**
   For example,

Environment	Subenvironments
Home	Den, bathroom, kitchen, bedroom, backyard
School	Special education class, music class, bathroom, cafeteria, playground

3. **List the activities for each subenvironment that the individual must conduct.**
   For example,

Subenvironment	Activities
Cafeteria	Go through food line
	Eat lunch
	Clean up self and area

4. **For each activity, list the requisite skills and the communication necessary for the student to participate in the activity.**
   For example,

Activity	Skills
Go through food line	Locate and obtain tray
	Locate and obtain plate and utensils
	Push tray through line
	Obtain desired foods
	Pay for lunch
	Communication: Indicate desired foods; ask for tray, utensils, napkin if not available; ask how much it costs

5. **Organize the activities and skills into areas or domains.**
   For example,

Domain: self-help
Environment: school
Subenvironment: cafeteria
Activity: go through food line
Skills: locate and obtain tray, etc.

Table 4.5 Informal Ecological Assessment Sample Questions

Questions to Ask to Determine Requirements of a General Education Class:

Physical arrangement of class:
How are desks arranged?
Where will your student's desk be located?
Where is the bathroom?
Where are his materials kept?

Teacher's instructional style
What type of instructional activities does the teacher use (e.g., large-group instruction, small-group instruction, independent work, lots of pencil-paper activities, group work)?
What type of instructional materials are used (e.g., basals, workbooks, manipulatives)?

Teacher's management style
What types of student behavior are and are not tolerated by the teacher? (For example: Is raising hand for permission to talk a requirement? Does teacher allow quiet talk among students? Are students allowed to leave seats without permission?)

Questions to Ask to Determine Requirements of a Work Situation:

Physical aspects of job site
Is the job performed primarily indoors or out-of-doors?
Is the job site crowded or noisy?
Is the job performed in a place that is accessible to the public?

Work requirements
Are there aspects of the job that require specific physical skills (e.g., strength, fine-motor dexterity, standing for long periods of time, sitting for long periods of time)?
Does the job require specific communication skills (e.g., greeting customers, answering the telephone)?
Does the job require specific cognitive skills (e.g., handling money, telling time, reading or writing)?
Does the job require knowledge of specific tools (e.g., copier, dishwasher, machinery, hand tools)?
Does the job require independent decision making or judgment?
Are there time constraints on the work to be completed?
How will the individual be supervised?

Social aspects of the job
Does the job require contact or interaction with the public?
Does the job require interaction with coworkers?
How and where are breaks taken, and what behaviors are permitted on break? (For example: Is there a designated break room? Are there usually several people on break at once? Are there snack machines? Is smoking allowed on break? If so, where?)

Questions to Ask to Determine Home Needs:

Leisure/recreational activities
What activities does the family enjoy doing together?
What skills would enable your child to participate more fully in these activities?
What activities would you like your child to do with his or her siblings (e.g., play board games, play outdoor games, etc.)?
What activities would you like your child to do independently (e.g., play video games, look at/read books, play with toys, etc.)?

Home jobs
What jobs would parents like their child to do independently (e.g., make his/her bed, carry dishes to the sink, clean room, etc.)?
What jobs would parents like their child to do with his/her siblings (e.g., wash dishes, wash the car, rake leaves, etc.)?

Home routines
What part of the child's daily routines need to be done independently (e.g., dress self, comb hair, fix a snack, etc.)?

Language/communication
How does the child let you know when he/she needs or wants something (e.g., tugs on your clothes, makes noises, cries, points, etc.)?
How should the child let you know when he/she needs or wants something (e.g., use words, use communication book, use sign language, etc.)?
Does the child express affection to parents or siblings? If so, how?
Should the child learn how to express affection to parents or siblings (e.g., give/receive hugs, kisses, etc.)?

Table 4.6 Formal Ecological Assessment Instruments

Classroom Ecological Inventory (Fuchs, Fernstrom, Scott, Fuchs, & Vandermeer, 1994)
  From: *Teaching Exceptional Children, 26*(3), 11–15.
  Designed to help identify important differences between special education and general education classrooms. This allows the special education teacher to take steps, such as teaching needed skills or modifying aspects of the general education class, that will enhance the likelihood of successfully integrating a student into the general education classroom.

Assessment for Integration into Mainstream Settings (AIMS) Assessment System (Walker, 1986)
  Available from: Hill M. Walker, Ph.D., Division of Special Education and Rehabilitation, University of Oregon, Eugene, OR 97403.
  Two of the instruments used in AIMS (SBS Inventory and Child Behavior Rating Scale) are available from Western Psychological Services, Los Angeles, CA. The purpose of AIMS is to help special education teachers (1) - select appropriate placement settings for integration of students with disabilities, (2) identify minimum behavioral requirements for those settings, (3) target specific skills to address in preparing students with disabilities for those settings, (4) assess the receiving teacher's needs for technical assistance in accommodating the included child, and (5) assess the included child's adjustment to the settings. AIMS actually consists of five different assessment instruments.

Virginia Commonwealth University Rehabilitation Research and Training Center Employer Interview Form (Moon, Inge, Wehman, Brooke, & Barcus, 1990)
  From: *Helping persons with severe mental retardation get and keep employment: Supported employment strategies and outcomes* (p. 41). Baltimore, MD: Paul H. Brookes.
  This is an interview form to use in interviewing potential employers to determine the demands of a specific job.

IMPACT: A Functional Curriculum Handbook for Students with Moderate to Severe Disabilities (Neel & Billingsley, 1989)
  Baltimore, MD: Paul H. Brookes.

Community Living Skills: A Taxonomy (Dever, 1988)
  Washington, DC: American Association on Mental Retardation

McGill Action Planning System (MAPS) (Vandercook, York, & Forest, 1989)
  From: *Journal of the Association for Persons with Severe Handicaps, 14*, 205–215.
  MAPS provides a systematic approach to planning school-based integration for students with disabilities. It uses a team process to address seven questions key to successful integration. Answers to some of these questions may highlight target skills to teach the student.

sample ecological inventory questions that might facilitate the planning process. Furthermore, published ecological inventories are available and provide a structure for team planning of individualized curricular sequences. The published inventories present a framework for obtaining the necessary information about specific environments such that the activities and skills for a particular student can easily be identified. Some sample published inventories appear in Table 4.6.

Obviously, developing an ecological inventory involves much more work than locating a curricular sequence that has already been delineated. Therefore, most teachers probably prefer working from a published curriculum. However, the advantage of the ecological inventory is that it directly matches an individual student's needs and

meets the curriculum considerations delineated previously, whereby a published curricula will need to be adapted to particular goals and communities. Whether a curricular sequence of skills and/or activities is developed individually or obtained from another source, the next step for curriculum development involves determining which of those skills/activities the student has already mastered.

Assess for Current Level of Functioning

After a desired curricular sequence has been established, we need to determine which of those skills a particular student needs to learn. If the curriculum itself is used for assessment purposes, we call this assessment technique **curriculum-based assessment (CBA).** A curriculum-based assessment can be conducted in several different ways: (1) Use sample indicators from the curriculum, (2) use formal assessment matched to the curriculum, (3) use observational recording techniques to measure performance on given objectives, and/or (4) devise a checklist whereby each behavior is coded as to whether the student can do it, can do it with help, or cannot do it at all. All curriculum-based assessments must include a few critical features: (1) ongoing assessment to determine progress in the curriculum, (2) use of valid assessment instruments or strategies, and (3) use of quantitative and qualitative data (Fuchs & Deno, 1994). The advantage of curriculum-based assessment is that the assessment results tie directly to the instructional objectives and materials.

An example of a published curriculum-based assessment is *The Brigance Inventories* (Curriculum Associates, North Billerica, MA). *The Brigance Inventories* include three separate components that measure a wide variety of academic (e.g., mathematics, decoding, comprehension, written language) and nonacademic (e.g., communication, health and safety, body image) skills from kindergarten through high school. Each test lists target objectives in different content areas that are assessed through graduated-difficulty skill sequences. The tests are sequenced according to grade level and, in some cases, age level. These tests are widely used for pretesting and post-testing and for developing and evaluating IEP objectives. In general, they are easy and quick to use and score and provide helpful information for planning and monitoring specific instructional areas.

Probably the most useful CBA technique is to develop a checklist and determine whether the child can perform the skill, perform some of the skill, or not perform it at all. This type of assessment is particularly preferred if an ecological inventory has been developed. Given a clear destination in the form of goals and a list of steps in the form of sequenced skills or activities leading to those goals, the teacher and other team members can, at that point, ask the child to perform each skill noting those that have already been learned and those that

need to be taught. Developing this list of skills and behaviors that a student needs to learn to meet predetermined goals is like developing a road map for a long journey. The next step is to determine exactly where to commence teaching.

Obtain Social Validity and Prioritize Activities and Skills

Determining what to teach a student with autism and related disorders should not only be based on long-term goals and current level of functioning, but also on what is viewed as appropriate by the child's family members and other significant people in that child's life. The concept of acceptability of a program by its consumer is known as **social validity** (Harris, Belchic, Blum, & Celiberti, 1994). Social validity is an important component of curriculum development. This is why we recommend that the planning procedure be a team process. School personnel and parents often differ in their perceptions of what a child needs to learn. It is important to obtain consensus about what is necessary and acceptable to teach. This type of consensus can be reached through mutual goal-setting and assessment, and frequent discussion. If teachers do not think it is important to teach something, they may not put much energy into teaching it. If parents do not see importance or relevance in a particular skill, they may not prompt it or reinforce it at home. In either case, the instructional program could be compromised. Thus, parents, advocates, and various school personnel should tackle the curriculum development procedure together.

Deciding what is important to teach leads to the determination of what to teach first, or prioritizing the skill and activities. Several considerations go into deciding in what order things should be taught. Certainly, the social validity process mentioned above will guide decisions regarding priority. Also, you should target those skills and activities that currently require large amounts of supervision and that will result in independent functioning. For example, if a child requires someone to help her get ready for bed each night, teaching those particular skills would give the parents time to do other household or family tasks. Additionally, teaching independent bed-time skills prepares the child for self-sufficiency in the future.

Determining the complexity of the skill or activity is another useful consideration for designating priorities. Usually, simple, basic, prerequisite skills are taught before more complex ones. For example, in learning to talk, children are taught receptive language (e.g., following simple directions like "Point to your head") before they are expected to produce expressive language (e.g., saying "Cookie"). Developmental sequences that delineate simple to complex skills can be found in developmental and adaptive behavior inventories and in published curricula. Some examples of published developmental inventories include:

- *Early Learning Accomplishment Profile and the Learning Accomplishment Profile—Revised* (Kaplan Press, Winston-Salem, NC). Both of these assessment profiles assess young children's development across a variety of developmental areas (e.g., gross motor, fine motor, cognitive, language, self-help). Items that the child does not pass become instructional targets.

- *Brigance Diagnostic Inventory of Early Development (IED)* (Curriculum Associates, North Billerica, MA). This is a criterion-referenced test that assesses areas such as preambulatory motor skills, gross motor skills, fine motor skills, self-help skills, prespeech, and speech and language. The IED is easy to use, and includes instructional objectives for each skill tested.

- *Behavioral Characteristics Progression (BCP)* (VORT Corporation, Palo Alto, CA). This is an assessment, instructional, and communication tool that is one of the most comprehensive programs available, a distinction that also makes it a bit unwieldy. The BCP includes 2,400 behaviors arranged in more than 50 strands. Instructional objectives are developed from the assessment information,

and progress through the skills is monitored continually.

- *Adaptive Behavior Evaluation Scale—Revised (ABES)* (Hawthorne Educational Services, Columbia, MO). This instrument is available in a home and school version and includes several subscales in the areas of communication, self-care, home living, social skills, community use, self-direction, health and safety, functional academics, leisure and work skills. This instrument can assist teachers in determining educational goals and objectives for individual students.

Those skills and activities that the child or adolescent performs frequently are also good first things to teach. For example, an individual needs to eat several times a day. Eating activities are good ones to teach if they have not been mastered. Furthermore, you should choose skills that are necessary to guarantee one's safety in current and future environments. For example, teaching the proper use of electrical appliances (e.g., a toaster) if the child is old enough to use them may take priority over teaching setting the table.

Another consideration for selecting priorities for students with autism has to do with behavior management. By choosing to teach a student to obtain what he wants or needs in socially appropriate ways, much inappropriate behavior can be prevented. This means that teaching functional communication and social skills is almost always a priority. For example, if a child loves flashlights, then it would be appropriate to teach the word "light" or the phrase "I want the flashlight." It is also important to teach skills that will result in natural reinforcement. What things does the child need to do to get people around her to like her and want to work with her? It is almost always a priority to teach people-pleasing behaviors. Finally, it is important to initially teach students with autism and related disorders basic learning behaviors such as compliance, attending, and imitating (motor and language imitation). If a student does not have these skills, little else will be learned.

Write Annual Goals and Objectives

Once the team has determined exactly what the student needs to learn, this information should be organized as goals and objectives. The ultimate goal for students with autism and related disorders is to achieve the ability to participate in their home, work, and community as independently as possible. Annual goals and objectives should lead toward that end. Goal statements communicate annual program intent, and behavioral objectives communicate the actual intent of instruction (Alberto & Troutman, 1999) or what the student is expected to achieve. Both goals and objectives should be written such that mastery can be determined. That is, teachers should be able to measure whether or not the goal and/or objective has been attained. We therefore

recommend that both goals and objectives be written in behavioral terms.

Usually, at least one annual goal is written for each domain or curricular area that has been targeted for teaching. The goals are then broken into smaller instructional components. These components are written as behavioral objectives. Several objectives are usually written for each goal. Table 4.7 provides some sample goals and objectives for students of various ages in various domains.

Note that behavioral objectives contain four pieces of information: who is doing the learning, what the student has to do to show learning, under what conditions this behavior must be performed, and the quality or quantity of behavior that signifies mastery. Identifying the learner, the target behavior, the conditions of the instruction, and the criteria for acceptable performance may

Table 4.7 Sample Goals and Objectives

Early Childhood

Communication
Goal: Henry will label common objects.
Objective: Given the command "What is this?" and the presentation of a (shoe, sock, toy, spoon), Henry will say the correct label 10 of 10 trials for 3 days.

Motor
Goal: Henry will demonstrate the correct use of scissors.
Objective: Given a drawn square, Henry will cut out the square along the lines using single-handle scissors with no more than two errors.

Self-Help
Goal: Henry will demonstrate the ability to dress himself independently.
Objective: Given a shoe lace tied in a bow, Henry will untie the shoelace by pulling with one hand until the loops disappear each time over 3 days.

Elementary

Cognitive
Goal: Mary will demonstrate the ability to identify colors.
Objective: Given randomly placed construction paper circles (green, yellow, red), one additional red circle, and the command "Match this," Mary will match the color red 9 of 10 trials.

Writing
Goal: Mary will reproduce written models.
Objective: Given a lightly drawn cross, Mary will use a pencil to trace the cross with no more than one error for each of 15 trials.

Social
Goal: Mary will participate in group activities.
Objective: During recess, Mary will remain with her group during the Red Rover game for 10 consecutive minutes each day this week.

Secondary

Vocational
Goal: Tad will complete laundry tasks.
Objective: When the dryer buzzer sounds, Tad will remove all clothes from the dryer, fold them, and place them in the laundry basket 10 consecutive times.

Monetary concepts
Goal: Tad will demonstrate knowledge of money values.
Objective: Given a quarter, nickel, dime, and penny and the request "Find the_____," Tad will pick up the correct coin with 90% accuracy.

Personal Management
Goal: Tad will demonstrate the ability to use the telephone correctly.
Objective: Given several scenarios and an unplugged phone, Tad will dial the correct number for assistance each time.

take some practice. For more information about the mechanics of writing goals and objectives, the reader is referred to Alberto and Troutman (1999), Gronlund (1978), and Mager (1997).

Remember that goals and objectives should be integrated into a total curricular approach rather than treated in isolation (Pfeiffer & Nelson, 1992). This means, for example, that if a goal in the self-help domain addresses toileting, there should be a corresponding goal in the communication domain of labeling things that pertain to toileting such as the words "toilet," "toilet paper," "pants," "up/down," "button," and "snap." Also, remember that the development of goals and objectives is an ongoing process in which the goals/objectives are modified as the student's progress is assessed and long-term goals are reevaluated. This dynamic longitudinal planning process should guarantee that the student is being taught essential skills at every opportunity.

Develop the Individualized Education Plan

The IDEA specifies that a document be developed for each special education student that prescribes and records appropriate educational services (Strickland & Turnbull, 1990). Each IEP should address the student's current level of academic and social functioning, student needs, assessment issues, and prescribed educational and related services. The IEP, however, should not just be viewed as a legal document, but as an "ongoing, flexible, and useful procedure from which a framework emerges to guide an ongoing educational program" (Smith, Slattery, & Knopp, 1993, p. 3). Smith and colleagues point out that viewing the IEP as a process rather than a product (1) allows for participation and program ownership by many "players" in the child's life, (2) can result in a broader, more comprehensive plan, and (3) can facilitate integrated placement decisions.

If the IEP is generated based on individualized assessment as opposed to a published curriculum, and if the IEP guides what happens in the classroom each day, the document is being used as intended. Teachers and other school personnel would

do well to develop a document that is a functional plan for instruction and the provision of related services. Daily lesson plans and class schedules should be derived directly from this document. Note that in some school districts, IEPs are generated by computer. Goals and objectives are prewritten and teachers simply designate which of those might pertain to an individual student. Allowing a published curriculum, whether computer generated or not, to dictate the IEP may preclude the individualized process mandated by law and recommended in this chapter. If computers are used to generate the IEP document based on a long-term vision, individualized assessment, and a social validity process, it might be useful. However, we recommend that computer-generated IEPs be used cautiously and that an ecological inventory be conducted to determine the appropriateness of objectives contained in the curriculum software.

The IEP, in fact, is the student's curriculum for a given year. The IEP can drive meaningful instruction if (1) it is developed through participation of professionals, parents, advocates, and students in a planning process that includes longitudinal goal determination, (2) it is a sequenced and organized list of functional community-referenced skills and activities, and (3) it includes personalized comprehensive assessment and well-written goals and objectives. For more specific information about developing IEPs, the reader is referred to Fiscus and Mandell (1983), Romanczyk and Lockshin (1981), and Strickland and Turnbull (1990). Falvey et al. (1987) recommend several questions for parents and professionals to consider when developing and prioritizing curricular content. Table 4.8 lists those questions. The answers to these questions will help to guarantee that the IEP is the most appropriate one.

CURRICULAR REFINEMENT

Developing a curriculum requires further refinement than just creating a list of prioritized skills and activities. Once this list has been created, the teacher

Table 4.8 Questions for Determining Curricular Content and Priorities

I. What skills need to be taught?
  A. Are the skills functional for the student?
    1. Are the skills being considered chronologically age appropriate?
    2. Are these skills required across a variety of environments?
    3. Can these skills be used often?
    4. Does someone have to do it for the student if he cannot?
    5. How do students without disabilities perform the skill?
    6. What skills would the student desire?
    7. What is the student's present level of performance on these skills?
    8. What family needs have been considered in choosing these skills?
  B. Will the skills result in more integration and independence?
    1. What skills does the society value?
    2. What are peers without disabilities being taught?
    3. What activities are peers without disabilities doing?
    4. What skills would reduce the discrepancy between student and peers?
    5. What skills would result in increased opportunities for interaction?
    6. What skills would lead to less restrictive placements?
    7. What skills would promote independence?
  C. What are the skill/task characteristics?
    1. What are the skills involved in this task/activity?
    2. What skills can be integrated across tasks?
    3. What skills can be recombined into other more complex skills?
    4. What skills will meet the largest variety of the student's needs?
    5. What family needs have been considered when determining skills?
II. Where should the skills be taught?
  A. Are the environments chronologically age appropriate?
  B. Are the environments accessible for teaching during school hours?
  C. Are the environments preferred by the student?
  D. Are the environments frequented by the student, peers, and family members?
  E. Are there opportunities to teach many skills in these environments?
  F. Are the environments appropriate for the student now and in the future?

needs to decide the level of competency necessary to meet the designated goal and needs to break down each skill and activity into small enough learning chunks for the student to grasp. In this section we will discuss levels of competency and task analysis—two concepts that facilitate pinpointing very specific curricular bits for each student.

Levels of Competency

The initial phase of curriculum development results in an individualized sequence of skills and activities in the form of goals and behavioral ob-

jectives. The second phase is to ensure that mastery of the objective will be useful to a particular student (Alberto & Troutman, 1999). Ensuring functional use requires an expansion of the curriculum such that each objective is taught to mastery at each of four hierarchical stages. These stages are **acquisition, fluency, maintenance, and generalization.**

Acquisition. Teaching a skill to mastery at the acquisition stage means that a student can perform two behaviors. He can identify the target behavior when someone else performs it correctly, and he can perform it correctly himself with some degree of accuracy. This is the lowest level of response competency. For example, let's say that a student is now able to pick the exact correct bus fare out of several coins given to him 8 times out of 10 during three consecutive sessions. We would say that he "acquired" the skill of designating his correct bus fare. However, it still takes him a long time to pick the correct coins, and we do not know yet whether he will be able to apply that skill when he needs to; that is, when he will be taking the bus to work. Teaching only to the acquisition level seldom results in functional, generalized learning.

Fluency. Fluency refers to the rate of performance of a behavior. If it currently takes the student 5 minutes to find the correct change, his behavior will not be functional. As a matter of fact, adults who see him taking that long to find change will probably come to the rescue and complete the task for him in order to expedite the process. Few bus drivers will wait 5 minutes for a fare. To teach the student to pick out the correct amount faster, the objective is changed to incorporate a time limit on the behavior. Now we want to teach "choosing correct bus fare within 20 seconds." Teaching a behavior at the fluency level demands some different strategies such as massed practice and reinforcing more timely responses.

Maintenance. Maintenance of a behavior implies that the student can perform the response at an acceptable rate over a long period of time without having to reteach it. For example, if our student can "pick the correct bus fare out of a group of coins within 20 seconds," we now want to make sure that he can display that same proficiency next month and the month after that. Teaching to maintenance does not necessarily require that the objective be written differently, but it does require some adjusted teaching strategies such as distributed practice and intermittent reinforcement. Again, teaching the bus fare skill is not finished if the student can only perform the skill for 2 weeks and then never again.

Generalization. If our curriculum goals target independent functioning in the community, which they should, then we must teach all functional skills to the level of generalization. Generalization means that the student can perform a behavior under different conditions, and that the student can adapt or change the behavior regardless of the conditions. The first type of generalization is known as **stimulus generalization.** Stimulus generalization means that even if things like instructional cues, materials, people, time of day, and settings change, the student will still perform the behavior at the same acceptable rate. For example, if the student mentioned above has to find bus fare standing at the bus stop rather than sitting in the classroom, we want to ensure that he can do that. Or if he has to find fare when the bus driver says "Good morning" one day and "Seventy-five cents, please" the next day, then we need to teach the student to respond accordingly. It does little good to assume that he can apply his new skill in a functional way without directly instructing him to do so. Several methods are available for teaching stimulus generalization including community-based instruction.

The second type of generalization is known as **response generalization.** Response generalization means that as one behavior is mastered, other related, similar behaviors may emerge. For example, once our student is choosing correct bus fare, he may also begin choosing correct change for doing his laundry. **Shaping** is a procedure based on response generalization whereby students are reinforced for successive approximations toward a target behavior. For example, each time a child makes a better attempt at saying "cookie," she is reinforced. First she says "caaaa" and receives a piece of the cookie. Next, after hearing the word again and being shown the cookie, she says "cooo," a related, but different behavior (response generalization) and receives a piece of cookie. No longer can she get the cookie for the "caaa" sound. In this way, correct pronunciation is taught. Unfortunately, response generalization is not easy to come by, especially for individuals with autism and related disorders.

Behavioral objectives will need to be altered to indicate instruction toward generalization. Usually the conditions statement is changed to indicate a new setting or person or cue. For example, the objective "Given the command 'What is this?' and the presentation of a (shoe, sock, toy, spoon), Henry will say the correct label 10 of 10 trials for 3 days" is changed to read "Given any of the following commands: 'What is this?' 'Say this,' or 'Label these,' Henry will say the correct label 10 of 10 trials for 3 days."

Note that students with autism and related disorders typically have extreme difficulty attaining generalization. Due to their tendency to overselect contextual cues, their overreliance on rote memory, their preference for routine and rejection of change, their restricted repertoire of behaviors, and their inattention to social cues and other's behavior, they will need well-planned instruction in order to generalize their responses. On the other hand, if they do not learn to generalize their response, little good has emanated from our instruction.

Task Analysis

An additional way to refine curriculum has to do with breaking skills down into subskills or breaking content down into subcontent so that the steps of learning are more accessible to the learner. This process is known as **task analysis.** The number of steps in a task analysis is related to a student's ability to grasp them. For one student, going through the cafeteria line may be broken into four steps (get tray, pick out food, pay the cashier, walk to table). However, for another student, going through the cafeteria line may require 20 steps (e.g., locate cafeteria, walk to line, wait in line, get tray, get silverware and napkin, get plate, pick out salad, point to meat and vegetable, hand server the plate, take it back, obtain glass, pick out drink, push tray to cashier, pay cashier, wait for change, put change on tray, carry tray, find table, place tray on table, sit down). Wehman and Kregel (1997) recommend the following guidelines for developing a task analysis:

1. Each step should be listed in specific behavioral terms so that mastery can be easily determined.

2. Write each step so that it can become a prompt for the next step.

3. If the step has the word "and" in it, determine if the learner can achieve it or whether it needs to be broken down further.

4. Pilot-test the task analysis with the student before finalizing it for instruction.

Many published curricula contain task analyses; however, they should be adapted for individual students. When developing a task analysis from scratch, it is recommended that the adult try the task and write down each step performed, watch another student perform the task, or interview someone who knows how to perform the task in order to delineate the necessary steps. The interview technique is best used for vocationally related tasks for which the teacher or parent has little information (e.g., assembly line procedures). It is also important to remember that task analyses assume certain conditions (e.g., a specific cafeteria) and will need to be adapted if conditions might change.

Once the task analysis has been written, it can become a curriculum-based assessment whereby the student is asked to perform each step in order to determine which steps need to be taught at the acquisition level, which at the fluency level, and which at the maintenance and generalization level. In a curriculum development procedure not only do we need to know what general skills need to be taught, but what specific subskills are yet to be mastered. A sample task analysis assessment checklist is provided in Figure 4.1.

Other ways to conduct task analyses are available. One way is to list steps where each specifies a change in the duration of a behavior (e.g., student will work independently for 2 minutes, 5 minutes, 15 minutes, 25 minutes, 40 minutes). Another task analysis is such that each step signifies a decrease in the amount of assistance needed (e.g., student will ask to leave the cafeteria with three prompts, two prompts, one prompt, no prompt).

Activity: Gathering grocery carts to return to store.

Date: _____

Task Analysis	Needs Assistance	Verbal Assistance Only	Independent
Exit store to curb.			
Look both ways prior to stepping off.			
Cross when clear.			
Walk along car row to cart return station.			
Push carts tightly together.			
Connect carts with clip harness and strap.			
Check for oncoming cars.			
Push carts to center of row.			
Push to store.			
Stop at drive and check for cars.			
Cross when clear.			
Push carts into store.			
Place carts into cart rows.			
Undo harness.			

FIGURE 4.1 Sample task analysis checklist. (From *Functional Curriculum for Elementary, Middle, and Secondary Age Students with Special Needs,* by P. Wehman and J. Kregel, 1997, p. 193. Austin, TX: Pro-Ed Publishing. Copyright 1997, by Pro-Ed, Inc. Adapted by permission.)

Finally, a task analysis could be such that each step indicates more complex conditions (e.g., student will attend to task for 10 minutes while alone with the teacher in a room, while 3 other students are in the room, while 10 other students are in the room). Behavioral objectives do not necessarily need to be written for each step of a task analysis. Rather, task analysis steps could simply be listed under a behavioral objective assuming that mastery of all the steps leads to mastery of the behavioral objective.

CURRICULAR FORMAT

Curricula can be compiled and presented in several different ways. A curriculum can be lists of activities and/or skills sometimes organized by domain. It can be presented as goals with accompanying objectives, also in lists, as is required on an IEP. It can be formatted in a matrix configuration such that additional information can be added. Additional information in the curricular document may include any of the following: (1) speci-

Interpersonal Relationships
Goal: Will be able to initiate a conversation.
Objective: Will maintain appropriate distance from another for conversational purposes.
Objective: Will face another, make eye contact, and smile.
Objective: Will verbalize a greeting (i.e., hi, how are you; nice day isn't it?).

Grooming
Goal: Will improve grooming skills.
Objective: Will conduct all steps of a toileting routine.
Objective: Will comb hair each morning.
Objective: Will wash face and hands each morning, noon, and evening.

Receptive Language Skills
Goal: Will improve receptive language skills.
Objective: Will follow two- and three-step commands.
Objective: Will identify alike objects.
Objective: Will identify objects that are different.

FIGURE 4.2 Curriculum arranged by domain, goals, and objectives.

Motor Skills
Sit down from standing position
Roll ball when seated on floor
Roll objects while on feet
Open and shut a door
Walk forward
Walk backward
Walk sideways
Roll on sides
Walk up and down stairs
Run
Toss and catch objects with both hands
Etc.

Self-Help Skills
Discriminate between being dry and wet
Indicate need to go to the toilet
Walk to the bathroom
Unbutton/unsnap pants
Unzip pants
Pull down pants
Etc.

FIGURE 4.3 Curriculum arranged by domain and skills.

fied environments in which a particular skill or objective will be taught, (2) the teaching activity description, (3) the person responsible for teaching the skill, (4) methods for evaluating the specific curricular item, (5) materials necessary for instruction, and (6) the current level of function-ing. Sometimes the skill or activity is displayed as a task analysis. A matrix design could also allow for the skills to be delineated at various learning levels (e.g., acquisition, fluency, maintenance, and generalization). Figures 4.2 through 4.8 provide examples of several curricular formats.

Objectives	Activities	Materials
The child will locate tissue.	Take child to tissue box. Label tissue box. Provide many tissue boxes around room.	Facial tissues (colored) Markers/paper/tape Facial tissues (colored)
The child will wipe nose.	Model procedure. Provide full physical prompt. Provide practice opportunities. Reinforce approximations.	Tissues Stuffed bear for rubbing
The child will dispose of tissue.	Label trash can and provide picture of throwing away tissue. Prompt to locate trash can. Model disposing of tissue.	Trash can, paper, tape, marker, Mayer-Johnson picture Colored trash can

FIGURE 4.4 Curriculum arranged by objectives, activities, and materials.

Domain	Objective	Activity	Environment
Domestic	Making cereal	Using supplies purchased in the community, makes cereal each morning.	Classroom kitchen
Communication	Making picture choices	Provide a list of picture choices for breakfast.	Classroom kitchen
Social	Greeting others	Greeting the bus driver, the teacher, fellow students.	Bus, hallway, classroom

FIGURE 4.5 Curriculum arranged by domain, objective, activity, and environment.

The important thing to remember is that a curriculum is the guide for all other instructional decisions. Thus, it should be developed in a format that illustrates its vertical and horizontal coordination. It should be obvious to all those who plan to use it how long-term goals will be reached through mastery of short-term objectives (i.e., activities and skills). The format should also depict the relationship among various domains (e.g., communication, self-help, vocational). In most in-stances, there will be more than one curricular document. A comprehensive curriculum might be prepared, either a published version or individualized version, that delineates goals, activities, and/or objectives for all domains until long-term goals are mastered. The IEP for each student should also designate some of these goals and objectives targeted for that particular year. Finally, a classroom document might be prepared in which each student's goals and objectives are paired with

Goal	Objective(s)	Person	Evaluation Technique
Will indicate needs and desires non-verbally.	Will point to desired object.	Teacher/aide/parent	Nonrestricted event recording (pointing behaviors)
Will improve understanding of verbal commands.	Will sit in response to verbal command.	Teacher, aide	Restricted event recording
	Will stop in response to to verbal command.	Teacher, parent	Restricted event recording
	Will come in response to verbal command.	Teacher, aide, parents	Restricted event recording
Will improve matching skills.	Will match pictures of objects to actual objects.	Teacher	Restricted event recording
	Find match for object among many objects.	Teacher	Restricted event recording

FIGURE 4.6 Curriculum arranged by goal, objective, person, and evaluation technique.

Curricular Area: Writing	Required: School/Home	Has Skill	Needs Training
Will grasp pencil.	X/X	10-20-01	

Will trace lines:
   Horizontal
   Vertical
   Diagonal
   Curved
   Letters
   Numbers.
	X		X

Will copy model.	X		X

Steps	Duration	Date	Date	Date
Exits bus.	30 secs	FP	FP	FP
Walks directly to front door.	5 secs	FP	FP	FP
Opens door.	3 secs	V	V	V
Walks through door.	3 secs	I	I	I
Proceeds down the hall.	60 secs	PA	PA	V
Walks directly into classroom.	4 secs	V	V	I

Key: FP, full physical prompt; V, verbal prompt; PA, partial physical; I, independent.

FIGURE 4.7 Curriculum arranged for formative assessment.

CONTENT	BEHAVIOR				
	Identification	Production			
	A. Acquisition	B. Acquisition	C. Fluency	D. Application	E. Generalization

1. Conversation skills
  (1) with employer
  (2) with coworker
  (3) with customers
	1(1)A
	1(2)A
	1(3)A
		1(1)B
		1(2)B
		1(3)B
			1(1)C
			1(2)C
			1(3)C
				1(1)D
				1(2)D
				1(3)D
					1(1)E
					1(2)E
					1(3)E

2. Task-related skills
  (1) asking for clarification
  (2) asking for assistance
  (3) volunteering to assist
	2(1)A
	2(2)A
	2(3)A
		2(1)B
		2(2)B
		2(3)B
			2(1)C
			2(2)C
			2(3)C
				2(1)D
				2(2)D
				2(3)D
					2(1)E
					2(2)E
					2(3)E

3. Personal appearance
  (1) appropriate grooming
  (2) appropriate dress
	3(1)A
	3(2)A
		3(1)B
		3(2)B
			3(1)C
			3(2)C
				3(1)D
				3(2)D
					3(1)E
					3(2)E

Sample Objectives:

1(1)A Students will identify the scenarios that exhibit an employee having appropriate conversation skills with an employer 10 out of 10 times.

2(2)C Students will ask for assistance in completing job-related tasks as often as appropriate during all of the role-play scenarios.

3(1)E Students will come to work after they have showered and neatly combed their hair.

FIGURE 4.8 Curriculum arranged by level of learning. (From *Effective Instruction for Special Education,* by M. A. Mastropieri and T. E. Scruggs, 1994, p. 328. Austin, TX: Pro-Ed Publishing. Copyright 1987, 1994 by Pro-Ed, Inc. Reprinted by permission.)

formative assessment data (e.g., a checklist format as in Figure 4.1, graphs, work samples). Because curricula appear in so many formats, they may be confusing to parents and others not familiar with school forms and procedures. We recommend that curricula be presented in a clear, coherent manner such that they will be useful currently and in the future. We also recommend that curricula be accessible to all interested parties so that they can understand the long-term ramifications of the annual IEP.

SUMMARY

This chapter has presented various considerations and procedures for developing an appropriate curriculum for students with autism. Given the large number of deficits typically displayed by these stu-

dents, developing the most effective curriculum is imperative. Everything we teach should be functional, chronologically age appropriate, well integrated, community referenced, and refined to such an extent that the student progresses at an acceptable rate. All other educational decisions pale in comparison to the importance of curricular decisions. If we do not choose to teach what the learner needs to learn and organize it in a way to ensure mastery, then decisions about instructional methods and placement become dubious. In Chapters 6 through 9 we will discuss specific curricular areas in terms of recommended sequences, instructional strategies, and specific assessment techniques. Preparing students with autism and related disorders to function independently in integrated adult environments is a difficult task only made easier by the knowledge that every step achieved is one step closer to the ultimate goal.

KEY POINTS

1. Curricular decisions should precede all other educational decisions including placement.

2. What a student is taught affects many life choices and may prevent the development of inappropriate behavior.

3. A team of people who know the student best should develop the individualized curriculum.

4. Many students with autism and related disorders cannot benefit from the general education curriculum.

5. Curriculum should be functional, chronologically age appropriate, longitudinal, horizontally integrated, and community referenced.

6. Communication and socialization goals are typically priorities for this population.

7. It is important to establish placement goals for the long-term, intermediate term, and for the current year, allowing those goals to guide curricular decisions.

8. Individualized procedures best guarantee the most functional goals and objectives.

9. Curriculum-based assessment provides a starting point when deciding what to teach next.

10. Refining curriculum includes teaching to fluency, maintenance, and generalization, and task analyzing content and skills when necessary.

11. Curriculum can be organized into several different formats. It is important to pick the format that works best for the team involved.

REFERENCES

Alberto, P. A., & Troutman, A. C. (1999). *Applied behavior analysis for teachers* (5th ed.) Columbus, OH: Merrill.

Brown, L., Branston, M. B., Hamre-Nietupski, S., Pumpian, I., Certo, N., & Gruenwald, L. (1979). A strategy for developing chronological age appropriate and functional curricular content for severely handicapped adolescents and young adults, *Journal of Special Education, 13*(1), 81–90.

Brown, L., Nietupski, J., & Hamre-Nietupski, S. (1976). Criterion of ultimate functioning. In M. A. Thomas (Ed.), *Hey, don't forget about me!* Reston, VA: The Council for Exceptional Children.

Falvey, M. A. (1989). *Community-based curriculum: Instructional strategies for students with severe handicaps* (2nd ed.). Baltimore, MD: Paul H. Brookes.

Falvey, M. A., Grenot-Scheyer, M., & Luddy, E. (1987). Developing and implementing integrated community referenced curricula. In D. J. Cohen, A. M. Donnellan, & R. Paul (Eds.), *Handbook of autism and pervasive developmental disorders* (pp. 238–250). New York: John Wiley & Sons.

Fiscus, E. D., & Mandell, C. J. (1983). *Developing individualized education programs.* St. Paul, MN: West Publishing Company.

Fuchs, L. S., & Deno, S. L. (1994). Must instructionally useful performance assessment be based in the curriculum? *Exceptional Children, 61*(1), 15–24.

Gronlund, N. (1978). *Stating objectives for classroom instruction.* New York: Macmillan.

Harris, S. L., Belchic, J., Blum, L., & Celiberti, D. (1994). Behavioral assessment of autistic disorder. In J. L. Mateson (Ed.), *Autism in children and adults: Etiology, assessment, and intervention* (pp. 127–146). Belmont, CA: Brooks/Cole.

Mager, R. (1997). *Preparing instructional objectives.* Atlanta, GA: The Center for Effective Performance, Inc.

Neel, R. S., & Billingsley, F. F. (1989). *IMPACT: A functional curriculum handbook for students with moderate to severe disabilities.* Baltimore, MD: Paul H. Brookes.

Peterson, J., Trecker, N., Egan, I., Fredericks, H. D. G., & Bunse, C. (1983). *The teaching research curriculum for handicapped adolescents and adults: Assessment procedures.* Monmouth, OR: Teaching Research.

Pfeiffer, S. I., & Nelson, D. D. (1992). The cutting edge in services for people with autism. *Journal of Autism and Developmental Disorders, 22*(1), 95–105.

Romanczyk, R. G., & Lockshin, S. (1981). *How to create a curriculum for autistic and other handicapped children.* Austin, TX: Pro-Ed.

Smith, S. W., Slattery, W. J., & Knopp, T. Y. (1993). Beyond the mandate: Developing individualized education programs that work for students with autism. *Focus on Autistic Behavior, 8*(3), 1–13.

Spooner, F., & Test, D. W. (1994). Domestic and community living skills. In E. C. Cipani & F. Spooner (Eds.), *Curricular and instructional approaches for persons with severe disabilities* (pp. 149–183). Needham Heights, MA: Allyn & Bacon.

Strickland, B. B., & Turnbull, A. P. (1990). *Developing and implementing individualized education programs.* Columbus, OH: Merrill.

Vincent, L. J., Salisbury, C., Walter, G., Gruenwald, L. J., & Powers, M. (1980). Program evaluation and curriculum development in early childhood special education: Criteria of the next environment. In W. Sailor, B. Wilcox, & L. Brown (Eds.), *Methods of instruction for severely handicapped students* (pp. 303–328). Baltimore, MD: Paul H. Brookes.

Wehman, P., & Kregel, J. (1997). *Functional curriculum for elementary, middle, and secondary age students with special needs.* Austin, TX: Pro-Ed.

Wilcox, B., & Bellamy, G. T. (1987). *A comprehensive guide to the Activities Catalog: An alternative curriculum for youth and adults with severe disabilities.* Baltimore, MD: Paul H. Brookes.

5

Teaching: General Strategies

Did you know that:

- Students with autism will learn little without effective instruction?
- The best teaching strategies emphasize clarity and order?
- Stimulating environments may impede learning?
- Visual supports facilitate learning?
- Applied Behavior Analysis (ABA) encompasses various teaching strategies?

Chapter 4 presented various aspects of the decision process regarding *what* to teach a specific student. This chapter will provide recommendations for *how* to teach the designated curriculum. Remember that autism tends to impair motivation to learn, the way sensory stimuli are received, and the ability to attend to and subsequently assimilate, retain, retrieve, and utilize various forms of information (Frith, 1989). Students with autism and related disorders typically feel overwhelmed by noise, light, movement, verbal commands, and tactile stimulation (Wing, 1981). They appear to rely on rote memory and spatial orientation to make sense of their world thus finding great comfort in routine and sameness. Additionally, most students with autism demonstrate complex language deficits and interfering behaviors. Typical teaching strategies that rely on

facilitating learning by providing a highly stimulating environment with various materials, experiences, and continuous dialogue have not been found to work well for such individuals. On the contrary, teaching strategies that seem to work best for students with autism, particularly those with low cognition, are highly structured ones that bring clarity, order, and predictability to their world (Donnellan, Gossage, LaVigna, Schuler, & Traphagen, 1976; Lovaas & Smith, 1989; Maurice, Green, & Luce, 1996; Quill, 1995; Schopler, Reichler, & Lansing, 1980; Simpson & Regan, 1986).

Many preferred instructional strategies for children with autism and related disorders are founded in behavioral theory (i.e., ABA), which includes teacher-directed learning with clear, repetitive presentations of small chunks of information, practice, feedback, and data collection. Other components of a highly structured environment pertain to the organization of classrooms and materials, consistent routines and procedures, and clear visual cues that serve as prompts for desired behaviors. Traditional approaches to teaching students with neurological impairment include such a structured approach to teaching because it assists students with attending to relevant stimuli, predicting what will happen next, and grasping new information (e.g., Wiederholt, Hammill, & Brown, 1978). In the case of autism, structured teaching strategies take advantage of the child's propensity for routine, sameness, visual learning, and spatial memory. As progress is documented, teachers are encouraged to gradually present more complex learning tasks using progressively less structure for the purpose of promoting maintenance and generalization.

STRUCTURE AND TEACHING

When we talk about teaching strategies we refer to everything a teacher does to facilitate learning. This includes the physical arrangement of the classroom, classroom procedures and routines, the types of materials utilized, the pace of instruction, student–teacher ratios, the type of activity, structure, or lesson presentation, and various assessment strategies. A highly structured approach to instruction would imply that the teacher develops the classroom, the materials, the schedule, and the lesson such that predesignated learner responses are cued and prompted, frequent performance feedback is provided, and student progress is regularly monitored. With this type of structure, students seldom make mistakes, instead receiving frequent opportunities to practice correct responding. The goal of highly structured teaching is **errorless learning.** In other words, students do not have to make mistakes in order to learn. Students with autism and related disorders tend to memorize what they are taught. If what they memorize is incorrect, it is extremely difficult for them to "un-learn" it, and memorize a correct response. Thus, it is imperative that these students learn correct responding without errors. Furthermore, because students with autism are not typically motivated to learn and cannot make sense of their world easily, structured teaching strategies are usually indicated (Heflin & Simpson, 1998; Maurice et al., 1996; Quill, 1995). All of the strategies for structuring that we present are related to the concept of stimulus control described in Chapter 2. The steps in establishing stimulus control also apply to teaching students to respond to different types of structure.

STRUCTURING WITH PHYSICAL ORGANIZATION

Some characteristics of students with autism that make teaching them difficult are (1) their apparent inability to transform information into meaningful coherent ideas, generalized over a wide range of contexts (Frith, 1989; Stokes & Baer, 1977), and (2) their failure to shift attention, especially to auditory stimuli (Courshesne, 1995). Because of these characteristics, students will need an overabundance of structure and support in order to learn and function independently. One of the best ways to help students with autism bring order to their world and to learn is by arranging environmental variables to act as cognitive organizers. Because these students apparently attend to and remember static visual cues, we specifically recommend constructing a visually organized room in order to communicate learning and behavioral expectations (Dalrymple, 1995; Donnellan et al., 1976; Quill, 1995; Schopler, Mesibov, & Hearsey, 1995).

Desks, chairs, dividers, shelves, rugs, and materials can be arranged in such a way that time demands, procedures, curriculum, and location are readily communicated. For example, if students are expected to function independently for cognitive, prevocational, and vocational skills, receive instruction in self-help skills and communication skills, and perform appropriate leisure time skills, then the classroom should be arranged to communicate these functions. Organize areas according to the activity and curriculum to be delivered. Clearly delineate physical boundaries and expected behaviors. To accomplish this, the teacher might:

- Design an independent work area containing a long table and chairs with various **workstations** requiring matching, assembly, job, and/or discrimination skills.

- Arrange a separate area with a stove, refrigerator, kitchen supplies, an ironing board, iron, and washing machine indicating that self-help lessons will occur.

- Create a leisure time area to support appropriate leisure activities. This area might contain computers and software games, a card table and chairs, age-appropriate toys, books, and magazines, and bean bag chairs.

- Indicate direct instruction in communication and academics with desks, chairs and small tables, mats, rugs, boxes for completed work, pencils, paper, and so forth.

- Designate one easily accessible area of each classroom as a transition area. This area should contain places for each student's belongings and picture or written activity schedule (another visual support indicating classroom procedures).

Figure 5.1 provides a sample room arrangement for older students with autism.

Younger students with autism may have areas of the room designated for snack time, play, direct instruction, and self-help skills (particularly toileting, grooming, and dressing skills). The point is that the room arrangement itself can cue response expectations. If the student is expected to work independently, then the area should be free of distracters such as noise and flickering lights. Furthermore, designated tasks (e.g., workstations) need to be self-explanatory for the student. For example, Schopler et al. (1995) recommend that independent tasks indicate to the student (usually with pictures) how much work must be completed, what work must be completed, when the

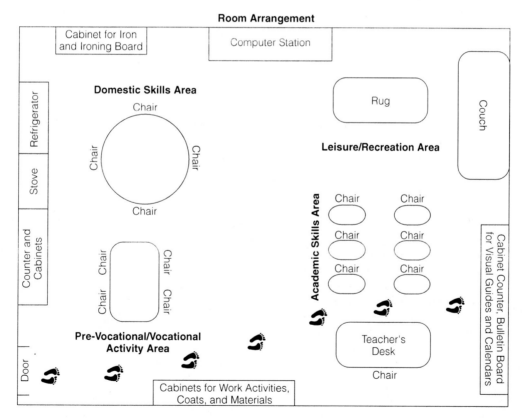

FIGURE 5.1 Room arrangement for older students with autism.

work is finished, and what happens when the work is finished.

When students are expected to work one-to-one with the teacher, then it might be best to place two chairs by a small table with instructional materials in proximity to the teacher's chair. If possible, this one-to-one instruction should be in a place somewhat visually isolated from everything else in the classroom. Of course, room arrangement is contingent on available resources, but access to a small, quiet work space for one-to-one instruction will be necessary for initial skill acquisition, for highly noncompliant and/or aggressive students, and for those who seem particularly distracted by noise and movement. Once instructional control has been obtained, students will be able to perform either one-to-one or within groups without as many environmental supports.

Group work is usually performed with students surrounding a table, with students in a horseshoe-shaped sitting arrangement, or with students sitting on one side of a table and the teacher working from the opposite side. For older students, working in rows of desks might be encouraged, particularly if inclusion in general education classrooms is a targeted placement. In any of these cases, student–teacher ratios are small. As more students are added to a group (student–teacher ratio becomes larger), structure correspondingly decreases and it is assumed that students can operate for longer periods of time without teacher support.

Additional visual support for behavioral expectations can be provided with dividers such as filing cabinets, partitions, bookshelves, carpet sections, masking tape on the floor, and pictures delineating areas. More visual cues are needed (higher structure) for students with lower cognitive functioning, young students, and those engaged in new learning. Materials pertaining to curriculum taught in a particular area of the room should be stored in that area. Color-coding of storage boxes, labeling everything with pictures or words, and keeping things in the same place over time will assist students to learn procedures and understand expectations. For example, storage boxes in the prevocational area may be green, as is the carpet and the masking tape to indicate where chairs are placed. Green paper lines the walls in that area. Another visual strategy might be to store each student's materials in color-coded boxes so that Jason's tasks are in the red box and Julie's are in the blue box. Labeling the boxes with Polaroid pictures and/or names will also help each child to recognize his or her own possessions. In other words, take advantage of the typical reliance on rote memory to help students with autism and related disorders come under the control of classroom stimuli and attain independence. Avoid rearranging the classroom unless it is absolutely necessary. Once students with autism learn visual cues, they can become very confused and anxious if those cues are altered or removed without warning and without teaching other ways to predict what should happen next. Table 5.1 provides some suggestions for visually organizing a classroom.

Organizing to Prevent Inappropriate Behavior

Because students with autism are easily distracted, masking irrelevant noises or visual distracters can be helpful. Teachers may want to cover windows or close blinds, close doors, use carrels, decrease noise by lowering voices, use earphones for tape recorders, place rugs to absorb noise, or add white noise if other methods do not work. Lighting might also need to be modified as needed. Some students with autism are distracted by the soft buzz of fluorescent lights, and lights that flicker are sure to be a distraction. In these cases, lamps might work better. However some students may also be distracted by shadows, so light placement is important. Observe individual students in order to target potential distracters. If self-stimulation or agitation increases under certain conditions, take the time to analyze what physical phenomena might need to be altered. Then, once the student is able to work calmly in carefully controlled environments, you should begin gradually introducing more natural environmental stimuli to the situation. For example, perhaps you use the classroom fluorescent

Table 5.1 Suggestions for Visual Organization

Use color-coding for:
- Organizing materials by area
- Organizing materials for each child (e.g., Jason's chair always has a red tape stripe, his cubby is marked with red tape, he sits on the red tape)
- Designating areas of the room (e.g., self-help is yellow, leisure is purple)

Use pictures for:
- Designating each child's place
- Destinations
- Daily schedules
- Delineating activities to perform in each area of the classroom
- Reminding students of desired behaviors
- Designating personal belongings
- Designating where things belong
- Designating tasks and activities

Use lists for:
- Reminding what things to take home or bring to school
- Reminding what to buy at the store or in the cafeteria
- Reminding what things to take on community outings
- Reminding what jobs to do
- Reminding what tasks need to be done

Use tape (e.g., wide electrician's tape) or paint for:
- Designating transition paths (e.g., painted footsteps)
- Designating line-up area
- Creating a "personal space" area for each student (e.g., taped square around desk, taped square around area where students are to sit)

Use dividers for:
- Designating transition paths
- Visually masking seductive stimuli (e.g., children playing outside)
- Providing obstacles for running away

---

lights rather than lamps for increasingly longer periods each day. Remember that the world in general is full of auditory and visual distracters so students must learn to deal with ever-increasing noise, movement, and visual stimulation if they are to function in integrated environments.

The physical environment can also be arranged so as to prevent inappropriate behavior. For example, students who run away should be placed distally from doors, or place obstacles such as a cabinet about 3 to 5 feet in front of the door to serve as a deterrent. Arrange aisles or walkways such that an adult can touch any student in the room within 3 seconds. If students are destructive, keep valuable items (e.g., computers, TVs, tape recorders) out of reach unless the student is supervised or until he learns alternate prosocial behavior. If students grab food, keep food reinforcers in an inaccessible place such as pockets of a carpenter's apron worn around the teacher's waist. If a student likes to lie on the floor or grab the teacher's shirt, then arrange the work table so that the student cannot get out of his seat or reach the teacher without the teacher moving the table. Keep favorite stim-toys (those things that students prefer to use for self-stimulation purposes) out of sight unless students have earned them. Basically, teachers should monitor students and arrange the environment to ensure maximum time on task and to prevent inappropriate behavior.

Organizing for Comfort and Safety

Everyone should be comfortable in the classroom. Small, cramped dark spaces are usually not conducive to learning. Messy rooms will fail to communicate learning expectations. Avoid excessive heat and cold. Allow easy access to bathrooms. Everyone should be able to move easily around the classroom and to obtain and return materials without many hassles. Teach students (and adults) to return materials to their designated place (indicating "finished"). Use safety precautions when working with stoves, irons, knives, or other such things. In sum, visually organizing the classroom to communicate expectations will create predictable and salient cues for designated behavior. Students with autism and related disorders will be more comfortable, more motivated, and more successful under such conditions.

STRUCTURING THROUGH ROUTINES AND SCHEDULES

Students with autism appear to find great comfort in routine. In fact, if routine is not imposed externally, many individuals with autism will impose it on their own. For example, a student may smell each bite of food before putting it in her mouth, or may touch all the pieces of a puzzle before putting it together, or may arrange the desk and chair in a certain fashion before sitting down to work. Because routine is so easily learned and often preferred, we recommend that teachers take great care in deciding what routines to establish in their classrooms such that they assist students to comply and learn.

Teaching Routines and Procedures

Generally, we recommend that teachers establish routine procedures for entering and leaving the classroom, monitoring a schedule and choosing activities, working, playing, toileting, and eating. For example, entering the classroom may entail walking to the central transition area, putting away coats, lunch boxes, and backpacks, and moving to an appropriate instructional area. This procedure will be facilitated if there are painted arrows or footsteps from the door to the transition area or some other visual cues such as dividers guiding students through the procedure. In any case, the teacher should prompt students to use established routines every time until the student can do it independently.

Students with autism typically have difficulty with new routines, particularly transitioning between activities or from one step of an activity to another. Due to their inability to shift their attention and to read social cues, these students will require instruction and support to master transition and activity procedures. First, teachers should establish procedures and routines for each transition and activity required during a day. For example, how will students determine where they should be and on what they should be working? How will they know when to change activities? What should they do if they finish their task and have free time? What are the procedures for going to lunch, the bathroom, and recess?

Schopler et al. (1995) recommend teaching students top-down and left-to-right routines so that they can "read" visual cues (regardless of where they may be posted) from top to bottom, and approach all tasks and activities in the classroom from left to right. For example, a student may be taught to work from a picture activity schedule, picking the top picture to indicate what activity he should complete first and working down the list until all activities are completed. A student may also be taught to sit down at a particular workstation which is arranged such that step 1 (pick up the first sheet of paper in a collating task) is positioned to the far left while the last step (stacking the stapled packets) is positioned to the far right.

It is also recommended that teachers establish routines and procedures for "waiting" (Dalrymple, 1995). For example, teach students to move to waiting chairs as part of the transition to new activities. This procedure will give the teacher a chance to set up workstations and to ensure that all students are in the correct place. It will teach students an appropriate behavior to display at other times when waiting might be required (e.g., waiting for a bus, waiting for dinner, waiting to go to the bathroom). Eventually, the student should be taught to respond to a verbal cue, "Please wait," by sitting nearby and possibly playing a handheld computer game, reading a comic book, or listening to a tape on a Walkman.

Another useful procedure or routine to teach is that of "finishing" activities and tasks. The concept of "finished" is a difficult one to teach to someone who translates the world in a literal fashion. Is one finished when a bell sounds? Or when the plate is empty? Or when the "finished" box is full? Depending on the activity, completion standards will vary. Dalrymple (1995) and Schopler et al. (1995) recommend several cues to help students determine completion. These cues include (1) using timers to indicate a time standard; (2) specifying the amount to be completed by using a counter, a card with a certain number of circles to be filled, a check-off strategy, or completing the exact number of tasks set out; (3) setting cues for completion such as the end of a music tape means put materials away, a teacher signaling completion of lunch, a teacher putting materials away as a signal for lesson completion; (4) using finished boxes that, when full, indicate completion; and (5) using peer models (e.g., when

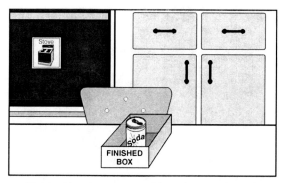

Finished box for concrete objects (e.g., soda can)

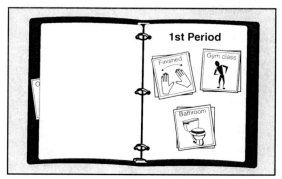

Picture activity schedule in notebook with
finished pictures to Velcro over pictures
of completed tasks

Picture activity schedule and finished box

FIGURE 5.2 Sample "finished" indicators.

a certain student puts his tray away, then lunch is finished). Figure 5.2 illustrates some sample "finished" indicators.

Finishing tasks can become a cue for changing tasks or transitioning. If actual task completion

does not initially cue students to transition, auditory cues (e.g., bells, music) might help to signal the time to change activities. For students who are first learning transition procedures, teachers might provide them with an object related to the next task (e.g., a pencil indicating academic time) to signal that it is time to move to the next activity. The student can carry the object to the appropriate place and in this way be able to transition with less prompting from the teacher.

It might also be useful to teach students the routine that work always precedes free time and attending always precedes work. By requiring task responses before awarding "play" time, the student not only learns to work for longer periods of time but pairing work with play enhances the motivation to participate in instructional tasks because the routine dictates that free time will follow. Asking the student for attention (e.g., "Look at me," "Pay attention," "Time to work") signals that work is to follow (which then leads to play time). Thus, promoting routines has the added benefit of activities cueing subsequent activities. For example, toileting may always precede lunch and snack times. After each instance of toileting, the student will learn quickly to wash his hands and make preparations for either snack or lunch. By following this routine every time, the student is better able to predict what activity comes next and perform independently.

Students with autism and related disorders will not typically do well if procedures or routines are suddenly changed because they have memorized what to do next. In cases where procedures or routines must change, students should be prepared well ahead of time, for example, with pictures of what will be happening, pictures with an X marked through the cancelled activity, or by role-playing behavioral expectations for the new routine. New routines demand much repetition, effective prompting, visual cueing, and advanced warning.

Establishing Schedules

To assist with consistent teaching routines (the adults will be less adept at this than the students) we recommend that teachers develop detailed schedules. The two types of schedules generally used are **whole-class schedules** and **individual schedules.** The first is for the benefit of teachers and others working with the students. The latter is for student use. A whole-class schedule is developed with several things in mind: (1) length of teaching sessions (10 to 20 minutes for young children; longer for older students, eventually approximating actual competitive employment expectations), (2) assignment of personnel (including teaching assistants, speech therapists, peer tutors, other related service personnel), (3) recess, lunch, snack and toileting breaks, (4) number of students scheduled with each staff member (one-to-one or grouping), (5) out-of-class activities (inclusion and/or community-based activities), and (6) students' specific scheduling needs (e.g., functioning level, IEP goals, learning preferences).

Whole-Class Schedules. Preparing a class schedule is a complex and necessary task. Start by filling in the "givens" such as lunch time and arrival and departure times. For young children, schedules are usually developed around half-hour blocks. This allows for transition time and up to 20 to 25 minutes of work time. Of course students can be given breaks during these blocks if necessary, but one curriculum area is usually designated for each time block. For older students, the time blocks may last 50 to 60 minutes. It is important to note that during a given time block (e.g., 9:00–9:30) one student could be working on communication, three could be receiving instruction in self-help skills, two could be working on motor skills, and the rest could be learning appropriate leisure time activities. A time block does not necessarily dictate that all students in the class work on the same curricular objective (remember instruction is individualized), but it does imply that there is an established routine for each student.

The scheduling of snacks and toileting at specified times each day is important. For students who are not toilet trained, toileting should happen frequently as a designated curricular goal (see Chapter 8). When establishing a schedule, consider whether students can work in a group or

whether they need one-on-one instruction for some skills and whether those who can work in a group need to master similar tasks. This part is tricky and is also related to the number of adults available to work with students. Group students when it is appropriate to do so. In some situations, the students may be grouped, but each given a different task and instruction while the others engage in guided practice. In other instances, students may be grouped and all taught the same thing (e.g., imitation or choral responding). For those students needing one-to-one instruction, consider the classroom space while scheduling so that they are not competing with other activities taking place in the classroom. If self-help skills necessitate the use of the rest room or the kitchen, avoid scheduling too many individuals in a particular area at the same time.

Additionally, consider when individual students work best. If most students begin fidgeting at 11:00 A.M. each day, schedule exercise or physical activities during that time. If some students respond best in the early morning, schedule communication training and socialization instruction for them during that time. Finally, consider integration opportunities. These may consist of time spent in general education classrooms (which may require one-to-one monitoring from a teaching assistant), community-based instruction (which may require monitoring from a job coach or the teacher), and peer tutoring (which might include peer volunteers from general education classes assisting in the special education classroom). Figure 5.3 provides a sample classroom schedule. Remember that schedules must be developed based on individual student needs and abilities and available resources. Each classroom schedule will differ.

Individual Schedules. Providing students with visual activity schedules is a widely used technique for assisting students with autism to understand expectations, predict ensuing events, make choices, anticipate changes, and operate independently (Dalrymple, 1995; Heflin & Simpson, 1998; Schopler et al., 1995). As with the "to do" list that most of us keep, a visual activity schedule

Teacher: Kay			Assistants: Debbie, Jan, Gloria		
Time	Kay	Debbie	Jan	Gloria	Other
8:00–8:30	Morning prep. Planning/ Charting	Morning prep.	Morning prep.	Morning prep.	
8:30–9:00	Child 3: Receptive lang.	Child 6, 7: Fine motor Socialization	Child 1, 4: Self-help	Child 2, 5: Imitation	Child 8: Speech therapy
9:00–9:30	Child 6,7: Independent matching	Child 1, 3, 4: Self-help	Child 8: Receptive lang. Cognitive	Child 2: Fine motor	Child 5: Speech therapy
9:30–10:00	Child 1, 2, 5: Independent cognitive	Child 4, 8: Leisure time skills	Child 3: Imitation	Child 6,7: Self-help	
10:00–10:30	Child 1, 2, 3, 5, 6, 7: Group language and socialization			Child 4, 8: Gen. ed. art.	
10:30–11:00	Conference w/ parents/staff	Child 1, 2, 3, 4, 5, 6, 7, 8: Outside break and toileting			
11:00–11:30	Child 1, 3: Expressive lang.	Child 8: Independent/ Matching	Child 4: Fine motor	Child 2, 5: Self-help	Child: 6,7: Speech therapy
11:30–12:00	Child 1, 2, 3, 4, 5, 6, 7: Leisure time activities				Child 8: Music
12:00–12:15	Lunch preparation, self-help: toilet, wash hands, comb hair				
12:15–1:45	Lunch supervision		Break	Break	
1:45–2:15	Child 1, 2, 3, 4: Kitchen		Child 5,6,7,8: Laundry		
2:15–2:45	Child 4: Expressive lang.	Break	Child 1, 2, 3: Laundry	Child 5, 7: Kitchen	Child 6, 8: Games with Peer tutors
2:45–3:00	Preparation for leaving: Toileting, wash hands, comb hair, put away materials				

FIGURE 5.3 Sample classroom schedule.

provides a way for students to understand what they are expected to do for the day, determine the order in which it should be done, and recognize when individual tasks are completed and how much is left to do. This type of cognitive organizer is particularly useful for anyone with neurological impairment.

Individual schedules (sometimes referred to as calendars) can utilize concrete objects or parts of objects (actual size or miniature), pictures (photos, three-dimensional drawings, line drawings), or written words. The schedule can be kept in cubby boxes, fastened to strips on the wall, on calendars, on cards filed in a box, in folders, in notebooks, or some other variation. The important thing is that the student be taught to use the schedule to determine what she is to do next or *not* to do next. Schopler et al. (1995) recommended several issues to consider when choosing a schedule system for a particular student. These include determining (1) whether the student can match objects, pictures, or words, (2) whether the student can read for comprehension, (3) whether the student can follow a sequence of activities using visual cues,

(4) the student's level of distractibility, (5) the best way to make the system portable, and (6) how the student can indicate that a task/activity has been completed.

Generally it is recommended that teachers initially use concrete objects (e.g., a soap bar to indicate time to wash hands), parts of objects (a piece of a pizza box to indicate lunch time), or miniature objects (e.g., a dollhouse toilet for restroom time) to signal an activity. For students who have matching skills, pictures, photos, three-dimensional pictures, or line drawings can be used for the schedules. Concrete objects are usually kept in single or multiple cubby boxes or on Velcroed

strips. The student is prompted to pick the first object (one at the top) and carry it to the appropriate area/activity where objects indicating steps in that activity are arranged left to right. After the activity is completed, the activity object is placed in a finished box and the next activity object is retrieved. Figure 5.4 illustrates some concrete object schedules on Velcro backings.

The same process is taught for a picture schedule. Pictures, such as photos or stick figures (like those obtained from Mayer-Johnson Company, 619-550-0084) may be fastened to a ribbon or strip of paper on the wall. The student can take the picture (usually top-down) to the designated

Concrete object activity schedule on Velcro backed by cardboard (Calendar time, PE, vocational: crushing cans, lunch)

Plywood backed Velcro activity schedule with pictures and concrete objects. Collating (folded paper), toileting (toilet paper), art (paintbrush), can crushing (can), lunch (spoon), newspaper sorting (news clipping), leisure time (audio tape), cooking (spoon), transition (backpack), bus

FIGURE 5.4 Sample concrete object schedules.

area/activity and then place it in a finished box on completion. Eventually, the student can work from a laminated picture strip without Velcro, simply looking to see what the next activity will be, marking an X through the picture when the activity is finished, and moving to the next picture (either top-down for the next scheduled activity or left-right for steps within an activity). These schedules can be kept in notebooks or wallets in order to allow for more portability and generalization. Eventually, students can be taught to match written words to tasks/activities, people, and destinations. Start with single words to indicate the next task/activity (e.g., "toilet" to indicate rest room activities) and move to phrases if the student learns to read and comprehend. Again, the student will need to be taught to cross off or place "finished" indicators on the tasks as they are completed. Written or picture schedules can also be kept in folders, card boxes, or tablets.

Not only can visual schedules be used to assist students through classroom procedures, but they can also be used to guide students through each step of an activity. For example, a recipe may be shown with pictures arranged left to right rather than written in its standard form. Or turning on a computer, inserting the computer disk, clicking on the appropriate icon, and turning off the computer can be communicated through left-to-right picture sequences. Additionally, pictures on a monthly calendar can indicate future events. For example, a picture of the zoo can be pasted onto the calendar on the day that the zoo trip is to occur. Students can mark off each day approaching the trip so that they can better understand when it is to occur. Similarly, if something is cancelled, pictures can be used to communicate the cancellation. By marking an "X" through the picture of the zoo because the bus drivers went on a strike, and placing a picture of a movie camera above it, a teacher can visually indicate the change and better prepare her students for it.

Pictures or written lists can also be used if the student is to be given a choice about the schedule. For example, leisure time might be scheduled for the 2:00–2:30 time slot. However, the student is given a "list" of five pictures indicating choices for a leisure time activity. The student can choose any one of the pictures and match it to the given activity. The schedule may also include destination pictures or words. For example, the student takes the picture of the gym or the library with him to the destination. This may prevent the student from forgetting where she is to go and assist her to become independent in this task. Figures 5.5 and 5.6 provide some samples of visual schedules. Picture communication in general will be covered in Chapter 6.

STRUCTURING THROUGH MATERIALS

Related to physical organization, procedures, and visual cues is the idea of learning or work systems (e.g., Schopler et al., 1995). In this case the work system informs the student what he is to be doing while in an independent work area. The system provides cues for what job students are to do, how much work they are to do, when they are finished, and what happens after task completion. For students who can read, the system may be a box of materials and written instructions (similar to learning centers in general education classrooms). For students who cannot read, instructions typically are given through pictures, shapes, colors, and alphabet or number matching.

Jigs and/or assistive devices are also encouraged. For example, a student may be expected to collate and staple office correspondence as a vocational task. Using number matching, the student is taught to put the paper stack marked "1" onto the taped square of the table marked "1," stack "2" on top of the taped "2," and so on, and to take one sheet from each stack in a left-to-right fashion. At this point, because straightening and holding the papers correctly for stapling is difficult, the student places the papers in an empty typing-paper box that has a cutout in the upper left corner with a stapler attached (a jig). The student is taught to place the papers as they were gathered, face up, in the jig and to push down on the stapler. The

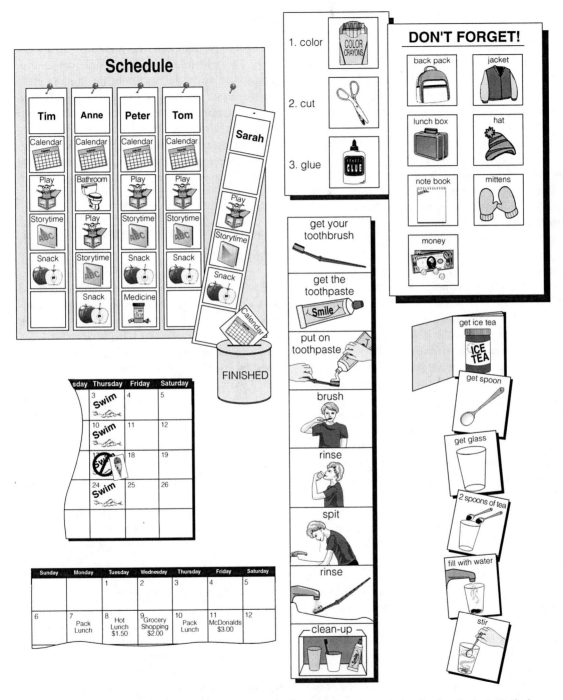

FIGURE 5.5 Sample visual schedules. (From *Visual strategies for improving communication,* by L. A. Hodgdon, 1995, pp. 32, 47, 80, 81, 83. Troy, MI: QuirkRoberts Publishing. Copyright 1995 by QuirkRoberts Publishing PO Box 71, Troy, MI 48099-0071. Reprinted with permission.)

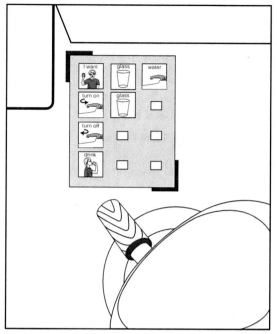

Picture cues for use of sink. They can be removed
in any order depending on the activity

Picture cues for use at kitchen sink

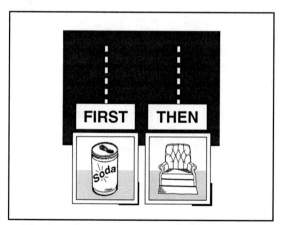

Visual cue for sequencing. Place any two pictures
in order to indicate work first (crushing cans),
then free time (favorite chair)

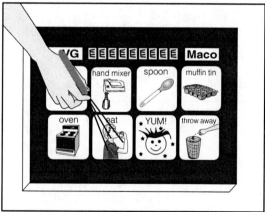

Lighted pointer to indicate which picture should be
pressed to receive verbal instructions from the
communication machine

FIGURE 5.6 Sample picture cues.

stapled stack is then removed and placed in the finished box to the far right. Figure 5.7 provides a diagram of this particular work system. Figure 5.8 shows a sample jig for folding paper to insert in an envelope.

The concept of organizing materials for the purpose of prompting correct responses is not new. Most first-grade teachers use large multiple-lined paper to encourage correct handwriting. Teachers use highlighting and underlining to facilitate students attending to relevant points in a passage. In many aspects of our lives, we rely on formatting to get us through tasks (e.g., filling out tax returns and IEP forms). The purpose of establishing work or learning systems is to encourage

independent functioning. It is important to gradually reduce the number of visual prompts necessary in order to encourage generalization; however, do not hesitate to add physical and visual organization as necessary for errorless learning.

STRUCTURING THROUGH LESSON PRESENTATION

Lesson presentation based on a behavioral model is somewhat similar to the direct instruction format often used with general education students. One example of a behaviorally based teaching strategy frequently recommended for students with autism and related disorders is called **discrete trial format (DTF),** or **discrete trial teaching (DTT)** (Donnellan et al., 1976; Maurice et al., 1996). This is a highly structured teaching method whereby skills are taught through repeated, structured presentations. The discrete trial format typically consists of (1) teacher directions, input, and prompting, (2) student responding, (3) teacher feedback relative to that response, and (4) some method of tracking student progress toward predesignated goals and objectives. By controlling the antecedents and consequences, teachers can bring clarity to the way information is presented for those students who have attention difficulties; and by regularly collecting data relative to student responses, teachers can make decisions about future teaching situations.

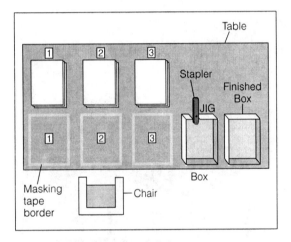

FIGURE 5.7 Sample structured workstation.

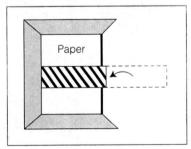

Flip over flap to hold paper while folding a letter

Folding box

FIGURE 5.8 Sample jig.

Discrete Trial Format

The theory governing discrete trial format is that we want students to respond with certain behaviors to external stimuli and *not* to respond other ways. For instance, given the word card "cat," we want a student to say (or read) "cat," *not* say or read "dog." Or if we give the command "Sit down," we want the child to sit down, *not* run around, stand up, or lay down. This is called discrimination training, or bringing responses under **stimulus control.** As you remember from Chapter 2, stimulus control occurs when certain antecedent stimuli cue particular behaviors (e.g., Alberto & Troutman, 1999). By providing a clear, discrete stimulus and reinforcing correct responses to that stimulus while *not* reinforcing incorrect responses, students learn that if they perform certain responses in specified conditions, reinforcement will usually follow. This sets the stage for teaching a myriad of skills.

The five steps to a discrete trial format lesson presentation are (1) presentation of a **discriminative stimulus (S^D),** (2) prompting, (3) student re-sponding, (4) presentation of consequences, and (5) an **intertrial interval.** The steps proceed in this set order and each presentation of these five steps is called a **trial.** A trial has a clear beginning and a clear ending. If one skill is being taught, several trials may be presented that require that skill. In this way, a student is able to practice a new response several times in a row. For example, if the student is learning to point to a pizza card to indicate that he wants pizza, the teacher may give 5 to 10 trials in a row requiring this behavior after which he gets pizza.

On the other hand, it might be more motivating to present alternating trials on different tasks. For example, a student may be given a trial requiring the identification of objects, then given a trial for saying his name, followed by a gross motor imitation trial. In this way, the child does not become bored, nor does the teacher; however, throughout the course of a day the student receives enough practice to acquire the desired skills. The rule of thumb is that difficult tasks require more clarity and repetition and, thus, are usually more conducive to trial-by-trial training. Table 5.2 provides a brief description of the components of a discrete trial format.

Table 5.2 Discrete Trial Format Components

1. *Instruction (S^D—discriminative stimulus):* The instruction given to the child.
2. *Prompt (optional):* Extra help to bring about a response.
3. *Response:* The observable and measurable behavior the child engages in after the instruction.
4. *Consequence:* A stimulus presented after a response to increase or decrease that response in the future.
5. *Intertrial interval:* A time period that provides for (a) a clear onset and end of each trial, (b) recording the outcome of trial, and (c) reinforcing good working behavior.

Things to Remember:

1. *Instruction (S^D)*
   a. Child must be attending.
   b. The instruction must be easily discriminable—clear and brief.
   c. The instruction must be appropriate and relevant.
   d. Be consistent in the instructions at first. Give a complete instruction.
   e. Do not give unintended prompts (e.g., looking at correct item).
2. *Prompt (extra help)*
   a. Must be effective (it actually helps achieve the response).
   b. It must eventually be faded. Within-stimulus prompts are easiest to fade.
3. *Consequation*
   a. Say "no" and turn head for incorrect response. In some instances, try prompting correct response before starting another trial.
   b. Praise and give a reinforcer for a correct response.
   c. Make the consequences contingent and immediate.
   d. Consequences must be consistent and clear.
   e. Consequences must be salient (prominent in the environment).
   f. Consequences must be effective—or else you need to change them.

Discriminative Stimulus. The discriminative stimulus (S^D) is the teacher's instruction to the child. A stimulus is anything that cues a response such as a picture, a command, a bell, or a red circle. A discriminative stimulus is a cue that indicates that a correct response will be reinforced and an incorrect response will *not* be reinforced. Before presenting an S^D, the teacher must ensure that the child is attending. This usually means that the child is sitting, facing the teacher, feet on floor, hands quiet, and looking at the teacher. These behaviors are typically cued with some verbal signal such as "do good sitting" or "ready" or "look." Once a student has learned to be attentive, these antecedent stimuli can be dropped and the trial may be started with the S^D only.

When the student is attending, the teacher presents the S^D, usually a verbal direction or command. The verbal direction should *consist of only a few words, be clear, be given only once,* and *be followed by a short pause.* For example, typical S^D's may include "Touch the circle," "Show me same," "Do this," "Point to *my* shoes," "Say 'I want a cookie,'" "Tell me what are you doing." Notice that most S^D's are *statements* that pertain directly to the desired response. Rather than ask a student "Where is the circle?" when differentiating a circle from a square, say "Point to the circle," which is the behavior that is required for reinforcement.

Additionally, an S^D should be *complete.* If there is an interruption while giving an S^D, stop the trial, obtain attention, and deliver the S^D again. When teaching new behaviors, particularly to young children or those with low cognition, it is recommended that the S^D stay consistent across trials. Say "Point to my shoes" for every trial rather than "Where are my shoes?" or "Can you find my shoes?" After the student is performing consistently to one S^D, then vary the S^D to promote generalization.

Prompts. Prompts are optional stimuli added to the S^D to increase the likelihood of correct responding and subsequent reinforcement (Billingsley & Romer, 1983). Prompts come in several formats and should be used when independent responding is not forthcoming. However, it is imperative that the prompts eventually be discontinued; otherwise, the student may become prompt dependent and never master the skill. Prompts can be verbal or non-verbal. Verbal or **auditory prompts** are typically additional directions or examples giving more information about responding. For example, a student may be given the S^D "What's your name?" and the auditory prompt "Sam." **Visual prompts** include gestures such as touching, tapping, or pointing and **modeling** or demonstration. For example, the S^D "Touch your nose" might be followed by the teacher touching her own nose. Visual prompts also include picture prompts. Many examples of these types of prompts were discussed earlier in this chapter.

Tactile or **physical prompts** are the most intrusive prompts. This type of prompting involves physically guiding a correct movement. For example, a student who is to "sign candy" may need the teacher to physically maneuver his hand into the correct position. Or if a student is to imitate gross motor behavior (e.g., hands up), the teacher, after giving the S^D "Do this," might need to physically guide the student's hands above her head. Physical prompts are the most difficult to fade and should be used only when necessary. Prompts can also be differentiated based on the amount of assistance provided. **Full prompts** require maximum assistance with the behavior. **Partial prompts** provide some assistance by requiring the student to do some of the behavior alone. Generally, prompts are faded by moving from full to partial assistance. For example, a teacher may initially use a full physical prompt to teach a student to comply with instructions to "stand up" and "sit down." This means that after the teacher gives the cue, she holds the student's arms or shoulders and guides him to stand up or sit down. After several trials using full physical prompts, the teacher begins using partial physical prompts if needed to cue the correct response. For example, if the student does not respond following the cue, the teacher might simply touch the student's elbow to prompt "stand up," or shoulder for "sit down." Eventually the partial prompts should no longer be necessary.

The types of prompts that have been very successful with students with autism are referred to as stimulus modification or **within-stimulu prompts** (Schoen, 1986; Schreibman, 1975). Within-stimulus prompting means that the stimulus is altered in certain ways (size, color, position, texture, or some other dimension) to make it more likely that the child will respond correctly. For example, while teaching a student to discriminate a circle from a square, the student may at first be presented a very large circle and a tiny square, making it more likely that he will point to the circle.

The type of prompting necessary for a particular student is determined through initial assessment. Give the student instructions or natural S[D]s and observe to see how much of the response the student performs independently. As a general rule, physical and verbal prompts may be necessary for learning a new task. As trials are repeated, less intrusive prompts should be used. Remember that independent functioning is a goal, so any procedure (even one-to-one instruction) that promotes student dependence on a person, procedure, or material will need to be eliminated, if possible, while natural cues and consequences are established for maintaining appropriate skills.

Before initiating a prompt, you should develop a system for fading the prompt. In this way, prompts will only be used when necessary and eliminated as soon as possible, thus facilitating independent responding. Billingsley, Liberty, and White (1994) list several prompt fading systems that can be used in discrete trial teaching as well as other teaching formats. Table 5.3 lists the common prompt fading procedures. In most instructional systems, prompted trials should be reinforced but recorded as incorrect or prompted responses. We do not want the student to experience undue frustration or become unmotivated. However, we are working with students who often attend to irrelevant stimuli, so we must be prudent in applying any technique that may detract from a desired performance.

Table 5.3 Prompt Fading Procedures

1. *Graduated guidance.* This technique is used with physical prompts. Initially, use as much prompting as necessary to obtain a correct response (e.g., in response to "Point to____" teacher takes student's hand and moves it to the correct item). Gradually, use less guidance by moving the location of the prompt (e.g., move student hand above item, student must touch it; move student arm toward item, student must use hand to touch it; touch student's arm, student must move hand to correct item; touch student's upper arm, student does response; shadow student's response; use no physical prompt). Prompted correct responses should be reinforced.

2. *Increasing assistance.* Increasing assistance begins with allowing the student to respond independently. If she does not, then give a verbal cue. If this does not get the correct response, add a gestural cue. Add physical prompt if these do not work. For example, given the S[D] "Sit down," student does not comply. Teacher says "Come to your seat"; teacher says "Sit down" and points to the chair; teacher says "Sit down" and moves the student to the chair. This type of prompting should not be used in dangerous situations. With increasing assistance, there is a high probability of incorrect responding at first so it might not work well with some students with autism. Prompted correct responses should be reinforced.

3. *Decreasing assistance.* Decreasing assistance, similar to graduated guidance, is a process of systematically using weaker prompts, regardless of whether or not they are physical ones. Begin by providing the amount of prompt necessary to obtain the correct response. Gradually (usually after three successful trials) use less prompting as long as the student is still responding correctly. If an error occurs, back up to the stronger prompt. Prompts are usually presented before the response occurs, not as a corrective strategy. For example, let's say you are teaching shape discrimination. Initially you use a larger version of the target shape (e.g., circle) than the distracter shapes (e.g., square, triangle). Gradually you reduce the size of the circle until size is no longer a prompt for correct responding. At this point, the student must discriminate by shape alone. Prompted correct responses should be reinforced.

4. *Probing.* Probing is an assessment strategy for determining if the student is able to respond independently, thus needing no further prompting. At regular intervals, give the S[D] and observe the student's responses. Use this information to plan further prompting strategies. For example, if a teacher has been using gestures to prompt the student to put his tray up before leaving the cafeteria, then try giving the S[D] only ("Line up") and see if the student takes his tray back with no gesture. If so, eliminate the gestural prompt thereafter.

Responses. Once the S^D (and the optional prompt) has been delivered, the student is then expected to respond, usually within 1 to 5 seconds. He may either respond correctly, incorrectly, or not at all. If the response is correct, he should be reinforced. In the case of incorrect responding, no reinforcement should be given. Thus, it is important to be able to distinguish when a response is correct or not correct. For example, if a student is told to "Sit in chair" and he sits sideways with his feet tucked under him, then we do not want to reinforce that behavior. What we want, and what must be operationally defined, is "good sitting." Good sitting usually means sitting in a chair, facing forward, feet on floor, head up, eyes open, hands in lap. If we do not operationally define the behavior in such a way that all trainers know when it is correct, then incorrect responding may be reinforced and maintained. Conversely, correct responding may not be reinforced consistently. Additionally, operationally defining responses will allow precise data collection regarding student progress.

Consequences. Consequences are teacher behaviors that follow student responses. For correct student responses, the teacher should reinforce enthusiastically with praise ("good") and other designated reinforcers (e.g., food, hugs, pats). It is important to obtain effective reinforcers to motivate students to attend and to respond correctly. See Chapter 2 for a discussion about reinforcers and ways to ensure effectiveness. For incorrect responding, the consequence should be no reinforcement (e.g. attention, touch, eye contact). Simply say "No" or "Wrong," frown or keep a straight face and monotone, and briefly turn your head away. Make sure to prompt a correct response on the next trial. Sometimes teachers correct an incorrect response right after it occurs within the same trial. However, in this instance, there is a danger of reinforcing an undesirable behavior chain (i.e., incorrect response—teacher corrected response—reinforcement). The teacher should make a judgment about whether to correct a response in a new trial (e.g., by prompting the correct response in the next trial) or immediately

after a mistake. If the child does not respond at all, begin another trial immediately, physically guiding the desired response following the S^D. Remember to reinforce all correct prompted trials. Prompt a few more trials, then try fading the prompt. If correct responding does not increase, check to see if the reinforcers are effective and if the prompting is occurring in a way that ensures errorless learning.

The student needs to recognize consequences as either reinforcement or no reinforcement. Because individuals with autism have a difficult time distinguishing social cues, the teacher must be very demonstrative in delivering rewards, while being bland after incorrect behaviors. Furthermore, it is recommended that consequences be immediate and contingent (Donnellan et al., 1976). Only give reinforcers for correct responses (contingent), and give some sort of feedback immediately after the student responds so that he learns that his behavior determines teacher behavior. If the consequence is presented too slowly, intervening behavior may occur (e.g., self-stimulation). In this case, if a reinforcer is given, the student may learn, for example, to respond and then self-stimulate to gain a reward. Timing in discrete trial training is crucial for avoiding inappropriate learning and ensuring successful responding.

Consequences should be applied consistently. Determine what schedule of reinforcement might be appropriate (see Chapter 2 for a discussion of reinforcement schedules) and systematically thin the schedule. The rule of thumb is to reinforce every correct response, prompted or not, for new learning, for young children, and for those with the most severe cognitive impairment. As fluency and maintenance are obtained, space the reinforced trials to approximate a natural reinforcement system. For generalization training, reinforcement temporarily may become more frequent, but eventually should be thinned to naturally-occurring schedules.

We recommend not using punishment as a consequence for incorrect responding when teaching skills to replace skill deficits. If prompts and reinforcers are effective, there should be little problem in obtaining instructional control in a discrete trial format. If students continue to display interfering behaviors, refer to Chapter 3 for recommended reductive procedures.

Intertrial Interval. The intertrial interval is a 3- to 5-second period during which no instructions are given. This time provides a distinct ending to the trial and sets the stage for a clear onset of the next trial. During this time period, the teacher can record data regarding the student's previous response, reinforce good attending, establish rapport with the student, allow the student to enjoy a reinforcer (e.g., food, stim-toy), and/or correct inappropriate behavior.

Assessing Student Progress

To determine whether students are learning what has been targeted, teachers need to gather data regarding their responding. Usually, teachers use event recording to count correct responses. This is similar to counting the number of correctly spelled words on the weekly spelling quiz. In the case of discrete trial teaching, the count reflects the number of correct verbalizations, or imitations, or correct responses. An accurate count of correct responding lets the teacher know whether the student is progressing toward the designated mastery criteria (as stated in the instructional objective). If the student is not progressing satisfactorily, then the teacher will need to adjust the instructional strategies (e.g., break the task into smaller steps, adjust the prompting system, assess to see if the student has necessary prerequisites, provide more practice, or select a more powerful reinforcer). Because mastery is defined as independent correct responding, our data collection also needs to reflect whether the correct response was a prompted or unprompted one. Progress is evident when unprompted correct responding increases. If data reflect a number of prompted incorrect responses, a stronger, more controlling prompt should be implemented.

Figure 5.9 provides a data collection sheet for discrete trial teaching. Each of the six sections represents 10 trials of a skill acquisition (i.e., "do this": clap; "do this": touch head; "do this": arms in air; "give me": elephant; "point to": bus). An "X" signifies an unprompted correct response; an "O" indicates an unprompted incorrect response; and "P" indicates prompted responses (either correct, "XP," or incorrect, "OP"). The teacher simply circles the appropriate indicator during intertrial intervals.

Progress is also evident when the teacher uses less intrusive prompts to elicit correct responding. Thus, it is often useful to gather data about not only correct/incorrect responding, but also about the type of prompt required to get correct responses. In this way teachers can detect progress even when independent correct responding has not been mastered. Figure 5.10 illustrates a form that indicates the use of full and partial physical prompts, gestural and verbal prompts, and those responses that only needed to be cued by the S^D (i.e., unprompted responses). Note that a visual graph can be drawn right on this dual-purpose data sheet.

We recommend graphing all recorded data to facilitate communication about student progress to parents and other personnel who are working with students. A graph is much easier to decipher than is a stack of data collection forms. Typically, we recommend graphing percentages of correct, unprompted responses. However, the raw number of correct responses could also be graphed if the number of trials/steps is held constant for each day that data are collected (called **controlled presentations**). See Chapter 2 for a discussion of data conversion and graphing.

Figure 5.11 is a simple graph constructed from Brett's data sheet in Figure 5.9 for April 19 and subsequent training sessions. Note that the teacher initially gave three trials without prompting in order to gather a baseline (an indication of correct responding before trial training began). In this case, Brett gave no correct responses, so the baseline was graphed as "0." Subsequent discrete trial training sessions resulted in an increasing number of correct, unprompted responses. This graph indicates 4 days of training; however, graphs should be constructed to show enough

Brett	Task 1 "Do this": clap				Task 2 "Do this": touch head				Task 3 "Do this": arms in air			
	Date 4/19/01				Date 4/19/01				Date 4/19/01			
1	XP	OP	(X)	O	XP	OP	(X)	O	(XP)	OP	X	O
2	XP	OP	(X)	O	XP	OP	(X)	O	XP	OP	(X)	O
3	XP	OP	(X)	O	XP	OP	(X)	O	XP	OP	(X)	O
4	XP	OP	(X)	O	XP	OP	(X)	O	XP	OP	(X)	O
5	XP	OP	(X)	O	XP	OP	(X)	O	XP	OP	(X)	O
6	XP	OP	(X)	O	XP	OP	(X)	O	XP	OP	(X)	O
7	XP	OP	(X)	O	XP	OP	(X)	O	XP	OP	(X)	O
8	XP	OP	(X)	O	XP	OP	(X)	O	XP	OP	(X)	O
9	XP	OP	(X)	O	XP	OP	(X)	O	XP	OP	(X)	O
10	XP	OP	(X)	O	XP	OP	(X)	O	XP	OP	(X)	O
Total			10				10				9	

Comments: *Excellent attendance — lots of smiles* →

	Task 1 "Give me": elephant				Task 2 "Point to": (bus) (baseline)				Task 3 "Point to": bus			
	Date 4/19/01				Date 4/19/01				Date 4/19/01			
1	XP	OP	(X)	O	XP	OP	X	(O)	(XP)	OP	X	O
2	XP	OP	(X)	O	XP	OP	X	(O)	(XP)	OP	X	O
3	XP	OP	(X)	O	XP	OP	X	(O)	(XP)	OP	X	O
4	XP	OP	(X)	O	XP	OP	X	O	(XP)	OP	X	O
5	XP	OP	(X)	O	XP	OP	X	O	XP	OP	(X)	O
6	XP	OP	(X)	O	XP	OP	X	O	XP	OP	(X)	O
7	XP	OP	(X)	O	XP	OP	X	O	XP	OP	(X)	O
8	XP	OP	(X)	O	XP	OP	X	O	(XP)	OP	X	O
9	XP	OP	(X)	O	XP	OP	X	O	XP	OP	(X)	O
10	XP	OP	(X)	O	XP	OP	X	O	XP	OP	(X)	O
Total			10				5				5	

Comments:

FIGURE 5.9 Discrete trial data sheet.

days to attain skill mastery (usually more than 3 to 5 days) and to also show maintenance (distributed trials over several weeks). Construct data collection forms and graphs such that they will be easy to use, give useful information, and clearly depict the student's progress.

Remember that this five-step discrete trial format can be repeated as necessary until the stu-

Student: _Baxter_   Staff: _Mr. McCorkel_

Trials					
Cue	1 2 3 4 5 6 7 8 9 10	1 2 3 4 5 6 7 8 9 10	1 2 3 4 5 6 7 8 9 10	1 2 3 4 5 6 7 8 9 10	1 2 3 4 5 6 7 8 9 10
Verbal	1 2 3 4 5 6 7 8 9 10	1 2 3 4 5 6 7 8 9 10	1 2 3 4 5 6 7 8 9 10	1 2 3 4 5 6 7 8 9 10	1 2 3 4 5 6 7 8 9 10
Gesture	1 2 3 4 5 6 7 8 9 10	1 2 3 4 5 6 7 8 9 10	1 2 3 4 5 6 7 8 9 10	1 2 3 4 5 6 7 8 9 10	1 2 3 4 5 6 7 8 9 10
Partial physical	1 2 3 4 5 6 7 8 9 10	1 2 3 4 5 6 7 8 9 10	1 2 3 4 5 6 7 8 9 10	1 2 3 4 5 6 7 8 9 10	1 2 3 4 5 6 7 8 9 10
Full physical	1 2 3 4 5 6 7 8 9 10	1 2 3 4 5 6 7 8 9 10	1 2 3 4 5 6 7 8 9 10	1 2 3 4 5 6 7 8 9 10	1 2 3 4 5 6 7 8 9 10

Date _4-18_

Time start/stop _9:15-9:30_

Task/step _4_

Cue(s) _"Hand me" array =_ _Cup_
Spoon
Dish
Fork

Criterion _8/10 Trials_

Observation
Comments

FIGURE 5.10 Data collection form for controlled presentations. (From *Applied behavior analysis for teachers*, by P. A. Alberto and A. C. Troutman, 1999, p. 115. Columbus, OH: Merrill, an imprint of Prentice-Hall. Copyright 1999, 1995 by Prentice-Hall, Inc. Reprinted with permission.)

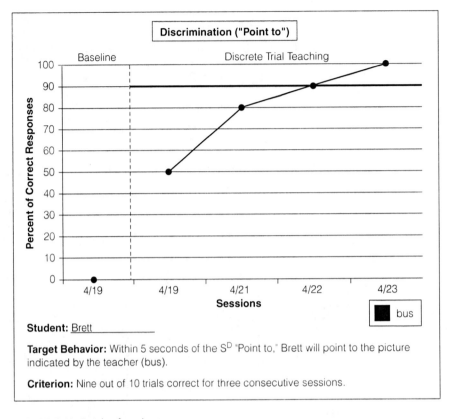

Discrimination ("Point to")

Baseline   Discrete Trial Teaching

Student: Brett

Target Behavior: Within 5 seconds of the S^D "Point to," Brett will point to the picture indicated by the teacher (bus).

Criterion: Nine out of 10 trials correct for three consecutive sessions.

FIGURE 5.11 Graph of student progress.

dent meets criterion on that particular step or task. It is best used for specific skill training at the initial stages of learning (i.e., acquisition and fluency). It may not, however, be an appropriate way of teaching to generalization in naturalized settings. Imagine learning to play tennis. For basic skills such as holding the racket, forehand/backhand swings, and serving, repetitious trials and practice (one-to-one) may be required. As the skills are acquired, however, and it is time to apply them in game situations, the coach uses a different type of instruction (incidental teaching, delayed feedback, corrective prompts/models). This is also true for teaching skills to students with autism and related disorders. Apply the discrete trial format for those skills needing an intensive, highly structured approach, but avoid using only discrete trial training because students might fail to generalize their learning and reach independence.

ADDITIONAL STRATEGIES FOR TEACHING SKILLS

Additional instructional strategies that are recommended for teaching students with severe disabilities can also be applied to students with autism and related disorders. These strategies, **shaping, chaining, generalization training,** and **milieu teaching,** are also based in applied behavior analysis. Shaping is essentially a reinforcement strategy. Chaining is a method for combining several response steps into a complex behavior. Generalization training methods are utilized when students need to learn to apply skills under a variety of conditions and to maintain skills over time, while a related technique, milieu teaching, refers to the process of instructing skills within a natural context based on student initiations and interest.

Shaping

Shaping is a procedure whereby the teacher systematically reinforces successive approximations toward a specific behavioral response. Beginning with behaviors that the student already performs, the teacher would reinforce slight changes in those behaviors as long as they more closely resemble a targeted response. At the same time, no reinforcement would be given for behaviors that do not move the student closer to the designated target. Shaping can be used for teaching various behaviors, particularly those that are difficult to prompt, such as articulation. For example, in teaching a student to say "mama," reinforce her for making any sound whatsoever, then reinforce for "mmm" sounds (and not for other sounds), then reinforce for a "ma" sound (but no longer for just "mmmmm" sounds), then reinforce for "mama" (and never again for "mmmmm" or "ma"). Shaping can also be used for other types of responses. For example, teach a student to compliment others by reinforcing his smiling at others, then smiling and saying "Nice," then smiling and saying "You're nice," then smiling and saying "You are a very nice person." Remember to always reinforce a behavior that more closely approximates the target behavior and do not reinforce a previous approximation once a more accurate one has been produced.

To implement a shaping procedure, the target behavior and successive steps toward that behavior must be operationally defined. Observe the student to determine which of those approximations are already being produced. In this way, the teacher will know where to begin reinforcing. Shaping is not an efficient technique by itself. The teacher may wait long periods of time for appropriate responses, and the student may go for long periods of time without reinforcement. Thus, it is often recommended that teachers apply prompting strategies, where possible, to the shaping procedures so that student and teacher motivation does not wane (Billingsley et al., 1994).

In terms of data collection, simply tally how many appropriate (unprompted and prompted) approximations occur per session or per day.

Transfer these responses onto a graph either as the total number of correct responses (e.g., the number of times the student said "mama" each day) or as a percentage of opportunities (e.g., the percentage of compliments during peer interactions).

Chaining

While shaping involves teaching one target behavior (e.g., saying "mama") through progressive approximations, chaining is a procedure for combining several distinct behaviors into a complex "chain" usually resulting in an activity or task (e.g., washing dishes, donning a jacket, proceeding through a cafeteria line). The first step in a chaining procedure is to conduct a task analysis for the task or activity. The task analysis provides a list of essential sub-behaviors required for mastery of the task or activity. Task analysis and chaining are often used to teach self-help, leisure, and vocational skills. You should ensure that the task analysis has resulted in sub-behaviors that can be attained by a particular student; otherwise, develop more steps with easier behaviors. Generally, the more steps produced in the task analysis, the more likely it is to apply to many different students.

Second, using the task analysis, assess whether a student can already perform any of the sub-behaviors (steps). The third step, once assessment is completed, is to begin directly teaching each step not currently mastered in the task analysis sequence. The sequence can be taught from step 1 to the last step **(forward chaining)** or from the last step to the first **(backward chaining).** For example, in teaching a student, Javier, how to write his name, the teacher could prompt and reinforce printing a "J" (step 1) and then physically guide the student through the other steps (letters). Step 2 (printing "a") would be taught when step 1 has been mastered (forward chaining). Alternately, the teacher could physically guide the student through all the steps until the last one (printing "r"). This last step would be prompted and reinforced and, when mastered (i.e., prompts are faded and the student is responding independently), the second to the last step would be taught (backward chaining).

Many self-help tasks are commonly taught using backward chaining (e.g., toothbrushing, dressing, tying shoes, opening and closing fasteners), as are certain basic academic skills (e.g., learning telephone number and address, writing letters and numbers). The repetition of steps and successful completion of the task provided by backward chaining seem to make this an effective strategy for such tasks. On the other hand, vocational and leisure skills may be best taught using forward chaining. For example, a student may learn to stuff envelopes by first collating papers, then collating and stapling, then collating, stapling, and folding, then collating, stapling, folding, and inserting into an envelope, and so forth. Or a student may learn to swim by blowing bubbles under water, then floating on her stomach, then floating and kicking her legs, etc. Choose either forward or backward chaining based on which sequence might be easiest to learn for a given student, and most logical given the nature of the task.

Some tasks are impossible or illogical to teach using forward or backward chaining. For example, it would be difficult to teach a student how to dive off the side of the pool using forward or backward chaining because some of the steps in this task could not be prompted. Likewise, it would make little sense to teach a student to go through the cafeteria line by having him first pick up his tray, but nothing else, then pick up his tray and silverware, but nothing else (that is, the teacher would then complete the task). For these tasks, we recommend another form of chaining, **total task presentation.** Like other forms of chaining, this type of chaining includes discriminative stimuli, prompts (if possible), and consequences. Total task presentation differs from forward and backward chaining in two ways. First, all steps in the sequence are performed by the student every time the task is presented. Second, partial prompts or verbal prompts are typically the only type of prompts that can be used, because the nature of the tasks precludes full physical prompts. Thus, the student would perform each step in diving off the side of the pool (stand with feet together and arms together over-

head, bend knees, lower chin, hold breath, push off in an outward and downward motion, keep form intact throughout dive) given only verbal prompts after the initial cue. Similarly, a student would learn to go through the cafeteria line by performing each step given only verbal or partial physical prompts.

For total task presentation, a data sheet should reflect notations for each step. Although mastery is indicated when all the steps are performed independently and correctly, progress can be noted as more steps are mastered or require less assistance. Again, it is wise to include some indicator of prompted steps and the types of prompts needed to ensure correct responses. Figure 5.12 illustrates a data collection form for a total task presentation. This data sheet also shows the type of prompt: gestural, verbal, or physical. A "+" indicates correct responding (unprompted) whereas a "−" indicates incorrect responding. This form also allows graphing. Percentages are provided in the column just to the right of the listed steps. Divide the number of unprompted correct responses ("+"s) by the total number of steps to be performed and multiply by 100 to find the percent of correct responses per day. Plot a point on this data sheet next to the correct percent for each day and connect the points to form a graph.

Eventually, each step in the behavior chain becomes an S^D for the next step and the student's behaviors are brought under control of the routine itself, thus not requiring teacher or parent directives. For example, when you get up in the morning, you may automatically (as a response to getting up) walk to the bathroom. After walking into the bathroom you may automatically (as a response to walking into the bathroom) pick up your toothbrush and reach for the toothpaste (as a response to holding your toothbrush) and so forth. In fact, many of our behaviors under such stimulus control happen with such little thought, we often do not remember if we performed them or not. Table 5.4 provides some sample complex tasks and activities that might best be taught with one of the techniques of forward chaining, backward chaining, or total task presentation.

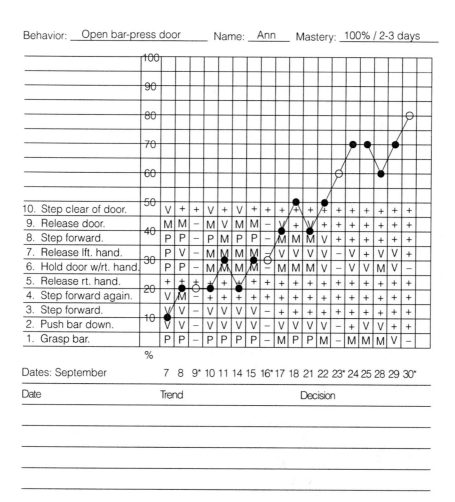

FIGURE 5.12 Total task presentation data form. (From *Assessment of individuals with severe disabilities: An applied behavior approach to life skills assessment* (2nd ed.), by D. M. Browder, 1991, p. 115. Baltimore, MD: Paul H. Brookes Publishing Co. Copyright 1991 by Paul H. Brookes Publishing Co. Reprinted with permission.)

In the case of individuals with autism and related disorders, teaching them a particular behavior chain will probably not be difficult. The difficulty will occur when some step in the chain cannot be performed or is interrupted (e.g., there is no toothpaste in the bathroom). In this case, many students with autism will just stop at that step in the sequence, failing to complete the rest of their grooming routine. The next two strategies are designed to address such an occurrence and involve loosening stimulus control.

Generalization Training

The concept of generalization (defined and discussed in Chapter 4) refers to the ability of an individual to apply skills and knowledge under various conditions and to adapt one's behavior

Table 5.4 Sample Skills Taught through Chaining Techniques

Forward Chaining

- Learning parts of a complex game (e.g., kickball, races)
- Most complex gross motor tasks (e.g., dribbling a ball, jumping rope, swimming)
- Reading tasks (e.g., reading letters, words, sentences)
- Writing name, address, etc.
- Increasing time on-task
- Increasing complexity of a task (e.g., complete a three-piece puzzle, then a four-piece puzzle, then a five-piece puzzle)

Backward Chaining

- Most self-help tasks (e.g., dressing and undressing, brushing teeth, washing hair)
- Verbalizing personal information (e.g., name, address, birth date, telephone number)
- Walking to destinations independently
- Rote memory tasks (e.g., counting, saying days of the week)

Total Task Presentation

- Many cooking tasks (e.g., making coffee, toast, a sandwich)
- Moving through line (e.g., cafeteria, fast food restaurant, theater)
- Many leisure activities (e.g., bowling, playing "Old Maid")

accordingly. Generalization is one of the most difficult things to teach students with autism. For most children, generalization occurs as a function of their ability to transfer their learning, attend to various types of models, and to distinguish similarities among social cues and situations. However, students with autism, who have complex attending difficulties, usually need deliberate instruction for generalization to occur. In 1977, Stokes and Baer presented several specific techniques for programming for the generalization of behavior. Table 5.5 summarizes those techniques. We recommend that teachers use these techniques to ensure that functional skills reach maintenance and generalization.

To address generalization, consider altering the antecedents, the required student responses, and the consequences. For example, vary the conditions under which a student should emit a behavior. Vary those who give instructions, the number of students in the classroom or a group, the tone of voice, and the S^D itself. Use different materials (three types of shoes, socks, coffeepots, toasters, etc.). Also require the student to give similar but different responses, especially language responses. Rather than reinforce rote production of a phrase or sentence (e.g., "How are you today?"), require the student to say it differently (e.g., "How are you doing, Carl?"). Finally, vary the reinforce-

ment schedule and fade to natural consequences. To do this, the student may need to be taught to recognize various types of reinforcers (head nods, smiles, winks) as positive feedback. For planning purposes, we recommend (1) identifying goals and objectives at the maintenance and generalization level, (2) monitoring student behavior under natural conditions, and (3) using graphs to communicate progress.

Failing to teach to generalization can have dire effects. Students may never attain independent living and/or working skills; the same goals and objectives may appear year after year on an IEP because skills learned in the classroom do not transfer to other school environments or home; or students may be compelled to remain in segregated settings because they cannot display appropriate behavior under integrated conditions. School personnel who do not aim for the generalization and maintenance of treatment gains for all their students are doing them a disservice.

Billingsley et al. (1994) recommend that teachers choose specific generalization training techniques based on particular student problems. For example, if a student fails to emit a response in a generalized setting, then teachers might try providing familiar S^D's in the new environment. Teachers should also provide prompts and cues in

Table 5.5 Generalization Training Strategies

1. *Sequential modification.* Implement a program that was successful in one setting in a different setting. For example, have parents reinforce communication responses at home (Lovaas, Koegel, Simmons, & Long, 1973). This is the most time-consuming technique. May need to provide cues (S^Ds) in the second environment (e.g., picture schedules, routines, recorded messages).

2. *Introduce natural reinforcers.* Teach students functional skills that will entrap natural reinforcers (e.g., asking for a stim-toy or something to eat, smiling, making eye contact, compliance). Also teach students to recognize natural reinforcers (a hug) as something positive. Need to determine age-appropriate skills that receive reinforcers in a particular setting and attempt to get others in that environment to provide high-frequency reinforcement at first.

3. *General case programming.* Known as loosening stimulus control, teach using many relevant examples (S^Ds). Once a response is learned to one S^D, begin to vary them so that the same response can be practiced in response to many S^Ds. For example, change the commands, the people giving the commands, the materials used, the setting, and so forth. In this way, the students do not remain stimulus bound. Vary the reinforcers. Also teach different versions of the same behavior. Milieu teaching is a procedure for varying routines, cues, sequences, and providing less structure.

4. *Use indiscriminable contingencies.* Thin reinforcement to intermittent schedules. This technique promotes the maintenance of behavior by providing unpredictable schedules of reinforcement (the slot machine schedule). Provide reinforcement for classes of behavior rather than specific behaviors (e.g., "You did a nice job at lunch").

5. *Program common stimuli.* Make settings more alike. Make the training classroom more like the general education classroom by adding more students, changing the classroom arrangement, and so forth. Or make the classroom more like the kitchen at home. Also introduce into the second setting something familiar from the first setting (e.g., the student's favorite chair) (e.g., Koegel & Rincover, 1974).

6. *Mediate generalization.* Teach students to monitor their own generalized behavior through self-recording or self-evaluation. Students can be taught to record each time that they finish a certain task, no matter where the task is to be performed. The recorded responses are then reinforced.

7. *Train to generalize.* Provide reinforcers for generalized behavior. A student can receive reinforcers for displaying a learned behavior in a different environment or under different conditions. This would be true for prompted or unprompted behavior.

From Stokes and Baer, 1977.

the generalized setting. For example, peers might be taught to prompt correct responses on the playground or in the cafeteria. Sometimes, the student herself might be taught to use picture prompts kept in a wallet to cue correct behaviors in generalized settings.

Sometimes a behavior is performed under conditions where it should not be performed (e.g., reaching for food in the cafeteria line because he was taught to self-serve at the salad bar). In this case, the teacher may need to spend time teaching when *not* to give that particular response. Sometimes inappropriate behaviors occur as a function of incorrect reinforcement strategies (i.e., inappropriate behaviors are reinforced and appropriate behaviors are not). For example, a student who puts his face in his plate of pasta at the restaurant is sent to the car for time-out (supposedly a punishment), where he self-stimulates (a reinforcer). A better procedure would be to deliver a favorite stim-toy contingent on sitting and eating properly. See Chapter 3 for more specific reductive techniques. If a student demonstrates a generalized behavior once but not again, then the problem may be one of maintenance. In this case, more frequent reinforcement should be delivered in the generalized setting. In some instances the student can be taught to give himself reinforcers through self-monitoring or to elicit reinforcers by asking questions such as "Didn't I do a good job on this?" (i.e., training natural contingencies of reinforcement).

Assessing for generalization differs from assessing skill acquisition and fluency. For generalization, we are interested in noting whether a student responds appropriately (or *inappropriately*) under a variety of conditions (White, 1988). Thus, the student must have an opportunity to respond in many situations. Each situation should be described on the data sheet. We are also interested only in unprompted first-time responses. Once someone emits a response, natural prompts and consequences may occur. In this case, subsequent responding is not a true measure of generalization. Generalization data should only reflect one entry per situation. The important thing to remember about generalization training is that when students are learning new behaviors, we usually recommend bringing them under stimulus control. That is, teach the students to respond certain ways to certain commands, materials, or settings. At first it is important to keep conditions fairly consistent until the student is regularly responding correctly. At some point, however, the teacher needs to systematically loosen stimulus control (general case programming) so that the student will be able to function under many conditions. Students with autism will need much support to make these changes. One teaching method that facilitates generalization utilizing several of the aforementioned techniques is milieu teaching.

Milieu Teaching

Very often, even when the teacher has not planned for it, a generalized response might be needed (e.g., a situation where the toothpaste is missing, a student sees something that he wants, a choice is to be made at the park, the bus is late). These are perfect situations to instigate milieu teaching (Kaiser, 1993). Milieu teaching involves taking advantage of a naturally occurring teaching opportunity (although it can also occur in situations staged by the teacher). According to Kaiser (1993), milieu teaching procedures are (1) short positive interactions, (2) administered in the setting in which the behavior naturally occurs, (3) used to teach a functional skill, and (4) guided by the student's interest in the task.

Milieu teaching involves four basic procedures that may be used individually or in combination:

(1) modeling desired responses and correcting responses, (2) providing an instruction (**mand**) and then modeling/correcting if necessary, (3) **time delay,** and (4) **incidental teaching.** Modeling, as in discrete trial training, refers to the process of providing a verbal or visual prompt to facilitate the behavior the student needs to perform. With milieu teaching, however, the teacher does not provide the S^D: it occurs naturally.

For example, while outside on the playground, a student tugs on the teacher's sleeve and looks at the swing (S^D). The teacher, noting the student's desire to swing, gains the student's attention and provides the verbal prompt for what she wants the student to say ("Want swing"). The student may respond by pointing. In this case the teacher provides a corrective model, "Want swing." The student says "Want swing." The teacher then reinforces this response with praise and expanded language ("Good talking. You want to swing. Go ahead and get on the swing") and the natural consequence of allowing him to swing. If the student does not respond correctly after the second model, provide another corrective model and award the desired activity regardless of the student's response. To keep the interaction natural, avoid excessive demands for correct responses before allowing the student to obtain the object/activity of his interest. The purpose of milieu teaching is to insert prompts and instructions into natural situations to promote responding without distracting from the natural context (i.e., during recess the students are typically allowed to swing without requesting it first).

The second type of milieu teaching procedure, mand-model, involves giving a direct instruction (mand) within natural contexts when the student is interested in responding, followed by a model if necessary (Kaiser, 1993). For example, a student is given Jell-O for lunch and reaches to pick it up with her hands. The teacher blocks her hands, gains the child's attention, and says "Use your spoon" (mand), places the spoon in the student's hand, and physically guides her through the initial bite (corrective model). If the student continues to eat with the spoon, the teacher should praise the student ("Good, you are eating with a spoon. I bet that Jell-O is good"). If the student puts the spoon down and reaches for the Jell-O again, the teacher should provide another instruction and a corrective model. A correct behavior receives praise plus uninterrupted Jell-O eating. An incorrect response may require instructions and physical guidance for the remainder of the eating procedure. The mand-model procedure provides more prompting than the model procedure alone, so it should only be used when modeling alone does not elicit correct responding.

Time delay (Kaiser, 1993) is a procedure whereby the teacher waits 5 to 15 seconds for a student-initiated response after a stimulus has occurred. If the student does not respond, the teacher provides a mand-model. The purpose of a time delay is to decrease the student's dependence on teacher instructions and models and to encourage the student to act independently. For example, a student has donned his jacket but needs help with his zipper. The teacher, aware that the student will need assistance, waits for a request for help. If the student says, signs, or points to the zipper (depending on his communication abilities), the teacher gives immediate praise, a correct model, "You want help with your zipper," and provides assistance. If the student does not initiate a response within about 15 seconds, the teacher can then provide a mand-model procedure. However, with a time delay procedure, the teacher runs the risk of losing student interest. Thus, the teacher should wait only as long as a student will tolerate while still remaining interested in the material/activity.

Incidental teaching incorporates the other three procedures but is only applied during situations when a student is verbally or non-verbally making a request (Kaiser, 1993). The teacher can stimulate such situations (e.g., not giving a student his milk with the cookie snack) or just be aware of those naturally occurring situations when a student may want something and not be able to get it independently. Request situations are very important opportunities for teaching new skills, promoting fluency, and expanding skills because students are motivated to perform under these conditions. The teacher, after noticing that the

student wants something, should apply modeling, mand-modeling, or time delay procedures in order to teach the student appropriate ways of getting what she wants.

Remember that students with autism typically do not want many things, except time to engage in self-stimulation. Thus, it is important that teachers become aware of desired objects/activities/situations for particular students and apply incidental teaching techniques under those conditions. It is also important for teachers to refrain from preempting requesting behavior by anticipating student needs and providing desired items or activities without requiring the student to request them (Westling & Fox, 1995).

When natural request situations are infrequent, teachers can create them. For example, a teacher may hide the toothpaste for the purpose of stimulating a request response. When the student, brushing his teeth after lunch, comes to the step requiring him to obtain the toothpaste, the teacher could model asking for some toothpaste (e.g., "I need some toothpaste, please"). Or the teacher could time delay, waiting until the student looks at the teacher and holds up his toothbrush, before prompting the language response. If the student still does not make a request appropriately, the teacher could say "Tell me what you want" (mand). Say "Want toothpaste" (model). A correct response should be followed by praise, a correct model, and the natural consequence of obtaining the desired object/activity. You will learn more about stimulating language and communication through environmental manipulation and milieu teaching in Chapter 6.

Milieu teaching requires data that reflect not only the various situations in which a student responded but also which teaching procedures were used or whether the student emitted a generalized response where no teaching procedures were used. Kaiser (1993) recommends using the data collection form in Figure 5.13 in addition to notes about specific situations and responses. This form provides a format to gather data about three students for three targeted behaviors each. In this example, the targeted behaviors are language

Student	Michael		Student	Kristie		Student	Caryn	
Setting	Times	Prompts/Conseq.	Setting	Times	Prompts/Conseq.	Setting	Times	Prompts/Conseq.
TARGET 1 want + noun			**TARGET 1** photo + label			**TARGET 1** two words		
breakfast	//	S,TD	breakfast	///	MQ,MQ,MQ	group	/	S/T
group	/	MQ	sm. grp.	/	MT	math	/	TD
TARGET 2 new noun labels			**TARGET 2** request assistance			**TARGET 2** action verbs		
math	/	M	arrival	/	S/T	group	/	M/T
hall	/	M	departure	/	S/T	self-help	/	M/T
transition								
bus	/	M/T(peer)				transition	/	M/T
TARGET 3			**TARGET 3**			**TARGET 3** req. assistance "help please"		
						breakfast	/	MQ/T
						self-help	/	TD/T

Setting: Specify activity when response occurred
Times: Use slash for each occurrence
Prompts: (Record one symbol for each occurrence): M = Model, S = Spontaneous,
T = Acknowledged by adult or peer, MQ = Mand or question, TD = Time delay

FIGURE 5.13 Milieu teaching data form. (From "Functional Language" by A. P. Kaiser, p. 354. In *Instruction of students with severe disabilities,* by M. E. Snell (Ed.), © 1993. Reprinted by permission of Prentice-Hall, Inc., Upper Saddle River, NJ.)

responses. Data consist of a notation of the situation, tallies of the target responses, and codes that indicate which milieu teaching procedure was utilized. Those marked "S" for spontaneous could be graphed by day to visually indicate progress over time. It is important to gather data when using milieu teaching to avoid the continued use of ineffective teaching strategies and the haphazard application of the procedures.

Notice that milieu teaching involves the application of applied behavior analysis in natural settings (e.g., Hart & Rogers-Warren, 1978). Both discrete trial teaching and milieu teaching include a stimulus (S^D), prompts and models, student responses, and consequences. The difference is that in discrete trial training, the teacher presents the S^D, and the consequences are often not directly related to the student's behavior (e.g., pats, hugs, food for counting to 10). Furthermore, several trials may be repeated at one time (massed trials) in order for students to acquire or become fluent at a specific skill. In milieu teaching, the environment naturally contains the stimulus (e.g., the light is off and it is dark), and the consequence is naturally related to the student's behavior (e.g., the light comes on when the student flips the switch). Milieu teaching does not typically include massed training trials, but rather the teacher must take advantage of naturally occurring situations or simulated situations in which responses can be extended and practiced across settings (i.e., the toothpaste example). In both teaching procedures, however, the teacher gives various types of prompts to ensure correct responding and strives for unprompted, independent functioning. Furthermore, in both types of teaching, it is important to chart and communicate student progress.

Grouping

One-to-one instruction is often recommended for students with autism because it provides undivided teacher attention and fewer distracting stimuli (Rotholz, 1990). However, students should eventually be able to learn new skills in small group situations. Grouping procedures allow for the teacher to decrease prompt dependency, loosen stimulus control, and promote generalization. Few, if any, adult work or living situations will afford a one-to-one instructional situation. So, if long-term goals for individual students include independent living and working, then students must be taught to work and function with others present. Furthermore, group arrangements are common to general education classrooms, if inclusion is of concern. Additionally, grouping students with autism with peers offer opportunities for interaction and modeling (Kamps et al., 1991). Group instruction is also more efficient than one-to-one instruction allowing teachers to provide more response opportunities and teacher-directed interactions rather than having students work by themselves as the teacher engages in one-to-one instruction with others.

Reid and Favell (1984) describe three general models of group instruction: (1) **sequential,** (2) **concurrent,** and (3) **tandem.** Sequential group instruction involves the teacher briefly

teaching each student individually while sitting in a group with others either watching or engaging in their own independent tasks. The students may be working on the same or similar objectives or very different ones. For example, three students may be sitting on one side of a curved table. The teacher, using DTF, instructs one to "Point to nose." The student does it and receives an edible reinforcer. The next student is asked to say "I want cereal," whereupon he receives a Fruit Loop. The third student is given a puzzle and told to complete it. The teacher then moves back the first student and so on. Students learn to wait their turn, work independently for short periods of time, and to attend to teacher cues with more distracters present. Figure 5.14 provides a sample of large group instruction activities where each student is working on individual objectives.

Large group lesson: all students with teacher

Student A

1. Read food names.
2. Match names to pictures.
3. Complete worksheet matching names.

Student B

1. Read food name.
2. Trace food name.
3. Identify by category: vegetable, fruit, etc.

Student C

1. Identify food name.
2. Identify letters of food name.
3. Sitting and hands down.

Student D

1. Identify food name.
2. Point to letters in left-to-right sequence while spelling.
3. Sitting behavior.

Student E

1. Point to picture.
2. Verbalize food name with model.
3. Verbalize food name without model.
4. Point to picture among selection.

FIGURE 5.14 Large group lesson activities. (From *Educational strategies for autistic children/youth: Autism teacher training program,* 1982, p. 333. Kansas City, KS: Department of Special Education, University of Kansas Press. Reprinted by permission.)

The concurrent group model uses procedures whereby the teacher instructs the entire group interspersed with individual responding. For example, the teacher may have the entire group imitate motor skills (e.g., hands up, hands out, tongue out) or social skills (e.g., shake hands, smile at me). If one student does not smile, the teacher can engage in one-to-one instruction with that student while the others continue to practice smiling at each other or shaking hands. The tandem model begins with one-to-one instruction and systematically expands to include more students. As more students are added, each needs to learn to work on a thinner reinforcement schedule, to remain seated, and to attend with more distracting stimuli. Koegel

and Rincover (1974) demonstrated that effective instruction could occur with up to eight children with autism in a group using the tandem model.

Continue to record student responses during group instruction. Collect data on each student's responses when giving individual cues or group cues. Data sheets might include the number of students in the group so that correct responding within groups can be evaluated. Figure 5.15 is a sample data collection sheet for sequential group organization. This data sheet could be adapted for concurrent and tandem group structures.

We recommend beginning instruction with a one-to-one procedure until attending and compliance skills are mastered. Then teach the student to

Date											
Student A											
Give 1–5 pennies											
Identify penny											
Identify nickel											
Student B											
Give 5–10 pennies											
Identify nickel											
Identify dime											
Student C											
Counts one object											
Counts two objects											
Counts three objects											
Student D											
Counts one object											
Counts two objects											
Counts three objects											

FIGURE 5.15 Group lesson data sheet. (From *Educational strategies for autistic children/youth: Autism teacher training program*, 1982, p. 333. Kansas City, KS: Department of Special Education, University of Kansas Press. Reprinted by permission.)

wait longer between trials, work for intermittent reinforcement, and emit multiple behaviors in response to one cue. At this point any of the aforementioned group formats may be introduced. Remember that students who can only work one-to-one with an adult and who never learn to work in group situations are not likely to be successful in integrated school or community settings.

Note that group instruction may have a few drawbacks. For example, teachers may find it more difficult to manage a group of students and to plan instruction for students of varying ability levels. It may also be more difficult for the students to attend to instruction with more noise, movement, and verbal interaction present. However, the benefits of group instruction in terms of generalization and integration are worth the effort. Related

to grouping is the procedure of **peer tutoring.** Same-age peers from general education classrooms have used modeling and reinforcement to teach students with autism and related disorders social skills, discrimination skills, matching, signing, prevocational skills, preacademic skills, and sight word identification (Rotholz, 1990). Chapter 7 discusses peer tutoring with regard to increasing social behavior.

In the preceding sections we have presented several instructional strategies for use with students with autism. These strategies are based on the assumption that providing structure and order will enhance the likelihood that students with autism will respond to the environment and learn new skills. Table 5.6 summarizes many of our suggestions. Structure correspondingly increases with

Table 5.6 Suggestions for Providing Structure in Learning Situations

Physical Arrangement

- Match the curriculum to the physical arrangement.
- Use visually clear boundaries.
- Make relevant stimuli salient (use color, shape, etc., matching).
- Arrange for group and/or one-to-one instruction.
- Mask interfering stimuli (auditory and visual).
- Arrange to prevent problem behaviors.
- Arrange convenient materials access and storage.
- Arrange to facilitate toileting.
- Include a transition area and "wait" chairs.
- Maximize comfort (size, lighting, temperature, traffic flow).
- Avoid rearranging the classroom once cues are learned.

Routines and schedules

- Establish routine for entering/leaving classroom.
- Establish routine for choosing activities.
- Establish routine for starting and completing activities.
- Establish routine for waiting.
- Establish routine for predicting times to work and play.
- Establish routine for toileting and eating.
- Establish routine for changing activities.
- Establish a classroom schedule.
- Establish individual schedules using visual guidance.

Structured Lessons

- Use trial-by-trial and milieu teaching for skill acquisition and fluency.
- Use generalization training to promote maintenance and generalization.
- Provide prompts and fade them systematically.
- Keep students engaged in learning activities 80 percent of the school day.
- Utilize group instruction as students progress.
- Collect and graph response data.
- Regularly evaluate learner progress.
- Construct detailed lesson plans.
- Maintain progress records/notebooks.
- Engage in self-evaluation.

the number of these suggestions that are implemented. Use more structure initially then move to natural classroom, community, and work conditions. Be aware, though, that many students with autism may never learn to work in unpredictable situations and may always be dependent on others bringing order to their world.

PLANS AND REPORTS

Essential to applied behavior analysis is planning and accountability. Once a teacher has made decisions about what to teach and how to teach it, the next step is to develop a written plan. Typical lesson plans in general education classrooms consist of a few notes about which activities students are to perform that day. However, when teaching students with autism, extreme care should be taken to specify each piece of the instructional process. Lesson plans should generally include (1) the goal/objective, (2) specific information about the conditions for responding (e.g., which S^D will be presented, which setting, which prompt system), (3) types of reinforcers and the reinforcement schedule, (4) mastery criteria (include baseline information), and (5) evaluation methods (e.g., probe technique, recording technique). Donellan et al. (1976) developed a lesson plan format directly related to discrete trial teaching. A sample lesson plan in this format is provided in Figure 5.16.

This particular lesson plan indicates that Brett is to master pointing to a picture of a bus when the teacher gives the S^D "Point to bus." Included on this lesson plan form are the dates for skill introduction and mastery, the procedures for gathering a baseline count and for probing for mastery, the prompt system and steps for fading the prompts, the reinforcement schedule and the type of reinforcer, the mastery criteria (as well as the criteria for failure), and the particular data recording strategy. Consistency across trainers and across time can be better ensured by specifying each component of the discrete trial format and the accountability system. Other lesson plans (e.g., Simpson & Regan, 1988) are not necessarily in a

discrete trial format but typically provide columns for expected behavioral responses, intervention procedures (teaching strategies and prompting system), consequences, mastery criteria, and special considerations. Regardless of the format utilized, it is generally believed that providing specific information about antecedents, expected responses, and types of consequences will cue teachers to remain consistent in their lesson presentation and to communicate exactly what is occurring during the teaching procedure.

Accountability (i.e., whether a student is learning what is being taught) is provided through formative assessment procedures such as data collection and graphing. Unfortunately, many teachers gather data relative to student progress but never present the data in a way that others can understand and evaluate. Some teachers may not systematically assess progress at all. Formative assessment is a key component of effective instruction and applied behavior analysis and should be incorporated into the daily instructional routine.

We have recommended various methods for gathering data and for graphing the results. To facilitate this type of record keeping, we also recommend that assessment information, lesson plans, and graphs be maintained in a notebook for each student. The first section of this notebook, entitled "Comprehensive Assessment," might contain all initial assessment information pertinent to what is to be taught (e.g., curriculum-based assessments, ecological inventories, adaptive behavior checklists). The comprehensive assessment section could be followed by separate sections for each designated curricular area or domain (e.g., language, self-help, leisure, social skills, prevocational skills).

In each of these curricular sections are the lesson plan(s) for particular skills, a graph depicting baseline performance and progress toward mastery, and any additional work samples or assessment information. A final section might be labeled "Behavioral Excesses." In this section, include a description of the targeted excesses, the functional assessment results and interpretation, a behavior management plan, and baseline/intervention graphs. This section might also include a list of

Discrete trial training lesson plan

Student: *Brett*

Date Introduced: *4-19-01*

Date Mastered: _____

Baseline Procedures: Present S^D "Point to" 3 times (bus). Calculate percentage of correct responses.

Probing Procedures: Present S^D "Point to" without prompt after every step of prompt fading procedure, within one program step. Change position of target picture after every other trial.

Target Behavior	Step	S^D	Response	Consequences & Schedules	Criterion	Data Recording Method
Within 5 secs. of the presentation of S^D "Point to," Brett will point to the picture indicated by the teacher (bus).	1.	Teacher places two pictures on table (train and bus) and says "point to bus."				Trial-by-trial: X = correct O = incorrect XP = correct prompted OP = incorrect prompted
	a.	Prompt: Physically take Brett's hand and point to correct picture.	Brett points to picture of train.	Correct: "Good job!!" plus primary (popcorn, soda, pieces of chocolate, etc.) 100%	Mastery: 9 out of 10 trials correct for 3 consecutive sessions. Fail: 3 consecutive incorrect responses.	
	b.	Prompt: Wait to see if Brett makes move to point, then provide light taps to arm until he points to picture.	Same as above	Same as above	Same as above	Same as above
	c.	Prompt: Wait to see if Brett makes move to point, then teacher gestures toward pictures on table.	Same as above	Same as above	Same as above	Same as above
	d.	No prompt	Same as above	Same as above	Same as above	Same as above

FIGURE 5.16 Discrete trial training lesson plan. (Adapted from *Teaching makes a difference: A guide for developing successful classes for autistic and other severely handicapped children,* by A. Donnellan, L. D. Gossage, G. W. LaVigna, A. Schuler, & J. D. Traphagen, 1976, p. 56. Santa Barbara, CA: Santa Barbara Public Schools. Copyright 1976 Santa Barbara Public Schools. Adapted by permission.)

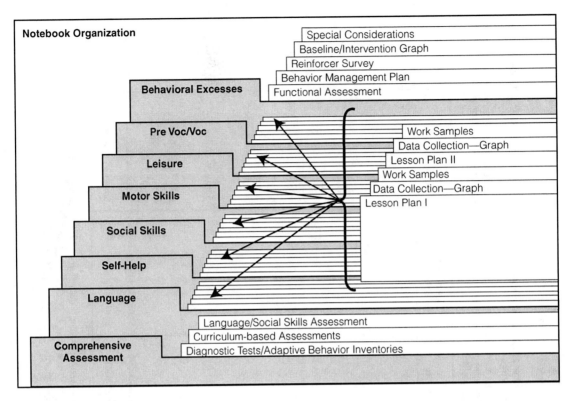

FIGURE 5.17 Sample notebook content.

effective reinforcers and notes about special considerations (e.g., avoid time-out in a closed room because it promotes extreme anxiety in this particular student). Figure 5.17 provides a drawing of sample content in a notebook. Keeping such precise information about skill attainment promotes effective communication, collaboration, and accountability.

EVALUATING TEACHING STRATEGIES

In Chapters 2 through 5 we suggested various ways for teachers to develop curriculum and instruct students. Good teachers master a variety of techniques and strategies, formulating a "toolbox" from which to choose what is best for an individual student at any given instructional point. This toolbox includes curriculum decisions and pedagogical applications for managing student behavior, structuring the classroom environment, and delivering instruction. It also includes formative assessment methods so that teachers know whether or not to use different tools in the future. We encourage teachers to regularly evaluate themselves in terms of their proficiency in utilizing the best teaching practices. We have provided a teacher self-monitoring form (Figure 5.18) to facilitate this self-evaluation process. This form can be adapted to include additional instructional strategies and procedures. We recommend that teachers rate themselves and paraprofessionals working in their classroom for a few days each month to ensure that all aspects of effective instruction are regularly applied. If teacher behavior reflects best practices, students are more likely to continue to learn and master necessary skills.

Place a check beside the behavior that was performed each day. Decide whether you are teaching what the students need to learn and whether you are using effective instructional strategies.

Teacher Behavior			Days		
	M	T	W	TH	F
1. I/we taught my students only things that are relevant to each one's short-term, intermediate, and long-term objectives.					
2. I/we taught communication skills at every possible opportunity.					
3. I/we targeted skills that will result in reinforcers for the students.					
4. I/we prompted effectively and only when necessary, encouraging independence whenever possible.					
5. I/we taught in generalized settings whenever possible.					
6. My students were engaged in relevant *learning* activities for 80 percent of the day.					
7. I used age-appropriate instructional materials adapted for independent use.					
8. My classroom was arranged to encourage independent functioning (schedules/ materials available/etc.).					
9. I provided opportunities for my students to interact with nondisabled students.					
10. I provided one-to-one trial-by-trial training for skill acquisition and fluency.					
11. I taught students in small groups when appropriate.					
12. All adults who are working with my students are familiar with the objectives and administer consistent antecedent stimuli and consequences.					
13. I/we systematically reinforced: —independent communication —correct responding —following directions —other:					
14. I/we did not reinforce inappropriate behavior.					
15. I/we used punishment ____ times.					
16. I collected data (correct responses) on each objective taught today for ____ students.					
17. I have adjusted my curriculum and instructional strategies for tomorrow as necessary.					
18. I have shared the results of my day's evaluation/assessment with people who will be working with my students tomorrow.					
OTHER:					

FIGURE 5.18 Teacher self-monitoring checklist.

SUMMARY

In this chapter we have provided descriptions of a variety of strategies that might be utilized to teach students with autism and related neurological disorders. Teachers are encouraged to arrange a classroom environment to promote learning and to prevent problem behaviors. Research has shown that students with autism learn best under highly structured conditions. That is, their learning is best promoted by adding structure through physical arrangements, visual supports, schedules and routines, materials adaptation, low student–teacher ratios, trial-by-trial and milieu teaching, and by data collection and evaluation. High structure will facilitate skill acquisition and fluency. Lower structure can be applied for skill maintenance. Generalization is enhanced by various structured applications that are "loosened" over time.

Chapters 6, 7, and 8 will provide information about curriculum and instructional strategies pertaining specifically to communication, social, and life skills. It is our opinion that teaching students with autism and related disorders demands a great deal of technical knowledge and diligent attention. We encourage teachers to evaluate their own practices and their students' progress on a regular basis. Self-evaluation and a willingness to alter one's own behavior for the improvement of student learning lead to master teaching. We hope all students with autism encounter master teachers throughout their school careers. The vignette *Putting It All Together* provides a view of a classroom for students with autism and related disorders. See if you can identify the various methods for providing structure in the classroom.

Putting It All Together

Ms. Miller (teacher) and Ms. Rogers (paraprofessional) greet students at the door each morning. As students take off their jackets, put away backpacks, and so on, Ms. Miller and Ms. Rogers monitor students' performance on target skills for that activity. For example, Jason is working on taking off his jacket with no assistance; he is currently on the next to the last step in this backward-chaining task. Hodari is learning to put his jacket on a hanger (using forward chaining; today he is on step 2). Each student's data forms for these tasks are kept on a clipboard hanging next to the coat closet.

Next, students sit in a semicircle in front of the calendar and jobs chart. Both Ms. Miller and Ms. Rogers have students' data forms on clipboards on their lap. Each student has from one to three skills targeted for instruction during this time. As Ms. Miller directs the group, she and Ms. Rogers record data on student responses on the appropriate form. Sample skills addressed during this activity include:

- *Erica:* Greet peers using two different greetings (e.g., "Good morning, Jason." "Hi, Chris."); recite days of week; state name, address, telephone, and birth date.

- *Michael:* Sign current day, given cue "What day is this?"; respond to yes/no questions; refrain from hand-flapping for 15 consecutive minutes.

- *Chris:* Use complete sentences; recite months; state name, address, telephone, and birth date; refrain from verbal self-stimulation for duration of the group time.

- *Jason:* Make eye contact when teacher is talking to him; sign preferred choice for job (given two choices), sign response greeting when greeted by peer.

- *Hodari:* Keep hands to self (no pinching peers) for 15 consecutive minutes; remain in seat for 5 consecutive minutes; point to desired job, given choice pictures; respond to yes/no questions for "Is this. . .?" (e.g., "Is this a chair? Is this your leg? Is this Erica?").

After morning group, students pick up their independent activity folder or box, which is color-coded by student. They sit at their desks for a 20-minute period, working on independent activities (e.g., assembling puzzles, handwriting, using a calculator to add grocery prices, matching words to pictures). Ms. Rogers supervises students during this time, while Ms. Miller takes students one at a time to work on discrete trial tasks for 5 to 10 minutes each. She will work with two or three students during this time. At the end of the 20-minute work period, it is time for class jobs. Each adult works with two or three students, supervising their assigned chore. Afterwards it is time for bathroom, snack, and play. Again, each of these are times during which the teachers monitor students' performance on target skills using data forms (e.g., wash hands after toileting with no prompts; pour milk into cup; butter toast; play cooperatively with toy).

At the end of these activities, teachers again work with two or three students; one group works on additional self-care and/or daily living tasks, the other on language tasks. After approximately 20 minutes, the groups move to the other teacher. During these teaching activities, teachers record data on students' data forms for target skills such as these:

- *Erica:* Use curling iron, iron flat items, sew on button; carry on conversation with a minimum of four exchanges, tell simple jokes selected from joke book developed by teacher, use appropriate intonation during speech.

- *Michael:* Brush teeth for 3 consecutive minutes, tie shoe; respond to yes/no questions, respond to

"what" questions by signing name of pictured object or activity shown.

- *Chris:* Wash load of clothes, fold clothes, iron pullover shirts; carry on conversations with a minimum of 4 exchanges, tell simple jokes selected from joke book developed by teacher, use appropriate intonation during speech, refrain from asking questions about vacuum cleaners.

- *Jason:* Put on pullover shirt, put shoes on correct feet; comb hair, looking at image in mirror; sign names of objects given cue "What is this?"; sign names of familiar people.

- *Hodari:* Follow directions without falling to floor and giggling; put plates in dishwasher, put shoes on correct feet, brush teeth without playing in water; point to imitate signed names of pictured objects (household objects, clothing, and play objects).

It is then time to get ready for lunch: use bathroom, wash hands, get lunch money, and so forth. Erica, Chris, and Michael each go to different general education classes to join those groups for lunch and recess. In the cafeteria, the teachers are monitoring data as Jason and Hodari point to desired lunch items, carry trays, and clean up correctly. Several general education students serve as peer tutors during this time. These students have been taught how to initiate with Jason and Hodari, how to prompt them on appropriate behavior (eating, looking at peers, responding to peers' comments, etc.), and how to interrupt inappropriate behavior (e.g., self-stims, playing with food). The teachers sit close to, but separate from, the students.

In the afternoon, Erica and Chris remain in their general education classes for special area activities (library, art, music, P.E.). Jason, Chris, and Michael have P.E. (with the adaptive P.E. teacher), more discrete trial tasks with both teachers, and play time (each student is learning specific play skills; they are joined by trained general education peers during this time).

The last activity of the day is vocational class. Erica and Chris return to Ms. Miller's class for this. Students first punch their "time card" in the time clock, then pick up their vocational assignment folder (color-coded by student). Erica and Chris are given verbal instructions for their vocational task, as well as the pictured task sequence in the folder. Sample vocational tasks include these:

- *Erica and Chris:* Work in school office sorting and delivering mail, making copies for teachers, collating papers, and shredding papers. Two days each week, Erica, Chris, and Michael work with Ms. Miller on various community-based instruction activities (e.g., shopping, riding bus, using library).

- *Jason and Hordari:* Wash tables in cafeteria, pick up trash on school grounds, do two- to three-step assembly tasks in classroom (e.g., collate and staple papers).

- *Michael:* Sweep floor in cafeteria with push broom, sweep gym and stage floor, shred documents using shredder, do three- to five-step assembly tasks in classroom.

By then, the day is almost over. Students once again gather in the semicircle for closing group. During this time, Ms. Miller works on language tasks and writes notes home (asking each student what they did that day). Students are sent to get their backpacks one at a time during this time, as Ms. Rogers assists.

Of course, throughout the day, teachers are also attending to reinforcement plans, correcting inappropriate behavior, prompting appropriate behavior, insisting on communicative responses, taking advantage of milieu teaching, especially for problem solving, and so forth. In addition, students receive various related services such as speech and language therapy and occupational therapy. Needless to say, teaching students with autism is a multifaceted job that requires good organization and planning, the ability to implement and monitor multiple activities simultaneously, adherence to routine while being flexible enough to accommodate the unexpected, good collaborative skills, and a well-developed sense of humor.

KEY POINTS

1. Due to the nature of autism, students with this disorder are best taught in highly structured, predictable environments.

2. Teaching techniques based in ABA and cognitive theories provide that type of structure.

3. Careful physical arrangement of the classroom is one way to provide cues for expected student behavior. Arrangement should match the curriculum, prevent unwanted behavior, and provide for comfort and safety.

4. One of the most important ways to add structure to a classroom is through routines and schedules. Schedules can be for the entire class or for individuals.

5. Visual cues add support for students who typically do not attend to auditory stimuli. Visual supports are used in various ways to enhance instruction.

6. Materials can be constructed to communicate expectations and assist students in becoming more independent.

7. Discrete trial format (DTF) is an effective format for delivering instruction for new skills and skills that need drill and practice.

8. Generalization is a problem for students with autism. Teachers need to plan and use specific strategies to facilitate generalization.

9. Milieu teaching is a method of teaching that better ensures generalization and spontaneous responding.

10. It is important to teach students with autism to work in groups and in natural environments.

11. Formative assessment is an important component of applied behavior analysis and effective instruction. Data regarding student progress can be collected and graphed in any of several various ways. Planning and reporting are important teaching functions.

12. Teacher self-evaluation is encouraged because instructing students with autism demands so much technical expertise.

REFERENCES

Alberto, P. A., & Troutman, A. C. (1999). *Applied behavior analysis for teachers* (5th ed.). Columbus, OH: Merrill.

Billingsley, F. F., Liberty, K. A., & White, O. R. (1994). The technology of instruction. In E. C. Cipani & F. Spooner (Eds.), *Curricular and instructional approaches for persons with severe disabilities* (pp. 81–116). Needham Heights, MA: Allyn & Bacon.

Billingsley, F. F., & Romer, L. T. (1983). Response prompting and the transfer of stimulus control: Methods, research, and a conceptual framework. *The Journal of the Association for the Severely Handicapped, 8,* 3–12.

Courshesne, E. (1995). Infantile autism, Part 2: A new neurodevelopmental model. *International Pediatrics, 10,* 155.

Dalrymple, N. J. (1995). Environmental supports to develop flexibility and independence. In K. A. Quill (Ed.), *Teaching children with autism: Strategies to enhance communication and socialization.* New York: Delmar Publishers.

Donnellan, A., Gossage, L. D., LaVigna, G. W., Schuler, A., & Traphagen, J. D. (1976). *Teaching makes a difference: A guide for developing successful classes for autistic and other severely handicapped children.* Santa Barbara, CA: Santa Barbara Public Schools.

Frith, U. (1989). *Autism: Explaining the enigma.* Worcester, England: Billings.

Hart, B. M., & Rogers-Warren, A. K. (1978). Milieu teaching approaches. In R. L. Schiefelbusch (Ed.), *Bases of language intervention* (Vol. 2, pp. 193–235). Baltimore, MD: University Park Press.

Heflin, L. J., & Simpson, R. L. (1998). Interventions for children and youth with autism: Prudent choices in a world of exaggerated claims and empty promises. Part I: Intervention and treatment option review. *Focus on Autism and Other Developmental Disabilities, 13*(4), 194–211.

Kaiser, A. P. (1993). Functional language. In Martha E. Snell (Ed.), *Instruction of students with severe disabilities.* New York: Macmillan.

Kamps, D. M. N., Walker, D., Dugan E. P., Leonard, B. R., Thibadeau, S. F., Marshall, K., Grossnickle, L., & Boland, B. (1991). Small group instruction for school-aged students with autism and developmental disabilities, *Focus on Autistic Behavior, 6*(4), 1–18.

Koegel, R. L., & Rincover, A. (1974). Treatment of psychotic children in a classroom environment: Learning in a large group. *Journal of Applied Behavior Analysis, 7,* 45–49.

Lovaas, O. I., Koegel, R., Simmons, J., & Long, J. S. (1973). Some generalization and follow-up measures on autistic children in behavior therapy. *Journal of Applied Behavior Analysis, 6,* 131–166.

Lovaas, O. I., & Smith, T. (1989). A comprehensive behavioral theory of autistic children: Paradigm for research and treatment. *Journal of Behavior Therapy and Experimental Psychiatry, 20,* 17–29.

Maurice, C., Green, G., & Luce, S. C. (1996). *Behavioral intervention for young children with autism.* Austin, TX: Pro-Ed.

Quill, K. A. (1995). *Teaching children with autism: Strategies to enhance communication and socialization.* New York: Delmar Publishers.

Reid, D. H., & Favell, J. E. (1984). Group instruction with persons who have severe disabilities: A critical review. *Journal of the Association for Persons with Severe Handicaps, 9*(3), 167–177.

Rotholz, D. A. (1990). Current considerations on the use of one-to-one instruction with autistic students: Review and recommendations. *Focus on Autistic Behavior, 5*(3), 1–6.

Schoen, S. F. (1986). Assistance procedures to facilitate the transfer of stimulus control: Review and analysis. *Education and Training of the Mentally Retarded, 21,* 62–74.

Schopler, E., Mesibov, G. B., & Hearsey, K. (1995). Structured teaching in the TEACCH system. In E. Schopler & G. B. Mesibov (Eds.), *Learning and cognition in autism* (pp. 243–268). New York: Plenum Press.

Schopler, E., Reichler, R. JH., & Lansing, M. (1980). *Individualized assessment and treatment for autistic and developmentally disabled children, Vol. 2: Teaching strategies for parents and professionals.* Austin, TX: Pro-Ed.

Schreibman, L. (1975). Effects of within-stimulus and extra-stimulus prompting on discrimination learning in autistic children. *Journal of Applied Behavior Analysis, 8,* 92–112.

Simpson, R. L., & Regan, M. (1986). *Management of autistic behavior.* Austin, TX: Pro-Ed.

Stokes, T. F., & Baer, D. M. (1977). An implicit technology of generalization. *Journal of Applied Behavior Analysis, 10,* 349–369.

Westling, D. L., & Fox, L. (1995). *Teaching students with severe disabilities.* Englewood Cliffs, NJ: Prentice Hall.

White, O. (1988). Probing skill use. In N. Haring (Ed.), *Generalization for students with severe handicaps: Strategies and solutions* (pp. 131–141). Seattle: University of Washington Press.

Wiederholt, J. L., Hammill, D. D., & Brown, V. (1978). *The resource teacher: A guide to effective practices.* Austin, TX: Pro-Ed.

Wing, L. (1981). Language, social, and cognitive impairments in autism and severe mental retardation. *Journal of Autism and Developmental Disorders, 11,* 31–44.

6

Remediating Deficits in Speech and Language

Did you know that:

- Speech does not guarantee effective communication?

- Better communication ability predicts better outcomes for students with autism?

- Not everyone agrees about how we learn language?

- Language development can help prevent learned helplessness and challenging behavior?

- Language ability is closely related to cognitive and social abilities?

- Teaching someone to communicate requires multiple strategies?

Mastering the ability to communicate with others is a fundamental aspect of healthy human development. Language allows us to form social relationships, obtain knowledge, and to live and work independently. Those who cannot understand or produce language usually remain dependent on others, having few or no means for making choices and expressing wants and needs. This phenomenon, known as **learned helplessness** (Guess, Benson, & Siegel-Causey, 1985), characterizes many individuals with severe cognitive and language deficits, including those with autism. Learned helplessness, in turn, results in reduced motivation to respond to the environment

and hampers the ability to recognize the link between one's behavior and contextual stimuli (Rosenhan & Seligman, 1989).

The inability to communicate wants and needs, and to influence the action of others through language, is also linked to inappropriate behaviors (Durand, 1993; Reichle & Sigafoos, 1994). Inappropriate behavior, in turn, increases the probability that an individual will receive punitive, restrictive, and segregated treatment. Restrictive and segregated treatment approaches typically prevent normal language development, thus creating a vicious communication deficit–behavioral excess cycle. Although typical children learn language without much help, children with cognitive disorders, including autism, will need systematic and comprehensive language instruction. Indeed, most of our time and effort should be spent on teaching children to effectively communicate.

WHAT IS LANGUAGE?

Teachers would do well to learn about the composition of language and the nature of normal language development because it is the primary tool by which most knowledge is transferred (e.g., Vygotsky, 1962). Understanding language development is particularly important for those who engage in direct language instruction with non- or low-verbal students. **Language** is composed of several complex elements but has basically been defined as "the use of arbitrary symbols, with accepted referents, that can be arranged in different sequences to convey different meanings" (Lefrancois, 1995, p. 228). Thus, in order to master language an individual will need to understand the notion of symbols and referents (something represents something else) and be able to learn what symbol stands for what. Additionally, the individual needs to learn rules about choosing and combining the symbols in such as way as to impart specific information. And, of course, the individual has to WANT to convey information to someone else. Speech and manual communication are examples of language systems.

Communication, on the other hand, requires less ability. Communication is defined as any set of interactions (e.g., self-injurious behavior, body language, crying) that transmits information. In this case the individual just needs to want to convey information. If this communication does not follow language rules, it is typically inefficient and often ineffective. The receiver often has to work hard to interpret meaning. In fact without a hard-working receiver, communication often fails. Although almost all children with autism communicate some of the time, they invariably have problems with one or more aspects of language. Because these students will have a difficult time using language to communicate, they may choose other means of conveying information. Therefore, teachers must observe all behavior for possible communicative intent, particularly aggressive or self-injurious behavior.

Communication and Language Components

The elements of language require a complex set of abilities and skills that allow people to understand what others are communicating **(receptive language)** and to produce communicative behaviors **(expressive language)** in a way that others can understand. Language demands the mastery of rules **(structure)** and the cognitive abilities to un-

Table 6.1 Language Components and Definitions

Phonemes: Individual speech sounds used within a language (in English we have approximately 40 phonemes).

Morphemes: The smallest units of meaning in a language resulting from a combination of phonemes (e.g., base ball s). Each morpheme must have a referent for which it clearly stands.

Syntax: Grammar rules in a given language (e.g., sentence structure, use of articles).

Prosody: Cadence, rhythm, and pitch in speech.

Semantics: The general meaning of language including discrete words and contextual connotations.

Pragmatics: Situational context of language including speaker–listener interaction and determining who says what to whom, how they say it, why and when they say it .

derstand the representation of objects and events with symbols, and to produce meaning for a wide variety of purposes. Table 6.1 lists and defines several components of language. The interaction of **phonology, morphology, semantics, pragmatics, prosody,** and **syntax** typically develops in an established sequence as a child matures so that most children have mastered oral language structure by 9 years of age (Gleason, 1997).

Additionally, language has **form** and **function.** Communicative form refers to the types of behaviors used to communicate (e.g., gestures, pointing, head movements, aggression, whining, speech). Many individuals with autism do not master the form of speech and must be taught to use different language forms (i.e., pictures, sign language). Function, or why an individual communicates, refers to the various communicative intents. Neel and Billingsley (1989) delineate several communicative functions common to individuals with mild to severe disabilities:

Requesting (also known as manding): To satisfy needs such as obtaining food, approval, or affection; to obtain help such as help putting on shoes.

Protesting: Saying "No" to tasks, toys, food, activities (such as going to bed).

Responding to social initiatives: A range of behaviors such as following someone who says "Come on."

Initiating and maintaining social interaction: Behaving in a way that causes and maintains social contact (e.g., sitting in someone's lap).

Seeking comfort: Behaviors such as running to mother when hurt or distressed.

Expressing interest in the environment: Such as pointing to something.

Communicating experiences not shared by others: Requires language such as telling someone about the zoo visit last month.

Play acting or pretending: Requires imagination.

As mentioned in Chapter 1, individuals with autism typically lack the motivation to communicate and, thus, do not master the use of language for many functions. As a matter of fact, many individuals with autism never learn speech, and those who do typically use it inappropriately and ineffectively. Because language disorders are a primary characteristic of autism and because lack of language is severely handicapping, teaching and facilitating language development should be a priority for parents and teachers.

Language Development

Historically, theorists have disagreed as to the exact nature of language development. Some theorists believe that children learn language by associating things and concepts with a word. Parents point to something and label it. The child then stores the associations for later use (Wallace, Cohen, & Polloway, 1987). Others believe that language develops through imitation of adult speech and grammatical rules (Bandura, 1977). In this case, adults act as language role models. Skinner (1957) essentially explained language development as a result of reinforced responses, first motivated by approval for verbalizations and later by natural consequences for the appropriate use of language.

Chomsky (1967), on the other hand, presented a biological view of language development claiming that humans, at birth, possess an innate understanding of grammatical rules (syntax) that unfolds with exposure to the environment. Finally, Bruner (1977) presented the interactionist orientation explaining language development, particularly the mastery of pragmatics, as a function of dialogue and frequent social interaction particularly between parents and children. This dialogue and interaction allows the child to understand the nature of language and its rules of application.

Why would it matter what theorists say about how language develops? Because in the field of autism there is much controversy about the best way to teach it. For example, some professionals recommend the use of natural social interactions and social role models, while others recommend straight skill training based on Skinner's work. In this book, we will recommend a combination of approaches to language training. We recommend that teachers (1) instruct students to label objects, people, and places (also known as **tacting**), (2) train and encourage imitation of correct language usage (also known as **echoing**), (3) reinforce students for the use of language, and (4) motivate students to use language by providing natural interactive opportunities. This type of instruction and facilitation requires adults to label things in the environment, to frequently model correct language usage, to reinforce communicative effort, and to provide a rich social context for children.

Developmental Sequence. Regardless of the theory, it is generally agreed that language develops in a sequence of simple to complex skills beginning in early infancy with gestures, crying, and cooing. At first the crying is not meant as communication but the infant soon learns, from adult reactions, to use various behaviors and vocalizations to control the environment. The intention to communicate usually develops between the age of 8 and 12 months (Berk, 1999). The second critical ability that develops in infancy is the knowledge that language relates to the real world. This means that things are designated by an auditory or signed symbol. Soon these early expressive and receptive abilities progress to sound imitation (echoing) usually through playful interaction with the parents. Interestingly, many individuals with autism continue echolalic responses beyond this initial developmental period; unfortunately, with little communicative intent.

As the desire to communicate for the purpose of meeting hunger, comfort, and affection needs grows, the infant develops a one- or two-word expressive language system. These few words are typically names of favorite objects and/or people and are known as **holophrases.** The holophrase is used for many functions such as socializing, requesting, or protesting. For example, the infant may say "Mama" with different intonations to mean "help me," "give me . . .," "stop that," and so forth. Understanding the communicative intent of a holophrase requires a listener who can interpret what the child is intending to communicate. This skill is also necessary for teachers of students with low language ability.

By age 2, the typical child begins using two-word phrases known as **telegraphic speech** (Berk, 1999). Telegraphic speech, like a telegram, leaves out unnecessary words. For example, it includes word combinations such as "Juice please," "Go play," "Come outside," and "Sit, mama." Once a child uses combinations of these phrases (e.g., "Baby sleepy. Go bed."), he is demonstrating grammatical rules. Also during this period, children appear to understand everything an adult says; that is, they seem to have an expansive receptive vocabulary or, at least, they have learned to respond to adult behavior and expressions. For example, a mother may say "See the doggy" and look over at the dog. Her child follows her gaze and gives the impression that she understands the sentence; or a child may imitate a routine and appear to follow directions (e.g., close the door). Note that the ability to follow another's gaze, share attention, and imitate modeled behavior—important skills for language development—are very often not demonstrated by young children with autism.

Between the ages of 2 and 5, children move from telegraphic speech to multiple-word sentences to adult-like speech structures (Lefrancois, 1995). They learn to use articles, word endings, correct inflection, and finally master most exceptions to grammatical rules (e.g., using "went" instead of "goed"). Their sentences become longer and more complex. Not only is their language more complex, but preschool-age children learn to express concepts and refer to events that are remote in time and space (Gleason, 1997). They use their language for a wider variety of functions such as pretending and conversing. During middle childhood, oral language development continues in the form of vocabulary expansion and syntactic development. Usually, at this point, emphasis shifts from oral language development to written language development (i.e., reading, writing, spelling, written expression). Table 6.2 lists the language milestones of a normally developing child.

Related Factors. Normal language development is influenced by many factors, including heredity (intelligence, physiology), environment (parenting, social class, familial factors), and maturation (neurological system) (Wallace et al., 1987). If a child is born with cognitive disorders (e.g., mental retardation) or physical impairments (e.g., vision, hearing impairments; cerebral palsy), then language development may be adversely affected. Similarly, if the family fails to provide adequate sociolinguistic interaction and support, or if the child has neurological problems that prevent typical developmental maturation, then language may be delayed or absent. In the case of autism, neurological problems appear to put them at risk for many language difficulties.

Very closely related to language development is cognitive development. Some believe that thought (cognition) must precede language development. For example, Piaget (1954) maintained that children must develop the ability to think symbolically before language can develop, that thinking ability precedes language development. On the other hand, Vygotsky (1962) believed that intelligence develops as a function of language,

Table 6.2 Language Development Milestones

Milestones	Behaviors	Sample
First year		
Prespeech	Gestures, cooing, crying, babbling	Looking at bottle. "Dadadadada."
Holophrase	Word plus gestures	"Dada" plus pulling stuck toy, meaning "Help me."
Second/Third Year		
Two-word sentences	Modifiers plus nouns	"No juice." "Where doggy?" "More cheese." "Baby sleep."
Multiple-word sentences	Subject plus predicate	"Shark bites water." "I want juice please." "No play with kids." "Shoes are upstairs."
Third/Fourth Year		
Complex grammatical structures are added	Nouns, verbs, prepositions Combined clauses	"I can't find it." "Give me some juice." "Where are my shoes?"
Adult-like structures	Structural distinctions	"He promised to help me make it."

that thought cannot occur without language. In either case, thinking and language abilities are intricately connected, particularly after age 2 when language becomes the primary method for transmitting and acquiring knowledge. Cognitive delays, therefore, appear to cause language disorders, and language disorders, in turn, may cause further cognitive delays.

Typical cognitive development in very young children is characterized by three main characteristics: (1) **egocentricism,** (2) **centration,** and (3) **transformation difficulties** (Yawkey, Askov, Cartwright, Dupuis, Fairchild, & Yawkey, 1981). Egocentric thought in characterized by a "here and now" worldview, preventing young children from taking another's perspective. For example, when a child hits another and the mother tries to explain that it hurts, he cannot understand because he himself is not hurting. Centration refers to a child's propensity to focus on superficial stimuli rather than on other salient characteristics (Wallace et al., 1987). This type of thinking is illustrated with an experiment whereby an adult shows a child two same-size glasses of water and then pours one glass of water into a long glass tube. When asked if the amount of water in the two different size containers are the same, a small child will say "no" because they no longer look the same. This child only considers the appearance of the water, not the more salient fact that no water was added or subtracted.

Transformation in thinking refers to the ability to associate a series of successive events across time and space. Young children are cognitively incapable of doing this. They tend to view all events as isolated. Thus, the child above treats the initial state of the water and final state as unrelated events neglecting the important feature of pouring the water into a different size container. In terms of complex language development, children must eventually develop the cognitive skills to (1) view the world from more than their own perspective, (2) develop an ability to focus on many features of physical phenomena at once, and (3) be able to connect related events across time. Interestingly, individuals with autism tend to have difficulties in all three cognitive areas. They typically remain egocentric thinkers, lack the ability to generalize learning, and may overselect various stimuli (remember the torn sleeve example in Chapter 1). Thus, we cannot ignore the cognitive deficits that may directly contribute to their language difficulties (Schopler & Mesibov, 1995; Tager-Flusberg, 1996).

Another cognitive ability typically developed in infancy is the notion of cause–effect, that certain behaviors cause things in the environment to be altered. Babies discover that hitting the mobile makes the fish move or the bells ring. They discover that pulling a string makes the toy move toward them. They learn that dropping food on the floor gets mother to pick it up and interact with them. Without the understanding of cause–effect, the motivation to communicate may be compromised (Layton & Watson, 1995). For example, if a child does not understand that sounds, words, and phrases impact the environment, then she is not likely to use those things to get needs and desires met. Learning about cause–effect typically happens through playing with toys and people. Because children with autism do not play in the typical manner, they are often delayed in acquiring prelinguistic cognitive abilities (Layton & Watson, 1995). Furthermore, even if a child develops communicative intent, based on cause–effect awareness, she still may not understand that objects are represented by sounds and words.

In addition to cognitive abilities, social ability is also closely linked to language development. Social interactions with the infant (i.e., eye-gazing, smiling, laughing) are behaviors that bring adults in proximity and cause reciprocal interaction often involving verbal communication. For example, a baby smiles and the mother says "Hi, little fellow, are you awake? Do you want to eat?" This type of verbal interaction then stimulates early language responses such as cooing. In fact, Bruner (1977) claims that language will only develop from such interaction. He claims that children learn to make eye contact, take turns, direct others' attention through gestures and eventually words, and to converse through interaction with others (Lefrancois, 1995). If the child is given little social contact and spends the majority of his time alone, as children with autism desire, then language development will be hampered. Further-

more, if children are given everything they want or need without having to communicate to get it, then there is little motivation to communicate. Thus, we will recommend that students with autism spend time around other verbal children and adults and that sociocommunicative interaction be encouraged through antecedent manipulation and reinforcement strategies. We will also recommend that social language be taught so that social interactions will be successful and not something to avoid.

Finally, for language to develop, an individual needs a form of communication that she can master. The best language form is speech because it is universally understood and has the greatest productivity potential. However, if children cannot develop speech due to cognitive or physical disabilities, then other forms of communication (visual systems, sign language, computerized devices) should be made available (Layton & Watson, 1995). The overriding goal is to teach functional communication while enhancing cognitive and social development and, in turn, preventing inappropriate behaviors.

LANGUAGE PROBLEMS IN AUTISM

Language and cognition do not seem to develop in a typical manner for individuals with autism. Many will show deficits in almost all aspects of language coinciding with deficits in cognition and social competence (e.g., American Psychiatric Association [APA], 1994; Frith, 1996; Hinerman, 1983; Paul, 1987).

Related Problems

In addition to severe language impairment, many cognitive prerequisites may be missing or impaired. For example, many children with autism (1) have mental retardation (APA, 1994), (2) fail to develop the awareness of cause–effect (Layton & Watson, 1995), and (3) lack the ability to think symbolically, interpret symbols in their environment, or use symbols to transmit messages to others (Hinerman, 1983; Kamhi, 1981). Evidence of cognitive deficits includes lack of toy play, non-functional use of objects, and lack of imitative play and pantomime (APA, 1994; DesLauriers, 1978; Menyuk, 1978).

Further evidence of cognitive impairment is apparent in infants or toddlers who:

- Do not imitate social behavior such as waving bye-bye, pat-a-cake, or other parental behaviors (Fay & Schuler, 1980)
- Fail to make eye contact
- Show no preference for their mother's speech ("Interview with ASAF," 1999)
- Fail to point to things of interest
- Do not readily respond to their names (Bartak, Rutter, & Cox, 1975; Staff, 1999)
- Show little or no desire to explore the environment
- Generally do not consider other people of interest (APA, 1994; Hinerman, 1983; Schopler & Mesibov, 1995; Wing, 1981)
- Have difficulty learning concepts (e.g., over, under, behind)
- Rarely refer to events that happened in the past or in various places

Compounding the apparent cognitive impairment, many individuals with autism also show disturbances in perception (APA, 1994). It appears that auditory input is distorted for these individuals. They either tend to be overly sensitive to sound or they need a higher intensity of sound in order to respond. Thus, they may ignore most auditory input or attend only to a relative few selected sounds (Lowell, 1976). This inability to process auditory stimuli, particularly rapidly occurring stimuli (Tallal, 1976), may explain their extreme difficulty mastering speech and social skills.

Receptive Language Problems

The inability to process auditory stimuli (i.e., attend to it, act on it, imitate it) contributes directly to problems in language comprehension (receptive language). Many individuals with autism perform poorly on tests of language comprehension (Paul & Cohen, 1995) and seem to have trouble understanding sentences. Sometimes, due to their perception and cognitive difficulties, children with autism may appear deaf (Giddan & Ross, 2001). Frequently, parents report that their child with autism is very "good" because she will spend hours in her crib and not demand attention. Unlike children who are deaf, however, children with autism also fail to respond to visual and tactile stimuli. Conversely, those children with autism who are very sensitive to sound may become very agitated in the presence of certain voice tones and pitches. In either case, it seems that learning to attend to the spoken word and to obtain meaning from it would be difficult if the ability to attend to contextual cues in general is impaired.

Additionally, children with autism appear to overemphasize syntactic structure rather than semantic content in their understanding of language (Paul, Fischer, & Cohen, 1988). For example, they will obtain meaning from the order of the words, rather than the meaning of the word itself. Thus, a child with autism will understand that "Come to dinner" means to come and eat, but will not understand "Dinner's on" as meaning the same thing. Receptive language seems to be enhanced with direct cues and consistent wording. In one study, children with autism tended to misunderstand the speaker's intention when indirect sentences such as "How about getting ready for lunch?" were used, and when sentences were uttered in nonstructured settings (Paul et al., 1988).

Unfortunately, language comprehension problems often result in increasingly restricted interactions and experiences, which, in turn, could potentially result in cognitive delays. For example, if parents and teachers do not think a child can understand what is being said, they themselves find no joy in interaction and often quit trying to provide the rich interactive experiences necessary for enhancing language. That is, adults may resort to only making requests of the children or only giving them directions rather than engaging in imitative play, conversational speech, complex social interactions, and new, interesting activities. Without the connection of various experiences to words and sentences, the child with autism will fail to develop appropriate language comprehension, functional expressive language, and social competence.

Expressive Language Problems

As mentioned in Chapter 1, the language problems most associated with autism are expressive language problems. In fact, expressive language problems are one of the primary identifying characteristics of the syndrome (APA, 1994). If low cognition is present, most individuals with autism will be mute and often noncommunicative (APA, 1994). In addition to the fact that almost half of the autistic population never acquires expressive speech, and might be limited in other language forms such as sign language, those who do master expressive language usually display limited and idiosyncratic speech patterns with problems manifested in many areas. Only about 30 percent of individuals with autistic disorder develop functional language (Miranda-Linne & Melin, 1997). Even those at the mild end of the autism spectrum may have an impaired ability to initiate and sustain conversation (Rappaport, 1996). If a child with autism does not acquire speech by the time she is 7 years old, the prognosis for oral language acquisition appears dim (Bondy & Frost, 1994; Maurice, Green, & Luce, 1996).

Word Use and Articulation. Individuals with autism, especially those with high cognitive functioning, often develop fairly large vocabularies because they can memorize what words mean; however, they may fail to use their knowledge of the meaning in order to retrieve correct vocabulary or to organize their speech (Paul, 1987). Many individuals may also show obsessive interest in certain words and/or their meanings resulting in perseveration (repeating words over and over). Articulation typically does not seem to be a problem for children with speech, although it may be somewhat delayed and imprecise (Needleman, Ritvo, & Freeman, 1980).

Syntax and Morphology. Individuals with autism seem to be able to use the common grammatical morphemes, but seem to have some trouble with verb tenses and articles, perhaps because referents change according to the point of view of the speaker (Bartolucci, Pierce, & Streiner, 1980). For example, present and past tenses may be altered as a function of which speaker is making the comment. Thus, children with autism may display some grammatical errors. Their syntactic ability (using rules to produce language) may be simplistic but most speaking children with autism use correct word order. Delays most often occur in the use of questions, negatives, conjoined sentences, and passive sentences (Giddan & Ross, 2001). Interestingly, many individuals with autism rely on questioning as their primary mode of initiating and maintaining conversations (Hurtig, Ensrud, & Tomblin, 1982).

Pronoun Reversal. A unique characteristic of children with autism is the propensity to misuse personal pronouns, especially "I" and "you." Children with autism will often fail to use the pronoun "I" correctly, instead repeating "you" as it was heard from another. For example, "You want to eat now?" means "I want to eat now." As previously mentioned, pronouns are connected to changing referents. For example, "father" is always one person, but pronouns do not always refer to the same person. This shifting reference may be especially difficult for individuals with autism (Fay, 1971).

Echolalia. Echolalia, the inappropriate repetition of words, phrases, or sentences, is one of the most classic characteristics of autistic speech. Generally, echolalia comes in three types: immediate, delayed, and mitigated (Hinerman, 1983). **Immediate echolalia** entails all or part of an utterance that is repeated following its occurrence. The repetition duplicates the intonation, pitch, and articulation patterns of the speaker and quite often is repeated several times. For example, a teacher tells a student to "wash your hands and sit down." The student repeats "wash your hands." **Delayed echolalia** is the duplication of an utterance that occurred some time before. This type of echolalia often comes in the form of repeated TV commercials, lines from jingles or songs, or radio announcements. **Mitigated echolalia** refers to repetitions that differ slightly from the original utterance. For example, a parent may tell a child to "stay away from the swimming pool," and the child repeats "no swimming pool" each time he goes outside.

As mentioned previously, normally developing children show echolalia in their early language development, usually repeating sounds slightly more advanced than their spontaneous language (Berk, 1999). Children with autism, however, are more likely to repeat questions and commands they do not understand or for which they know no appropriate response (Lovaas, 1977). Echolalia, however, does appear to be used to acquire language. Additionally, it is believed that echolalia serves a communicative function for children with autism (Prizant & Rydell, 1984; Wetherby, Prizant, & Hutchinson, 1998). These authors proposed that immediate echolalia may serve the purposes of self-stimulation, turn-taking, assertions, affirmative answers, requests, rehearsal to aid processing, and self-regulation. Delayed echolalia may serve the purposes of getting an adult to do a task, labeling, providing new information, gaining attention, requesting, a "yes" answer, and protesting. Interestingly, delayed echolalia seems to follow nondemand-type interactions while immediate echolalia seems to follow specific, complex demands (Rydell & Mirenda, 1994). Furthermore, echolalia may represent concrete, literal thinking patterns (Paluszny, 1979).

Another explanation for echolalia may be that there are two primary ways of learning to speak: analytic and gestalt (Giddan & Ross, 2001). **Analytic learners** progress from one- to two- to multiple-word sentences. **Gestalt learners** memorize multiple-word units. The analytical method allows for more flexibility and creativity in language. Children with autism appear to engage at an extreme level of gestalt processing. They may, however, eventually move from this echolalic responding to an analytical learning approach as evidenced by the appearance of mitigated echolalia described above (Schuler & Prizant, 1985). The

important thing to remember is that echolalia may assist with language development, providing a way for the individual to interact and acquire additional knowledge.

Prosody. Prosody refers to intonation, speech rhythm, inflection, voice volume, intensity, quality, and pitch. This aspect of language may also be impaired or abnormal for individuals with autism. These individuals are often described as having "wooden" speech (Hinerman, 1983) and flat affect. They tend to speak in a monotone (Giddan & Ross, 2001), often in a consistently high-pitched tone with muttering, loud outbursts, and poor volume control. Sometimes they use a sing-song rhythm; when echolalic, they typically duplicate the prosody of the original speaker. In some instances, these children display hoarseness, harshness, and hypernasality (Pronovost, Wakstein, & Wakstein, 1966).

Non-verbal Communication. Typical non-verbal communication includes bodily contact, proximity, physical orientation, appearance, posture, head nods, facial expressions, gestures, and eye contact. These features, in conjunction with speech production, convey interpersonal attitudes and assist in establishing relationships and conveying information. Individuals with autism often fail to use gestures, eye movements, and facial expressions in conjunction with speech to convey meaning. In fact, these individuals often display facial grimaces and tics and may actively avoid eye contact (Wing, 1996).

Problems with Pragmatics

For those individuals with autism who do master a language system, one of the most debilitating deficits is that pertaining to language "use" or pragmatics. Mastery of pragmatics involves following conversational rules such as turn-taking, relevant responses, maintaining a topic, on-topic responses, being clear and unambiguous, and using cohesive sentences. Pragmatics also involves taking another's perspective and using language for various functions such as greeting, predicting, referring to things, narrating, commenting, explaining, comparing, and joking (Rappaport, 1996). Individuals with autism typically show sparse verbal expression and lack of spontaneity (Giddan & Ross, 2001). They have historically been characterized as persons who:

- Fail to reciprocate in speech

- Fail to listen

- Fail to move from an obsessive topic to a topic of interest to the listener

- Fail to take turns in conversations

- Display highly rigid and contextually inappropriate speech (Dewey & Everard, 1974; Shapiro, Huebner, & Campbell, 1974)

One study revealed that, when responding to adult verbalizations, children with autism were less likely to make relevant responses, to expand the discussion, or to add new information; more typically they spent their time imitating responses or failing to respond at all (Tager-Flusberg, 1996). They seem to have very little to say and seem not to know how much to say, usually giving one-word answers when two or three sentences would be socially appropriate. One of the overriding pragmatic problems in this population is the apparent inability to utilize contextual cues. Individuals with autism fail to recognize and understand the speaker's intent, monitor their listeners' needs, or use contextual stimuli (e.g., looking, pointing, holding something up) in order to convey meaning. They have a propensity to interpret and produce language literally without attention to variations and connotations. Additionally, they utilize few language functions, choosing instead to use instrumental functions such as requesting, responding, and directing, as opposed to social functions such as commenting or joking (Prizant & Schuler, 1987a). Finally, individuals with autism often fail to match the content of their speech to their meaning. For example, a child may say "Want to go in the green Volvo?" which means "Let's go for a ride in the car." This lack of pragmatic ability is directly tied to the essential autistic characteristic: lack of social competence and inability to relate to people.

Problems with Language Form

Due to problems in acquiring and utilizing language, individuals with autism often resort to idiosyncratic ways of communication. Instead of imitating adult speech and learning communicative forms through natural reinforcers, children with autism may display a wide range of behavior to convey meaning. These various language forms may include aggressive behavior (particularly to protest), speech (one-word to complex), pointing, pulling others to something, self-injury, tantrums, crying/whining, echolalic behaviors, sign language, or proximity (Prizant & Schuler, 1987a).

Even for those who can speak, and speak well, speech is not always used to convey meaning and is often used in noncommunicative ways, as evidenced with some echolalia. Accepted non-verbal communication forms (e.g., facial expressions, intonation, body orientation) are rarely used by individuals with autism; instead they may resort to self-injurious behavior or aggression in order to get what they want or to get out of difficult situations and tasks (Prizant & Schuler, 1987a). This propensity to use idiosyncratic forms of communication and not use conventional forms means that we need to assume communicative intent in most behavior, while shaping more appropriate means for interacting with people. In fact, the complex and varied language/communication, cognitive, and social problems displayed by those with autism clearly indicate assessment and intervention in all of these areas as early as possible and for as long as possible. Table 6.3 summarizes language problems in autism.

ASSESSING LANGUAGE AND COMMUNICATION

Because students with autism tend to have problems in all aspects of language and communication, extensive language/communication assessment is indicated. Such an assessment facilitates instruction in essential and functional skills. Given the

Table 6.3 Language/Communication Problems in Autism

Receptive Language Problems

Inability to attend to auditory stimuli
Inability to act on auditory stimuli
Inability to imitate auditory stimuli
Inability to use contextual cues to obtain meaning
May appear deaf

Overly sensitive to sounds
Obtain meaning from word order, not semantic content
Failure to understand indirect or complex sentences

Expressive Language Problems

Mutism
Word use and articulation
Imprecise articulation

Obsessive use of vocabulary
Incorrect use of vocabulary

Syntax and Morphology

Trouble with verb tenses and articles
Failure or delay in use of syntactic rules

Perseverative use of questions
Pronoun reversal

Echolalia

Immediate
Delayed

Mitigated
Noncommunicative echolalia

Prosody

Wooden speech and flat affect
Monotonal speech
High-pitched tone

Poor volume control
Sing-song speech
Hoarseness, harshness, hypernasality

Non-verbal Communication

Fail to use non-verbal communication to enhance communicative intent
Facial grimacing
No eye contact or appropriate body orientation

Pragmatic Problems

Limited language uses
Lack of spontaneity
Failure to reciprocate and take turns in conversation
Respond with inappropriate amount of communication

Failure to maintain a conversation
Failure to recognize the speaker's intent
Failure to match speech content to meaning
Rigid and contextually inappropriate speech

Form Problems

Idiosyncratic communication forms
Often use aggressive behavior or self-injurious behavior to communicate
Failure to use appropriate non-verbal forms of communication

Speech often not used to communicate
May use crying, tantrums, echolalia, physical manipulation, gestures to communicate

Related Problems

Mental retardation
No awareness of cause–effect
Failure to understand symbolic representation
Lack of toy and imitative or imaginative play
Nonfunctional use of objects
Do not attend to environmental stimuli
Failure to take turns or another's perspective

Egocentric thinking
Little interest in exploring the environment
Little interest in people
Little response to communicative models
Overselection of stimuli
Failure to transfer or adapt learned skills

complexity of language, assessment should occur in several areas:

1. The social domain, including ways in which the child initiates interaction and responds to others. Non-verbal social behaviors also need to be assessed.

2. The communicative domain, including the degree of communicative intent and verbal and non-verbal communicative functions displayed. The frequency of communication and the various communicative forms utilized should also be assessed. This area of assessment may be the most important.

3. The linguistic domain, including all receptive and expressive language components. Assessment might also include analysis of echolalic speech if present.

4. The cognitive domain, including the ability to understand symbolic representation. Also include an assessment of other developmental areas to establish a performance profile (Parker, 1996; Prizant & Schuler, 1987b).

Assessing language and communication can be a daunting task because so many components are involved and because language is so closely related to social and cognitive skills. Thus, we recommend that teachers and parents seek assistance from a Speech-Language Pathologist (SLP), particularly in the areas of linguistic and cognitive assessment. Note, however, that not all SLPs are trained to assess children who are non-verbal or low verbal; rather, SLPs are typically trained to target articulation problems, which individuals with autism rarely display. Teachers, SLPs, and parents should work together to acquire the necessary knowledge to conduct a comprehensive language/communication assessment. The more comprehensive and accurate the assessment, the more likely that appropriate communication goals and objectives will be targeted. Because so many language/communication abilities must be assessed, it might be best to include both formal (published) and informal procedures. Consult the SLP about formal language tests that will be most useful for assessing the linguistic domain with verbal students. Some

formal language assessment instruments also contain components pertaining to social, communicative, and cognitive domains. Additionally, several autism diagnostic instruments (e.g., *ASIEP*), adaptive behavior scales, and developmental profiles provide such information.

Remember that formal norm-referenced language tests for children with autism and related disorders may not provide useful information (Prizant & Schuler, 1987a). Due to the discontinuity with which these individuals develop, comparing them to normally developing children may give erroneous information. For this reason, we suggest you use tests that have been specifically developed for individuals with autism. Furthermore, children with autistic disorder often display noncompliant and challenging behavior that may make it difficult to obtain reliable results in a testing situation. Failure to understand directions or to read social cues may also negatively impact formal test scores.

Formal Language/Communication Assessment Instruments

Many formal language assessment instruments are available, some of which pertain specifically to individuals with autism. Table 6.4 lists a few formal language assessments.

The *Assessment of Basic Language and Learning Skills (ABLLS)* (Partington & Sundberg, 1998) is a criterion-referenced assessment instrument, curriculum guide, and skills tracking system for children with language delays. This means that no age norms are provided. Rather the purpose of this instrument is to determine what the child with language delays can already perform and what skill is to be targeted. The instrument is based on B. F. Skinner's analysis of verbal behavior, which focuses on the different conditions in which language occurs and purports to identify the skills necessary for a child to become more capable of learning from everyday experiences. The *ABLLS* uniquely assesses a variety of language skills: the child's motivation to respond, her ability to attend to verbal and non-verbal stimuli and to generalize language skills, and spontaneous language use.

Table 6.4 Examples of Published Language/Communication Tests

1. *Peabody Picture Vocabulary Test*
   American Guidance Service
   Publishers Building
   Circle Pines, MN 55014
2. *Environmental Language Inventory*
   Charles E. Merrill
   445 Hutchinson Avenue
   Columbus, OH 43235
3. *Receptive-Expressive Emergent Language Scale*
   Pro-Ed Publishers
   8700 Shoal Creek Boulevard
   Austin, TX 78757-6897
4. *Communication Programming Inventory*
   From: L. Sternberg (Ed.)., Educating students with
   severe or profound handicaps (2nd ed., pp. 345–363).
   Pro-Ed Publishers
   8700 Shoal Creek Boulevard
   Austin, TX 78757-6897
5. *Psychoeducational Profile-Revised (PEP-R)*
   Pro-Ed Publishers
   8700 Shoal Creek Boulevard
   Austin, TX 78757-6897
6. *Goldman-Fristoe Test of Articulation*
   American Guidance Service
   Publishers Building
   Circle Pines, MN 55014
7. *The Assessment of Basic Language and Learning Skills (The ABLLS)*
   Behavior Analysts, Inc.
   3329 Vincent Road
   Pleasant Hill, CA 94523
8. *Preschool Language Scale*
   Charles E. Merrill
   445 Hutchinson Avenue
   Columbus, OH 43235
9. *Test of Language Development—Primary (TOLD)*
   Pro-Ed Publishing
   8700 Shoal Creek Boulevard
   Austin, TX 78757-6897
10. *"Let's Talk" Inventory for Adolescents*
    Charles E. Merrill
    445 Hutchinson Avenue
    Columbus, OH 43235
11. *Test of Adolescent Language-2 (TOAL-2)*
    Pro-Ed Publishing
    8700 Shoal Creek Boulevard
    Austin, TX 78757-6897
12. *Communication and Symbolic Behavior Scales (CSBS)*
    Paul H. Brookes
    P.O. Box 10624
    Baltimore, MD 21285

The *Autism Screening Instrument for Educational Planning, second edition, (ASIEP 2)* (Krug, Arick, & Almond, 1993), includes a subtest for assessing non-verbal or low-verbal communicative ability and a subtest specifically designed to assess social interaction in individuals with autism. Language scores are computed and plotted on a profile for the purpose of comparing the target student's utterances to typical individuals with autism and those with mental retardation but no autism. Social interaction scores indicate the extent to which the child initiates interactions and the general methods for doing so. Again, comparative sample population scores are provided.

The *Psychoeducational Profile—Revised (PEP-R)* (Schopler & Reichler, 1995) has a communication section that assesses communicative ability across a variety of settings as well as in clinical situations. Several of the questions obtain information about communicative intent. The *Adolescent and Adult Psychoeducational Profile* (Mesibov, Schopler, Schaffer, & Landrus, 1988) is geared toward the older

autistic population. The *Autism Diagnostic Observation Schedule (ADOS)* (Lord, Rutter, Dilavore, & Risi, 1999) provides various activities during which assessors can make direct observations of social and communication behaviors. This instrument can be used with all ages and with those who are non-verbal as well as those who are verbally fluent.

For children who are verbal, the *Let's Talk Inventory for Adolescents* (Wiig, 1982) and the *Let's Talk Inventory for Children* (Bray & Wiig, 1987) assess pragmatic and linguistic functioning. In these tests individuals are shown pictures depicting situations in which communication is required and a brief narrative is read to the student. The student responds by saying what the speaker in the picture would say under the circumstances. For young children (ages 3–8), the *Test of Pragmatic Skills* (revised) (Shulman, 1986) includes a variety of scripts (accompanied by puppets) designed to elicit responses from students. Requests, greetings, and rejection/denial are a few of the functions assessed.

Informal Language Assessment

Informal procedures such as direct observations, notations, and interviews might be the most appropriate assessment method for students who are non-verbal or low-verbal, particularly when assessing the communicative domain. These instruments can be constructed by teachers, parents, or SLPs, or may be found in other sources such as this book. To assist teachers and parents in their understanding of language and communication assessment, sample assessment questions for each domain are listed in Table 6.5.

Two of the primary purposes of informal language/communication assessment as it pertains to individuals with autism and related disorders are to determine the range of communicative functions and forms, and record and/or describe the conditions and contexts under which the various types of communication occur (Quill, 1995). Figure 6.1 provides a sample informal assessment checklist for determining what communicative forms the student utilizes for various functions. Note that the checklist has a comment section for information about contextual conditions. This type of checklist could also be adapted to include specific questions about the conditions under which various communicative behaviors occur (e.g., when the most and least communication occurs). Analyses of linguistic quality and related social and cognitive skills are important but we recommend assessing the communicative domain first. Once this type of analysis has been conducted, teachers, SLPs, and parents can begin to shape existing responses into complex functional language.

Informal assessments, particularly observations in naturally occurring or simulated situations, can provide excellent information about language ability. For children with autism who may not attend well to their surroundings, naturally occurring situations typically do not stimulate language production. In these cases, the teacher, SLP, or parent might need to intentionally set up situations that stimulate communication responses in order to assess their quantity and quality. For example, a teacher may engage in an interaction whereby she repeatedly opens a container with a favorite stim-toy. Once the student seems to be anticipating the opening, the teacher neglects to open it. At this point many students may gaze at the container, gesture toward it, pull the teacher's hand toward it, produce vocalizations, echolalia, or perhaps aberrant behavior. In this way, the teacher is able to record the various communicative behaviors and make judgments about their appropriateness and functionality.

Familiar routines are also a good time to structure assessment interactions. For example, a student may be accustomed to having his milk handed to him once he sits down for lunch. In an assessment situation, the teacher could, on purpose, engage in something else and "forget" to give the student the milk. Often communicative behavior will result. However, teachers must be cautious because aggressive behavior may also be part of that repertoire. Functional behavioral assessment, as described in Chapter 3, provides useful information about how communicative attempts relate to environmental conditions, and about the relationship of communication to challenging behavior.

Likewise, interviews with parents and others who know the child well can provide information regarding those situations in which the target child is most likely to be socially interactive, whether they interact with peers or adults, types of current communicative behaviors, and a list of activities that the child likes to do with others. Neel and Billingsley (1989) include questions about communication form and function on their environmental inventory questionnaire. They also ask about a target child's cognitive abilities such as how well he handles situations such as change when interrupted, new people or activities, the termination of activities, and notification about impending changes. If target children display little interactive behavior, you might want to videotape them in comfortable surroundings with familiar people. Check the tapes for basic non-verbal communication such as head and mouth movements, intentional vocalizations, upper extremity movements, and facial expressions.

Table 6.5 Sample Language Assessment Questions

Social Domain

- How often and in what way does the child initiate interaction?
- How does the child respond to others' initiations?
- What types of non-verbal behaviors are used in social and conversational situations?
- How often does the child desire to interact?
- Under what conditions does the child interact the most?
- Under what conditions does the child interact the least?
- What does the child communicate about?
- Does the child maintain communicative exchanges? If so, how?
- Does the child terminate interaction? If so, how?
- Does the child play? If so, how interactive is the play?
- Who does the child typically interact with?

Communicative Domain

- What communicative functions does the child display? (Consider whether the child makes various requests, protests, declares, makes choices, asks for help, expresses affection, communicates emotion, shares information.)
- How does the child communicate each of the functions? (Consider aberrant behavior, gazing, pointing, reaching, vocalizations, nodding, signs, pictures.)
- How do different conditions affect the ways a child communicates?
- How often does the child communicate each function?

Linguistic Domain

Language Comprehension:

- Does the child follow simple directions?
- Does the child look at objects that might be the topic of discussion (ie., joint attention)?
- Does the child follow new or complex directions?
- Under what conditions does language comprehension seem best? (Consider focused attention, speed of speech, intonation, length of utterance, gestures, pictures).

Expressive Language:

- What are the primary forms of communication? (Consider echolalia, signs, aberrant behavior, vocalizations.)
- Does the child use correct grammar?
- Does the child use correct meanings?
- Does the child carry on appropriate conversations?
- How much vocabulary is evident?
- Does the child use nouns, verbs, word combinations, "wh" questions, articles, prepositions, adverbs, negating?
- Does the child articulate well? (Consider use of plurals and verb tenses.)
- Is appropriate prosody evident?(Consider accent, timing, and vocal intonation.)

Echolalia:

- What functions might the child communicate through echolalia?
- Is there flexibility in the echolalic responses (i.e., mitigated echolalia)?
- Does the echolalia seem to be self-stimulatory or nonfocused?

Cognitive Domain

- Does the child refer to or show awareness of objects and people that are out of sight?
- Does the child show interest in a variety of people and things?
- Does the child categorize objects based on various dimensions?
- Does the child discriminate color, shape, size, and so forth?
- Does the child move to get what he wants?
- How well does the child handle change? (Consider conditions such as interruptions, new people, type of activities, ending activities.)
- Does the child insist on routines and rituals?
- Does the child imitate adult behaviors? If so, are they novel actions or learned ones?

Name _____ Date _____

Examiner _____

Indicate ways the child communicates for the various purposes.

Functions   **Communicative Forms**

	Complex speech	Phrases	Single words	Signs	Echolalia	Gestures/pointing	Nods yes or no	Moves another	Crying or whining	Tantrums/SIB	Aggression	Other	Comment
Requests objects/ food/event.													
Requests adult to act.													
Requests out of activity/task.													
Requests help.													
Requests to leave.													
Chooses person/ activity/object.													
Protests change in routine.													
Protests adult action.													
Protests loss of something.													
Indicates pain.													
Indicates affection.													
Shares information.													
Initiates interaction.													
Other.													

FIGURE 6.1 Sample informal language and communication checklist.

Assessment across the various social, communication, linguistic, and cognitive domains will provide a profile of the likely conditions under which a given child will communicate, and the quality and functionality of current verbal and/or non-verbal behaviors. This information, in turn, provides a starting point for subsequent communication and language instruction. Finally, it might be wise to assess the characteristics of the people who interact with each child because language training will require a great deal of effort from all of them. Responsive communication partners and motivating social contexts are necessary to stimulate spontaneous interactions (Schuler & Prizant, 1987).

LANGUAGE AND COMMUNICATION TRAINING

Comprehensive language/communication assessment is necessary to the development of appropriate curriculum (what the student needs to learn) and to decisions about effective instruction (how the student will learn best). Goals and objectives should be established before deciding the best way to teach, and they should be based on the interrelationship of social, cognitive and linguistic abilities, and the overriding purpose of fostering independence and competence.

Deciding What to Teach in a Language/Communication Program

In deciding what to teach in the area of language and communication, you must consider both structural and functional goals. Although it is important to teach linguistically appropriate communication forms, it is an even higher priority to teach a means of achieving sociocommunicative functions for meeting one's own needs. Without functional communication, students' motivation to learn may wane, aberrant behavior may escalate, and intellectual development may stagnate.

Structural Goals and Curriculum. Structural goals in language/communication training pertain primarily to the linguistic and cognitive domains and include abilities in the following areas: prelinguistic cognitive skills, receptive comprehension, expressive vocabulary development, correct grammar, articulation, and appropriate prosody. Most of these goals also apply when teaching students to use alternate language forms such as sign language or visual communication systems. Specific structural goals for early language development might include these:

1. Create an association between objects/activities and symbols for those objects and activities (i.e., referentially).

2. Increase receptive language skills (e.g., following simple directions).

3. Teach relevant and simple vocabulary, beginning with meaningful concrete nouns.

4. Teach protest words (e.g., "no").

5. Pair nouns and verbs or nouns and adjectives into phrases.

6. Add pronouns and proper nouns to make simple sentences and phrases.

7. Systematically add grammatical categories and more vocabulary.

8. Work on articulation or correct sign formation, while not discouraging communicative intent.

It is extremely important to begin language training by teaching vocabulary words the student can use frequently and is motivated to use. (Cheryl describes her experiences with this caveat in her story in Chapter 9.) For students with autism, these are typically favorite objects, places, or foods. Initial vocabulary from the categories of self-care, identities, time, activities, animals, body parts, colors, number, and time may also be included. Vocabulary, particularly initial vocabulary, should be directly related to an individual's environment. For example, if the student's parents call a soft drink "pop," then teach the student to request or label it "pop," not "soda."

Before beginning language training, ensure that students have the ability to attend and imitate motor responses. Once imitation is acquired, teaching language responses will be easier. Typically, begin with receptive comprehension ("put in"), and receptive labeling (e.g., point to the cookie), moving next to expressive labeling (e.g., "What do you want?" "What is this?"). As one-word responses are mastered, add two-word combinations (e.g., adding "want," "eat," "give," "go"). Initial vocabulary may also include a word to protest (i.e., say "no") because there are many activities in which these students do not want to participate and many situations they do not prefer (e.g., changes in routine). Teaching students an appropriate way to express refusal should reduce or eliminate challenging behavior that serves that function.

At this point, the teacher must also decide whether general vocabulary (e.g., "food," "more," "want," "hey," "clothes") might serve the individual better or whether specific vocabulary (e.g., "cookie," "orange juice," "red sweater") should be emphasized (Reichle & Sigafoos, 1994). The advantage of general vocabulary is that, for those students who learn slowly, these words serve a variety of functions in a variety of settings. The advantage of specific vocabulary is that the individual can more clearly communicate, especially with unfamiliar listeners. Usually explicit vocabulary is taught after mastery of general vocabulary although some question the wisdom of this sequence (Sundberg & Partington, 1998).

Typical structural curricular sequences can usually be obtained from SLPs who have been specifically trained to facilitate such curriculum. Published language curricula also provide lists of developmental goals and objectives. These lists are convenient guides for teachers and parents who

Table 6.6 Sample Published Communication and Language Curricula

Teach Me Language: A Language Manual for Children with Autism, A.S., and Related Developmental Disorders	*Language Time: Autism and PDD*
SKF Books 20641 46th Avenue Langley, B.C. Canada V3A 3HA	LinguiSystems 3100 4th Ave East Moline, IL 61244-9700
Communication-Based Intervention for Problem Behavior: A User's Guide for Producing Positive Change	*Early Language Concept Kits* *Building Language Photo Library* *Magnetic Story Sequencing Kit*
Paul H. Brookes P.O. Box 10624 Baltimore, MD 21285	*Lakeshore Listening Lotto* Lakeshore Learning Materials 2695 E. Dominguez St. Carson, CA 90749
Teaching Developmentally Disabled Children: The ME Book	*Syntax Flip Book—Revised edition*
Pro-Ed Publishing 8700 Shoal Creek Boulevard Austin, TX 78757-6897	Pro-Ed Publishing 8700 Shoal Creek Boulevard Austin, TX 78757-6897
Behavioral Intervention for Young Children with Autism	*Wh- Programs*
Pro-Ed Publishing 8700 Shoal Creek Boulevard Austin, TX 78757-6897	Pro-Ed Publishing 8700 Shoal Creek Boulevard Austin, TX 78757-6897
Individualized Assessment and Treatment of Autistic and Developmentally Disabled Children II. Teaching Strategies for Parents and Professionals	*Beginning ASL VideoCourse* Sign Enhancers 1535 State St. Salem, OR 97301
Pro-Ed Publishing 8700 Shoal Creek Boulevard Austin, TX 78757-6897	*Building Communication Competence with Individuals Who Use ACC*
The Sounds Abound Program *SPARC for Grammar* *HELP for Vocabulary*	Paul H. Brookes P.O. Box 10624 Baltimore, MD 21285

are deciding what an individual student needs to learn. Table 6.6 provides a list of some sample language curricula.

New teachers or those conducting lengthy comprehensive assessments may temporarily rely on published curricular lists. However, overreliance on published curriculum should be avoided. By law, school personnel must develop individualized goals and objectives based on comprehensive assessment results. Furthermore, published curricula reflect typical language milestones and students with autism, given their related cognitive disorders, may not master skills in a typical order. Refer to Chapter 4 for ideas about developing individualized curriculum goals based on individual environmental demands and opportunities. As illustration, a sample structural curricular sequence is presented in Table 6.7.

Table 6.7 Sample Curricula for Structural Communication Goals

Receptive Language

Discriminates nonlanguage sounds (TV vs. lawn mower).
Discriminates voices (goes to who is talking).
Follows one-step instructions.
Identifies body parts, objects, people.
Identifies pictures.
Identifies possessions.
Identifies objects by function.
Identifies environmental sounds.
Identifies places.
Identifies emotions.
Follows two-step instructions.
Retrieves objects out of view.
Identifies attributes and categories.
Follows directions with prepositions.
Answers yes/no questions about objects and actions.
Follows three-step instructions.
Identifies item that is missing.
Answers Wh- questions about objects and pictures.
Follows complex instructions from a distance.
Identifies items as same or different.
Identifies plural vs. singular.
Answers Wh- questions about short story or topic.
Follows instructions: "ask" vs. "tell."

Expressive Language

Points to desired object in response to "What do you want?"
Spontaneously points to desired objects.
Imitates sounds/words.
Labels objects and pictures (nouns).
Says or gestures yes/no for items.
Verbally requests desired items.
Labels verbs and possession.
Imitates two- and three-word phrases.
Uses elicited sentence to request items.
Spontaneously uses sentence to request items.
Calls parent from a distance.
Labels body parts, places, emotions, categories.
Uses present progressive verbs.
Uses simple sentences ("It's a . . .").
States "I don't know."
Asks Wh-questions.
Uses prepositional forms.
Uses appropriate plural forms.

Uses correct form of "to be."
Answers general knowledge questions.
Describes picture in a sentence.
Recalls immediate past experience.
Answers "where" and "when" questions.
Describes sequence of pictures.
Retells a story.
Recalls past events.
Describes topics and objects not in view.
Tells own story.
Uses correct verb tense.
Uses appropriate passive forms.
Asserts knowledge.
Answers advanced general knowledge questions.
Describes how to do something.
Answers "which" questions.
Uses appropriate contractions.
Move to abstract language skills.

Articulation

Produces isolated sound.
Produces sound in words (initial, medial, final positions).
Produces sound in one of two words.
Produces sound in sentence.
Produces sound in sentence in response to questions.
Produces sound in sentence in conversation.

Syntax

Nouns (chair).
Simple verbs (want).
Uses noun phrases with intransitive verb.
Indefinite pronouns (that).
Personal pronouns (I, you).
Main verbs (is).
Uses noun phrase with transitive verb plus noun phrase.
Uses noun phrase and form of "to be" and noun object.
Secondary verbs (want to see).
Uses irregular past forms of verb tenses.
Negatives (no).
conjunctions (and).
Wh-questions ("What is that?").
Prepositions (in/on).
Adjectives (red).
Possessives (hers).
Adverbs (fast).

Functional Goals and Curriculum. The many structural aspects of language may be difficult to teach to students who typically have little motivation to communicate. Thus, functional language and communication goals may be even more important. Teaching students to spontaneously use communicative behaviors to achieve various purposes better serves the individual in everyday activities. Typical functional goals might include these:

1. Expanded use of communicative functions and semantic categories

2. Increased frequency and variety of interactive experiences

3. Increased spontaneous and self-initiated communication

4. Use of appropriate non-verbal communication

5. Use of appropriate social conventions (manners)

The overriding goal in teaching functional language is to move from elicited responses (the teacher says "What do you want?" and the child responds "Sandwich") to spontaneous language (the child comes to the teacher and says "I want a sandwich"). Functional language curricula such as the sample sequence provided in Table 6.8 typically list semantic and pragmatic skills that may first be elicited from the student, but are ultimately produced spontaneously in appropriate contexts. It is important to teach language uses that match students' desires and their environmental demands. For example, if a student is currently most interactive when she is hungry, facilitate spontaneous requesting during these times. The important thing to remember is that the skill being taught should be potentially useful to a particular student. Published curricula may or may not provide

Table 6.8 Sample Functional Communication Curricular Sequence

Semantics (Move from elicited to spontaneous)

Uses nouns as agents and objects.
Uses action words appropriately.
Uses appropriate social words in greetings, farewells, apologies.
Describes attributes of people or things.
Uses agent–action–object constructions.
Indicates location of objects with three-word sentences.
Correctly uses common pronouns.
Responds verbally to questions.
Uses proper nouns appropriately.
Uses possessives appropriately.
Uses negatives appropriately.
Verbally affirms or agrees.
Coordinates two ideas into a sentence.
Identifies time or duration of an event.

Pragmatic Functions
(Move from elicited to spontaneous)

Requests food or object.
Requests attention, affection, assistance.
Requests information, permission, peer/adult interaction.
Refuses.
Protests.
Expresses cessation of an activity.
Affirms in answer to a question.
Comments about an object, action, mistake.
Expresses humor.
Expresses confusion or fear.
Expresses frustration or anger.
Expresses happiness or sadness.

Functional Communication

Asks appropriate questions.
Interrupts appropriately.
Initiates greetings and farewells.
Uses eye contact, gesture, or name to identify the next speaker.
Responds appropriately with smiling, frowning, and other facial expressions.
Modifies voice volume for various situations.
Clarifies a topic for discussion.
Asks for clarification of a topic.
Takes turns in a conversation.
Accepts momentary silence in a conversation.
Uses short responses (why, really, oh) to keep a conversation going.
Closes conversations appropriately.
Is polite and tactful.
Adjusts the formality of language for various situations.
Resists topic change when more discussion is desired.
Facilitates a positive social interaction.
Communicates negative statements appropriately.

useful skills for each student. Further, functional goals should be taught concurrently with structural goals so that the individual can receive natural reinforcement for using language.

Cognitive Goals and Curriculum. As previously mentioned, many in the field of language development believe that language cannot be mastered without cognitive prerequisites (e.g., Snyder & Lindstedt, 1985). Prelinguistic cognitive skills may include the following: (1) imitation (motor and speech), (2) attending to things in the environment and what others attend to, (3) guiding others' behavior (e.g., placing adult's hand on the cabinet door), (4) using simple gestures for communicative purposes, (5) tool use and symbolic play, and (6) taking another's perspective. A more specific sample prelinguistic cognitive sequence appears in Table 6.9.

For very young children with autism or those with more severe cognitive delays, you might need to teach prelinguistic cognitive skills. It is usually recommended that cognitive, structural, and functional language skills be taught concurrently (Maurice et al., 1996). However, in the case of very young children, early cognitive development may need to precede language training. In either case, cognitive and language development will be enhanced by both specific skill training and a context rich in interaction and instructional support. Language acquisition, as complex as it is, will necessitate instructional techniques emanating from more than one language theory.

Strategies for Teaching Language and Communication

Best practices for teaching language and communication skills to students with autism continue to be controversial. The reason for disagreement about effective instructional approaches is directly related to the variation among language development theories. One's philosophy about how language develops dictates training methods. Those

Table 6.9 Sample Prelinguistic Curricular Sequence

Attending	Play
Makes eye contact when prompted or called.	Explores toy operations.
Sits in seat on command.	Hands toy to adult if needing help.
Responds to simple motor direction.	Pretends (sleeping and eating).
Sustains eye contact for up to 5 seconds in response to prompt.	Uses common objects and toys appropriately.
Makes eye contact in response to name from a distance.	Plays with dolls.
Responds verbally when name is called.	Pretends with more than one person or object (brushes doll's and mother's hair).
Makes eye contact during conversation.	Combines two toys in pretend play (pours from pitcher into cup).
Makes eye contact during group instruction.	Plays house.
Imitation	Stacks and knocks down blocks.
	Plays with sand and water (filling, pouring, dumping).
Imitates gross motor movements.	Pretends external events (store shopping, doctor, teacher).
Imitates actions with objects.	Pretends in sequences (combs hair, gives bath, puts to bed).
Imitates fine motor movements.	Associative play.
Imitates oral motor movements.	Imaginative play.
Imitates sequenced gross motor movements.	Uses dolls and puppets to act out scenes.
Imitates sequenced actions with objects.	Plans a sequence of pretend events.
Imitates actions paired with sounds.	Full cooperative play.
Imitates block patterns and drawings.	
Imitates complex sequences.	
Imitates peer play.	
Imitates verbal responses of peers.	

From Maurice, C., Green, G., & Luce, S. C. (1996). *Behavioral intervention for young children with autism: A manual for parents and professionals* (pp. 66–69, 306–309). Austin, TX: Pro-Ed.

who believe it must unfold would advocate an indirect, facilitative approach. Those who believe language is acquired through reinforcement and imitation would advocate a more direct approach. The methods presented in this book are based on two theoretical models, behavioral (ABA) and interactive, because the two have been shown to be effective with individuals with autism (Kaiser, 1993; Lovaas, 1977, 1987; Prizant & Wetherby, 1998). Thus, we recommend strategies based on a combination of these models. The interactive model is based on Bruner's (1977) view that language is learned through social interactions. The behavioral model is based on Skinner's (1957) view that language needs to be directly shaped and reinforced.

Behavioral Model. Discrete trial training, also known as discrete trial format (DTF), which was discussed in detail in Chapter 5, is the primary teaching strategy associated with the behavioral model. With DTF, students are taught predominantly discrete behaviors in an Antecedent→Response←Consequence format through massed repetitive trials. Reinforcement and data collection are an integral part of the program. In a discrete trial format, the student responds to teacher cues, receiving immediate feedback from the teacher as to whether the response was correct or not. Although DTF has been found to be effective in teaching many components of language (Carr, 1985; Heflin & Simpson, 1998; Lovaas, 1977, 1987; Maurice et al., 1996), it has been criticized for not resulting in spontaneous speech and generalization (Gresham & MacMillan, 1997; Reichle & Keogh, 1986).

Therefore, we recommend that teachers use DTF for teaching language skills at the acquisition and fluency levels (initial learning), and for teaching any skills that dictate drill and practice for mastery (e.g., receptive and expressive labeling). Although natural social interactions typically stimulate language development, many children with autism fail to participate in natural interactive contexts. In these cases, a highly structured behavioral approach such as DTF will most likely be more effective initially. After mastery of early structural and prelinguistic cognitive skills, teach-

ers and parents should begin to apply interactive and generalization strategies toward complex structural and functional goals.

Using DTF for language training has the advantages of (1) creating a predictable routine in which to learn, (2) providing consistency in terms of cues and feedback, and (3) being more efficient. As a result, children with autism may find this type of training preferable to less structured strategies; even teachers may prefer the scheduled teaching. For example, a teacher may want to teach a student receptive labeling. Rather than awaiting a natural opportunity to label, the teacher may structure a DTF session as follows:

The teacher has a sock, shoe, and shirt on the table in front of the student.

Teacher: Jason, look at me. Point to shoe.

Jason: (Looks away.)

Teacher: Jason, look at me (physically moves head to face her).

Teacher: Point to shoe (takes Jason's hand and points to shoe).

Jason: (Complies.)

Teacher: Good pointing (gives Jason a raisin and marks response on data form).

This teaching trial would probably be repeated several times in a row or interspersed with other teaching trials. At some point the prompts would be faded and, presumably, Jason would learn to point to each named item, regardless of its position on the table. Similarly, teaching a student to make a request using a DTF session may go like this:

The teacher has a lemon, a cookie, and some juice on the table in front of the student:

Teacher: Diane, look (teacher sweeps hand over items). What do you want?

Diane: Juice.

Teacher: Use a sentence. What do you want? I. . . .

Diane: I want juice, please.

Teacher: Good talking! (gives a sip of juice and marks response on data sheet).

The teacher may continue trials until no verbal prompting is necessary, and should soon move to interactive procedures for maintaining and generalizing the responses.

Many language behaviors can be taught using massed trials of DTF, and adults can be taught to apply DTF effectively. Some formal DTF programs insist that DTF be conducted according to a designated format with no variation (e.g., 40 hours per week, nonuse of pre-attending cues, or rigid adherence to time constraints) (Lovaas, 1987). It has been our experience that DTF can be flexibly applied and still result in skill mastery. However, it is important to be consistent in the presentation of antecedent stimuli, prompts, and consequences until generalization and spontaneity are targeted. For generalization and spontaneity, antecedent stimuli should be "loosened," prompts faded, and reinforcement thinned.

DTF can often result in learning when used in a less than 40-hour-per-week regimen (Gresham & MacMillan, 1997). Of course, the more DTF is used, typically the more the child learns. But overly intensive training may actually have detrimental effects on the learner, the trainers, and the parents (Gresham & MacMillan, 1997). The decision about how much time should be spent with DTF sessions should be based on a comprehensive needs assessment, environmental demands, and learner tolerance. For example, a student who has speech and occasionally interacts with others would probably not need endless hours of one-to-one drill and practice in order to improve his language. However, a child who rarely interacts, shows little or no desire to communicate, and has no speech may very well benefit from intensive training. DTF can also be effective for teaching alternate communication systems (i.e., visual communication systems, sign language, computerized devices).

One example of a published language program based in behavioral theory is *TALK* (*Training for Acquisition of Language in Kids*) (Drash & Tudor, 1991). This highly structured program is applicable for children aged 6 months to 2 years (Scott, Clark, & Brady, 1999). The program addresses both cognitive and language skills and aims for normal language functioning. The curriculum includes goals for increasing vocalizations, shaping desired speech sounds, shaping words, and then naming objects and pictures. Ultimately, sentences are shaped and reinforced. Two key elements of the program are that it be initiated with young children (under age 4 preferably) and that parents learn the structured training approach and remain consistent.

Interactive Model. Contrary to the rather clinical trial training approach, the interactive model of language development is based on the assumption that language develops through social interactions in natural contexts and, therefore, "language should always be presented to the child in a meaningful situation" (Snyder & Lindstedt, 1985, p. 31). In this approach, teachers and parents would engage children in functional activities that allow them to manipulate the environment, and training would occur in natural settings such as the cafeteria, the bus, the rest room, or the kitchen. The interactive model also implies that language develops as a function of cognitive development and, in turn, promotes cognitive development. Thus, language acquisition is facilitated through play, exploring and manipulating the environment, motor imitation, and prelinguistic non-verbal interactions (e.g., Harris & Vanderheiden, 1980).

Many important aspects of the interactive model are important to communication in children with autism (i.e., internal motivation, teaching in natural contexts, individual control of the environment, frequent social interactions, and teaching prelinguistic skills). However, utilizing the interactive approach alone is not recommended. The problem with this methodology is that it assumes internal motivation to communicate and natural acquisition of prelinguistic skills. Because most children with autism do not typically display these attributes, a combination of interactive and behavioral methodology is indicated, especially for eliciting more spontaneous and generalized language use (e.g., Hart & Rogers-Warren, 1978; Kaiser, 1993; Neel & Billingsley, 1989; Ogeltree & Oren, 1998). Milieu teaching as described in Chapter 5 illustrates this combination of behavioral and interactive models (the reader is referred to Kaiser, 1993, for a detailed description of milieu teaching as a strategy for increasing functional language).

Milieu teaching is based on the assumption that language is a social communication medium, not just a formal linguistic system (Kaiser, 1993; Ostrosky, Drasgow, & Halle, 1999). The emphasis is on finding a communication system that is easy to learn, teaching responses that are immediately useful to an individual, and training in natural contexts to ensure generalization. As you might remember, milieu teaching consists of four basic procedures: (1) **model,** providing a cue for a student to respond in certain situations; (2) **manding** or instruction-model, giving an instruction about how to respond; (3) **time delay,** waiting for response initiation; and (4) **incidental teaching,** which is used only in requesting situations. In incidental teaching, the teacher arranges items such that an individual wants them, then uses the other milieu teaching techniques to elicit a request, more complex language, or a conversation. With milieu teaching, the teacher is expected to establish a stimulating teaching environment. Such a classroom might include language paired with routines; interesting materials and activities; adults and peers who insist on communication and reinforce spontaneous initiations; and assistance, materials, and/or activities only in response to communication (Kaiser, 1993).

Table 6.10 lists the procedures for milieu teaching as it applies to language development. Particular milieu teaching procedures should be chosen based on the amount of assistance required. Providing models and instructions are a form of prompting. Avoid using too few or too many prompts and be ready to fade them as soon as possible. Also, pick the procedure that matches the natural flow of the activity. For example, if a student wants a Beanie Baby but does not know what it is called, the teacher should model ("Beanie Baby. Say, Beanie Baby"). On the other hand, if a student has requested the Beanie Baby in the past but now only points, the teacher might use time delay, because the student knows how to correctly respond without prompts. Note that milieu teaching still requires direct instruction or the components of DTF (i.e., cueing, prompting, responding, consequating, data collection). The difference is that in milieu teaching the teacher arranges the environment so that the child is intrinsically motivated to communicate, instruction occurs in natural situations, and natural consequences provide reinforcement.

A sample milieu teaching session might go something like this:

The teacher places Tommy's stim-toy out of reach and tells him it is time for work (incidental teaching).

Tommy: (Goes to the shelf and reaches for the stim-toy.)

Teacher: What do you want, Tommy? (mand/instruction.)

Tommy: (Signs "toy.")

Teacher: Good signing, Tommy. You can have the toy after we work for fifteen minutes. Do you want to work with the puzzle or with the word cards (holds one in each hand)?

Tommy: (Turns to the teacher and reaches for the puzzle.)

Teacher: Pauses (time-delay).

Tommy: (Points to the puzzle.)

Teacher: Signs "Want puzzle." (model).

Tommy: (Imitates signs.)

Teacher: Good signing, Tommy! (Hands him the puzzle and tells him to sit down at the table.) (reinforcement).

The primary component of incidental teaching, and milieu teaching in general, requires school personnel to arrange environments in such a way as to stimulate requesting and commenting. Kaiser (1993) recommends several strategies for arranging the physical environment such that a student *wants* to communicate and so that many opportunities occur in which to prompt and reinforce language responses. Table 6.11 lists some ideas for arranging the environment for the purpose of stimulating communication.

Furthermore, a stimulating classroom should contain interesting, reinforcing activities and mate-

Table 6.10 Milieu Teaching Procedures for Language Development

Model

1. Present model related to child's interest (say "Drink water").
   a. Correct response: praise, expand, access to object.
   b. Incorrect response: move to step 2.
2. Repeat model (say "Drink water").
   a. Correct response: praise, expand, access to object.
   b. Incorrect response: move to step 3.
3. Provide corrective feedback ("Drink water") and access to object.

Mand Model

1. Present instruction related to child's interest ("Tell me what you want").
   a. Correct response: praise, expand, and access to object.
   b. Incorrect response: move to step 2.
2. Provide a second instruction/mand ("Tell me what you want").
   a. Correct response: praise, expand, and access to object.
   b. Incorrect response: move to step 3.
3. Go back through the steps in the model procedure.

Time Delay

1. Present time delay of approximately 5 seconds.
   a. Correct response: praise, expand, and access to object.
   b. Incorrect response: move to step 2.
2. Present second time delay (about 5 seconds).
   a. Correct response: praise, expand, and access to object.
   b. Incorrect: move to step 3.
3. Present steps back in mand/model procedure.
   a. Correct response: praise, expand, and access to object.
   b. Incorrect response: move to step 4.
4. Present steps back in the model procedure.

Incidental Teaching

1. Arrange the environment such that there is a favorite item that the individual can see but cannot reach.
2. Obtain joint attention.
   a. If the individual requests the item, use time delay, mand/modeling, or modeling to elicit an expanded response or engage the student in a conversation.
   b. Correct response: give the item and answer with expanded language.
   c. Incorrect response: Use time delay, mand/modeling, or modeling to obtain an attainable imitation.
   d. Correct response: give the item and answer with expanded language.

rials and be staffed with adults who are ready and able to respond appropriately to language attempts by their students. This means that the adult must immediately attend, give feedback, provide the requested material or assistance, and provide expanded language and appropriate affect (e.g., smiling, touching, warm tone of voice, positive interactive style). Note that adults should refrain from providing too much help in the absence of communicative responses. An interactive model will not work if adults do not attend to, cue, prompt, and reinforce students for communicating.

Additional Language Strategies. Many teaching strategies are appropriate for language training that can be used in conjunction with DTF and milieu teaching. One such strategy involves the notion of observational learning (Charlop, Schreibman, & Tryon, 1983), a primary method for language development in typically developing children. **Observational learning** is based on the premise that children learn by watching others (modeling). Because children with autism typically do not naturally attend to relevant models in their environment nor learn to imitate easily,

Table 6.11 Ways to Arrange the Environment to Elicit Language

- *Interesting materials.* Entice students to attend to and want materials and activities that are known to interest them. For example, a teacher purposely activates a computer game that includes ringing bells when Delise is sitting on the couch self-stimulating. Delise stops and looks at the computer.

- *Out of reach.* Not being able to reach a desired object often results in communication attempts. For example, the teacher places a banana on the shelf above the sink when Tommy is washing his hands. Tommy finishes washing and reaches for the banana.

- *Inadequate portions.* Language can be elicited when students want to participate in an activity but lack the material(s) to do so. For example, everyone is handed headphones for music listening except Dylan. The teacher turns on the tape recorder and Dylan says "No."

- *Choice making.* It is very likely that students will communicate when given a choice. For example, Tomas is asked whether he wants a lemon or a cookie. Tomas says "Cookie."

- *Assistance.* Often students will communicate when they want to do something and need assistance doing it. The teacher locks the door then announces that it is time to go outside. Sara reaches the door first and cannot open it. "Open door," she says.

- *Silly situations.* Often language can be stimulated by doing something unexpected and silly. For example, when folding towels with Phillip, the teacher wraps the towel around her head. Phillip looks at the teacher and says "No, fold it."

using language models has not been a primary intervention technique. Nevertheless, Coleman and Stedman (1974) used peer models to increase receptive labeling and increase verbalizations in individuals with autism. These authors reinforced a peer model for appropriate voice tone and for using different vocabulary. The target student with autism also improved voice tone and vocabulary usage after watching the other student receive reinforcement. In some instances, video modeling has been found to be effective in teaching conversation skills and question-asking in students with autism (Charlop & Milstein, 1989). If a student with autism has a propensity to echo, then modeling may be a useful strategy to try.

Expansion is another method of facilitating language development (Rappaport, 1996). Expanding the student's language means repeating a child's utterance or gesture and adding one word or sign for more complex grammar. Next, have the student repeat the expanded sample. For example, a student may say "Airplane" while looking up at the sky. The teacher then says "Airplane flying." If the student does not repeat the utterance, the teacher prompts by saying "You say 'Airplane flying'. " Rappaport further recommends the use of (1) short, clear sentences, (2) exaggerated intonation and volume, and (3) slow talking.

Children with autism often respond to music, so phrases or words spoken with rhythm and exaggerated intonation may be easier for them to imitate. For example, saying "All gone" with arm gestures, raised eyebrows, and a sing-song intonation might best facilitate correct responding. Adults might try varying their own intonation, speaking softly, then loudly so students can discern the difference, and modifying their verbal pace.

Classroom or home routines provide another means for stimulating language production, particularly for making choices, requests, and protesting. *Joint Action Routines (JARs)* (Neel & Billingsley, 1989; Snyder-McClean, McClean, Etter-Schoeder, & Rogers, 1984) is a program that describes how to use routines in such a manner. In this program, teachers arrange certain routines (those ending in a product, those relating to an activity, and those related to cooperative turn-taking) such that they occur in a set sequence each day. Language responses are then embedded in the routine. For example, a student may be required to wash hands, come to the snack table, request a snack, request more, clean up his trash, say thank you, and go to the next activity. The language and self-help behaviors result in natural reinforcment (the snack), so additional reinforcement is generally unnecessary. However, be careful not to over-structure the day, thus preventing spontaneous communication (Ogletree & Oren, 1998).

Neel and Billingsley (1989) recommend that adults allow students to express their wants and needs, thus promoting spontaneous communication. To facilitate spontaneous communication, teachers should take a "listener's" role, observing and attending to students. Spontaneous communication posits that rather than the teacher initiating language learning, the child is instructed to initiate interactions that result in various learning opportunities. For example, Koegel (1995) recommends teaching individuals to make queries as a method for enhancing child-initiated and spontaneous interactions. Queries such as "What's that?" are common in typically developing children and usually result in interaction and labeling, both opportunities for learning. Queries can be used across settings, providing a learning tool and an opportunity for expanded language. Koegel recommends the following teaching queries:

- **Teach "What's that?"** Place favorite objects in a sack and prompt the child to say "What's that?" If the response is given, the teacher removes the item, labels it, and gives it to the child. Gradually fade the prompt. Once the query is produced unprompted, prompt and require the child to label the item before receiving it. Fade the sack and place items on a table. Elicit the query and label for each while verbally praising for correct responses. Prompting can occur in generalized environments so that ultimately the child has acquired a method for learning vocabulary without adult initiation.

- **Teach "where" questions.** Place favorite items in various locations without the child's knowledge. The child is then prompted to ask "Where is it?" Given that question, the adult, using prepositions, tells the child where it is and the child is allowed to retrieve it. The child is next prompted and required to not only ask where it is, but to state the appropriate preposition (e.g., under, on, behind) before being allowed to retrieve it.

- **Teach "whose" questions.** Using attractive items, prompt the child to say "Whose is it?" before being given the item. Next require the child to give the possessive before receiving the item (Mama's, baby's, yours, mine). The first-person possessives will be the most difficult to teach.

- **Teach "What happened?"** Using a pop-up book or other interactive toy, prompt the child to say "What happened?" after the adult manipulates the toy. Reinforce for correct responding and next require the child to repeat the past tense of the verb (e.g., the cow jumped). In this way, students can learn verb tenses through a structured yet self-initiated procedure.

Language training techniques should be embedded within every activity throughout the day. Teachers and parents should take advantage of every opportunity to elicit, expand, motivate, and reinforce communication and language. However, it is also important to avoid frustrating children to the point of inappropriate behavior (e.g., teacher puts the dessert on the shelf and forgets about it).

Dealing with Echolalia. Traditionally, it was thought that eliminating echolalia would facilitate language. However, some think that echolalia may be a necessary stage between language comprehension and production and may also serve various communicative functions (Prizant & Rydell, 1984; Prizant & Schuler, 1987b; Wetherby et al., 1998). Thus, it may be best to use echolalia to shape spontaneous language (Manning & Katz, 1991). Rydell and Prizant (1995) recommend the following intervention procedures for students with echolalia:

1. Assess the student's echolalic responses for communicative intent, for initiations, and for flexibility (i.e., mitigated echolalia).

2. Establish individualized language goals based on assessment results.

3. Initially encourage echolalia as legitimate communication.

4. Expand the uses of echolalia.

5. Facilitate using echolalia to communicate across people and settings.

6. Prompt mitigated echolalia and productive utterances.

7. Prompt productive utterances used for a variety of purposes in a variety of contexts.

Manning and Katz (1991) describe a procedure whereby the teacher responds to and reinforces peer models for correct language responses as a way to decrease echoed responses in students with autism. Additionally, these authors recommend consistent attention to the intent of the child who echoes, while providing a simplified correct language version in place of an echoed utterance. For example, a child may repeat the peer's model "I want a cookie" when he really wants juice. The teacher would attend to the echoed response and say "Want juice," followed by the juice. Donnellen, Gossage, LaVigna, Schuler, and Traphagen (1976) used **volume cueing** as a way to prompt correct nonechoed responses. In this technique, teachers give the stimulus (e.g., "How are you?") in a very soft voice, while prompting the answer ("I'm fine") in a very loud voice. The student learns to echo the loud portion but not the soft portion. The prompt is gradually faded to a whispered prompt (while the cue is given in a regular conversational pitch). If necessary, the teacher might place his fingers on the student's mouth to prevent echoing until the desired prompt is given.

Carr, Schreibman, and Lovaas (1975) suggested that students be taught to say "I don't know" or "I don't want to" as a way to decrease their echolalic responses. This suggestion is based on the assumption that echolalia increases in situations of high anxiety, distraction, or fatigue, and decreases in familiar situations in which the child understands what is expected and can easily emit requested behaviors. Rydell and Prizant (1995) recommended that teachers use simplified language to ensure the child understands, assuming auditory comprehension difficulties are also connected to heightened echolalic responses. Finally,

it is suggested that if teachers use nondirective cues (low-constraint interactions), as opposed to teacher-directed high-constraint interactions, within a predictable context, echolalia may likely decrease. Although a directive interaction style may be used to instruct various language skills, a facilitative style may be best for decreasing echolalia.

For those students who exhibit high-frequency noncommunicative echolalic and perseverative speech, the best approach may be to teach alternate forms of communication. This is also true for older students who have no speech at all or very few vocalizations. Not only can alternate communication forms eliminate noncommunicative echolalia, they may facilitate verbal production, while immediately providing a more accessible means of communicating (Rydell & Prizant, 1995).

Augmentative and Alternative Communication Systems

Because speech is so difficult to prompt and shape, some students who have not responded to intensive speech training may need to be taught alternative ways of communicating. These are typically individuals who require intensive drill and practice to master even the most basic skills, who seem unmotivated to use speech for communicative purposes, and/or who never acquire speech at all. Typical augmentative and alternative communication (AAC) systems include (1) sign language, (2) visual communication systems using objects, pictures, or words, and/or (3) computerized devices. Deciding when to use AAC systems and which particular system to use requires deliberate consideration. Speech is the much preferred communication form because it requires no physical aids and is universally understood. However, if a student does not seem able to master speech such that she or he can use it for various communicative functions, then another system may be considered. Above all, it is important to provide each student with some means of useful communication.

Decisions about the type of AAC system to teach must be based on individualized assessment. Consider such factors as developmental abilities, age, cognitive skills, environment, vocabulary needs, communication partners, and functional skills. AAC systems were not originally designed for individuals with autism; rather, they were designed for individuals with severe sensory, cognitive, and/or physical disabilities. Thus, matching a particular AAC system to an individual who has no physical or sensory impairment means thinking through several issues. Consider:

1. Whether the system is portable

2. Whether the student may be motivated to use it

3. Whether the system is flexible, allowing a wide variety of vocabulary and functions

4. How easy it is to prompt responses

5. Whether others will understand communicative responses

6. The potential for expanded language

7. Whether the system will be useful for a particular individual (Layton & Watson, 1995)

Very often, the communication program will be one consisting of a variety of language systems rather than a singular approach.

Sign Language. In the 1970s, probably out of frustration from trying to teach speech, several researchers attempted to teach individuals with autism to communicate using **sign language** (Carr, 1979; Creedon, 1973; Schaeffer, Musil, & Kollinzas, 1980). Instead of using sign language as though the child were deaf, signs were paired with speech as **total communication** or **simultaneous communication.** In many instances, total communication resulted in better speech ability for children with autism (Carr, 1979; Miller & Miller, 1973). These positive results may be due to the visual nature of this system. Additionally, many signs directly illustrate the referent. This means that some signs look like what they symbolize (e.g., combing hair, crying, drinking) and, thus, are perhaps easier to comprehend than speech symbols.

From an instructional point of view, signs are much easier to prompt and shape than are speech responses. Thus, children may acquire functional language at a faster rate. Sign language, like speech, is an **unaided language system.** This means that no physical aids are required in order for communication to take place. So, sign language is portable (the language system follows the child) and flexible (various concepts can be communicated). Signs can be delivered rapidly and constructed into sentences with complex meanings. However, mastering sign language, as with speech, presupposes that those with whom the child interacts model sign language and understand it. Because most people outside of the classroom do not comprehend sign language, the potential for naturally occurring expansion and reinforcement is usually limited. A language system that others do not understand may also inhibit integration efforts and most certainly will not be functional across contexts. In fact, many students with autism who are taught sign language essentially remain mute and acquire relatively little functional language (Layton & Watson, 1995).

Nevertheless, communicating with even a few signs is superior to not communicating at all or communicating with inappropriate behavior. Sign language is generally recommended for use with older students who have failed to acquire speech rather than with very young students who may simply be language delayed. It is also important to determine if a student has the motoric capabilities to make discrete signs. If fine motor development is delayed and the child does not readily imitate motor responses, then sign language may not be a viable choice. Sign language can be taught through discrete trial and milieu teaching procedures using similar curricular sequences as those developed for speech acquisition. The most common manual communication systems are American Sign Language (ASL) or Signing Exact English (SEE 2). For more information regarding specific strategies and resources for teaching sign language, we recommend Carr (1982, 1983), Layton and Watson (1995), and Goetz and Hunt (1994).

Visual Communication Systems. Speech and sign language rely on transient auditory and visual stimuli. This means that language components are speedily delivered and the listener/viewer must be able to comprehend quickly and remember after only fleeting exposure. Many students with autism have difficulty processing (attending to, discriminating, comprehending, and remembering) transient stimuli, and appear to respond better to static visual cues. **Visual communication systems** that rely on objects, pictures, symbols, or printed words for transmitting messages provide such cues. Visual systems allow students to scan options and take the necessary time to select appropriate responses. Additionally, visual communication systems do not require eye contact or imitative skills (difficult skills for many individuals with autism). Furthermore, responses can be easily prompted. Students can be taught to point to or hand pictures to a person in order to acquire a desired object or activity, to make choices, or to cue themselves about tasks, destinations, or time. For initial language acquisition, visual systems have been shown to be effective (Bondy & Frost, 1994; Miranda & Schuler, 1986).

Visual communication systems are **aided systems** because they require the use of physical paraphernalia. Either the student must carry pictures in a wallet or notebook or be able to access a communication board. This means that visual systems are not particularly portable. Communication boards, particularly, are not easily transported. The board or notebook will need to be durable and lightweight and the student will need to remember to take it with him. Otherwise various boards will need to be constructed and remain in each appropriate environment. Certainly, generalization is hampered by the necessity of this physical aid. Although most people understand when a picture of an object is shown, pictures of actions or concepts may not be as readily discernible. Furthermore, communication partners (e.g., teachers, parents, siblings) do not use picture communication, so modeling and expansion may be limited. Visual communication cannot be quickly delivered, and it is difficult to form sentences or complex meanings with visual aids.

However, many children with little or no communicative ability have been taught to use pictures for various communicative functions. Visual systems, which were discussed in Chapter 5, usually consist of boards, paper, or cloth containing objects or object symbols (e.g., fork for "lunch"); photographs of people, places, and things; or line drawings arranged for communicative use. Using Velcro to attach the symbols allows teachers to change or rearrange the symbols, to use symbols in various environments, and to require the student to remove or place symbols as a signal to do something or that they are finished doing something. The most widely used symbolic pictures are the *Picture Communication Symbols* (Mayer-Johnson, 1992) in both book and software format. The pictures can be used for communicative purposes as well as for environmental supports.

Aided language stimulation. (Goosens, Crain, & Elder, 1992) is an example of a visual communication strategy whereby speaking partners point to symbols on a communication board as they say a word. Cafiero (1998) recommends that board symbols be chosen using an ecological assessment approach (see Chapter 4) and that individual communication boards be constructed for a specific environment or activity. Estimates are that students who establish **joint attention** (shared attention to a common item or activity) and point may be able to handle up to 50 symbols on a language board. Others may be limited to two to six symbols (Cafiero, 1998). Symbol arrangement on the board should resemble correct grammar (i.e., subjects, verbs, objects, descriptors) and should make sense to the user. Communication boards can provide a means of interaction simply by providing visual cues to aid verbal comprehension or by allowing students to initiate interactions by pointing to or handing symbols to another.

Frost and Bondy (1994) have developed a picture communication system, the *Picture Exchange Communication System (PECS),* which initially teaches children to request objects or activities by handing others pictures symbolizing the desired item. They reason that requesting, rather than labeling, should be taught first is because students will be much more motivated to request things.

Requesting further requires an interaction, often a spontaneous interaction, and will most often result in natural reinforcers. Picture requesting is gradually shaped into other language functions and, in some cases with young children, functional speech develops (Bondy, 2000). Bondy and Frost (1994) also claimed that children previously using sign language developed a larger vocabulary with pictures. For additional ideas and recommendations for increasing communicative functions with visual strategies, the reader is also referred to Hodgdon (1995a, 1995b).

Some students with autism may be able to comprehend the printed word even though speech eludes them. Because words, like pictures, provide a static visual cue, non-verbal individuals with autism have sometimes developed reading skills (LaVigna, 1977; Wolff & Chess, 1965). An advantage of using the printed word is that most people will understand what is being communicated. Students may be taught to carry word cards or sentence strips and to produce them for various functions. Again, portability is a problem. Students will have to carry word cards in a pocket, on a key ring, or in a notebook. Speed of language production is also a problem and the student will have to comprehend oral input, because others do not use the printed word to communicate as they are talking. However, reading can enhance other language skills such as sentence structure and concept development (Layton & Watson, 1995).

Computerized Devices. Many types of computers have speech output capability and can translate pictures, symbols, or word formats into speech. These devices are available in a range of sizes and weights and can display various combinations of letters, symbols, pictures, and words. Some computerized devices have monitors displaying a few items at a time, whereas others may have a static display for visual scanning. Some allow for recording voices, whereas others are programmed with a computer voice. In some cases, students might need to be taught to select among many displays for specific occasions, thus making their use more complicated. Computerized de-

vices range in price from several hundred to several thousand dollars.

The biggest challenge with the use of computerized devices for students with autism is portability. Unless the device is lightweight, small, and durable, it will not be practical as an interaction tool in various contexts. An additional challenge may be teaching a student how to use the device. Many students may become more intrigued with the apparatus itself (pushing buttons for a sound) and hence fail to recognize its communicative potential (Layton & Watson, 1995). Some popular computerized devices are the *Wolf* (Wayne County Regional Education Service Agency, Wayne, MI), the *Intro Talker, Touch Talker,* and *Light Talker* (Prentke & Romich Co., Wooster, OH), the *McCaw* (Zygo Industries, Inc., Portland, OR), *Alltalk* (Adaptive Communication Systems, Inc., Pittsburgh, PA), and the *DynaMyte* (Sentient Systems Technology, Inc., Pittsburgh, PA.). Computers, as with other AAC systems, may stimulate speech production while providing some form of functional communication so the computerized vocabulary should be chosen through an individualized ecological assessment process. Remember that aided language systems will only be useful if the aid is present and working when the child wants to communicate. Absent, damaged, neglected, or ill-conceived language aids will do little to facilitate functional communication.

All AAC systems can be taught using discrete trial and milieu teaching techniques in natural contexts. Work still needs to be done to develop AAC systems for very young and very active children. However, AAC systems have been effective in reducing and preventing problem behavior and providing individuals with an appropriate means of interaction. None of these language systems needs to be used exclusively. In most instances, using a combination of AAC systems and speech may be best, and in some cases speech production might improve with the use of AAC systems (Reichle & Keogh, 1986).

Choosing which language system to utilize is a difficult process. The danger lies in insistence on one particular language form to the exclusion of others, thus possibly depriving individuals of communicative ability. There is also a danger in choosing a form that may not be functional, thus wasting precious instructional time. A third danger pertains to generalizability. This is a particular problem for manual communication and the use of nonrecognizable symbols. For more information about speech and AAC training we recommend contacting:

American Speech-Language-Hearing Association, 10801 Rockville Pike, Rockville, MD 20852; 301-897-5700

Communication Aid Manufacturers' Association (CAMA), P.O. Box 1039, Evanston, IL 60204; 800-441-2262

SUMMARY

Language and communication skills may be the most important thing to teach. Without such skills, a student is often powerless to affect his environment and may resort to inappropriate and bizarre behavior for which he will be punished and segregated. The individual's prognosis, not to mention immediate well-being, is dependent on functional communication ability. However, the complexity of language and its interaction with cognitive and social development make for an instructional challenge. With a myriad of skills across several domains, teachers will do well to read and learn as much about language/communication training as possible. This chapter has provided a brief overview of language development, problems specific to individuals with autism, ways to assess communication and language for instructional purposes, curricular sequences, best practices in terms of teaching strategies, and alternate and augmentative communication systems. As with all instructions, teachers must consider long-term, intermediate, and short-term goals and remember that independence across settings is the ultimate target.

KEY POINTS

1. Teaching individuals to communicate in appropriate and functional ways is one of our most important tasks and should be addressed at every opportunity.

2. Speech is only one form of communication. It includes many receptive and expressive components.

3. The structure of language is important; however, for individuals with autism, communicative forms and functions may be better assessment and intervention targets.

4. There are many theories about how language develops. The theories directly relate to methods of assessment and intervention. Behavioral and interactive theories are recommended.

5. Language typically develops from prespeech in infants to complex language understanding and use in the first 4 to 5 years of life.

6. Language development is closely related to cognitive development. Debate exists about exactly how they are related. Students with autism typically show many problems in both areas.

7. Assessment and intervention for language/communication development needs to occur in four areas: social domain, linguistic domain, communicative domain, and cognitive domain. Both formal and informal assessment methods can provide useful information in these domains.

8. Published language curricula can provide ideas for structural and functional goals for students. However, it is important to ensure an individualized education plan.

9. Discrete trial format is a behavioral technique useful for initial language skill training. However, it seldom produces spontaneous language use or generalization.

10. Milieu teaching combines the interactive and behavioral model to provide opportuni-

ties for spontaneous language and generalization. It is not, however, as efficient as DTF for skill acquisition.

11. Echolalia is a form of communication and might be used to enhance language development.

12. AAC systems include sign language, visual systems, and computerized devices. These systems may be used when speech does not develop and may result in more speech production.

13. Each individual should be provided with a means to communicate his needs and desires. This may mean combining strategies and language systems.

REFERENCES

American Psychiatric Association. (1994). *Diagnostic and statistical manual of mental disorders* (4th ed.). Washington, DC: Author.

Bandura, A. (1977). *Social learning theory.* Englewood Cliffs, NJ: Prentice-Hall.

Bartak, L., Rutter, M., & Cox, A. (1975). A comparative study of infantile autism and specific developmental receptive language disorder: 1. The children. *British Journal of Psychiatry, 126,* 127–145.

Bartolucci, G., Pierce, S., & Streiner, D. (1980). Cross-sectional studies of grammatical morphemes in autistic and mentally retarded children. *Journal of Autism and Developmental Disorders, 10,* 39–50.

Berk, L. E. (1999). *Infants, children, and adolescents.* Needham Heights, MA: Allyn & Bacon.

Bondy, A. S. (2000). Picture exchange communication systems. In J. Scott, C. Clark, & M. Brady (Eds.), *Students with Autism: Characteristics and instruction programming.* San Diego: Singular (pp. 209–211).

Bondy, A. S, & Frost, L. A. (1994, August). The picture exchange communication system. *Focus on Autistic Behavior, 9*(3), 1–18.

Bray, C. M., & Wiig, E. H. (1987). *Let's talk inventory for children.* San Antonio, TX: The Psychological Corporation.

Bruner, J. S. (1977). Early social interaction and language acquisition. In H. R. Schaffer (Ed.), *Studies in mother-infant interaction.* New York: Academic Press.

Cafiero, J. (1998). Communication power for individuals with autism. *Focus on Autism and Other Developmental Disabilities, 13*(2), 113–121.

Carr, E. G. (1979). Teaching autistic children to use sign language: Some research issues. *Journal of Autism and Developmental Disorders, 9,* 345–359.

Carr, E. G. (1982). Sign language. In R. Koegel, A. Rincover, & A. L. Egel (Eds.), *Educating and understanding autistic children* (pp. 142–157). San Diego, College-Hill Press.

Carr, E. G. (1983). *How to teach sign language to developmentally disabled children.* Austin, TX: Pro-Ed.

Carr, E.G. (1985). Behavioral approaches to language and communication. In E. Schopler & G. B. Mesibov (Eds.), *Communication problems in autism.* New York: Plenum Press.

Carr, E., Schreibman, L., & Lovaas, O. I. (1975). Control of echolalic speech in psychotic children. *Journal of Abnormal Child Psychology, 3,* 331–351.

Charlop, M. H., & Milstein, J. P. (1989). Teaching autistic children conversational speech using video modeling. *Journal of Applied Behavior Analysis, 22,* 275–285.

Charlop, M. H., Schreibman, L., & Tryon, A. S. (1983). Learning through observation: The effects of peer modeling on acquisition and generalization in autistic children. *Journal of Abnormal Child Psychology, 11,* 355–366.

Chomsky, N. (1967). The formal nature of language. In E. Lenneberg (Ed.), *Biological foundations of language* (pp. 397–442). New York: John Wiley.

Coleman, S. L., & Stedman, J. M. (1974). Use of a peer model in language training in an echolalic child. *Journal of Behavior Therapy and Experimental Psychiatry, 5,* 275–279.

Creedon, M. P. (1973, March). *Language development in non-verbal autistic children using a simultaneous communication system.* Paper presented at the biennial meeting of the Society for Research in Child Development, Philadelphia.

DesLauriers, A. J. (1978). Play, symbols, and the development of language. In M. Rutter & E. Schopler (Eds.). *Autism: A reappraisal of concepts and treatment.* New York: Plenum Press.

Dewey, M., & Everard, M. (1974). The near normal autistic adolescent. *Journal of Autism and Childhood Schizophrenia, 4,* 348–356.

Donnellan, A., Gossage, L. D., LaVigna, G. W., Schuler, A., & Traphagen, J. D. (1976). *Teaching makes a difference: A guide for developing successful classes for autistic and other severely handicapped children.* Santa Barbara, CA: Santa Barbara Public Schools.

Drash, P. W., & Tudor, R. M. (1991). Language and cognitive development: A systematic behavioral program and technology for increasing the language and cognitive skills of developmentally disabled and at-risk preschool children. In M. Hersen, R. M. Eisler, & P. M. Miller (Eds.), *Progress in behavior modification* (Vol. 26, pp. 173–220). Newbury Park, CA: Sage.

Durand, V. M. (1993). Functional communication training for challenging behaviors. *Clinics in Communication Disorders, 3,* 59–70.

Fay, W. (1971). On normal and autistic pronouns. *Journal of Speech and Hearing Disorders, 36,* 242–249.

Fay, W., & Schuler, A. L. (1980). *Emerging language in autistic children.* Baltimore, MD: University Park Press.

Frith, U. (1996). Social communication and its disorder in autism and Asperger syndrome. *Journal of Psychopharmacology, 10,* 48–53.

Frost, L. A., & Bondy, A. S. (1994). *PECS: The picture exchange communication system: Training manual.* Cherry Hill, NJ: Pyramid Education Consultants.

Giddan, J. J., & Ross, G. J. (2001). *Childhood communication disorders in mental health settings.* Austin, TX: Pro-Ed.

Gleason, J. B. (1997). *The development of language* (4th ed.). Needham Heights, MA: Allyn & Bacon.

Goetz, L. & Hunt, P. (1994). Augmentative and alternative communication. In E. C. Cipani & F. Spooner (Eds.). *Curricular and instructional approaches for persons with severe disabilities* (pp. 263–288). Needham Heights, MA: Allyn & Bacon.

Goosens, C., Crain, S. S., & Elder, P. (1992). *Engineering the preschool environment for interactive symbolic communication 18 months to 5 years developmentally.* Birmingham, AL: Southeast Augmentative Communication Conference Publications.

Gresham, F. M., & MacMillan, D. L. (1997). Autistic recovery? An analysis and critique of the empirical evidence on the Early Intervention Project. *Behavioral Disorders, 22,* 185–201.

Guess, D., Benson, H., & Siegel-Causey. (1985). Concepts and issues related to choice making and autonomy among persons with severe disabilities. *The Journal of the Association for Persons with Severe Handicaps, 10*(2), 79–86.

Harris, D., & Vanderheiden, G. (1980). Augmentative communication techniques. In R. Schiefelbusch (Ed.), *Nonspeech language and communication: Analysis and intervention* (pp. 259–302). Austin, TX: Pro-Ed.

Hart, B., & Rogers-Warren, A. (1978). Milieu teaching approaches. In R. Schiefelbusch (Ed.), *Language intervention strategies* (pp. 193–236). Austin, TX: Pro-Ed.

Heflin, L. J., & Simpson, R. L. (1998). Interventions for children and youth with autism: Prudent choices in a world of exaggerated claim and empty promises. Part I: Intervention and treatment option review. *Focus on Autism and Other Developmental Disabilities, 13*(4), 194–211.

Hinerman, P. S. (1983). *Teaching autistic children to communicate.* Rockville, MD: Aspen.

Hodgdon, L. A. (1995a). *Visual strategies for improving communication: Practical supports for school and home.* Troy, MI: QuirkRoberts Publishing.

Hodgdon, L. A. (1995b). Solving social–behavioral problems through the use of visually supported communication. In K. Quill (Ed.), *Teaching children with autism* (pp. 265–286). Albany, NY: Delmar Publishers.

Hurtig, R., Ensrud, S., & Tomblin, J. B. (1982). The communicative function of question production in autistic children. *Journal of Autism and Developmental Disorders, 12,* 57–69.

Interview with ASAF grant winner Dr. Ami Klin. (1999). *Advocate: The Newsletter of the Autism Society of America, 32*(3), pp. 12–14.

Kaiser, A. P. (1993). Functional language. In M. E. Snell (Ed.), *Instruction of students with severe disabilities.* New York: Macmillan.

Kamhi, A. G. (1981). Nonlinguistic symbolic and conceptual abilities of language-impaired and normally developing children. *Journal of Speech and Hearing Research, 24,* 446–453.

Koegel, L. K. (1995). Communication and language intervention. In R. L. Koegel and L. K. Koegel (Eds.), *Teaching children with autism* (pp. 17–32). Baltimore, MD: Paul H. Brookes.

Krug, D. A., Arick, J. R., & Almond, P. J. (1993). *Autism screening instrument for educational planning.* Austin, TX: Pro-Ed.

LaVigna, G. W. (1977). Communication training in mute autistic adolescents using the written word. *Journal of Autism and Childhood Schizophrenia, 7,* 135–149.

Layton, T. L., & Watson. L. R. (1995). Enhancing communication in nonverbal children with autism. In K. A. Quill (Ed.), *Teaching children with autism: Strategies to enhance communication and socialization.* Albany, NY: Delmar Publishers.

Lefrancois, G. R. (1995). *Of children: An introduction to child development* (8th ed.). Belmont, CA: Wadsworth.

Lord, C., Rutter, M., Dilavore, P. C., & Risi, S. (1999). *Autism diagnostic observation schedule (ADOS).* Los Angeles: Western Psychological Services.

Lovaas, O. I. (1977). *The autistic child: Language development through behavior modification.* New York: Irvington.

Lovaas, O. I. (1987). Behavioral treatment and normal educational and intellectul functioning in young autistic children. *Journal of Consulting and Clinical Psychology, 55,* 3–9.

Lowell, M. (1976). Audiological assessment. In E. R. Ritvo (Ed.), *Autism: Diagnosis, current research and management.* New York: Spectrum.

Manning, A. L., & Katz, K. B. (1991). Facilitating functional communication with echolalic language users. *Focus on Autistic Behavior, 6*(3), 1–7.

Maurice, C., Green, G., & Luce, S. C. (1996). *Behavioral intervention for young children with autism: A manual for parents and professionals.* Austin, TX: Pro-Ed.

Mayer-Johnson, R. (1992). *The picture communication symbols* (Books I–III). Solana Beach, CA: Mayer-Johnson Co.

Menyuk, P. (1978). *Language and maturation.* Cambridge, MA: The MIT Press.

Mesibov, G., Schopler, E., Schaffer, B., & Landrus, R. (1988). *Individualized assessment and treatment for autistic and developmentally disabled children.* Austin, TX: Pro-Ed.

Miller, A., & Miller, E. E. (1973). Cognitive-development training with elevated boards and sign language. *Journal of Autism and Childhood Schizophrenia, 3,* 65–85.

Miranda, P., & Schuler, A. L. (1986). Teaching individuals with autism and related disorders to use visual symbols to communicate. In S. Blackstone (Ed.), *Augmentative communication: An introduction.* Rockville, MD.: American Speech-Language-Hearing Association.

Miranda-Linne, F., & Melin, L. (1997). A comparison of speaking and mute individuals with autism and autistic-like conditions on the autism behavior checklist. *Journal of Autism and Developmental Disorders, 27,* 245–263.

Needleman, R., Ritvo, E. R., & Freeman, B. J. (1980). Objectively defined linguistic parameters in children with autism and other developmental disabilities. *Journal of Autism and Developmental Disorders, 10,* 389–398.

Neel, R. S., & Billingsley, F. F. (1989). *IMPACT: A functional curriculum handbook for students with moderate to severe disabilities.* Baltimore, MD: Paul H. Brookes.

Ogletree, B. T., & Oren, T. (1998). Structured yet functional: An alternative conceptualization of treatment for communication impairment in autism. *Focus on Autism and Other Developmental Disabilities, 13*(4), 228–223.

Ostrosky, M. M., Dragow, E., & Halle, J. W. (1999). How can I help you get what you want? A communication strategy for students with severe disabilities. *Teaching Exceptional Children, 31*(4), 56–61.

Paluszny, M. J. (1979). *Autism: A practical guide for parents and professionals.* Syracuse, NY: Syracuse University Press.

Parker, R. (1996). Incorporating speech-language therapy into an applied behavior analysis program. In C. Maurice, G. Green, & S. C. Luce (Eds.), *Behavioral intervention for young children with autism.* Austin, TX: Pro-Ed.

Partington, J. W., & Sundberg, M. L. (1998). *The assessment of basic language and learning skills (The ABLLS).* Pleasant Hill, CA: Behavior Analysts.

Paul, R. (1987). Communication. In D. J. Cohen & A. M. Donnellan (Eds.), *Handbook of autism and pervasive developmental disorders.* New York: John Wiley & Sons.

Paul, R., & Cohen, D. J. (1985). Comprehension of indirect requests in adults with mental retardation and pervasive developmental disorders. *Journal of Speech and Hearing Research, 28,* 475–479.

Paul, R., Fischer, M. L., & Cohen, D. J. (1988). Brief report: Sentence comprehension strategies in children with autism and specific language disorders. *Journal of Autism and Developmental Disorders, 18,* 669–677.

Piaget, J. (1954). *The construction of reality in the child.* New York: Basic Books.

Prizant, B., & Rydell, P. (1984). Analysis of functions of delayed echolalia in autistic children. *Journal of Speech and Hearing Research, 27,* 183–192.

Prizant, B. M., & Schuler, A. L. (1987a). Facilitating communication: Theoretical foundations. In D. J. Cohen, A. M. Donnellan, & R. Paul (Eds.), *Handbook of autism and pervasive developmental disorders.* New York: John Wiley & Sons.

Prizant, B. M., & Schuler, A. L. (1987b). Facilitating communication: Language approaches. In D. J. Cohen, A. M. Donnellan, & R. Paul (Eds.). *Handbook of autism and pervasive developmental disorders.* New York: John Wiley & Sons.

Prizant, B. M., & Wetherby, A. M. (1998). Understanding the continuum of discrete trial traditional behavioral to social pragmatic developmental approaches in communication enhancement for young children with autism/PDD. *Seminars in Speech and Language, 19*(4), 329–353.

Pronovost, W., Wakstein, M., & Wakstein, D. (1966). A longitudinal study of speech behavior and language comprehension in fourteen children diagnosed as atypical or autistic. *Exceptional Children, 33,* 19–26.

Quill, K. A. (1995). *Teaching children with autism: Strategies to enhance communication and socialization.* Albany, NY: Delmar Publishers.

Rappaport, M. (1996). Strategies for promoting language acquisition in children with autism. In C. Maurice, G. Green, & S. C. Luce (Eds.), *Behavioral intervention for young children with autism* (pp. 307–319). Austin, TX: Pro-Ed.

Reichle, J., & Keogh, W. J. (1986). Communication and instruction for learners with severe handicaps: Some unresolved issues. In R. H. Horner, L. H. Meyer, and H. D. B. Frederick (Eds.), *Education of learners with severe handicaps: Exemplary service strategies.* Baltimore, MD: Paul H. Brookes.

Reichle, J., & Sigafoos, J. (1994). Communication intervention for persons with developmental disabilities. In E. C. Cipani & F. Spooner (Eds.), *Curricular and instructional approaches for persons with severe disabilities* (pp. 241–262). Needham Heights, MA: Allyn & Bacon.

Rosenhan, D. L. & Seligman, M. E. P. (1989). *Abnormal psychology* (2nd ed.). New York: W. W. Norton.

Rydell, P., & Mirenda, P. (1994). The effects of two levels of linguistic constraint on echolalia and generative language production in children with autism. *Journal of Autism and Developmental Disorders, 21,* 131–157.

Rydell, P. J., & Prizant, B. M. (1995). Assessment and intervention strategies for children who use echolalia. In K. A. Quill (Ed.), *Teaching children with autism: Strategies to enhance communication and socialization* (pp. 105–129). New York: Delmar Publishers.

Schaeffer, B., Musil, A., & Kollinzas, G. (1980). *Total communication.* Champaign, IL: Research Press.

Schopler, E., & Mesibov, G. B. (1995). *Learning and cognition in autism.* New York: Plenum Press.

Schopler, E., & Reichler, J. (1995). *Individualized assessment and treatment for autistic and developmentally disabled children. Vol. 1: Psychoeducational profile-revised (PEP-R).* Austin, TX: Pro-Ed.

Schuler, A. L., & Prizant, B. M. (1985). Echolalia. In E. Schopler & G. B. Mesibov (Eds.), *Communication problems in autism.* New York: Plenum Press.

Schuler, A. L., & Prizant, B. M. (1987). Facilitating communication: Prelanguage approaches. In D. J. Cohen, A. M. Donnellan, & R. Paul (Eds.), *Handbook of autism and pervasive developmental disorders.* New York: John Wiley & Sons.

Scott, J., Clark, C., & Brady, M. (1999). *Students with autism: Characteristics and instruction programming.* San Diego: Singular.

Shapiro, T., Huebner, H. F., & Campbell, M. (1974). Language behavior and hierarchic integration in the psychotic child. *Journal of Autism and Childhood Schizophrenia, 4,* 71–90.

Shulman, B. B. (1986). *Test of pragmatic skills, revised edition.* Tuscon; AZ: Communication Skill Builders.

Skinner, B. F. (1957). *Verbal behavior.* New York: Appleton-Century-Crofts.

Snyder, L. S., & Lindstedt, D. E. (1985). Models of child language development. In E. Schopler & G. B. Mesibov (Eds.), *Communication problems in autism.* New York: Plenum Press.

Snyder-McClean, L., McClean, J., Etter-Schoeder, R., & Rogers, N. (1984). Structuring joint action routines: A strategy for facilitating communication in the classroom. *Seminars in Speech and Language, 5,* 213–228.

Staff. (1999). Video study hints that autism can be spotted in babies. *Autism Research Review International, 13*(1), 1.

Sundberg, M. L., & Partington, J. W. (1998). *Teaching language to children with autism or other developmental disabilities.* Danville, CA: Behavior Analysts.

Tager-Flusberg, H. (1996). Brief report: Current theory and research on language and communication in autism. *Journal of Autism and Developmental Disorders, 26,* 169–172.

Tallal, P. (1976). Rapid auditory processing in normal and disordered language development. *Journal of Speech and Hearing Research, 19,* 561–571.

Vygotsky, L. S. (1962). *Thought and language* (E. Hanfman & G. Vakar, Trans.). Cambridge, MA: The MIT Press.

Wallace, G., Cohen, S. B., & Polloway, E. A. (1987). *Language arts: Teaching exceptional students.* Austin, TX: Pro-Ed.

Wetherby, A. M., Prizant, B. M., & Hutchinson, T. A. (1998). Communicative, social/affective, and symbolic profiles of young children with autism and pervasive developmental disorders. *American Journal of Speech-Language Pathology, 1,* 79–91.

Wiig, (1982). *Let's talk inventory for adolescents.* San Antonio, TX: The Psychological Corporation.

Wing, L. (1981). Language, social, and cognitive impairments in autism and severe mental retardation. *Journal of Autism and Developmental Disorders, 11,* 31–44.

Wing, L. (1996). *The autistic syndromes.* London: Constable.

Wolff, S., & Chess, S. (1965). An analysis of the language of fourteen schizophrenic children. *Journal of Child Psychology and Psychiatry, 6,* 29–41.

Yawkey, T., Askov, E., Cartwright, C., Dupuis, M., Fairchild, S., & Yawkey, M. (1981). *Language arts and the young child.* Itasca, IL: F. E. Peacock.

7

Remediating Deficits in Socialization

Did you know that:

- To improve social performance for children with autism, you must provide opportunities to socialize?

- Inclusion does not necessarily result in better social skills for children with autism?

- Sometimes we need to teach children how to be friends?

- Direct instruction of social skills does not necessarily result in improved friendships?

Children and youth with autism characteristically display low levels of social engagement, usually preferring to be left alone. In fact, Kanner (1943) chose the term *autism,* from the Greek *autos,* meaning "self," to reflect this cardinal symptom of the disorder. So great is the desire to be left alone that attempts to interact by teachers or nondisabled peers may produce strongly negative behaviors such as self-abuse, aggression, tantrums, or crying from a child with autism. Social initiations by a student with autism are usually for the purpose of meeting needs or wants. For example, a child may take the teacher's hand and lead her to the refrigerator, then place her hand on the refrigerator door. This behavior does not reflect a desire for physical contact or social interaction; it is simply the child's way of communicating that he

wants something to eat or drink that is in the refrigerator. Even children and youth with autism who exhibit higher levels of social behavior (e.g., they watch people in their environment, initiate limited conversations, or respond to greetings) typically do not use high-quality skills. For example, a student who initiates conversations may use unusual syntax or may talk only about one or two preferred topics. As students with autism grow older, they may display more socially oriented behavior (Scott, Clark, & Brady, 2000), but without intervention, continue to lack the skills needed to effectively participate in social situations. These individuals will probably never achieve the level of social competence of nondisabled individuals. However, well-planned and comprehensive interventions will increase opportunities for integrated placements, and will increase options for independent functioning.

Children and youth with autism may have impairments in a variety of aspects of socialization. Socialization impairments in the population of individuals with autism may include deficits in social skills and peer interactions (Stone & Lemanek, 1990), lack of acknowledgement of or response to the emotions of others (i.e., lack of empathy)(Howlin, 1986), deficits in social aspects of communication, as you learned in Chapter 6, and a general apparent lack of interest in social interactions (i.e., lack of motivation). Additionally, children with autism exhibit an absence of joint attention, a characteristic that appears to be unique to autism (Mundy, 2000) and is one of the four primary social symptoms of autism in the DSM-IV (American Psychiatric Association [APA], 1994). **Joint attention,** or shared attention, is a social experience shared by two or more people, often initiated by one person. For example, a toddler who is enjoying a toy will typically look away from the toy to the parent in the room, and back to the toy, as if to share the experience with the parent. Young students watching a magic act may look at and direct expressions of amazement toward their teacher on the conclusion of a dramatic trick. When adults experience a powerful stimulus (e.g., a good joke, a beautiful painting, a disturbing site, a surprise) they often look at other people who are sharing the same experience and smile, nod, shake their heads, or exhibit other appropriate, shared responses.

One of the most challenging aspects of improving social skills in students with autism is generalization of newly learned skills. As you know, students with autism usually do not automatically generalize new skills to different environments, unfamiliar peers or adults, or any other change from the original learning conditions. Effective social behavior is almost entirely a process of generalizing skills to novel conditions. For example, young children learn to say hello in response to a greeting. They probably exhibit this skill fairly predictably in the presence of familiar adults, but may turn away shyly or simply not respond when greeted by an unfamiliar adult. Eventually, with practice, and informal prompting and reinforcement, children learn to respond not only to unfamiliar adults, but to novel greetings (e.g., "Hi there!" or "Good morning") and in new settings. Children with autism will not generalize most skills without structured interventions to achieve that goal.

Many believe that socialization deficits are related to—even rooted in—cognitive and communication deficits. Kanner (1943) attributed the characteristic social isolation of children with autism specifically to insufficient language skills.

Furthermore, development of joint attention skills in infancy is thought to be an important prerequisite to cognitive and communication development in preschoolers. Perhaps most importantly, higher level skills in joint attention in very young children appear to be predictive of better language development later (Mundy, 2000).

Social skills are important for successful functioning in all aspects of life at home, school, and work (Lovaas, 1987; McEvoy & Odom, 1987). Even many daily living tasks require some degree of socialization: riding the bus, shopping for groceries, making telephone calls, interacting with fellow employees and supervisors, leisure activities, and so forth. The degree to which a child with autism exhibits social skills and social interest is an important predictor of successful functioning later in life (Matson & Swiezy, 1994; Schopler & Mesibov, 1983). Indeed, individuals who exhibit better social skills are more likely to be accepted in and benefit from integrated settings in school and the community, are more likely to live at a higher level of independence, and are more likely to work in more integrated settings. One significant correlate of social skills is peer acceptance: Children who exhibit good social skills are likely to be accepted by peers, whereas children who exhibit poor social skills are more likely to be overlooked or actively rejected. Research suggests that having meaningful friendships is important to the development and well-being of children (Hurley-Geffner, 1995). For typical children, friends not only provide companionship, but also serve as a context for development of complex social skills (e.g., play, social communication, self-control, cooperation, perspective-taking) and may facilitate children's reasoning ability (Nelson & Aboud, 1985) and mental health (Crockett, 1984).

In addition to the importance of friendships, the long-term ramifications of poor social competency and few friendships in childhood have been well established. A substantial body of research has documented that children who have weak or negative peer interactions are at greater risk than their peers for delinquency, poor school performance, and mental health problems in adulthood. Although these studies examined the effects of poor social skills in nondisabled children, Hurley-Geffner (1995) advises that it is likely that children with autism and developmental disabilities would experience benefits from meaningful friendships. Given the important role friendships play in children's social development, clearly teachers of children with autism and developmental disabilities should pay careful attention to teaching needed social skills and developing opportunities for meaningful social interactions.

Access to integrated environments and nondisabled peers, and thus opportunities for social interaction, was the purpose of the P.L. 94-142 mandate that children with disabilities be educated in the **least restrictive environment** (LRE) (Kellegrew, 1995). This mandate was predicated on three principles: (1) that children with disabilities have a civil right to participate in the same activities and environments as nondisabled students, (2) that integration would result in improved attitudes of nondisabled children and general education teachers toward children with disabilities, and (3) that children with disabilities would benefit from exposure to nondisabled peers who model appropriate social, academic, play or leisure, and language skills. The interpretation and implementation of LRE has evolved over the years from simply sending a child with disabilities to lunch or recess with typical age-peers to full-time placement of a child with disabilities in an age-appropriate general education class, with a variety of support services. In addition, our understanding of the instructional procedures that are essential for children with disabilities to gain maximum benefit from integrated placements has grown tremendously. We now know, for example, that improving socialization outcomes for students with autism and developmental delays requires structured interventions (directed both toward the child with disabilities as well as nondisabled peers), along with carefully designed opportunities to interact in meaningful contexts with nondisabled peers. When program philosophies and practices emphasize socialization interventions, and provide

a wide array of opportunities for socialization, and when these practices are supported by effective intervention procedures, children and youth with autism can be expected to achieve improved social performance (Strain, 1982).

In this chapter we will describe interventions for improving social competence in children and youth with autism, including methods for determining students' current socialization deficits and the demands of social environments, generic social intervention strategies, and intervention strategies specific to different age groups. This is an exciting area of study that is changing our views of "best practices" for improving social behavior in students with autism. Socialization interventions have evolved from rather simplistic interventions designed to improve discrete social skills in students with autism to interventions that emphasize the importance of the contexts in which those students participate and the social actions of nondisabled peers in relating to students with autism. In this chapter we will describe a variety of different types of socialization interventions, from direct instruction to peer-mediated interventions as part of milieu instruction. For most students, a combination of interventions will probably produce the strongest outcomes.

SOCIAL COMPETENCE VERSUS SOCIAL SKILLS

According to Frea (1995), "The specific level of social skills exhibited by a child may not be as important as the effect these skills have for producing positive and reinforcing interactions for all concerned" (p. 66). This quote nicely describes the difference between **social competence** and **social skills.** Social competence refers to other people's perceptions of the social performance of an individual (Hops, 1983). Socially competent individuals are typically able to initiate and maintain friendships and personal relationships, interact appropriately with authority figures, and effectively manage stressful situations. Social skills are those discrete social behaviors that are typically exhibited by socially competent individuals (e.g., eye contact, asking questions, giving compliments, responding appropriately to negative feedback).

The distinction between social competence and social skills is an important one. Appropriate use of discrete social skills does not necessarily result in social competence. This means that efforts focused only on changing the behaviors of students with autism (teaching the child to make eye contact, to respond to adults' greetings, etc.) may be misguided; the child's skills must be considered with regard to contexts in which he or she must function, and desired social outcomes within those contexts. For example, nothing is accomplished by teaching a child with autism to respond to peers' greetings if no peers then initiate greetings. Nor is it useful to teach a child with autism how to participate in leisure activities if he is then excluded from those activities by nondisabled peers. These *contexts,* then, become targets for intervention, as well as the child with autism.

In addition, adding appropriate social skills to a child with autism's behavioral repertoire probably will not result in that child being viewed as socially competent if he continues to engage in high levels of bizarre self-stimulatory behaviors, aggression, or any other behaviors that peers would find annoying or offensive. The child's inappropriate behaviors would no doubt overshadow the correct social behaviors, with the result that peers would not wish to interact with the student, regardless of the quantity or quality of her social skills.

ASSESSMENT STRATEGIES FOR DETERMINING SOCIALIZATION CURRICULUM

The first step in intervention for any area of instruction is to determine what the child needs to learn. Determining what a youngster needs to learn in the area of socialization means evaluating three areas: (1) contexts in which the child functions to determine the social demands in each, (2) the social culture of those contexts to determine socially valid skills to teach, and (3) the child's level of socialization in those contexts to determine skills the child needs to learn.

Assessment of Contexts and Determining Socially Valid Skills

Assessment of contexts means determining contexts in which the student will—or could—potentially function and the types of opportunities for social interaction within each of those contexts. However, identification of social contexts alone is insufficient. In addition, you must identify what skills are needed within those environments and what skills are reinforced (or punished). As we described in Chapter 4, the demands of specific target environments should be identified using ecological assessment. This process will result in an inventory of socialization demands, as well as skills needed for communication, work, self-direction, self-care, and so forth. The nature of the target context influences the type of socialization opportunities and skills needed to succeed in those environments. For example, the socialization demands of using a library probably revolve around initiating interaction with librarians for assistance. By contrast, having lunch with age-peers would require the far different social skills of responding to peer social initiations and possibly adult directives and initiating social interactions with peers.

Ecological assessment may be done informally, by observing in target environments or asking questions of the teachers and parents who supervise the environment. Using an informal approach, we recommend that the following five questions be answered:

1. What activities occur within this environment? For example, activities in the cafeteria might include waiting in line, getting food, moving to a table, eating, clearing the place and returning the tray, and then exiting the cafeteria.

2. How are these activities structured? Activities may be teacher directed (e.g., small-group instruction or a teacher-led game), structured but not teacher directed (e.g., peer tutoring

or cooperative learning activities, lunch, bus rides, a work activity involving two or more students), or unstructured (e.g., free time, passing in hall between classes, break time at work). Each type of structure requires slightly different social skills.

3. What types of interactions are directed to students from teachers or other adults in the environment? For example, do adults mostly give directives that require no response or directives that require a response? Or do they initiate social conversation with children in the area (e.g., a cafeteria monitor asking a student what she did over the weekend)?

4. Are interactions with peers primarily conversational or are they more activity oriented? In the cafeteria, interactions between peers probably consist mostly of engaging in conversation while eating. On the playground, interactions may include initiating a request to participate in an activity or share equipment, giving directions during a game, or having conversations. For adolescents, interactions would undoubtedly be far more verbal and less oriented to an ongoing activity.

5. What is the nature of peer interactions? This question, in particular, addresses the important issue of selecting socially valid skills to teach. For example, what are common topics of conversation? What types of activities do students participate in that involve socialization? What words and phrases are commonly used? What type of humor do students use? What gestures or movements do students use as a part of social interactions?

Along with interviewing key adults to determine needed social skills, we also recommend direct observation of same-gender age-peers in target environments. The behavior observation methods described in Chapters 2 and 3 can be used for this purpose. For example, you might first observe using anecdotal recording during a free-time period. From information gathered in the anecdotal report, you could extrapolate specific social behaviors that are likely to be exhibited by

the target group. Next, you could use event recording (or duration recording as appropriate) to determine at what rate certain skills are demonstrated or for how long. For example, you might measure the average rate at which students initiate verbal interactions with one another or the average duration of a conversational exchange. This information will help teachers establish valid target skills and criteria.

Ecological assessments can also be conducted using formal ecological inventories, such as those listed in Table 4.6 in Chapter 4. These instruments will aid in identifying a wide variety of skills, including socialization skills, needed for success in other environments: general education contexts, home, leisure activities, work, and so forth.

Information gathered through formal or informal ecological assessment will constitute the framework for skills needed by a given student to facilitate full participation in social contexts. This information will help in the curriculum development process described in Chapter 4. For example, as described in Table 4.2, the first step is to establish goals. Here are some sample goals for socialization:

Long-term goal: The student will live semi-independently with a roommate.

Intermediate goal: The student will engage in cooperative cooking and cleaning activities (e.g., making cookies, making a bed).

The student will initiate conversations with others.

The student will exhibit joint attention during mutual leisure activities (e.g., watching videos, playing a game, bowling).

Short-term goals: The student will initiate greetings to peers and teachers.

The student will share supplies during a cooperative activity.

The student will ask for supplies as needed.

The student will exhibit joint attention when an adult provides an interesting stimulus (e.g., using a yo-yo).

Teachers will need to task-analyze target skills to facilitate instruction. For example, one of the skills identified as important to success in the cafeteria might be "carrying on a conversation with a peer who initiates." This general skill could be task-analyzed into the following steps:

- Look at the person who spoke.

- Think about what he or she said.

- Respond appropriately (e.g., answer question or make a comment on the same topic).

- Listen for peer to respond.

- Continue.

Understanding the discrete steps involved in a complex skill such as "carrying on a conversation" will help you better identify what needs to be taught, prompted, and/or reinforced.

Once the requisite skills have been identified, the next step is determining the student's level of proficiency in those skills (Bambara & Browder,

1991). Skills that the student lacks become targets for instruction. Skills that are present, but weak, need to be strengthened, either through increased opportunities for practice or stronger reinforcement for exhibiting the skills.

Assessment of Student Skill Levels

Student proficiency in target skills may be evaluated directly, using direct observation techniques; indirectly, using rating scales; or via a combination of the two approaches. Direct observation techniques use event recording or duration recording to measure the number, rate, percent, or duration of discrete skills. Table 7.1 lists the steps used in direct observation to assess the use of social skills.

Another way to evaluate students' use of social skills is with formal assessment instruments, including adaptive behavior scales and developmental scales. Table 7.2 lists commercially available scales in each of these areas. Note that some of

---

Table 7.1 Steps in Assessing Social Skills Using Direct Observation

1. Determine the skills you wish to assess, described operationally. Here are some examples of operational definitions of social skills:
   - Taking turns: Student waits while other students take their turns in an activity; student participates without prompting when it is his turn.
   - Initiating interactions with peers: Student stands 2 to 3 feet from peer; within 5 seconds of approach, student says peer's name, and makes a comment appropriate to the situation: asks a question, asks peer to play a game, asks to join a game, gives a compliment, and so on, then waits for peer's response.
   - Responding to peers' initiations: Given an initiation from a peer (question, invitation, etc.), student responds appropriately (answers question, says "yes" or "no" to the invitation, etc.) within 5 seconds.
   - Playing with a friend: Student participates appropriately in an activity that requires turn-taking and/or sharing with one or more peers (e.g., playing four-square, jumping rope, playing a video game, playing a board game, using the slide).

2. Determine the most appropriate measurement system for each skill. For the skills described above, appropriate measurement systems would include these:
   - Taking turns: Restricted event recording
   - Initiating interactions: Nonrestricted event recording
   - Responding to peers' initiations: Restricted event recording
   - Playing with a friend: Duration recording

3. Select a time and place to observe. Remember that you should observe when and where the skill is needed. Therefore, if you wish to increase a student's participation in social interactions during recess, you should observe during recess.

4. As you observe your target student, collect data for the same skills on a typical peer selected at random. This will provide an indication of the level of socialization that may be required for successful participation. Data on peers' skills may also help determine a target criterion for your student(s).

   - Once data have been gathered, the last step is to compare your student's data against that of peers and then develop objectives for intervention.

these instruments have not been normed on students with autism and developmental delays, but may provide helpful information, particularly about the student's level of socialization in environments outside of school. For example, the teacher could have the student's parents, job coach, or after-school caregiver complete a rating form periodically. This may give the teacher some indication of the degree to which the student is generalizing social skills being taught at school.

Discrepancies between social demands of target environments and a student's level of proficiency in those skills becomes the basis for determining the social skills curriculum for that child. Target skills need to be taught, shaped, prompted, and reinforced in all pertinent environments.

Thus, the first step in designing socialization interventions is to decide what the student needs to learn. This should be a process that begins with both formal and informal ecological assessment methods. Ecological assessment will help teachers identify activities that occur in target socialization contexts, and specific social behaviors that are reinforced—or punished—in those contexts. Another purpose of ecological assessment is to determine whether support is available in target contexts and to what extent support is provided. Next, direct observation or rating scales should be used to determine each student's level of competence in skills needed for success in target environments. Any discrepancies between skills needed for success and individual student skill levels become targets for instruction. The remainder of this chapter will focus on empirically based interventions for improving social performance.

Table 7.2 Rating Scales for Assessing Social Skills

Adaptive Behavior Scales

- *The AAMD Adaptive Behavior Scale—School Edition* (ABS-SE) (Lambert & Windmiller, 1981)
  Publishers Test Service
  CTB/McGraw-Hill
  Del Monte Research Park
  Monterey, CA 93940

Part Two of the ABS-SE assesses behavior in the following domains: Aggressiveness; Antisocial versus Social Behavior; Rebelliousness; Trustworthiness; Withdrawal versus Involvement; Mannerisms; Interpersonal Manners; Acceptability of Vocal Habits; Acceptability of Habits; Activity Level; Symptomatic Behavior; and Use of Medications.

- *The Vineland Adaptive Behavior Scales* (VABS) (Sparrow, Balla, & Cicchetti, 1984)
  American Guidance Service
  4201 Woodland Road
  P.O. Box 99
  Circle Pines, MN 55014-1796

The VABS is intended for use with individuals from birth to age 18. The Socialization Domain assesses interpersonal relationships, play and leisure skills, and coping skills (e.g., following rules).

Developmental Assessments

- *Early Learning Accomplishment Profile* (ELAP) (Glover, Preminger, & Sanford, 1978) (birth to age 3)
- *Learning Accomplishment Profile—Revised* (LAPR) (Sanford, 1975) (ages 3–6)
  Kaplan Press
  Winston-Salem, NC

NOTE: Both the ELAP and the LAP-R assess young children's development across a variety of developmental areas, including social skills. Items that the child does not pass become instructional targets.

- *Behavioral Characteristics Progression* (BCP) (VORT Corporation, 1973)
  VORT Corporation
  P.O. Box 60132
  Palo Alto, CA 94306

This is one of the most comprehensive programs available, a distinction that also makes it a bit unwieldy. The BCP includes 2,400 behaviors arranged in more than 50 strands. Social-emotional skills are addressed throughout the BCP.

INTERVENTIONS FOR INCREASING SOCIAL SKILLS AND SOCIAL COMPETENCE

Attention to socialization is considered an important part of the best practices for children with severe disabilities. Meyer, Eichinger, and Park-Lee (1987), in a comprehensive study designed to delineate quality indicators in instructional programs, identified 11 indicators of quality programming in socialization (see Table 7.3). These 11 indicators described specific practices in three major areas: (1) The program philosophy emphasizes the importance of socialization experiences; (2) social skills objectives are included in IEPs and are, therefore, targets for instruction; and (3) opportunities for social interaction with nondisabled peers are carefully developed.

General Considerations for Socialization Interventions

Several approaches have been shown to be promising for improving the social skills, and ultimately social competence, of students with autism. These approaches will be described later in this chapter. However, no matter what techniques are chosen to increase social skills, educators are more likely to achieve desired outcomes if certain considerations, many of which relate to contextual factors associated with socialization interventions, are observed. Many of these recommendations revolve around the importance of providing opportunities for practicing social behaviors in actual social contexts that involve nondisabled peers.

Start early. Children with autism often exhibit characteristics of social withdrawal at a very young age (Osterling & Dawson, 1994; Scott et al., 2000). Given the correlation between socialization, cognition, and communication, and the predictive aspects of socialization, the earlier socialization interventions are implemented, the better the outcomes (Frea, 1995; Strain, 1983). Inclusion in general education environments at a young age helps children with autism better learn social and play behaviors. Many early intervention programs (birth to age 3) and early childhood programs (ages 3–5) provide structured opportunities for interaction with nondisabled peers or with peers who have disabilities but exhibit developmentally appropriate social skills.

Teach social skills in context. Socialization interventions are far more effective when

Table 7.3 Quality Program Indicators in Socialization and Social Skills Instruction

1. The program philosophy emphasizes the goal of maximum participation in integrated environments.
2. The program philosophy emphasizes the goal of social acceptance and adjustment.
3. Each individualized education plan (IEP) contains objectives to develop social skills.
4. Each IEP includes objectives to teach the learner to interact with and help others.
5. Each IEP includes at least one measurable behavioral objective involving interactions with a peer who is not disabled.
6. Nondisabled peers spontaneously interact with students when passing them in the hall or meeting them in central areas, such as the lunchroom.
7. Students eat lunch in the cafeteria with peers.
8. Students participate in extracurricular activities typical for their age range with nondisabled students.
9. Students participate in daily social and leisure activities with the same-aged peers, such as recess or sports.
10. The program includes planned daily interactions with same-aged nondisabled peers.
11. Students participate in heterogeneously grouped instruction with nondisabled peers at least three times per week.

SOURCE: From Meyer, Eichinger, and Park-Lee, 1987.

provided in socially rich contexts where peers, and naturally occurring social stimuli and reinforcers, are present (Breen, Haring, Pitts-Conway, & Gaylord-Ross, 1985; Frea, 1995). It is difficult, if not impossible, to accurately imitate natural social contexts outside of those contexts. For example, it is probably not possible to duplicate those social stimuli present in a play group of children without disabilities (e.g., requests to play, comments about ongoing play activities, peer-to-peer instructions regarding a play activity) in a group comprised solely of children with autism. Teaching children with autism to recognize and respond to those stimuli requires that they have repeated exposures to natural social stimuli and naturally occurring social reinforcers.

Teach activities preferred by nondisabled peers. Students with autism should be taught to use the materials that are commonly part of the social repertoire of nondisabled students. For example, Gaylord-Ross and colleagues (1984) found that teaching students with autism to engage in activities preferred by nondisabled peers, such as playing video games, using stereos, and chewing gum, resulted in more frequent social interactions that were longer in duration than when students with autism were not taught to use those materials. In addition, these social interaction behaviors generalized to unfamiliar peers. Therefore, as part of the ecological assessment process, teachers should carefully observe the types of toys, games, activities, verbal expressions, and perhaps even clothing that are preferred by nondisabled peers. Then, children with autism should be taught typical use of these materials and activities as part of socialization interventions.

Reduce inappropriate behaviors. Seriously inappropriate behaviors should be reduced or eliminated prior to, or at least concurrent with, socialization interventions (Simpson, Myles, Sasso, & Kamps, 1991). Highly aberrant behaviors such as self-stimulation, self-abuse,

or aggression will undoubtedly result in fewer social initiations from nondisabled peers. Furthermore, children with autism who exhibit such behaviors may become targets for negative social interactions (e.g., name calling, taunts). Simpson and colleagues advise that children with autism do not need to be completely free of negative behaviors prior to socialization interventions, but they must be basically compliant. Furthermore, we would advise that social interaction programs involving nondisabled peers should never be implemented with an aggressive child with autism. Aggressive behaviors must be controlled before exposing peers to potentially dangerous behavior.

Teach pivotal behaviors. Koegel and his colleagues recommend targeting **pivotal behaviors,** or behaviors that are central to many areas of functioning (Moes, 1995). Pivotal behaviors are behaviors that serve a similar purpose in a variety of areas of functioning, including social functioning (Koegel & Koegel, 1995). As such, these behaviors can lead to higher quality social interactions and can improve generalization across behaviors and environments. Potential pivotal behaviors include initiating interactions, using appropriate affect, responding to initiations, terminating interactions, and so forth.

Strive for quality socialization experiences, not just quantity. Strive for high-quality social interactions, not just high quantity (Simpson et al., 1991). A large number of initiated greetings exhibited at odd times during the day in a monotone, expressionless fashion, are less meaningful than three or four greetings exhibited at appropriate times with enthusiasm and a smile! We believe that decisions to place students with autism, particularly older students, in general education classes on a full-time basis are decisions that are sometimes based on the quantity of social interactions rather than quality. If improving social behavior is the goal for placement with general education students, perhaps 1 or 2 hours of well-structured time, in carefully selected contexts, with peers who have been trained in peer mediation strategies would be more beneficial than full-day placement.

Emphasize generalization. Children can be taught to exhibit discrete social skills in structured situations rather easily. The challenge is teaching students to use those skills in new situations, where all of the familiar original learning conditions have changed. Generalization is, after all, the most essential component of learning: If skills do not generalize to real-life conditions, the student has gained nothing. A large body of research has delineated specific strategies for facilitating generalization, some of which were described in Chapter 5. In this chapter, we will present generalization strategies that are specific to social skills.

Intervention Approaches

Three general categories of interventions have been used successfully to improve social behavior in students with autism: **teacher-mediated interventions, self-mediated interventions,** and **peer-mediated interventions.** These are generic approaches that are appropriate for students of all ages and socialization levels. Although each of these procedures has been shown to improve the social performance of students with autism, the most effective interventions will employ two or more of these procedures within or across these categories in combination (Simpson et al., 1991). In the following sections we describe specific interventions in each of the categories described above.

Teacher-Mediated Techniques. Two types of teacher-mediated interventions have been used to increase socialization in children and youth with autism and developmental disabilities. The first is direct instruction of target skills, which typically involves discussion, modeling, and role-playing target skills. The second is social stories, a rather

new technique that is showing promise as a strategy for improving social behavior.

Direct Instruction of Social Behaviors. The first teacher-mediated approach to improving socialization is direct instruction of social skills. In a direct instruction approach, specific social skills are taught using procedures much like those used to teach academic skills. Generally this means that a curriculum is used which delineates skills to be taught and provides guidelines for instruction; that skills are taught in a teacher-led small-group format using explanation, demonstration, practice, and feedback; and that other behavioral procedures (e.g., self-monitoring, prompting, reinforcement) are used to facilitate generalization of skills. The vignette describing Ms. Jacobs' class illustrates a direct instruction approach.

Ms. Jacobs Teaches Social Skills

Ms. Jacobs teaches an intermediate class for students with autism, ages 9–11. Each of her students participates in a number of different general education activities, such as lunch, music, science, and reading. Despite having many opportunities to interact with general education peers, Ms. Jacobs' students typically interact little. They respond minimally to peer initiations and do not initiate interactions.

Ms. Jacobs believes that her students do not know many basic social interaction skills. To remedy the problem, she has implemented a social skills instruction program. First, she made careful assessments to determine skills to teach. She observed both her students and their peers in general education environments, and interviewed peers and teachers. This assessment indicated approximately 15 skills that seemed to be critical for social success. Skills targeted for instruction included answering questions, asking questions, carrying on a conversation, using humor, and sharing.

Next, Ms. Jacobs solicited four peers from general education classes to assist with social skills instruction. These peers were students familiar to her students and were selected because they had been observed attempting to interact with the students with autism. The general education peers simply participated in the group instruction, just as the students with autism.

Finally, Ms. Jacobs began instruction. The social skills group met daily, for 20 minutes per session. One or two of the four peers attended each group. The first skill taught was "answering questions." Ms. Jacobs first explained what "answering questions" meant, and she gave several examples from her students' daily lives. Next, Ms. Jacobs and her paraprofessional, Ms. Rogers, modeled the skill: The paraprofessional posed questions to Ms. Jacobs similar to the types of questions peers might ask. Ms. Jacobs would "think out loud" ("She asked me a question. I need to look at her and answer her."), then would reply to the question. Ms. Jacobs and Ms. Rogers demonstrated several examples of "answering questions." After each example, Ms. Jacobs asked for feedback from students ("Did I answer the question? Did I look at my friend?"). Next, one of the general education peers role-played the skill with either Ms. Jacobs or Ms. Rogers. Again, after each role-play, Ms. Jacobs asked other students for feedback about the peers' use of the skill. After that, the peer and the students with autism (one at a time) role-played the skill, with other students giving feedback. The peer was instructed to ask questions similar to those typically posed at lunch or other noninstructional situations. Ms. Jacobs

provided some examples. Each successful role-play was accompanied by praise from the teachers.

As she was teaching the skill, Ms. Jacobs used a chart with a picture representing the skill and listing the steps, to serve as a reminder for her students to use the skill. This chart was used at the start of each group to review the steps in the skill.

Once every student had successfully demonstrated the skill in role-play situations, students were shown a form that had the picture representing the skill at the top of the page, and five blank boxes at the bottom. Students were informed that Ms. Jacobs or Ms. Rogers would be watching them at various times, and when students used the skill of answering questions, they would earn a sticker. When all five boxes were filled, they could take the form to the principal for a special treat.

Each time a student left the classroom to attend a general education activity, he or she was reminded about using the skill of answering questions, and the steps involved. Ms. Jacobs and Ms. Rogers observed students at random times throughout the day. After each observation (e.g., at lunch), the adult gave the student feedback about his or her use of the skill and, if appropriate, gave a sticker for the student to apply to the form. In addition, any time any student was observed using the skill in any situation, Ms. Jacobs or Ms. Rogers would place a star on a chart that had a picture depicting the skill in the middle. When all the empty boxes on the chart were filled with stickers, the class could select a special group activity to do that day (e.g., make popcorn, play a game, go for a walk).

The last component of the direct instruction approach was that Ms. Jacobs informed the general education teachers and peers as skills were being addressed. She asked these individuals to praise her students any time they observed the students using the skill correctly.

Ms. Jacobs spent approximately one and one-half weeks on each skill. In addition, from time to time, she conducted review sessions for all previously learned skills. According to Ms. Jacobs' data, her students' use of the targeted skills increased dramatically after instruction. Although work remained to be done to improve her students' socialization skills, Ms. Jacobs knew her students were now far better prepared to interact with their general education peers.

Including nondisabled age-peers who are skilled in the social behaviors being taught can increase the effectiveness of direct instruction social skills lessons (e.g., Breen et al., 1985; Haring & Ryndak, 1994). Peers serve as models and help with the role-play practice. The advantages of using peers are the increased likelihood of students with autism modeling peers' use of the skills being taught (e.g., Bandura, 1977), more realistic practice scenarios, and more realistic responses to target students' use of skills during role-play practice.

Table 7.4 describes the steps in a direct instruction approach to teaching social skills. One major disadvantage of a direct instruction approach is that skills acquired and demonstrated in the instructional setting often fail to generalize. That is, students may demonstrate proficiency in a skill during the social skills lesson, but never use the skill in natural environments (e.g., the cafeteria, playground, hallways, inclusion classes). Teachers can increase the likelihood of generalization by incorporating the strategies for enhancing generalization described in the next section and by observing the general recommendations for socialization interventions noted earlier in this chapter.

Social Skills Curricula. Several commercial social skills curricula use a direct instruction approach and may be helpful in guiding social skills instruction (see Table 4.3 in Chapter 4 for a listing of social skills curricula). The *ACCEPTS* and *ACCESS* curricula are highly structured, even providing a script for teachers to follow. These are easy to use, and teachers who have never taught social skills appreciate the guidance that the script offers. The *Skillstreaming* series (*Skillstreaming in Preschool, Skillstreaming the Elementary School Child,* and *Skillstreaming the Adolescent*) are less structured, presenting each lesson in a brief outline form. Helpful features include the fact that each skill is task-analyzed, and several self-monitoring forms are included for use with each skill. *The Social Skills Intervention Guide: Practical Strategies for Social Skills Training* is coordinated with the *Social Skills Rating Scale* (Gresham & Elliott, 1990). However, commercial curricula should be used with three caveats in mind. First, none of the curricula listed in Chapter 4 have been field-tested with students with autism. Second, the skills included in each curriculum may not match the skills needed by your students, according to your ecological assessment data. Finally, the instructional procedures recommended may need to be slightly modified, depending on your students' language levels.

Instructional Scripts. One variation on the direct instruction approach involves using social scripts as a part of social interaction training. Haring and Ryndak (1994) describe social scripts as "routine social interaction patterns that can be repeated many times in a variety of contexts" (p. 303). As you have learned, social skills deficits and communication deficits are strongly interrelated. Children and youth with autism may have difficulty generating situation-appropriate words and phrases due to their language and communication deficits. Social scripts are useful in that they provide students with appropriate words to use in social interaction situations. Students are able to focus on other variables of the social situation without the obstacle of not having the words to say. Social scripts have been shown to be an effective intervention component with both preschoolers and adolescents with autism (e.g., Breen et al., 1985; Gaylord-Ross et al., 1984; Goldstein & Cisar, 1992).

Table 7.4 Direct Instruction Sequence for Teaching Social Skills

Direct instruction of social skills typically involves the following steps:

1. *Describe the skill and why it is important (rationale).* The description should include the task-analyzed steps of the skill being taught.

    EXAMPLE: "Today we're going to learn how to ask a friend to play with you. When you know how to ask a friend to play, you can play games that you like during recess and after school. Toni, you like to jump rope. You might ask a friend to play jump rope with you. Blake, you like to run. You could ask a friend to play tag with you." (Teacher would continue giving an example of how this skill could benefit each student.)

    "Here's how you ask a friend to play" (pointing to a chart with written or pictorial steps of the skill):

    - Think about what game you would like to play.
    - Decide which friend you want to ask.
    - Walk over to your friend.
    - Look at your friend and say in a nice voice, "Would you like to play _____ with me?"
    - If your friend says "no," choose another friend to ask.

2. *Demonstrate the skill.* Usually the paraprofessional or another adult assists the teacher with this step. You should demonstrate the skill several times; the more examples, the more likely students are to understand how to perform the skill.

    EXAMPLE: "Let me show you how you ask a friend to play. Let's pretend we're on the playground. I'm standing here by myself but I want to play." (Now teacher begins to act the part of a student on the playground as the other adults or nondisabled students are engaged in "playground" activities away from her.)

    (Teacher talks aloud to herself): "I'd really like to play catch. I think I'll ask Alicia if she wants to play with me. . . ."

    (Teacher approaches "Alicia"): "Alicia, do you want to play catch with me?"

    (Other adult or peer): "Sure! I'll get the ball."

    (NOTE: If nondisabled students are participating, they can be called on to demonstrate the skill).

3. *Solicit student feedback on the skill.* The teacher asks individual students to identify whether she correctly performed each step.

    EXAMPLE: "Did I decide what game I wanted to play?" (get student responses);

    "Did I ask someone to play?" (have students name the friend); and so forth.

4. *Have students role-play the skill.* Each student should practice the skill at least once, and more if needed. During the students' role-play, other participants are needed to play the roles of other students. These can be the adults in the class or, preferably, nondisabled peers. Each role-play situation should reflect individual student preferences, styles, and so forth. If nondisabled peers are participating, they should demonstrate the skills first.

    EXAMPLE: "Toni, it's your turn to practice asking a friend to play. Let's pretend we're on the playground after lunch. What game do you like to play?" and so forth. Teacher arranges the role-play to reflect the situation on the playground.

5. *Provide feedback on student performance of the skill.* After each role-play, the teacher should solicit feedback from other students in the group about the role-play. The teacher should also give feedback to the student doing the role-play.

    EXAMPLE (to other students): "Did you see Toni decide what game she wanted to play? What did she want to play? Did she ask her friend nicely?" and so forth.

    Role-play continues until each student has had the opportunity to practice the skill.

6. *Do generalization activities.* Generalization activities take place after each student has demonstrated proficiency in the skill during the role-play sessions. The purpose of generalization activities is to facilitate use of target skills in natural settings. Generalization activities might include games that require students to use target skills, self-monitoring procedures in which students keep track of their use of skills in generalized settings, and reinforcement contingencies for use of target skills in generalized settings. One important generalization strategy is to conduct social skills lessons in environments in which skills are to be used (Frea, 1995). For example, the skill of asking a student to play might be taught on the playground. The skill of responding to greetings might be taught in the hallway and at the bus area.

To use social scripts, first identify situations in which scripts may be beneficial to facilitating social interaction. For example, perhaps the teacher's assessment reveals that nondisabled peers often extend verbal greetings to one of his students in the halls as the student is walking to class in the morning, but the student does not respond. The teacher could develop a generic script that would enable the student to respond appropriately to any greeting, such as "Hi, how are you?" or "Hey, how's it going?" or "Hi, see you later!" The teacher could then use a direct instruction approach to teach the student to say these words in response to greetings.

Gaylord-Ross and colleagues (1984) used scripts as part of an intervention to increase social interactions with peers. First, they taught adolescents with autism age-appropriate games and activities (e.g., playing video games, chewing gum). Next, these researchers taught students to invite peers to join them in those activities. This was accomplished using scripts in role-play situations with socially competent peers. Another use of scripts to promote social interaction was used by Goldstein and colleagues (1988). The authors provided scripts for preschoolers with disabilities and those without to use in performing skits (e.g., a store skit and a magic show), complete with props. Each student was assigned a role and followed the script developed for that role, while encouraged by the teacher to ad-lib on the script. Resulting data showed significant increases in social interaction and the use of social language.

Social Stories. A relatively new addition to the collection of social skills interventions is **social stories.** Social stories are brief, structured stories that describe specific social situations a student will encounter and appropriate responses to the social stimuli that will be encountered in that situation (Gray & Garand, 1993). Social stories are individualized to each student's social needs and can be developed for virtually any social situation the student will encounter (initiating greeting, waiting turns, sharing, responding to social initiations, etc.).

To create a social story, a target social situation is identified, along with the social stimuli the student will encounter in that situation and desired student response(s) to those stimuli. Next, the stories are put in written format, using approximately two to five sentences, and written using language and print size appropriate for the student. For students who need visual cues, one or more pictures or icons should be used to represent each sentence. Gray and Garand (1993) recommend including three types of sentences in a social story: (1) **descriptive sentences,** which provide information about the social context (setting, people, activities, etc.); (2) **directive sentences,** which tell the student what to do; and (3) **perspective sentences,** which describe feelings of individuals involved in the situation. For example, let's say you need to teach a student how to transition from a preferred activity to a less preferred one without tantrums. Figure 7.1 shows an example of a social story that might be used for that purpose.

 We play with toys in center time every day.

 When the bell rings, I put the toys back on the shelf.

 Ms. Kathy says, "Good cleaning up, Brent!" and puts a sticker on my chart.

 Then I walk quietly to group and sit in my chair.

 Ms. Kathy says, "Good sitting, Brent!" and puts a sticker on my chart.

FIGURE 7.1 Example of a social story.

The teacher reads the story to the student just before the target social situation several days in a row. In the example shown in Figure 7.1, the story should be read to the student just before center time. Once the story has been introduced, students should be allowed access to it throughout the day. In addition to these guidelines, Scott et al. (2000) recommend having the student practice the target behavior in conjunction with reading the story. For example, the story in Figure 7.1 might be read to Brent, then during or after the story, he should practice the target behaviors (putting a toy back on the shelf, walking to group, sitting in his chair).

Social stories are thought to be beneficial because they combine information about needed social skills with visual cues (pictures and/or words). To date, little empirical evidence of their effectiveness is available. However, emerging research suggests that social stories are a promising intervention for improving social behavior (e.g., Kuttler, Myles, & Carlson, 1998).

Antecedent Prompting Procedures. According to Simpson and his colleagues (1991), antecedent prompting is a strategy in which the teacher uses one or more types of prompts to facilitate the student exhibiting an interactive behavior, which is then reinforced by peers and the teacher. **Antecedent prompting** requires placing the student in a natural context that involves social interaction with one or more socially competent peers (e.g., sharing a toy, sharing a video game, playing a game, sharing a snack). The teacher remains in proximity to the child with autism and provides prompts to the child to initiate or respond to a social interaction. Although verbal prompts are the most common, other prompts could be used as well (gestures, pictures, etc.). Typically, peers are instructed to respond positively to any initiations by the student with autism.

Ms. Jacobs, whom you met earlier in this chapter, uses antecedent prompting, in addition to direct instruction, as part of her socialization program. The vignette titled *Ms. Jacobs Uses Antecedent Prompting* describes how she uses this technique.

Ms. Jacobs Uses Antecedent Prompting

Remember Ms. Jacobs? In addition to directly teaching social skills, she also uses antecedent prompting procedures with all of her students. To do this, she and her paraprofessional, Ms. Rogers, accompany their students to activities that involve social interaction with nondisabled peers and adults. In these situations, any time there is an opportunity for their students to initiate or respond to a social initiation, they first wait 5 to 10 seconds to give their students an opportunity to respond independently. If they do not, Ms. Jacobs or Ms. Rogers prompt the correct behavior. Some of the many instances in which they use antecedent prompting include the following:

- During game time, in which general education students join the class for a variety of games and leisure activities. Stations are set up around the room, and students choose their preferred activity. During the game or activity, students are expected to make appropriate social initiations ("Do you want to play checkers?"; asking questions pertinent to the game) and responses (answering questions pertinent to the game).

- While waiting for the bus, students are expected to interact with their classmates and nondisabled peers by making greetings, asking questions, and responding to questions.

- In the lunch line, students are expected to indicate their food choices either verbally or by pointing. At the end of the line, they are to say "Thank you" when given their tray, and "You're welcome" when the cashier says "Thank you."

Antecedent prompting has been found to effectively increase social interaction, particularly when the intervention includes multiple interaction opportunities with competent peers in natural contexts (Simpson et al., 1991). However, potential negative aspects of the procedure have been noted. These include interruption of a naturally occurring social exchange (Strain & Fox, 1981), and children with autism becoming prompt dependent, exhibiting social behavior only when prompted to do so (Odom & Strain, 1986). Remember to follow the guidelines for using prompts described in Chapter 5:

1. **Do not overprompt.** Prompt only if the student has not initiated or responded within a reasonable period of time (e.g., 5 to 10 seconds).

2. **Do not interrupt the natural flow of social interaction to provide a prompt.** The prompt is used only if the student *fails* to respond.

3. **Use the least intrusive prompts needed to solicit target behaviors.** Do not use physical prompts if verbal prompts will suffice. Do not use full verbal prompts if partial verbal prompts will result in the desired behavior.

4. **Fade prompts as soon as possible.** Use prompts as needed at first, then gradually increase the time that elapses between the opportunity for a social behavior and the teacher prompt. Also fade the level of prompts used. For example, if you begin training using full verbal prompts ("Eric, say 'Yes, I'd like to have a turn.' "), move to partial verbal prompts as soon as possible ("Eric, what do you say?" or "Eric . . .?").

5. **If you detect that students are becoming prompt dependent, switch to another intervention, or add a contingency in which unprompted initiations or responses are reinforced, using reinforcers in addition to naturally occurring social reinforcers.** For example, a prompt-dependent student might earn tickets for each unprompted social initiation or response. Prompted social behaviors do not earn tickets. When he has accumulated 10 tickets, he may exchange them for use of a preferred material or activity for 10 minutes.

Self-Mediated Techniques. Self-mediated techniques use strategies that involve the student doing something to facilitate the use of target skills. For purposes of this discussion, the self-mediated technique we present is self-monitoring.

Self-Monitoring. **Self-monitoring** involves targeting a specific behavior, then teaching the student to systematically record each time that behavior is performed. Self-monitoring should also be considered a generalization strategy. It would not be appropriate to have students self-monitor skills that have not yet been taught. Once students have attained the acquisition level in a given skill, self-monitoring of that skill can be introduced as one tactic for facilitating attainment of fluency, maintenance, and generalization levels of performance.

Examples follow of self-monitoring systems that would be easy for students to use to record each time a target social skill is exhibited:

- Record a tally mark on an index card. The card can be kept on the student's desk, or carried in a pocket.

- Place a poker chip in a jar.

- Place a star on a chart.

- Drop a small block in an egg carton section.

- Use a handheld digital counter, or a golf stroke-counter that is worn on the wrist.

These items are easy to use in generalization settings such as the playground or cafeteria.

Once the student has learned to use the system, a target performance criterion can be set, with reinforcement delivered upon attainment of the criterion. For example, the student could be encouraged to make 10 social greetings during the day. If the self-monitoring system indicates 10 or more greetings were exhibited by the end of the day, the student earns a special reinforcer.

Self-monitoring has been used to effectively increase social behavior in children and youth with autism and developmental disabilities (e.g., Koegel & Koegel, 1990; Koegel, Koegel, Hurley, & Frea, 1992). In addition, collateral decreases in disruptive behavior, such as self-stimulation, as a result of self-monitoring procedures have also been reported (Koegel et al., 1992), as have generalized improvements in untargeted behaviors (Koegel & Frea, 1993).

One major consideration in using self-monitoring as an intervention to improve social behavior is the probability that many students will be able to self-monitor only one response at a time, rather than multiple, complex responses (Haring & Ryndak, 1994). Because of this, the nature of the behavior targeted for self-monitoring is especially important. Robert Koegel and his colleagues recommend that students self-monitor pivotal behaviors. For example, students may be taught to self-monitor the number of social questions initiated during the day. Social questions are pivotal because they invite responses and may result in extended social interactions. Even self-monitoring is considered a pivotal behavior (Haring & Ryndak, 1994) because it can be used to facilitate generalization of a number of different behaviors across a wide variety of natural contexts. Other examples of pivotal behaviors that students might self-monitor include eye contact, appropriate facial and verbal affect, initiating interactions, functional communication skills, and awareness and responsivity to environmental stimuli (Haring & Ryndak, 1994; Moes, 1995).

Peer-Mediated Interventions. Peer-mediated interventions involve using socially competent peer confederates to initiate and maintain social interactions with students with autism. The **peer confederates** typically receive training in effective methods for accomplishing these outcomes prior to intervention. Peer initiations have been used successfully to increase social behavior in a variety of age groups of students with developmental disabilities, from preschool through secondary (e.g., Haring & Breen, 1990; Odom & Strain, 1986; Sasso, Mundshenk, Melloy, & Casey, 1998).

A substantial research base provides strong support for using socially competent peers as social change agents for students with autism. Within this research base, a variety of intervention formats have been used to increase social behavior in students with autism. Following are descriptions of some of the formats.

Peer Social Initiations. In this format, peers are taught to initiate and maintain social interactions with children and youth with autism. The trained peers and the students with autism are then placed in natural social activity settings (e.g., playing games, listening to music, sharing a snack). During the activity, the peer confederates initiate social interactions and respond positively to any appropriate social behaviors from the students with autism. For example, peer confederates may be taught to ask game-related questions; how to provide prompting, reinforcement, and encouragement; and how to respond to social behaviors exhibited by a student with autism. The peer and a student with autism would then engage in a game such as the Go Fish card game, providing the peer confederate with a natural context in which to encourage social responding from his or her partner with autism.

At the secondary level, peer confederates were employed by Breen, Lovinger, and Haring (1989, as cited in Haring & Ryndak, 1994) in an intervention designed not only to increase social behaviors of students with severe disabilities, but also to create friendships between these students and nondisabled peers. Their intervention, called the "Partners at Lunch (PAL) Club," recruited nondisabled peer groups (a few students at a time) to commit to a minimum of one to three lunch periods per week during which they will eat lunch with a student with a disability "assigned" to them. In addition, one afternoon each week, the PAL Club meets after school with their peers with disabilities and the teacher for leisure activities. In addition, during this intervention, teachers discuss with the peer groups how the lunch interactions are proceeding and provide suggestions for any identified problems.

According to an emerging database, the number of socially competent peers paired with a student with autism seems to affect the level of social behaviors exhibited by the students with autism. Using dyads (one nondisabled peer with one student with autism) seems to result in a greater level of social responding than do triads (two nondisabled peers with one student with autism) (Sasso, 1989; Sasso et al., 1998). This suggests that when more than one nondisabled peer is present, those students tend to interact more with one another than with the student with a disability (Sasso et al., 1998).

An added benefit to the use of peer confederates was demonstrated by Sasso and Rude (1987), who found that teaching high-status, socially competent peers to initiate interactions resulted in increased social responding from students with autism. An unplanned generalization effect occurred when untrained nondisabled peers in the same setting increased their social interactions with the students with autism. The students with autism demonstrated longer response rates, more initiations, and longer interactions following intervention.

Peer Expressions of Affection.

One interesting alternative to traditional peer confederate initiations was implemented by McEvoy and colleagues (1988) in an integrated early childhood education class. Rather than specifically train nondisabled peers to initiate interactions, the researchers modified group activities to involve expressions of affection. They found increases in both the number of interactions directed by nondisabled peers toward children with autism, and increases in initiations made by the children with autism.

Implementation of a similar intervention for preschoolers or elementary-age children would involve first establishing an integrated, structured play or activity period. During this activity period, children would be led in games that involve expressions of affection (hugs, pats) or other social initiations. Games and activities that would be suitable include games such as "Duck, Duck, Goose" or "London Bridge" or simple square dances. Other games can be modified to include more socialization activities. For example, "If You're Happy and You Know It" could include activities such as tickle your friend or hug your friend. A game of

freeze tag could include a provision that once you're "tagged," you can be "unfrozen" if a peer hugs you. Another activity possibility is that each child in turn sings "My friend is _____" (to the tune of *Frere Jacques*). While singing, the child goes to the named peer and gives him or her a hug or handshake. To make it equitable, students could draw names of the friend they will greet before the game begins.

Peer Tutoring.

In **peer tutoring,** students with autism are paired with socially competent peers, with the peers serving as tutors and the student with autism as the tutee. Peer tutoring as a socialization intervention should be considered with some cautions in mind. Some studies have shown peer tutoring to produce positive socialization increases, as well as increases in learning in a variety of areas, in children with autism (e.g., Breen et al., 1985; Egel, Richman, & Koegel, 1981). However, Sasso and his colleagues argue that those interactions have little positive effect on long-term social competence (Sasso et al., 1998; Sasso, Garrison-Harrell, & Rogers, 1994). Indeed, in pairing nondisabled students with peers with autism for instructional purposes, educators run the risk of creating hierarchical status differences, with the nondisabled student in a "superior" or more powerful role than the student with autism. In a study comparing peer tutoring to peer social initiations, Sasso and his colleagues (1998) found peer social initiations to be superior in increasing desired social behaviors in elementary-age students with autism.

This does not necessarily mean that peer tutoring programs should not be used, particularly given the effectiveness of such arrangements in increasing desired learning behaviors. It does mean, however, that if socialization is the outcome, other interventions should perhaps be used in place of, or in addition to, peer tutoring. Haring and Ryndak (1994) recommend stressing the benefits of friendship between tutors and tutees. To that recommendation we would add that teachers could facilitate friendship development through activities such as parties and other social activities for peer tutoring pairs (e.g., peer tutoring pairs might also be "lunch buddies" two or three times a week).

Peer Prompting. A final peer confederate intervention relates to strategies to generalize initiation behaviors to untrained nondisabled peers. Studies have shown certain techniques can increase the likelihood of untrained peers extending social interactions to children with autism. For example, Sasso and Rude (1987) showed that training socially skilled, high-status peers to initiate to students with autism was likely to influence other nondisabled peers to initiate interactions with the student with autism. In another study, Sasso and his colleagues (1987) showed that training nondisabled peers to reinforce untrained nondisabled peers for initiating interactions with students with developmental disabilities resulted in higher levels of interaction on the part of students with disabilities.

FACILITATING GENERALIZATION OF SOCIAL SKILLS

We next discuss strategies that should increase the likelihood of generalization of social skills. These include the Stokes and Baer (1977) generalization strategies (described in Chapter 5) as they relate to social skills, as well as some additional recommendations that were not presented in Chapter 5.

1. Teach skills that are naturally reinforced in target environments. In school, these might include smiling, responding to peers, greeting teachers, and extending invitations to play. Baer and Wolf (1970) call this **trapping reinforcement.** Many pivotal behaviors are selected because they typically result in natural reinforcement.

2. Teach peers (and teachers) to respond appropriately to students' correct social behaviors and to ignore or redirect inappropriate behaviors (Walker & Buckley, 1972). This is especially important as students begin to exhibit new skills. In our experience, peers often do not respond spontaneously to these new skills, perhaps because peers do not recognize them as appropriate social behaviors that warrant a response or because the new behaviors are "out of character" for the student with autism.

3. Use many examples in the teaching process (Baer, 1981). We would never teach long division by using only one example. Each social skill taught should be demonstrated several times, in several different contexts.

4. Program **common stimuli,** or make the training situation as much like real-life situations as possible (Stokes & Baer, 1977). This might mean having role-players use similar language, topics, even mannerisms, as would be used in the actual situation.

5. Once students demonstrate acquisition of target behaviors in the instructional setting, begin to vary the components of instructional lessons, what Stokes & Baer (1977) refer to as **general case programming.** For example, different teachers could conduct the social skills group at a different time of day and in a different setting. New students could be introduced into the group, and the instructional session might be conducted in a slightly different format (different order for role-players, for example).

6. Teach students to actively recruit their own reinforcement (Morgan, Young, & Goldstein, 1983). General education teachers, secondary teachers especially, often do not provide the high levels of reinforcement familiar to students with autism. Students can be taught to ask teachers "How did I do today?" or "Did I do a good job playing today?" as a way of soliciting reinforcement, in case it is not provided automatically.

7. Teach students to recognize the types of reinforcers used by general educators (Graubard, Rosenberg, & Miller, 1974). Teachers should study the types of reinforcers used in general education environments, then apply those in the special education setting as well.

Incorporating well-planned generalization strategies as part of an overall socialization program will increase functional use of social skills, including a greater likelihood that social behaviors will be used in appropriate contexts, with reinforcing social consequences from peers and adults.

SUMMARY

Perhaps one of the most critical areas of intervention for students with autism is socialization. While children and youth with autism characteristically do not exhibit functional social behaviors that lead to social competence, intervention efforts to remediate socialization deficits can result in significant improvements in social behavior, particularly when applied to preschool-aged children.

A variety of socialization interventions have been shown to produce desired outcomes, including teacher-mediated techniques (direct instruction, antecedent prompting, and social stories), self-mediated techniques (self-monitoring), and peer-mediated techniques (peer initiations, peer affection activities, peer tutoring, and peer prompting). The most robust outcomes will occur when two or more of these techniques within or across these categories are used in combination, and when these techniques are used in conjunction with well-planned generalization strategies. For example, a teacher might direct students in initiating social questions (a pivotal behavior) and would provide scripts for the students to follow in specific situations. Next, students could be taught to self-monitor their initiations involving social questions. In addition, the teacher would be available to prompt students to use the target behavior when appropriate situations arise. Finally, nondisabled peers might be taught to respond to these social questions in such a way that extends the social interaction.

The goal of socialization interventions is social competence. Students with autism may never be viewed as highly socially competent and will probably never desire the levels of social interaction common among nondisabled peers. However, careful instruction of critical skills with attention to generalization should result in desirable social outcomes, including a greater likelihood of social relationships, even friendships, between students with autism and peers.

Effective social behavior is necessary for successful functioning in all areas of life, and has been shown to be an important prerequisite to mental health and happiness. As educators, we must begin addressing socialization deficits in children with autism and developmental disabilities at a young age and continue applying effective interventions to continually expand these students' repertoires of social behaviors. Anything less may increase the likelihood of more restrictive placements for students, especially in adulthood.

KEY POINTS

1. Students with autism typically have one or more of four common types of socialization deficits: (1) lack of interest in others, (2) impaired social communication, (3) impaired social imagination and perspective-taking, and (4) lack of joint attention.

2. Social competence refers to other people's perceptions of the social performance of an individual. Socialization interventions must address social competence of students with autism, as well as social skills.

3. Assessment of socialization needs of students with autism requires evaluation of three areas: (1) contexts in which the child functions, (2) social culture of those contexts, and (3) the child's skills with respect to the demands of those contexts.

4. Programmatic emphasis on socialization may be characterized by (1) a program philosophy that emphasizes the importance of socialization experiences, (2) including social skills objectives on IEPs, and (3) providing carefully developed opportunities for social interaction with nondisabled peers.

5. Socialization interventions include teacher-mediated interventions, self-mediated interventions, and peer-mediated interventions. Interventions are most effective when used in combination.

6. Generalization of social skills can be enhanced through careful planning and inclusion of specific strategies.

REFERENCES

American Psychiatric Association. (1994). *Diagnostic and statistical manual of mental disorders* (4th ed.). Washington, DC: Author.

Baer, D. M. (1981). *How to plan for generalization.* Austin, TX: Pro-Ed.

Baer, D. M., & Wolf, M. M. (1970). The entry into natural communities of reinforcement. In R. Ulrich, T. Stachnik, & J. Mabry (Eds.), *Control of human behavior* (Vol. 2). Glenview, IL: Scott, Foresman.

Bambara, L. M., & Browder, D. M. (1991). Assessment in and for the home. In D. M. Browder (Ed.), *Assessment of individuals with severe disabilities* (pp. 137–176). Baltimore, MD: Paul H. Brookes.

Bandura, A. (1977). *Social learning theory.* Upper Saddle River, NJ: Prentice Hall.

Breen, C., Haring, T. G., Pitts-Conway, V., & Gaylord-Ross, R. (1985). The training and generalization of social interaction during breaktime at two job sites in the natural environment. *Journal of the Association for Persons with Severe Handicaps, 10,* 41–50.

Breen, C. G., Lovinger, L., & Haring, T. G. (1989). Effects of friendship-based and instructional aide experiences on attitudes of junior high students. Manuscript in preparation.

Crockett, M. S. (1984). Exploring peer relationships. *Journal of Psychosocial Nursing and Mental Health Services, 22,* 18–25.

Egel, A. L., Richman, G. S., & Koegel, R. L. (1981). Normal peer models and autistic children's learning. *Journal of Applied Behavior Analysis, 14,* 3–12.

Frea, W. D. (1995). Social-communicative skills in higher-functioning children with autism. In R. L. Koegel & L. K. Koegel (Eds.), *Teaching children with autism* (pp. 53–66). Baltimore, MD: Paul H. Brookes.

Gaylord-Ross, R. J., Haring, T. G., Breen, C., & Pitts-Conway, V. (1984). The training and generalization of social interaction skills with autistic youth. *Journal of Applied Behavior Analysis, 17,* 229–247.

Goldstein, H., & Cisar, C. L. (1992). Promoting interaction during sociodramatic play: Teaching scripts to typical preschoolers and classmates with disabilities. *Journal of Applied Behavior Analysis, 25,* 265–280.

Goldstein, H., Wickstrom, S., Hoyson, M., Jamieson, B., & Odom, S. L. (1988). Effects of sociodramatic script training on social and communicative interaction. *Education and Treatment of Children, 11,* 97–117.

Graubard, P. S., Rosenberg, H., & Miller, M. B. (1974). Student applications of behavior modification to teachers and environments or ecological approaches to social deviancy. In E. A. Ramp & B. L. Hopkins (Eds.), *A new direction for education: Behavior analysis.* Lawrence, KS: Support for Development Center for Follow Through.

Gray C. A., & Garand, J. D. (1993). Social stories: Improving responses of students with autism with accurate social information. *Focus on Autistic Behavior, 8*(1), 1–10.

Gresham, F., & Elliott, S. (1990). *Social skills rating system.* Circle Pines, MN: American Guidance Service.

Haring, T. G., & Breen, C. G. (1990, May). *A peer mediated social network to enhance social integration for persons with severe disabilities.* Paper presented at the 16th Annual Convention of the Association for Behavior Analysis, Nashville, TN.

Haring, T. G., & Ryndak, D. (1994). Strategies and instructional procedures to promote social interactions and relationships. In E. C. Cipani & F. Spooner (Eds.), *Curricular and instructional approaches for persons with severe disabilities* (pp. 289–321). Needham Heights, MA: Allyn & Bacon.

Hops, H. (1983). Children's social competence and skill: Current research practices and future directions. *Behavior Therapy, 14,* 3–18.

Howlin, P. (1986). An overview of social behavior in autism. In E. Schopler & E. G. Mesibov (Eds), *Social behavior in autism* (pp. 101–131). New York: Plenum.

Hurley-Geffner, C. M. (1995). Friendships between children with and without developmental disabilities. In R. L. Koegel & J. K. Koegel (Eds.), *Teaching children with autism* (pp. 105–125). Baltimore, MD: Paul H. Brookes.

Kanner, L. (1943). Autistic disturbances of affective contact. *Nervous Child, 2,* 217–250.

Kellegrew, D. H. (1995). Integrated school placements for children with disabilities. In R. L. Koegel & J. K. Koegel (Eds.), *Teaching children with autism* (pp. 127–146). Baltimore, MD: Paul H. Brookes.

Koegel, R. L., & Frea, W. D. (1993). Treatment of social behavior in autism through the modification of pivotal social skills. *Journal of Applied Behavior Analysis, 26*(3), 369–377.

Koegel, R. L., & Koegel, L. K. (1990). Extended reductions in stereotypic behavior of students with autism through a self-management treatment package. *Journal of Applied Behavior Analysis, 23,* 119–127.

Koegel, R. L., & Koegel, L. K. (Eds.) (1995). *Teaching Children with autism.* Baltimore, MD: Paul H. Brookes.

Koegel, L. K., Koegel, R. L., Hurley, C., & Frea, W. D. (1992). Improving social skills and disruptive behavior in children with autism through self-management. *Journal of Applied Behavior Analysis, 25,* 341–354.

Kuttler, S., Myles, B. S., & Carlson, J. K. (1998). The use of social stories to reduce precursors to tantrum behavior in a student with autism. *Focus on Autism and Other Developmental Disabilities, 13*(3), 176–182.

Lovaas, O. I. (1987). Behavioral treatment and normal educational and intellectual functioning in young autistic children. *Journal of Consulting and Clinical Psychology, 55* (1), 3–9.

Matson, J. L., & Swiezy, N. (1994). Social skills training with autistic children. In J. L. Matson (Ed.), *Autism in children and adults* (pp. 241–260). Pacific Grove, CA: Brooks/Cole Publishing Co.

McEvoy, M. A., Nordquist, V. M., Twardosz, S., Heckman, K. A., Wehby, J. H., & Denny, R. K. (1988). Programming autistic children's peer interaction in an integrated early childhood setting using affection activities. *Journal of Applied Behavior Analysis, 21,* 193–200.

McEvoy, M. A., & Odom, S. L. (1987). Social interaction training for preschool children with behavioral disorders. *Behavioral Disorders, 12* (4), 242–251.

Meyer, L., Eichinger, J., & Park-Lee, S. (1987). A validation of program quality indicators in educational services for students with severe disabilities. *Journal of the Association for Persons with Severe Handicaps, 12,* 251–263.

Moes, D. (1995). Parent education and parenting stress. In R. L. Keogel & L. K. Koegel (Eds.), *Teaching children with autism* (pp. 79–93). Baltimore, MD: Paul H. Brookes.

Morgan, D. P., Young, K. R., & Goldstein, S. (1983). Teaching behaviorally disordered students to increase teachers' praise and attention in mainstreamed classrooms. *Behavioral Disorders, 7,* 265–273.

Mundy, P. (2000). Understanding the core social deficits of autism. In J. Scott, C. Clarke, & M. Brady, *Students with Autism* (pp. 18–20). San Diego: Singular.

Nelson, J., & Aboud, F. E. (1985). The resolution of social conflict between friends. *Child Development, 56,* 1009–1017.

Odom, S. L., & Strain, P. S. (1986). A comparison of peer-initiation and teacher-antecedent interventions for promoting reciprocal social interaction of autistic preschoolers. *Journal of Applied Behavior Analysis, 19*(1), 59–71.

Osterling, J., & Dawson, G. (1994). Early recognition of children with autism: A study of first birthday home videotapes. *Journal of Autism and Developmental Disorders, 24,* 247–257.

Sasso, G. M. (1989). *Promoting social relationships in individuals with autism.* Paper presented at the meeting of

the Council for Children with Behavioral Disorders, Charlotte, NC.

Sasso, G. M., Garrison-Harrell, L. G., & Rogers, L. (1994). Autism and socialization: Conceptual models and procedural variations. In T. Scruggs & M. Mastropieri (Eds.), *Advances in learning and behavioral disabilities* (pp. 161–175). Greenwich, CT: JAI Press.

Sasso, G. M., Hughes, C. G., Swanson, H. L., & Novak, C. G. (1987). A comparison of peer initiation interactions in promoting multiple peer initiators. *Education and Training in Mental Retardation, 22,* 150–155.

Sasso, G. M., Mundshenk, N. A., Melloy, K. J., & Casey, S. D. (1998). A comparison of the effects of organismic and setting variables on the social interaction behavior of children with developmental disabilities and autism. *Focus on Autism and Other Developmental Disabilities, 13*(1), 2–16.

Sasso, G. M., & Rude, H. A. (1987). Unprogrammed effects of training high-status peers to interact with severely handicapped children. *Journal of Applied Behavior Analysis, 20,* 35–44.

Schopler, E., & Mesibov, G. B. (Eds.). (1983). *Autism in adolescents and adults.* New York: Plenum.

Scott, J., Clark, C., & Brady, M. (2000). *Students with autism.* San Diego: Singular.

Simpson, R. L., Myles, B. S., Sasso, G. M., & Kamps, D. M. (1991). *Social skills for students with autism.* Reston, VA: Council for Exceptional Children.

Stokes, T. F., & Baer, D. M. (1977). An implicit technology of generalization. *Journal of Applied Behavior Analysis, 10,* 349–367.

Stone, W. L., & Lemanek, K. L. (1990). Parental report of social behaviors in autistic preschoolers. *Journal of Autism and Developmental Disorders, 20,* 513–522.

Strain, P. S. (1982). *Social development of exceptional children.* Rockville, MD: Aspen Publishers.

Strain, P. S. (1983). Generalization of autistic children's social behavior change: Effects of developmentally integrated and segregated settings. *Analysis and Intervention in Developmental Disabilities, 3,* 23–34.

Strain, P. S., & Fox, J. (1981). Peer social initiations and the modification of social withdrawal: A review and future perspectives. *Journal of Pediatric Psychology, 6,* 417–433.

Walker, H. M., & Buckley, N. K. (1972). Programming generalization and maintenance of treatment effects across time and across settings. *Journal of Applied Behavior Analysis, 5,* 209–224.

8

Remediating Deficits
in Life Skills

Did you know that:

- Many basic skills don't "just come naturally" for children with autism?

- Independence in basic life skills is critical to long-term outcomes for students with autism?

- Students with autism may need to be taught how to play?

- Creativity often plays a role in job development for students with autism?

Children and youth with autism and pervasive developmental disorders typically have difficulty learning skills that their nondisabled peers learn with little or no formal instruction. So far, we have discussed characteristic deficits and recommended remediation procedures in behavior, speech and language, and socialization. Three other areas that present problems for many children and youth with autism will be discussed in this chapter: self-help skills, leisure skills, and vocational skills. We refer to these areas as "life skills."

Independence in self-help tasks, engaging in appropriate leisure activities, and the ability to perform meaningful work are all critical prerequisites to living full lives as part of mainstream society. Each self-help task a child or youth cannot do alone increases his or her dependence on others. Students who are allowed to engage in bizarre

self-stimulatory behaviors rather than being taught to participate in age-appropriate leisure activities are likely to be shunned or teased by peers and to call undesirable attention to themselves in public places. Young adults who are unable to participate in work activities, particularly competitive employment, miss one of the most important aspects of typical adults' lives. Most children learn most self-help tasks with little systematic, formal instruction. Most children typically choose age-appropriate and socially acceptable leisure activities. Most young people learn to work by having responsibility for chores at home, having part-time jobs, perhaps taking vocational classes at school, and finally pursuing formal postsecondary vocational training or full-time apprenticeship-type employment. Unfortunately, most children with autism do not learn these skills through typical developmental channels. Thus, they need long-term, formal, comprehensive, and systematic instruction if they are to gain any degree of independence in these areas.

This chapter will address what and how to teach in these three essential life skills areas: self-help skills, leisure activities, and vocational skills. For each area, we will describe general considerations, guidelines for developing curricula, and instructional recommendations, but first we will address assessment considerations.

ASSESSMENT OF SELF-HELP, LEISURE, AND VOCATIONAL SKILLS

As you know by now, the first step in teaching is to conduct assessment to determine what the student needs to learn. The three approaches to assessing life skills are ecological assessment, inventories and checklists, and direct observation. Teachers may need to use more than one of these strategies to delineate each student's life skills curriculum.

Ecological Assessment

Remember that ecological assessment means evaluating target environments to determine the skills needed for success in those environments. The result is an individualized set of potential target skills. This approach applies to assessing self-help, leisure, and vocational skills. For example, to determine what self-help skills 8-year-old students should be able to perform independently, observe 8-year-olds from general education classes or talk to general education teachers. Can most 8-year-olds tie their shoes? If so, your 8-year-olds should be able to do that task, or be well on their way to learning it. Virtually all nondisabled 8-year-olds are toilet trained. Students with autism who are about that age should be toilet trained as well. If not, toilet training must be a priority unless there is a physical or health reason why the child cannot learn self-toileting skills. Most 8-year-olds can feed themselves using forks and spoons correctly. Likewise, students with autism should exhibit similar eating skills and should not be allowed to engage in unusual, compulsive, or self-stimulatory eating habits (e.g., Raymond eating with a toothpick in the movie *Rain Man,* or a student who will eat only mashed potatoes, bologna, and mustard).

Ecological assessment is a useful tool for identifying target leisure skills as well. As discussed in Chapter 7, leisure activities that involve social interaction should be selected with regard to the norms of the local peer group. Target solitary leisure activities should also be similar to those engaged in by age-peers. Therefore, teachers of students with autism should observe nondisabled peers on the playground and during other self-directed activities and also ask general education teachers about their students' leisure preferences. Your students may show no interest in the activities identified. Research has shown that children with autism have both quantitative and qualitative differences in their play behavior as compared to children with other handicapping conditions or nondisabled children. This may be partially attributable to deficits in representational thought, language, sensorimotor skills, and cognitive skills (Rettig, 1994). Therefore, it is essential to teach students how to engage in play activities. As we discussed in Chapter 3, and as we will discuss further in this chapter, it is often possible, even desirable, to adapt students' preferred self-stimulatory behaviors to socially acceptable and peer-preferred leisure activities.

Ecological assessment in the area of vocational skills means identifying potential work environments, then determining what skills are necessary for success in those environments. Target work environments may be in school, in the home, or in the community. Some of the ecological assessments listed in Table 4.6 in Chapter 4 could be used to assess vocational skills in target environments. However, ecological assessment often is done informally, simply by observing and asking questions. The questions shown in Table 4.5 can guide informal ecological assessment efforts to determine requirements of a vocational setting, leisure activities, or home routines and chores. Once answers to these questions are obtained, determine which skills are essential and which skills are lacking. Perform a social validity check and repeat interview at least annually.

Inventories and Checklists

To assess self-help and leisure skills, teachers can also use adaptive behavior checklists or developmental checklists, such as those listed in Table 7.2 in Chapter 7. Skill deficits identified through the use of one of these instruments should then be compared to information gathered through eco-logical assessment to identify which of those skills the student needs in target contexts. If missing from a student's repertoire, those skills then be-come targets for instruction.

In addition to adaptive behavior and develop-mental checklists, many commercial vocational assessments are designed to help educators deter-mine vocational preferences and abilities (see Table 8.1). Most of these vocational assessments also include self-help tasks that are work related (e.g., appropriate grooming and dressing) and even leisure skills (e.g., appropriate behavior dur-ing breaks). Be sure to examine results of formal assessments to ecological assessment results in order to obtain an individualized, functional curriculum.

Table 8.1 Commercial Instruments for Career/Vocational Assessment

Brigance Employability Skills Inventory (Brigance)

- Publisher: Curriculum Associates
  153 Rangeway Road
  North Billerica, MA 01862
- A criterion-referenced test of skills needed to obtain employment and to assess students' career awareness. Like all the Brigance tests, this inven-tory is easy to use and results translate to instruc-tional objectives.

Reading-Free Vocational Interest Inventory—2 (Becker, 2001)

- The Psychological Corporation
  555 Academic Court
  San Antonio, TX 78204
- This inventory uses pictures to assess students' vocational interests across employment areas such as automotive trades, building trades, food service, animal care, and housekeeping.

Wide Range Interest-Opinion Test (Jastak & Jastak, 1979)

- Publisher: Jastak Associates
  P.O. Box 3410
  15 Ashley Place, Suite 1A
  Wilmington, DE 19804
- This instrument uses pictures to assess student work-related interests and attitudes for a wide variety of employment areas.

Direct Observation

Direct formal and informal observation of stu-dents' strengths and weaknesses in life skills may also play a role in the curriculum development process when determining normative standards for performance and initial instructional criteria. The behavior measurement methods described in Chapter 2 can be used to assess life skills as well. Examples of direct observation methods as ap-plied to life skills include the following:

- **Restricted event recording:** how many bites a student takes before she spits one out, how many times a student begins brushing his teeth within 2 minutes of being asked to do so; the number of times a student begins work within 5 minutes of clocking in; number of bites of food eaten with a fork rather than hand.

- **Nonrestricted event recording:** number of different sand toys used appropriately; number of items placed correctly in the dish-washer; number of times a student asks for help during work time.

- **Duration recording:** time spent brushing teeth; time spent engaged in appropriate interactive play behavior; time spent working on assigned vocational activity; time on-task while ironing; engaged time during assigned document-shredding task; how long it takes a student to finish eating his lunch, how long a student looks at a magazine, or how long a student tolerates sitting on the toilet.

Of course, behavior measurement methods can be combined with ecological assessment and checklists. For example, if stocking shelves in a grocery store is a target job for a student, the teacher might count how long it takes a typical employee to place all items from a carton onto the shelf. The teacher then times the student doing the same task for baseline data. The duration time for the nondisabled employee (or something close to that time) then becomes the target criterion for the student.

Brockett (1998) described an interesting approach for developing independent play activities in young children with autism or, with some adaptations, for leisure or vocational activities for older students as well. We will describe this method later in this chapter. At this point, however, we wish to explain the assessment process Brockett recommends for guiding selection of leisure materials for independent use. This is a structured approach to evaluating the child's or adolescent's response to toys or other items in three categories: skill, interest, and independence. "Skill" refers to the child's current ability to use the toy or material correctly. "Interest," of course, refers to the child's level of curiosity toward the item or the appeal the item seems to have for the student. "Independence" is an evaluation of the child's potential for independent use of the toy or material. The steps in the assessment portion of this structured play approach are as follows:

1. Collect a box of toys or leisure materials that you believe will interest the student and that the student may be able to use appropriately and independently to some degree. Table 8.2 lists toys and materials that can be used for this purpose.

2. Prepare a checklist for evaluating the child's response to each item in terms of skill, interest, and independence (see Table 8.3 for an example). "Skill" should be evaluated as *failing* (the child did not use the material correctly), *emerging* (the child appeared to know what to do with the item and attempted to use it correctly), or *passing* (the child played appropriately with the toy). "Interest" and "independence" are evaluated as *high, medium,* or *low,* depending on the child's level of interest and how quickly the child might be able to use the item independently.

3. To conduct the assessment, sit with the student and hand him one item at a time. Observe the student for about 1 minute per item, evaluating each of the three areas. If the student shows no signs of being able to use the item independently, model the correct

Table 8.2 Ideas for Independent Play Activities

Early Childhood

- Beads on a string
- Nesting cups or rings on a dowel
- Pop beads
- Shape boxes (putting shape blocks into matching holes)
- Nuts and bolts
- Large-piece puzzles, puzzles with knobs on pieces for holding
- Duplo blocks
- Blocks for stacking
- Bristle blocks
- Sand or water play with toys (shovels, buckets, pitchers, cups, sieve, etc.)
- Shapes with Velcro to be matched to shape outlines on poster
- Large plastic vehicles (cars, trucks, dump trucks, cranes, etc.)
- Dolls to dress and feed
- Play-Doh with cookie-cutter shapes, Play-Doh Factory, etc.
- Fisher-Price Little Schoolhouse, Farm, or Parking Garage
- Sorting activities

Intermediate

- Wooden or cardboard jigsaw puzzles
- Three-dimensional puzzles
- Lite-Brite
- Legos
- Remote-controlled cars
- Art activities (chalk, markers, paint, poster board, construction paper, etc.)
- Origami
- Dot-to-dot pictures
- File folder activities (matching pictures, letters, words, numbers, vocabulary words, math facts, etc.)
- Computer games or activities
- Handheld video games
- Karoake machine
- Etch-a-Sketch
- Books, magazines

Secondary

- Jigsaw puzzles with smaller pieces
- Exercise equipment (stationary bicycle, treadmill, weight machine, rowing machine, small trampoline, etc.)
- Crossword puzzles, find-a-word puzzles, etc.
- Art activities
- Computer games or activities
- Handheld video games
- Karoake machine
- Operating audiovisual equipment (TV, stereo, VCR)
- Magazines

Table 8.3 Sample Assessment Form for Structured Independent Play

Student _____Jackson_____   Date ____10/19/01____

Test conducted by _____Ms. Lockhart_____

Item	Skill	Interest	Independence
Lite-Brite	Fail	High	High
Play-Doh, with Factory	Pass	High	High
Art activities			
Chalk	Pass	Low	Low
Paint	Emerging	Low	Low
Markers	Pass	Medium	Medium
Handheld video game (Tetris)	Emerging	Medium	High
Remote-controlled car	Emerging	High	High
Puzzles	Fail	Low	Low
File folder activities (match words, addition facts)	Pass	Low	Low
Sticker book	Pass	Medium	High
Etch-a-Sketch	Emerging	High	High

From S. Brockett (1998) Developing successful play activities for individuals with autism. *Advocate*, 31(6), 15–17. Reprinted with permission.

use of the item several times. If the student then attempts the correct use of the item, "skill" should be scored as *emerging*.

4. Continue in this fashion until all items have been presented. Of course, if the student's attention wanes, the activity can be stopped and resumed at another time.

5. Finally, once all items have been evaluated, select one item to teach the student to use independently. Any toys or materials rated as passing (skill), high (interest), and high (potential for independence) should be the first ones considered for developing into independence. While that item is being targeted for independence, correct use of other toys or materials that were rated at an emerging skill level, high interest, and high potential for independence could be taught.

Given the information shown in the evaluation results in Table 8.3, using Play-Doh with the Play-Doh Factory would be the logical first choice to teach as an independent activity. Using sticker books might be the second choice. Given the student's high interest and emerging skills in

the remote-control car and Etch-a-Sketch, either of those toys could be targets for teaching.

This approach could also be used for selecting leisure materials and activities for older students by simply choosing different age-appropriate stimulus items. Likewise, for skill-interest vocational assessment, follow the same procedure with vocational materials and tasks.

As you know, assessment of critical skills is an essential step in curriculum development. The following sections discuss each of these three curricular areas (self-help, leisure, and vocational) in terms of issues and considerations, what to teach, and strategies for teaching.

SELF-HELP SKILLS

Self-help skills are critical to success in almost any area of functioning, as well as to overall independence. Individuals are more likely to gain acceptance in mainstream environments if they are adequately groomed, toilet trained if physically able, and can take care of basic personal hygiene needs in socially acceptable ways. According to Snell

(1993), toileting, eating, and dressing are the most critical self-care areas. To this list we would add personal grooming and hygiene as an essential self-care category, based on research that indicates children who are unkempt in appearance are more likely to be rejected by their peers (e.g., Coie, Rabiner, & Lochman, 1992).

General Considerations for Teaching Self-Help Skills

Three general considerations should guide instruction in self-help skills (Westling & Fox, 1995). First, choosing appropriate self-help skills should be the result of close collaboration between school personnel and parents. The personal nature of many self-help tasks requires that parents be informed and involved in selecting target skills. Also, parents can provide information about family practices that may shape how skills are taught. For example, when family members brush their teeth, is it standard practice to use a glass for rinsing or not? Do the parents plan for their son to use a safety razor or electric shaver? The teacher should teach skills in the same way that youngsters will perform them at home. An ecological assessment (parent interview or direct observation in the home) should provide this type of information.

Second, self-help skills should be taught in natural contexts and at natural times whenever possible (e.g., milieu teaching). Thus, eating skills are best taught at breakfast, snack, and lunch times. Toileting skills are taught during toileting breaks (more frequently during the toilet training process). However, some self-help tasks do not naturally occur at school (e.g., dressing, shaving, washing hair, filing fingernails). For these skills, the teacher should provide instruction at the most natural time possible. For example, dressing skills for older students could be taught before and after changing clothes for PE. For any self-help skills, if naturally occurring opportunities do not offer sufficient learning time, the teacher should, of course, integrate additional instruction in contexts and at times that are the most natural.

Third, teachers must remember that many self-help tasks are very personal (e.g., dressing and undressing, toileting, caring for menstrual needs), and should be taught with respect for the student's privacy, regardless of the age of the student. This means that instruction in these tasks should be done individually, not with several students at a time. It also means that the student's privacy should be ensured by teaching target skills in a bathroom, separate room, or at least behind a screen. Finally, the person doing the instruction should be of the same gender as the student. Whereas we believe this is true for students of any age, it is particularly critical for adolescents.

Sometimes, self-help skills are more efficiently taught if the task or the materials are modified in some way. Occupational therapists, specialists who work to improve students' fine motor and functional skills, can offer good suggestions for these types of modifications. Tasks may be modified by (1) eliminating steps, (2) combining steps, (3) changing how steps are done, or (4) modifying the materials used in the task. Materials may be modified for the purpose of (1) making them easier to use, (2) reducing the likelihood of errors, or (3) highlighting salient aspects of the material, or those aspects that students must attend to in order to correctly use them. Materials may be modified by using larger or smaller versions; changing the appearance or form; or using color-coding to highlight salient components. Task or material modification may be permanent, meaning the student will always use the modified approach, or temporary, in which a modified form is used during acquisition and modifications are gradually faded as the student becomes more proficient in the skill. Some examples of how to modify tasks or materials using the types of modifications just described follow:

- To teach drinking from a straw, use short straws (just a few inches long) to minimize the time and intensity of sucking that is required before reinforcement is obtained (the liquid). Gradually increase the length of the straw.

- Toothbrushes, hairbrushes, spoons, forks, and so on may be easier to hold if handles are fat and nonslippery. Gluing foam padding around the handle is one way to accomplish this.

- Tying shoes is easier when the laces are large and flat (such as laces used in athletic shoes) and not too long or short. Using two different color laces may help the student distinguish laces at each step. Of course this task may be eliminated entirely by replacing the laces with Velcro straps.

- Tube socks may be easier to learn to pull on at first. In addition, socks that are one size larger than the child's foot may be easier to put on.

- Color-coding may help the student differentiate right from left shoes, and fronts and backs of clothes. For example, make a green foot shape for the right foot and a red foot shape for the left foot. Then place a green stick-on dot on the right shoe, and a red dot on the left shoe. Placing dots on the rounded outer edge of the shoe will help draw the student's attention to that part of the shoe (for discriminating right and left). Gradually fade use of the dots by cutting them smaller and smaller.

- It is easier to teach beginning dressing skills by using clothing that is slightly larger than the child's normal size.

- Beginning drinking skills may be more successful (i.e., result in less spilling) when thickened liquids are used in place of typical liquids, such as juice combined with yogurt, applesauce, or baby cereal (Alexander, 1991), or commercial thickening agents that do not alter the taste of the liquid.

Before we begin discussion of specific categories of self-help skills, we would like to remind you that all of the instructional strategies presented in Chapter 5 will be used for teaching self-help skills. Following are a few specific examples of how these strategies might apply to teaching self-help skills:

- Everything the student uses for hygiene might be color-coded. For example, a student's toothbrushing supplies (toothbrush, toothpaste, and cup) might have green dots and be stored in a green box, while shaving supplies for that student would have red dots and be stored in the red box. Each box would have the student's picture on it.

- Use a timer to let the student know how long she is to remain on the potty.

- Provide pictures to remind students of the steps in washing hands.

- Use a jig for setting the table. For example, placemats that have utensils, napkins, plates, and drinking glasses drawn in their proper spots could be used to prompt correct table setting.

- Making a sandwich might be taught using discrete trial training as part of total task presentation. Each day at lunchtime, the student is directed through four trials (one trial for a sandwich for each student in the class); the teacher records whether the student performed each step or not (e.g., needed assistance or prompting). The task is taught in the kitchen (milieu teaching), with data kept on a clipboard in the kitchen area.

- Using backward chaining and discrete trial teaching, a student is taught to put on her shoes and fasten the Velcro straps. The teacher begins by placing a shoe on the student's foot, tightening the strap, and positioning it close to the Velcro closure strip. The teacher gives the cue "Put on your shoe." If the student responds by pressing the strap down correctly, the teacher records a "+" on the data sheet, then begins another trial with the other shoe. Later in the day the process is repeated. Once the student correctly presses the strap down in five consecutive trials, she is required to do the last two steps of the task—tighten the strap and press it down. This process continues until the student is able to put her shoe on and fasten it independently.

Toileting Skills

Most children are toilet trained between ages 2 and 3. Typically, this is a developmental process during which children exhibit signs of readiness for toilet training, and parents teach their child toileting skills. With patience, perseverance, and perhaps a sense of humor, the child soon is using the toilet with little direction from parents.

Children with autism, due mostly to their cognitive and language deficits, often do not show the signs of readiness for toileting exhibited by nondisabled children. Sometimes, they even exhibit challenging behavior in opposition to efforts to teach them toileting skills. However, it is critical that children learn toileting skills, and the closer this occurs to the developmentally appropriate window of time, the better. Regardless of how old a student is, if he or she is in school and not toilet trained, and if there is no physical reason why the student cannot use the toilet normally, toilet training must be a priority. Children who are not toilet trained have a much poorer prognosis than those who are, particularly in terms of integrated placement.

Snell (1993) presented three criteria for determining whether a student is ready for toileting instruction:

1. The student eliminates on a regular, and thus predictable, schedule.

2. The student can remain clean and dry for a minimum of 1 to 2 hours, thus indicating some degree of voluntary control.

3. The student is at least 2½ years old.

Whereas nondisabled students may learn many toileting-related skills without formal instruction, students with autism and PDD may not learn such skills without direct instruction. Table 8.4 provides a partial list of toileting and toileting-related skills, listed in approximate developmental order. These skills may need to be adapted depending on environmental demands (e.g., potty seat on toilet versus a small child's potty chair; bathrooms that are shared by other students in the school).

Table 8.4 Toileting and Toileting-Related Skills

- Indicates discomfort when wet or soiled.
- Defecates when placed on potty.
- Urinates when placed on potty.
- Indicates a need to go to the bathroom.
- Goes to the bathroom with little or no assistance.
- Uses the urinal or raises toilet lid to urinate (boys).
- Returns toilet seat and lid to proper position.
- Uses toilet paper.
- Flushes toilet.
- Pulls pants down without assistance.
- Pulls pants up without assistance.
- Washes and dries hands.
- Differentiates between the men's and women's restroom by looking at signs on the doors.
- Obtains assistance or uses appropriate adaptive behaviors if there are problems in the bathroom (e.g., toilet is overflowing, a toilet is labeled "Out of Order," there are no paper towels).

Teaching Toileting Skills. The following steps describe a recommended toilet training process (Westling & Fox, 1995). Note that some tactics recommended in the past are no longer considered appropriate (e.g., punishment for toileting accidents, giving large quantities of liquids to promote urination, spending long hours in the bathroom) (Westling & Fox, 1995). Instead, recommendations generally revolve around shaping toileting behavior under natural conditions and differentially reinforcing desired toileting behaviors.

1. Collect data to determine the child's patterns of elimination. A chart such as the one shown in Figure 8.1 can be useful in this regard. Continue data collection until elimination patterns are discerned.

2. Take the child to the toilet during the times when he or she is most likely to void. According to the data in the chart shown in Figure 8.1, the child regularly eliminates between 8:30 and 9:30 A.M. Therefore, this child should be taken to the bathroom when he arrives at school, and allowed to sit on the toilet for approximately 5 minutes. If the child does not void during this time, have the child get up, and try again in 10 or 15 minutes (or less, depending on the age of the child).

Toileting/Pants Check Record — Baseline: 9/6–9/17 — Intervention 9/20

Name: Jacob

Locations: gym, classroom, north hall, cafeteria, bathrooms

Time	9/6	9/7	9/8	9/9	9/10	9/13	9/14	9/15	9/16	9/17	9/20	9/21	9/22	9/23	9/24	9/27	9/28	9/30	10/1	10/2
8:30		(WB)					(W)	W+	W+	A		W+		W+		W+	(W)	W+	A	(W)
8:45		D		(W)	(W)	W+	D	D	D	B		D	W+	D	W+	D	D	D	B	D
9:00	(W)	D		D	D	D	D	D	D	S	W+	D+	D	D	D	W+	D	D+	S	D
9:15	D	D	(BW)	D	D	D	D	D	D	E	(B)	D	D	D	D	D	D	D	E	D
9:30	D	D	D	(W)	(W)	D	D	(W)	D	N	D	D+	D	D+	D	D+	D+	D+	N	D+
9:45	P.E.	P.E.	P.E.	P.E.	P.E.	P.E.	P.E.	P.E.	P.E.	T	P.E.	P.E.	P.E.	P.E.	P.E.	P.E.	P.E.	P.E.	T	P.E.
10:00	D+	D	(WB)	(W)	W+	D	D	D	(W?)		D	D+	(W)	D+	W+	W+	WB+	D+		WB+
10:15	D	(WB)	D	D	D	D	D	D	D		D	D	D	D	D	D	D	D		D
10:30	D	D	D	D	W–	D	D	D	D		D	D+	D+	D+	D+	D+	D+	D+		D+
10:45	D	D	(W)	D	W+	W+	D	D	(W)		D	(W)	D	(W)	D	D	D			D
11:00	W–	D	D	D	D	D	D	W	D		D	D+	D	D+	D	W+	D+	D+		W+
11:15	D	D	(W)	(W)	D	D	D	D	D+		D	D	D	D	D	D	D	D		D
11:30	D	D	D	D	(W)	D	D	D	D		D	D+	D+	D	D+	D+	D	BW+		D
11:45	L	L	L	L	L	L	L	L	L		L	L	L	L	L	L	L	L		L
12:00	D	D	D	D	D	D+	D	D	D		D	B+	B+	D	D	D	D?			D
12:15	(WB)	(W)	D	(WB)	W+	(W)	WB+	D	(WB)		D	D	D	B+	WB+	B+	WB+	D–		WB+
12:30	D	D	(WB)	D	D	D	D	B+	D		(WB)	(W)	D	D	D	D+				D
12:45	D	D	D	D	(BW)	D	D	D	D		D+	D	D	D+	D+	D	D			D
1:00	D	D	D	D	D	D	D	D	D		D	D	(WB)	D	D	D1	D+		A	D+
1:15	D	D	D	D	D	D	D	D	D		D	D	D	D	D	(W)	D		B	D
1:30	D	(W)	D	D	D	D	D	D	D		D	D+	D	D+	D	D+	D+		S	W
1:45	D	D	D	D	D	D	W	D+	D		D	D	D	D	W–	D	D		E	D
2:00	(BW)	(W)	D	(W)	D	D–	W	D	D+		D	D–	D+	W+	W+	W+	D+		N	D
2:15	D	D	(B)	(WB)	(W)		(W)					W–		D		W–			T	D
2:30				D																
# Self initiations / # Accidents	1/3	0/5	0/5	0/7	2/4	3/2	2/2	2/3	4/2		2/3	9/1	5/3	9/0	7/1	11/1	9/1	7/0		6/2

Key
D = Dry
L = Lunch

Student Initiated
W+ = Wet on toilet
B+ = BM on toilet
D+ = Self-initiated, no elim.

Teacher Assisted
W– = Wet on toilet
B– = BM on toilet
D– = Teacher-initiated, no elim.

Accidents
(W) = Wet
(B) = BM

FIGURE 8.1 Data collection form for toilet training. (From Snell & Farlow, 1993. Reprinted by permission of Pearson Education, Inc., Upper Saddle River, NJ 07458).

3. If the child voids while on the toilet, praise enthusiastically.

4. Continue to check for dryness during periods when the child is not on the toilet. Comment on and praise dry pants ("Good for you—you are clean and dry! I'm proud of you!").

If the child has an accident during training, the teacher should make a brief comment of mild disapproval ("I'm disappointed that you are wet! Next time I hope you'll tell me when you need to go."), change the student into dry clothes, and nothing more. There should be no punishment for accidents (Westling & Fox, 1995).

Eating Skills

Mealtimes offer not only rich opportunities for practicing a variety of skills, but are also natural contexts for integration with nondisabled peers, and have the advantage of being centered around food, which functions as a strong primary reinforcer for many students. Eating skills include everything from finger feeding to using knives to cut and spread. Furthermore, mealtimes are good times to teach a number of eating-related skills, including appropriate behavior in restaurants, using different types of restaurants correctly (ordering from a menu, ordering at a counter, etc.), using transportation to and from public eating venues, money skills, home meal preparation and cleanup, grocery shopping, and nutrition. Table 8.5 provides a partial list of eating and eating-related skills that students with autism may need to learn, listed in approximate developmental order. Please note that the skills listed in Table 8.5 are not meant to be a complete curriculum. They should serve simply as examples of the types of skills that may be targeted. As described in Chapter 4, all self-help curricular areas will depend on each student's individual needs.

Teaching Eating Skills. The instructional strategies of task analysis, chaining, shaping, and prompting are commonly used to teach eating skills. Teach skills in sequence from the most basic, such as appropriate finger feeding, to more complex, such as cutting food with a knife and fork. In addition, target skills should be age appropriate, such as drinking from a cup for young children to using straws and drinking from soda cans for older students. Table 8.5 lists skills according to appropriateness for different age groups. However, you should remember that a 14-year-old who still has not learned basic eating skills may need to start by learning skills that are typical for much younger students.

The following list describes recommendations for teaching eating skills:

1. Teach skills during meals and snacks consisting of foods that are highly motivating for the student. It would be a mistake to try to teach a new skill (e.g., using a spoon) with a food the student dislikes (e.g., tomato soup)!

2. Reduce inappropriate behaviors that will interfere with correct eating (e.g., leaving the table during mealtime, self-stimulatory behaviors that involve the hands) or that will draw negative attention to the student during mealtime (e.g., self-stimulatory behaviors or idiosyncratic eating habits such as smelling each bite before eating or regurgitating food).

3. In the early stages of learning new skills, use food that makes the skill easier. Following are some examples of foods that work well for students who are not yet skilled in the stated tasks:

   - **Finger feeding:** cheese cubes, raw vegetables, peanuts, grapes (foods that are not slippery, and chunky enough to be easily picked up)
   - **Using a spoon:** mashed potatoes, pudding, soft ice cream, oatmeal (foods that cling to the spoon)
   - **Using a fork:** meat cubes, oven-roasted potato cubes, cooked carrots (foods that are easily speared, and likely to stay on the fork tines)
   - **Spreading with a knife:** soft butter on tortillas, sturdy crackers, or thick toast; soft peanut butter on toast (foods that

Table 8.5 Eating and Eating-Related Skills

Young children (preschool, primary) typically are able to:

- Self-feed appropriate finger foods.
- Drink from a cup.
- Drink with a straw.
- Use a spoon (fist grasp acceptable).
- Use a spoon to eat soup, with some spilling.
- Spear food with a fork.
- Use a knife for spreading (incomplete spreading, may tear bread or break crackers).
- Use a napkin with reminders.
- Remain seated for duration of meal (with reminders).
- Ask for drinks and snacks, and more of particular foods at mealtime.
- Eat independently, probably with food remaining on mouth and hands after eating, and crumbs on table, chair, and floor.
- Wash and dry hands with reminders, and possibly assistance.
- Clean hands and face after eating with reminders and assistance.
- Talk to others at table while eating.
- Ask for and use condiments (ketchup, steak sauce, salsa, etc.).
- Self-serve some foods (mashed potatoes, yogurt, applesauce, etc.).
- Pour from a pitcher with some spilling; may need reminders when to stop.

Primary–intermediate age children typically are able to:

- Use fork and spoon with correct grasp.
- Drink, without spilling, from any type of cup, can, or bottle.
- Cut foods with a knife and fork with no assistance.
- Use a napkin.
- Eat soup with a spoon, with little spilling.
- Use a knife for spreading with little difficulty.
- Ask for and use most condiments, including salt and pepper.
- Request foods to be passed.
- Pass food to others at the table on request.
- Self-serve from serving bowls.
- Pour liquids from a pitcher or carton with little spilling.
- Select desired items and place order at restaurants.
- Prepare snacks.
- Use kitchen utensils and appliances with supervision (mixer, blender, oven, etc.).
- Perform most cleanup tasks (clear table, wash dishes, load dishwasher).
- Adjust behavior to a variety of restaurant settings, with prompts (e.g., drive-in, cafeteria, formal restaurant).
- Assist parents with grocery shopping (help make list, retrieve items in store).
- List foods that are good for you, and foods that have no nutritional value.
- Describe, at least in part, elements of a nutritionally sound diet.

Adolescents typically are able to:

- Fix snacks and some meals.
- Perform meal-preparation tasks, including chopping, measuring, cleaning, peeling, etc.
- Do cooking and cleanup activities.
- Use kitchen appliances without supervision.
- Set table.
- Verify accuracy of restaurant tab and calculate tip.
- Adjust behavior to a variety of public eating settings.
- Work in eating-related jobs (wait tables, bus tables, cook, wash dishes, etc.).
- Use public transportation to get to eating establishments.
- Go to restaurants with friends, without supervision.
- Do grocery shopping independently.
- Describe and plan nutritionally sound meals.

spread easily or foods that do not crumble or break easily during spreading)

- **Cutting with a knife:** fish filets, tender boneless chicken, omelet (foods that cut easily).

4. Enlist nondisabled peers to serve as peer buddy tutors during snacks and mealtimes. Peers should be taught to model target skills, to prompt their partners in correct use of skills, to interact with their partners socially (see Chapter 7), and to reinforce correct use of skills. Teachers should also reinforce students with autism for imitating their partner's eating habits ("You're eating just like Cameron! Good for you!").

5. As discussed in Chapter 6, teach relevant vocabulary such as favorite foods, labels for eating utensils, napkins, place mats and so forth, appropriate verbs (e.g., eat, cut, drink), functional adjectives (e.g., hot, cold, slimy, wet, spicy), and how to ask for, or refuse, more food.

6. Use picture prompts to cue students to engage in target behaviors, such as using utensils and napkins.

7. Mealtimes should be completed within a reasonable time. One student we know typically takes a minimum of 1½ hours to finish his lunch! On the other hand, students should not be allowed to gulp their food so that they are finished in a few minutes. For slow eaters, finishing meals within a specific time (use a timer) should be differentially reinforced. It might be appropriate to remove food when the timer rings. Be sure to consult with parents and obtain their approval before using this strategy. Students who eat too fast might be taught to put their fork down after every bite, or reinforced if they take longer than a specified time to finish a meal.

8. Students should eat a sufficient range of foods to ensure good nutrition. Some students refuse to eat anything other than a few foods or refuse to eat foods of certain textures. One student we know insists on eating only white foods. If increasing the variety of foods a student will eat is a goal agreed on by teachers and parents, disliked foods should be presented in very small amounts (e.g., one or two peas, one small piece of apple). Favorite foods would not be given until the student eats the disliked food. We wish to point out that we do not necessarily think the goal of getting students to eat a greater variety of foods is important *unless* the student's diet is severely deficient in certain food groups or the student is not getting sufficient nutrients. Like nondisabled peers, children with autism should be allowed their preferences, within reason.

9. Educators should teach socially valid skills, and determine socially valid criteria as standards for those skills (Alper, McMullen, McMullen, & Miller, 1996). Observing nondisabled age-peers in a variety of meal and snack contexts will help teachers determine socially valid eating and eating-related skills. Furthermore, this type of ecological assessment will help teachers determine acceptable levels of performance. For example, do most children regularly use a napkin? Do most children eat pizza with their fingers or a fork? What are peers' conversational topics at lunch? These skills and standards may become targets for students with autism.

10. Finally, most school contexts do not present naturally occurring opportunities to practice some skills, such as eating meals family style (passing bowls, serving self, etc.). Therefore, teachers will need to create opportunities if these skills are instructional targets. Cafeteria staff in most schools are eager to help students with special needs. The authors used to have "class lunch" one day each week. On these days, cafeteria staff cheerfully served our students' lunches in bowls and on platters to allow students opportunities to practice serving themselves, passing dishes, and asking for desired items. Each lunch, three or four special guests were invited, including nondis-

abled peers, other teachers, school staff, and administrators. In addition to providing good opportunities for eating skills instruction, these lunches also served as venues for socialization. Not only did the students with autism benefit, but other people in the school came to know the students with autism a little more personally. This resulted in spontaneous social initiations outside of the classroom, such as greetings in the hall, initiations on the playground, and reciprocal invitations to other classes' activities.

Dressing Skills

Children with autism may have little difficulty learning dressing skills within typical developmental ranges. However, if a student is unable to tie shoes, put on a coat, remove a pullover sweater, put on socks, or any of the many other dressing skills required for independence, school personnel should work collaboratively with parents to target age- and skill-appropriate goals in this area.

Like the other self-help areas discussed so far, dressing skills also include related skills, such as changing clothing regularly; choosing clothing items that match and are appropriate for the weather; recognizing when clothing needs to be laundered, does not fit properly, or is in need of repair, and so forth. As you will see from the list of dressing skills given in Table 8.6, many of these skills are typically acquired in late childhood and adolescence.

Teaching Dressing Skills. The general guidelines discussed above for teaching self-help skills also apply to teaching dressing skills. These include:

- Use effective teaching techniques (task analysis, chaining, data-based instruction, and prompts).
- Teach skills in context as much as possible. This may be difficult because nondisabled children typically do not work on most dressing skills at school, especially older students. However, opportunities for such instruction do exist (arriving at and leaving school, changing clothes for gym class).

Table 8.6 Dressing and Dressing-Related Skills

Young children (preschool, primary) typically are able to:
- Put on all basic clothing items (socks, shoes, pullover shirt, button-down shirt, pants, underwear).
- Remove all basic clothing items.
- Identify own clothing.
- Pick out clothing they like and wish to wear; clothing may not be coordinated or appropriate for weather or occasion.
- Fasten most closures: large (front) zippers, buttons, snaps, hooks.

Primary–intermediate age children typically are able to:
- Put on all clothing items.
- Remove all clothing items.
- Choose their own clothing for play and school.
- Fasten all closures (including belts, shoelaces).
- Tell someone when clothing does not fit comfortably.
- Fold clothing simply (match socks, fold underwear, fold shirts and pants in half).
- Place items of clothing on hangers (button-front shirts, coats).
- Polish or clean shoes.

Adolescents typically are able to:
- Care for own clothing (wash and dry, iron, fold or place on hangers).
- Make some clothing repairs (sew on missing button, sew small seam rips).
- Select own clothing for purchase.
- Create a personal style with clothing.

- Teach skills with regard to students' privacy when necessary (e.g., putting on undergarments).

- Teach appropriate vocabulary.

- Use stimulus modification methods to make the dressing task easier. Examples of stimulus modification for dressing tasks were described earlier.

- Use actual clothing to teach dressing skills. Commercial materials such as dressing boards, dressing vests, shoe-tying boards, and so forth are of little use for students with autism. These materials, while appealing in appearance, are different than what the child must actually button, zip, tie, snap, and so forth. Plus, fastening buttons on a button board in front of you requires a different orientation than fastening buttons on your shirt. Skill generalization is always a priority and is much more likely to occur when instructional materials are the real thing, not a clever-looking commercial imitation.

Personal Grooming and Hygiene Skills

The last self-help area to consider for students with autism is personal grooming and hygiene (PGH). Having some degree of proficiency in these skills is important to independence, dignity, and social acceptance. Table 8.7 provides a partial list of PGH skills that students with autism might not learn without direct instruction.

Teaching Grooming and Hygiene Skills.
One of the goals in teaching these skills is for students to not only do PGH tasks without assistance, but to do them without reminders as well. Few nondisabled adolescents need to be reminded to brush their teeth at least twice a day, wash, blow their nose, comb their hair, and so forth. Therefore, teaching PGH skills should include attention to *when* to perform the grooming tasks. Of course, many of the PGH tasks listed in Table 8.7 are normally done at home in the morning or before bed. Because students may need more practice in these

Table 8.7 Grooming and Personal Hygiene Skills

Young children (preschool, primary) typically are able to:
- Wash and dry hands and face.
- Bathe or shower with supervision.
- Brush teeth.
- Comb hair.
- Use tissue to blow nose.

Primary–intermediate age children typically are able to:
- Bathe or shower independently.
- Wash and dry own hair.
- Request certain hairstyles.
- Trim nails.
- Polish nails.
- Cover mouth to cough or sneeze.

Adolescents typically are able to:
- Bathe or shower daily without reminders.
- Tell barber or stylist how they want their hair cut or styled.
- Comb their hair into a variety of styles (if appropriate for hair length).
- Curl own hair with rollers or curling iron.
- Take care of fingernails, toenails, and cuticles.
- Apply makeup.
- Shave.
- Apply deodorant daily.
- Care for menstrual needs.

skills during the day, teachers should schedule grooming tasks at appropriate times during the day. For example, "morning tasks" such as washing face, brushing teeth, combing hair, and shaving could be done first thing in the morning. Washing and styling hair and applying makeup could be done after PE or swimming.

Part of teaching students when to engage in PGH skills involves teaching them to recognize when those tasks are needed. For example, a student should be taught to examine his or her hair to see if it needs combing. Rather than just telling a student "You need to blow your nose," students should be taught to pay attention to the sensation that means they need to blow their nose. For example, the teacher might say "A.J., do you feel something on your nose? What do you need to do?" (e.g., the mand/model strategy described in Chapter 5).

Perhaps as important as teaching students when it is appropriate to engage in grooming tasks is teaching them when it is *inappropriate* to do so. Students should be taught that many PGH tasks should be done in the privacy of one's home, bedroom, or bathroom. Even some tasks that some people do in public (e.g., comb hair, file nails) should not be done in certain situations (restaurants, at the table, in formal situations such as church or class).

Teachers and parents should work collaboratively to plan instruction in grooming tasks. Parents may wish for teachers to take the lead in teaching certain skills, such as shaving. If so, parents could tell their son before he leaves, "You need a shave! Good thing you'll do that at school." Also, parents and teachers should discuss vocabulary, basic steps, and materials to be taught in grooming tasks. For example, does a student use both shampoo and a separate conditioner? Does the student need to learn to blow-dry hair? Does the student have access to a curling iron? These types of potential skills should be identified through ecological assessment. Communication about what is to be taught, and how, regarding tasks students will typically perform at home will facilitate acquisition and generalization of target skills.

PLAY, LEISURE, AND RECREATION SKILLS

Attention to developing age-appropriate and socially acceptable play, leisure, and recreation skills is another important instructional area for students with autism. Participation in recreational activities plays an important role in all of our lives, and provides many social, emotional, cognitive, and physical benefits (Heyne & Schleien, 1994). Recreational activities provide relaxation and renewal, as well as opportunities to explore new skills and interests, engage in social relationships, and develop physical fitness. Most individuals report feeling better both physically and emotionally when they regularly engage in physical activity, and the health benefits of physical activity are well established. Most of us do not require formal instruction to participate in recreational activities, pursue leisure time interests, and de-

velop specific skills and talents. However, this is not the case for children with autism. Without systematic instruction in leisure and recreation skills, it is unlikely that individuals with autism will learn them on their own, due to their overriding cognitive, language, and social deficits (Schleien & Ray, 1988). Given undirected free time, most students with autism would either sit doing nothing or engage in inappropriate behavior, unless they are taught desirable leisure and play skills and are provided with structured opportunities to practice these skills. As you learned in Chapter 7, decreases in maladaptive social behavior have been associated with increases in appropriate play skills. This suggests that, for individuals with autism, in addition to the benefits of leisure and recreation activities already described, developing these skills may also have desirable effects that can help mitigate socially unacceptable behaviors.

General Considerations for Teaching Play, Leisure, and Recreation Skills

One of the more challenging aspects of teaching (and parenting) children with autism is that these children characteristically do not engage in appropriate activities when left on their own. Even without specific instruction, when nondisabled children are on the playground they choose to interact with one another, swing, and play games. A young child with autism in the same situation would isolate herself and probably self-stimulate (sift dirt, twirl, talk to herself, etc.). During free time in the classroom, nondisabled adolescents would undoubtedly talk to one another or the teacher, sleep, write notes, or work on homework. An adolescent with autism, without specific instruction and prompting, probably would do none of these, but rather sit alone and self-stimulate. Because of this, teachers of students with autism cannot afford to give their students "free time." Instead they must schedule leisure and recreation times during the day, then provide systematic instruction in appropriate skills during those times. Following are curriculum and instruction recommendations for teaching leisure and recreation skills.

Curriculum. An important consideration for leisure/recreation instruction is skill selection. Like every other curricular area, skill selection must be individualized and based on ecological assessment. This means that part of the process of selecting recreation and leisure activities for instruction is determining what types of activities age-peers in the school and community engage in and what students' families do in the way of leisure activities. However, skill individualization also means accommodating student preferences and interests and perhaps family recreation interests. One unique aspect of leisure and recreation for the general population is the wide range of activities that are characterized as "leisure and recreation activities." Just in your own circle of friends, you may know people who prefer reading as a relaxation activity, while others find relaxation by preparing for and participating in triathlons! Some acquaintances may like playing cards, while others love golf, fishing, or watching baseball. Some people prefer solitary leisure activities; others seek group pursuits. Some individuals like spectator sports, whereas others want to engage in the sport! The point here is that, given such a wide array of possibilities, teachers and parents should be able to find activities that each student enjoys and that reflect varying skill levels. Because of their apparent lack of awareness and lack of interest in their environment, personal interests of children and youth with autism probably will not be obvious. You may have to expose the student to a variety of activities and gauge his responses to determine likes and preferences.

One option for selecting leisure activities is to choose activities that incorporate a student's self-stimulatory behaviors or obsessive preferences. We discussed this in Chapter 3 with regard to finding appropriate alternatives for these behaviors. This concept can be expanded to target potential leisure skills as well. For example, a child who engages in proprioceptive self-stimulation would probably be a good candidate for activities that result in considerable sensation in the muscles and joints, such as lifting weights, gymnastics, yoga, Tae-Bo, ballet, swimming, or aerobics. A student who likes to touch different textures may do well with finger painting, clay or ceramics, creating fabric collages, making bread or dough for pizza crusts, or making cookies that require forming the dough into small balls. A student who sniffs as a self-stim could make potpourri mixtures (and sell them perhaps) or experiment with combining fragrances and essential oils to create new fragrances. A student who obsessively lines up objects might be a natural at setting up domino paths in intricate patterns. Like many other aspects of teaching students with autism, determining leisure activities requires collaboration with parents and significant creativity.

Remember that it is important to target age-appropriate skills for instruction. However, in leisure and recreation areas, perhaps a little more leeway is seen with regard to this caveat. For one thing, many leisure/recreation activities are age appropriate for all ages, such as swimming, reading, watching movies, running, playing badminton, bowling, cycling, cooking, art projects, and so on. Also, it is not unusual for adolescents and adults to sometimes engage in "youthful" leisure activities: jumping rope, swinging on a park swing, building sand castles, collecting dolls or baseball cards, or building model cars or airplanes. Therefore, we urge teachers and parents not to be overly stringent in the "age-appropriate" rule when it comes to leisure/recreation activities. Two general rules of thumb: If the activity preferred by the student is clearly age inappropriate (e.g., a 10-year-old student loves playing with an infant's busy box), try to find a more age-appropriate version of the activity or more age-appropriate material for the preferred activity. Second, good leisure instruction means teaching a variety of skills: solitary activities, group activities, passive as well as active participation, and social communication skills. If one activity is a bit unusual for the child's age (e.g., a teenager who likes to play jacks), developing more age-appropriate activities in other areas would be in order.

Research suggests that the type and number of toys chosen for play instruction with young children are important considerations. Children are more likely to engage in social play when provided with social toys (e.g., vehicles, blocks, dolls) than when given isolated toys (e.g., puzzles, crayons, books) (Rettig, 1994). Also, it appears that greater social interaction occurs when children are given fewer toys, rather than more (Rubin & Howe, 1985). Remember, however, that simply providing toys may not be sufficient. Most children will need specific instruction in how to use those toys for typical play activities.

Instruction. In addition to *what* skills are taught, *where* and *how* skills are taught are also important. In this section, we describe preferred strategies for teaching leisure and play activities.

Direct instruction is an essential component of teaching play and leisure skills. Specific leisure time activities should first be task analyzed, then taught using one of the chaining techniques in discrete trial format (Brockett, 1998; Rettig, 1994). For example, after task-analyzing the activity of assembling a puzzle, a logical instructional choice would be backward chaining. To teach the skill, the teacher would assemble all pieces of the puzzle (except for the last piece), then give the cue "Martin, put your puzzle together." When Martin responds, he is reinforced, and the trial is repeated either with the same puzzle (but a different final piece), or a different puzzle. Eventually the student will complete the puzzle by inserting the last two pieces, then the last three pieces, then the last four, and so forth until he is able to do the puzzle independently. This type of instruction provides the structure students need to learn the target skills and the data teachers need to monitor student progress. Once skills are acquired, generalization should be addressed by then providing opportunities for the student to engage in target activities or use target toys in social contexts.

Brockett (1998) recommends a procedure for teaching independent play and leisure activities using instructional and organizational strategies described in Chapter 5. The steps in this procedure are as follows:

1. Choose a target activity using the systematic observational assessment methods described earlier in this chapter.

2. Determine a system to guide the student through the routine. The system should include a signal to the student that he has finished the activity. For example:

   - **Left to right with Finish Box.** In this system, individual activities are placed in separate boxes and arranged from left to right. The student completes the activity in each consecutive box, then selects the Finish Box, which contains a reinforcer. According to Brockett, this is the easiest system for students to use. For example, during leisure time, the student would complete each activity in order (e.g., a puzzle, a Legos activity in which the student designs a Legos structure to match a pattern provided), then obtain the reinforcer from the Finish Box.

   - **Matching.** This system requires the student to select activities by matching activity cards labeled with a number, letter, or color to the appropriate activity boxes. Once all cards have been used (e.g., activities completed), he chooses the reinforcer box.

   - **Written.** The child's play or leisure activities are written on a card. He uses the card to guide selection of materials or activities, perhaps crossing off each item as he finishes it.

3. Determine what type of visual cueing system will help the student complete activities independently, such as picture systems or jigs.

4. Devise an organizational structure to store the activities. This might be cardboard shoeboxes, clear plastic shoeboxes, manila envelopes, expanding file folders, dress boxes, and so forth. For example, an activity box for making a bead necklace would include the string, beads (in a small packet, with a small bowl to put the beads in), and perhaps pattern cards. An activity box for listening to

an audio tape might include the Walkman, a tape, and the picture sequence card to direct the student through the activity. A large tub for finished activities should be part of the routine, so that when the student finishes the activity (e.g., completes the necklace patterns, the tape ends, or finishes the puzzle), he places the completed product (or used materials) in the finish tub.

5. Teach the activity, cueing system, and organizational system using direct instruction.

6. Once students have learned the activity, have them use the activity boxes in context (e.g., during play time). Prompt as needed.

7. Begin by having the student complete one activity box. When she is able to do this independently, add a second box to the routine (using the left to right system, matching system, etc.), then a third, and so forth, as appropriate for the student's age and developmental level.

Once students learn this system, parents could implement the same system at home. This would address parents' frequent request that teachers help their son or daughter learn how to "entertain himself/herself." Remember to teach relevant vocabulary and to use parents' input when planning leisure activities. It is important to teach activities, vocabulary, and materials that the student will have access to at home.

With the exception of solitary activities, most leisure pursuits take place with other people, often in public places. Therefore, at some point, skill instruction should occur in the environments in which the activities typically occur, or in multiple environments to facilitate generalization, and with other individuals, including nondisabled peers. So, croquet may be taught in the park, at the school, and in a student's backyard, with a group of young people consisting of some students with autism and some nondisabled peers. Cycling might be taught along bike pathways in the park. Board games or card games (e.g., checkers, chess, Monopoly, Uno, Spades) could involve nondisabled peers and could be taught in any classroom, the cafeteria, or the student lounge.

Much like socialization interventions, both peer-mediated and adult-mediated approaches have been used to teach play behaviors to young children with autism. In peer-mediated programs, nondisabled children are taught to initiate, model, prompt, and reinforce social interactions with autistic peers (e.g., Lord & Hopkins, 1986; Strain, Hoyson, & Jamieson, 1985). Rogers and colleagues (1986) used adult-mediated play interventions to increase the social, communicative, cognitive, and symbolic play skills of young children with autism. In these programs, adults first worked individually with children, teaching play skills. Next, peers were introduced to the play setting; the adult prompted the autistic child to attend to peers' play behavior. Results showed significant improvements in developmental social/play behaviors, with increases in skills such as symbolic play, turn-taking, and extending interactions.

Adaptive physical education teachers are good resources for assistance with skill selection, obtaining materials, and advice on instruction of leisure/recreation skills. If your district does not employ adaptive physical education teachers, you might consult your regional education service center or the physical education department of a local university. General education PE teachers may also be helpful sources for teaching advice, materials, or information about developmental skill sequences.

Types of Leisure and Recreation Activities

As we discussed earlier, leisure and recreation activities cover a broad spectrum. Most of us participate in both solitary leisure activities as well as recreation pastimes involving one or more partners. Some of our leisure pursuits are passive (e.g., reading in a hammock) while others require significant expenditures of energy. In developing a leisure curriculum, we advise targeting both low-energy and high-energy skills, as well as solitary activities, partner activities, and group activities. Table 8.8 lists sample activities by age group in each of these areas.

Table 8.8 Sample Leisure and Recreation Activities

Preschool–Primary

Solitary or Partner Activities

- Look at books.
- Play with toys.
- Ride riding toys.
- Watch TV or videos.
- Fingerpaint, play with clay, draw pictures, color.
- Play imagination games.
- Card games (e.g., Old Maid, Go Fish).
- Board games (e.g., Candyland, Mouse Trap).
- Jump rope, play hop scotch.

Group Activities

- Hide-and-Seek.
- Duck, Duck, Goose.
- Various forms of Tag.
- Four-Square.

Intermediate

Solitary or Partner Activities

- Collect and organize items (e.g., baseball cards, Matchbox cars, glass figurines).
- Read books, magazines, comics.
- Ride bike.
- Practice sports (e.g., dribbling and shooting baskets, hockey, kicking soccer ball, playing catch).
- Practice dance, instruments, singing, etc.
- In-line skating.
- Fishing.
- Swimming.
- Computer games or video games.
- Board games (e.g., Monopoly, Sorry, Life, Risk).
- Camping.
- Taking care of pets.
- Listening to music.

Group Activities

- Organized sports.
- Lessons (e.g., dance, karate, art).
- Roller skating.
- Organizing and performing skits, puppet shows, etc.

Adolescent

Solitary or Partner Activities

- Reading.
- Computer games or surfing the web.
- Writing letters or sending Email.
- Talking on the telephone.
- Listening to music.
- Shopping.
- Attending sporting events, music shows, plays, etc.
- Engaging in physical fitness activities (e.g., aerobics, lifting weights, Tae-Bo).
- Playing tennis, golf, racquetball, bowling.
- Dating.

Group Activities

- Group sports.
- Giving and attending parties.
- Clubs and service organizations.
- Theater, band, dance group, cheerleading.

VOCATIONAL SKILLS

Work is a central part of most adults' lives. Whether paid or unpaid (e.g., parents who stay home to take care of their children, individuals who do volunteer work), the work we do is one of the characteristics that defines who we are. For example, when adults meet for the first time, one of the first questions asked is often "What type of work do you do?" For this reason, it is important to establish long-term work goals for students with autism. Although formal work training typically begins in high school (e.g., vocational education classes, after-school jobs) or after high school

(e.g., college, vocational schools, on-the-job training), work training for children with autism probably will need to begin much earlier, in the form of teaching skills that are necessary prerequisites to successful employment. For example, preschoolers with and without disabilities typically learn to clean up their work/play areas, put away their toys, and follow directions (Westling & Fox, 1995). Elementary school students learn to do classroom and home chores, be on time for classes, ask for help when needed, work and play with peers, and possibly travel around the community independently. By middle school, various types of vocational assessments are usually begun with students with disabilities to determine aptitudes and interests and to identify potential employment possibilities in the community. Intense and focused vocational training for students with disabilities occurs in high school, with students spending the majority of their day in some type of vocational preparation, including on-the-job training.

Long-term vocational planning is required by law as part of **transition planning.** The passage of P.L. 101–476 (IDEA) in 1990 initiated the requirement that needed transition services must be delineated in each student's individualized education plan (IEP) no later than the student's 16th birthday. For students with severe disabilities, transition planning must begin by age 14. The goal of transition planning is to prepare for and facilitate smooth transfer for students with disabilities from public school services into adult services. To achieve this, a committee consisting of school personnel who work with the student, the student's family, the student, and sometimes representatives from adult service agencies meets to plan long-term adult goals for the student. This meeting usually occurs in conjunction with the annual IEP meeting. The team takes the following steps as part of the transition planning process:

■ Set long-term goals in the areas of employment, independent living, recreation, and community participation.

■ Identify community and family resources to help achieve and maintain those goals; this includes delineation of services by adult service agencies (e.g., rehabilitation agencies, employment agencies, mental health/mental retardation agencies, health agencies).

■ Task analyze each long-term goal into annual goals and short-term objectives.

■ Regularly monitor progress toward those long-term outcomes.

■ Reevaluate the transition plan on an annual basis.

The IEP team often delineates transition-related goals and supports in a document separate from the IEP called the **individual transition plan (ITP).**

General Considerations for Teaching Vocational Skills

The long-term goal of vocational training is work placement in the community (Westling & Fox, 1995). Therefore, all instruction should be designed with this goal in mind. Curriculum and instruction guidelines for vocational training follow.

Curriculum. Several general rules apply to development of a vocational curriculum. First, vocational tasks should be age appropriate and functional. Sorting blocks by color may be age appropriate for preschoolers, but not for adolescents. A more age-appropriate, functional task would be to sort laundry into whites, dark colors, and light colors. Likewise, having an older student sort items using commercial "mailbox center" material is less functional than having the student sort and place school mail into teachers' mailboxes.

Second, vocational tasks should reflect the types of jobs that parents and other members of the IEP committee feel are appropriate and available for a given student, rather than designing vocational instruction around appealing commercial vocational materials. For example, it is of little benefit to teach assembly tasks if only a few jobs in the community require assembly skills. On the other hand, if a large number of office worker positions are available, IEP team members may decide a position as an office aide is an appropriate goal for a student. Therefore, this student's vocational instruction should consist of learning to operate different types of office machines such as photocopiers, fax machines, and shredders.

Third, vocational goals and instruction should reflect the interests and aptitudes of individual students. A student who is highly active will probably do better in a job that allows for movement (e.g., working outside, cleaning, delivery) than a job that is more sedate (e.g., sitting at a desk or work center). Creativity is an asset when it comes to developing vocational goals and designing vocational instruction. It is often possible to design vocational tasks around students' self-stimulatory behaviors or obsessive behaviors. For example, one teacher we know had a student who shredded paper as a form of self-stimulation. The teacher channeled this "interest" into a job for the student: hand-shredding confidential documents from the school counselor's office. The student's highest on-task time was during work time! A student who insists on lining up items may do well straightening canned and boxed items on shelves in a grocery store. A student whose self-stimulation is dropping little bits of lint and paper and watching them float through the air could have the job of emptying all of the school pencil sharpeners on a daily basis.

Instruction. All of the instructional methods described in Chapter 5 will be needed for vocational instruction. Task analysis of target jobs is an important first step in planning vocational instruction. Many of those tasks can then be taught using forward or backward chaining or total task presentation. Teaching target skills using discrete trial teaching will allow educators to closely monitor the student's progress toward independence in the task and to make data-based decisions about task or instructional modifications. Prompts will undoubtedly be necessary in the acquisition stages of instruction, but should be faded in a timely manner to facilitate fluency and generalization. If tasks are initially taught at school, prompts may again be needed temporarily to facilitate generalization in target contexts outside of the school.

Vocational tasks should be taught in settings as close to the target environment as possible. Much like the concept of milieu teaching, this approach is known as **community-based instruction.** For example, if the goal is for a student to bus tables at a local restaurant, initial skills might be taught in the school cafeteria (e.g., carrying the bin for dirty dishes, placing dishes in the bin gently to avoid breakage, wiping the table thoroughly), but as soon as the student is able to perform these tasks with or without verbal prompts, she should begin learning to do the job at the restaurant. Begin on-site instruction at times when the restaurant is less busy, gradually moving toward working during peak times. Likewise, if

the vocational goal for a particular student is to stock shelves at a grocery store, instruction should take place in the grocery store.

Teachers and parents should consider ways in which tasks or materials can be adapted to increase student independence (Sowers & Powers, 1991). For example, some tasks may lend themselves to the use of a jig. Other examples of task modifications include placing a bright green stick-on dot on the "print" button of the photocopier, and covering other buttons not frequently used; drawing outlines on storage shelves to delineate where products should be placed; and highlighting the last names of staff persons on mailboxes.

Many of the visual organization strategies described in Chapter 5 can be applied to increase success in vocational tasks. A picture sequence could be used to prompt a student whose job is to prepare utensil bundles (a knife, fork, and spoon wrapped in a napkin). A student whose tasks vary from day to day could pick up a picture schedule of the day's tasks when he checks in at work. This schedule might be a file folder with pictures attached with Velcro. A student who works at a grocery might have a folder that contains several lines of pictures representing the day's assigned tasks. The first line might show cartons of cake mixes in the storage room, then a picture of the student placing boxes of cake mix on the shelf, then the student flattening the carton, and placing the carton in the recycling bin. The student can be taught that after he completes a pictured task (or portion of a task), he removes the picture and places it in the "Finished" folder, or even in the pocket of a carpenter-type apron to be worn while on the job.

Employment Options

The ultimate vocational goal is for the student to obtain paid competitive employment, with little need for external supports to maintain that employment. However, many students may not be able to achieve that level of independence. This does not mean these students are destined for unemployment; it simply means we have to explore and develop supports to help individuals with disabilities obtain and maintain employment. This is called **supported employment.**

Supported employment is an umbrella term that refers to a number of different models. According to the Rehabilitation Act Amendments of 1992 (P.L. 102-569), supported employment is:

> . . . competitive work in integrated work settings for: (a) individuals with severe [disabilities] for whom competitive employment has not traditionally occurred; or (b) individuals for whom competitive employment has been interrupted or intermittent as a result of severe [disabilities], and who, because of their [disability], need ongoing support services to perform such work. (Title I, Sec. 103, i)

All of the supported employment models involve a **job coach,** who provides training and supervision for individuals with disabilities on the job until they are able to do the job independently, at which point the job coach provides intermittent ongoing support (Westling & Fox, 1995). The following are the most common supported employment models (Agran, Test, & Martin, 1994; Westling & Fox, 1995):

1. **Individual placement model.** Individuals with disabilities are placed in regular job settings and trained and supervised by a job coach. Although this model offers the greatest integration with nondisabled workers, it is not available to all who could benefit from it because of cost and a shortage of job coaches (e.g., Wehman & Revell, 1996).

2. **Enclaves.** Small groups of individuals with disabilities work together in a job setting and are trained and supervised by either a job coach or an employee of the business. A hotel we stayed in recently used an enclave arrangement: Rooms were cleaned by a group of individuals with disabilities.

3. **Work crews.** This arrangement is similar to enclaves, except that the workers with disabilities travel from job site to job site. For example, a work crew might provide lawn maintenance services or janitorial services. Both enclave and work crew models have been criticized because they usually pay less than minimum wage (Westling & Fox, 1995) and tend to keep workers with disabilities isolated from nondisabled workers and the public (e.g., Rusch, Johnson, & Hughes, 1990).

4. **Group placements.** This model offers the benefits of the individual placement model, with the economical aspects of enclaves and work crews. A group of individuals with disabilities is placed at the same work site, but are assigned separate jobs throughout the work setting rather than working in proximity (such as in an enclave model). For example, rather than the individuals with disabilities working together as a group to clean rooms, some of those individuals might be paired with nondisabled employees to clean rooms, while others might be assigned to work in the restaurant or on grounds maintenance.

5. **Entrepreneurial model.** This model is represented by, for example, a small business that employs both individuals with and without disabilities. The business provides specific products or services (e.g., a bakery, a cleaning service, a workshop that sells handmade furniture, a commercial laundry).

Educators and parents need to determine what types of supported services are available in their community because preparation may take a different slant for the various models.

Job Development. Finding jobs for students with autism may pose an interesting challenge for teachers and parents. We say interesting because employment opportunities, particularly for students with more severe disabilities, may not be immediately obvious. Teachers and parents may need to be creative in designing, creating, or modifying jobs for students with disabilities. In addition, the teacher (or other professional) or parent may have to convince the employer that hiring an individual with autism may benefit his or her business (Nietupski, Verstegen, & Hamre-Nietupski, 1992), as well as quell fears or concerns about hiring an individual with autism. Some examples of jobs that teachers or parents we know created for their children with autism and other severe disabilities are listed next:

- Straighten books at library.

- Wipe off tables in grocery store cafe.

- Deliver intrabuilding mail at the state capitol building.

- Sell notecards and matching envelopes made by students from heavy white paper (folded), then stamped with a variety of stamp designs (dipped in paint); sold at school and school-related meetings.

- Wipe off menus at a local restaurant.

Of course, part of job development for students with autism will probably involve informing potential employers and fellow employees about autism, and teaching them simple strategies for cueing, prompting, redirecting, and reinforcing.

Vocational Preparation. As we said earlier, preparing for employment actually begins in early childhood, and continues through adulthood, with instructional emphasis gradually becoming more focused on training for specific job tasks. Vocational training includes teaching not only specific job tasks, but teaching work-related skills as well (Sowers & Powers, 1991). For example, many of the socialization and communication tasks described in Chapters 6 and 7 are important for successful job placement. In addition, Table 8.9 lists skills that, while not actual job tasks, may be important for obtaining and maintaining employment.

If you are unsure as to the exact job a student may eventually have (e.g., the student is too young to determine a potential job, the student is moving to another community on completion of school), you should teach generic tasks that have widespread application. Although the details of these tasks may vary with contexts, there is enough similarity to justify them as targets for instruction. Table 8.10 lists vocational skills that may be applicable in a variety of employment situations.

Table 8.9 Skills Related to Vocational Success

- Follows directions, rules, and routines.
- Works independently on assigned tasks.
- Produces satisfactory quality of work.
- Works at appropriate speed.
- Works cooperatively with other employees.
- Interacts appropriately with customers.
- Behaves appropriately both on the job and during breaks (e.g., no self-stimulatory behavior, inappropriate hygiene behaviors, inappropriate language).
- Accepts negative or constructive feedback.
- Accepts interruptions in routine.
- Accepts new tasks, routines, or procedures.
- Solves problems independently or asks for help.
- Tells times, or has time awareness skills (e.g., gets to work on time, takes breaks of appropriate length).

Table 8.10 Vocational Tasks with Wide Applicability

- Answering phones
- Filing
- Photocopying
- Faxing
- Shredding
- Collating, stapling
- Folding letters, stuffing envelopes, applying address labels
- Distributing mail
- Intrabuilding or intraoffice delivery (e.g., faxes, supplies, messages, documents)
- Caring for plants (watering, trimming, dusting)
- Tidying offices, lobbies, public areas
- Cleaning bathrooms, break rooms
- Vacuuming
- Sweeping exterior areas of buildings
- Making coffee, setting out coffee supplies
- Loading, unloading commercial dishwashers
- Filling napkin holders, resupplying condiment bins and plastic utensil bins
- Emptying trash
- Straightening items on shelves
- Gathering shopping carts from parking lot
- Washing cars, trucks

SUMMARY

Teaching students basic life skills is an essential part of teaching students with autism. These students characteristically do not learn these skills on their own. Without ongoing, systematic instruction, most individuals with autism will require assistance with basic self-care tasks; will miss out on the many benefits that leisure and recreational activity provides; and will not participate in one of the most basic of life activities: work. All of this also means that unless these skills, along with related communication and social skills, are taught, individuals with autism will be relegated to more restrictive environments and will be unable to function as part of mainstream society.

KEY POINTS

1. Youth with autism often do not learn life skills without formal instruction.

2. Life skills curricula should be developed through ecological assessment of target environments and comparison of those skills against students' current skill levels. Commercial curricula are helpful guides, but may not be sufficient for all students' individual needs.

3. Life skills must be systematically taught, using a combination of state-of-the-art instructional procedures and should include related language and social skills.

4. Developmental appropriateness should be a prime consideration when selecting life skills for instruction.

5. An important component of life skills instruction is assessing how target skills can be modified, or prompts added, to facilitate acquisition. This means modifying materials, adjusting how the skill is performed, or adding visual prompts to remind students of what to do.

6. Teaching in context is especially important for life skills. These skills are useless unless the student is able to use them in a variety of environments, under a variety of conditions. On-site instruction of leisure and vocational skills, particularly, will enhance generalization.

7. Employment should be a goal for older adolescents and adults with autism. Creativity in job development in a variety of employment arrangements will increase the likelihood that students will be employed as adults.

REFERENCES

Agran, M., Test, D., & Martin, J. E. (1994). Employment preparation of students with severe disabilities. In E. Cipani & F. Spooner (Eds.), *Curricular and instructional approaches for students with severe disabilities* (pp. 184–212). Needham Heights, MA: Allyn & Bacon.

Alexandar, R. (1991). Prespeech and prefeeding. In J. L. Bigge (Ed.), *Teaching individuals with physical and multiple disabilities* (pp. 175–198). New York: Macmillan.

Alper, S., McMullen, V., McMullen, R. D., & Miller, P. J. (1996). Application to special education curricular areas with no general education parallels. In D. L. Ryndak & S. Alper (Eds.), *Curriculum content for students with moderate and severe disabilities in inclusive settings* (pp. 215–226). Needham Heights, MA: Allyn & Bacon.

Brockett, S. (1998, November–December). Developing successful play activities for individuals with autism. *Advocate, 31*(6), 15–17.

Coie, J. D., Rabiner, D. L., & Lochman, J. F. (1992). Promoting peer relations in a school setting. In L. A. Bond, B. E. Compas, & C. Swift (Eds.), *Prevention in the schools.* Newbury Park, CA: Sage.

Heyne, L. A., & Schleien, S. J. (1994). Leisure and recreation programming to enhance quality of life. In E. C. Cipani & F. Spooner (Eds.), *Curricular and instructional approaches for persons with severe disabilities* (pp. 213–240). Needham Heights, MA: Allyn & Bacon.

Lord, C., & Hopkins, J. M. (1986). The social behavior of autistic children with younger and same-aged nonhandicapped peers. *Journal of Autism and Developmental Disorders, 16,* 249–261.

Nietupski, J., Verstegen, D., & Hamre-Nietupski, S. (1992). Incorporating sales and business practices into job development in supported employment. *Education and Training in Mental Retardation, 27,* 207–218.

Rehabilitation Act Amendments of 1992, 29 U.S.C. § 701 *et seq.* P.L. 102–569.

Rettig, M. A. (1994). Play behaviors of young children with autism: Characteristics and interventions. *Focus on Autistic Behavior, 9*(5), 1–6.

Rogers, S. J., Herbison, J., Lewis, H. C., Pantone, J., & Reis, K. (1986). An approach for enhancing the symbolic, communicative, and interpersonal functioning of young children with autism or severe emotional handicap. *Journal of the Division for Early Childhood, 10,* 135–145.

Rubin, K. H. & Howe, N. (1985). Toys and play behavior: An overview. *Topics in Early Childhood Special Education, 5*(3), 1–9.

Rusch, F. R., Johnson, J. R., & Hughes, C. (1990). Analysis of co-worker involvement in relation to level of disability versus placement approach among supported employees. *Journal of the Association for Persons with Severe Handicaps, 15,* 32–39.

Schleien, S., & Ray, M.T. (1988). *Community recreation and persons with disabilities: Strategies for integration.* Baltimore, MD: Paul H. Brookes.

Snell, M. E. (1993). *Instruction of students with severe disabilities* (4th ed.). New York: Merrill.

Snell, M. E., & Farlow, L. J. (1993). Self-care skills. In M. Snell, *Instruction of Students with Severe Disabilities* (4th ed.). New York: Macmillan College Publishing.

Sowers, J., & Powers, L. (1991). *Vocational preparation and employment of students with physical and multiple disabilities.* Baltimore, MD: Paul H. Brookes.

Strain, P. S., Hoyson, M., & Jamieson, B. (1985). Normally-developing preschoolers as intervention agents for autistic-like children: Effects on class deportment and social interaction. *Journal of the Division for Early Childhood, 9*(2), 105–115.

Wehman, P., & Revell, W. G. (1996). Supported employment from 1986–1993: A national program that works. *Focus on Autism and Other Developmental Disabilities, 11*(4), 235–242, 250.

Westling, D. L., & Fox, L. (1995). *Teaching students with severe disabilities.* Englewood Cliffs, NJ: Merrill/Prentice Hall.

9

Understanding Intervention Controversies

Did you know that:

- Americans spend more than $14 billion each year on unproven treatments for medical and psychological disorders (Trachtman, 1994)?

- Probably more unproven treatments are tried with children with autism than are tried with children who have other disabilities (Cohen & Volkmar, 1997)?

- Assigning a one-on-one assistant to a child with autism may inhibit learning and socialization?

- School districts that create "autistic programs" are setting themselves up for litigation?

The attention being given to understanding and treating individuals with autism is unprecedented in scope and magnitude. Never before has there been such awareness of the disability or so many suggestions for treating the disorder. Popular press books, television news shows, journalistic writing, and postings on the World Wide Web spread the notion that the effects of autism can be eliminated. Of course, each book, news bulletin, and Internet posting is fairly spe-

cific about what it takes to "cure" an individual of autism. Even some articles that are referred to as scholarly (because they appear in journals after a team of reviewers has scrutinized the writing) promote the idea that if one just applies the right treatment, an individual with autism can become "normal." Controversy arises when these various sources promote treatments that are quite different and even contradictory to each other. For example, using close physical "hugging" in order to help the individual develop attachment to another person (Tinbergen & Tinbergen, 1983) is quite different from targeting specific behaviors to be decreased or increased in order to help the individual acquire useful skills (Lovaas, 1987); however, both methods have been described as enabling a child to recover from autism. This lack of agreement regarding which treatment is best has resulted in confusion and conflict among persons advocating for positive outcomes for individuals with autism. Nowhere is this conflict more apparent than at individualized education plan (IEP) meetings. It is not uncommon for school personnel and parents to find that they disagree on what constitutes a free, appropriate public education, resulting in IEP meetings that last for many

Written by L. Juane Heflin and Richard L. Simpson, with contributions from Cheryl Archer.

hours across multiple days and end—not with an agreed-on IEP—but with one party or the other requesting due process. Nor is it uncommon for both sides to involve lawyers in discussions of appropriate programming, resulting in the development of programs that favor the side that presents the most compelling legal argument, rather than on what is in the best interest of the student involved.

Chapter 1 presented an analysis of three theories that explain skill deficits and some of the common symptoms associated with autism. Belief in one or the other of these theoretical perspectives would influence which skills would be targeted for intervention. For example, adherence to the perceptual/cognitive theory results in an emphasis on teaching attending and imitation as well as teaching how to take another person's perspective. Adherence to the developmental theory results in an emphasis on creating an environment to facilitate skill emergence in a typical developmental sequence. Finally, adherence to a behavioral perspective results in targeting skills that enable the individual to function as independently as possible. All three theoretical perspectives require evaluation of an individual's performance so that specific skill deficits or excesses can be selected and addressed in order to improve adaptive functioning.

All treatments and interventions frequently used for individuals with autism can be categorized based on underlying theoretical constructs. Because of the different constructs, each category is theoretically driven with specific rationales and each promotes different outcomes for the individual. Controversy may occur when one advocate (e.g., a parent) approaches program development from one theoretical construct and another advocate (e.g., a teacher) promotes a program based on a different theoretical construct. Both advocates can create strong arguments for implementing a desired approach, even though the subsequent programming will be significantly different. For this reason, it is critical to be able to analyze theoretical constructs that underlie different interventions. Table 9.1 provides a synopsis of some of the interventions that garner attention in sources of information about autism. The synopses do not provide complete descriptions of the programs, but merely highlight distinguishing features. Readers are encouraged to consult the references provided for more complete information. Interventions are categorized in the table according to the theoretical explanations presented in Chapter 1, as well as two additional categories that address two different theoretical perspectives from those already discussed. These remaining two categories are relationship-based interventions and physiologically-based interventions.

The relationship-based construct attributes the cognitive, behavioral, and language differences common to autism to relationship and emotional deficits (Ricks & Wing, 1976; Sigman & Ungerer, 1984), the lack of ability to demonstrate empathy (Gillberg, 1992), or take another person's perspective (Wimmer & Perner, 1983). Relationship-based interventions stress the development of affect, attachment, bonding, and a sense of relatedness as priorities for treatment and intervention (Ricks & Wing, 1976; Sigman & Ungerer, 1984). Toward this end, the focus is either on enticing the individual with autism to interact and relate or on communicating unconditional acceptance so that the individual with autism feels safe to interact and relate.

Physiologically-based approaches address the underlying neurologic dysfunctions that are believed to be at the core of autism. Physiologically-based approaches attempt to modulate how the brain receives information, alter how information is processed in the neurologic system, and/or impact behavioral output. The emphasis is on changing internal neurologic functioning.

While Table 9.1 includes a wide range of intervention approaches with varying theoretical underpinnings, remember that the most compelling evidence for intervention effectiveness is based on behaviorally-based approaches, such as those listed in Table 9.1 and described in detail throughout this book.

Table 9.1 Synopsis of Intervention Approaches Categorized by Theoretical Perspective

Perceptual/Cognitively-Based Interventions

Program	Purpose	Authors	Method	Research
Social Stories	Improve socialization and social competence in individuals functioning on the higher end of the autism continuum.	Gray, 1995; Gray & Gerand, 1993	Social situations and appropriate responses are described in clear, concrete, and personal terms using descriptive, directive, and perspective sentences, using no more than 1 directive sentence for every 5 of the other types; stories are read as often as needed.	A promising practice with some existing research (Hagiwara & Myles, 1999; Kuttler, Myles, & Carlson, 1998; Swaggart et al., 1995), but more validation is needed.
Visually Cued Instruction	Assists students to organize their world, predict scheduled events, understand expectations, anticipate changes in routine, make choices and function more independently.	Dalrymple, 1995; Earles, Carlson, & Bock, 1998; Hodgdon, 1995; MacDuff, Krantz, & McClannahan, 1993; Quill, 1997	Visual cues are selected, based on the abilities of the student, on a continuum from objects to words; cues are then used to create schedules, label environments, give directions, allow for choices, communicate expectations, and so forth.	The use of visual systems for persons with autism is well-supported (Boucher & Lewis, 1989; Grandin, 1995; Hermelin & O'Conner, 1970; Layton & Watson, 1995; Mirenda & Santogrossi, 1985; Wolfberg & Schuler, 1993) although additional research is needed to determine who is most likely to benefit and which forms of representation are most beneficial.

Developmentally-Based Interventions

Program	Purpose	Authors	Method	Research
van Dijk Approach	Develop sensory perception, organizational skills, and communication.	van Dijk, 1967; van Dijk, 1986; MacFarland, 1995	Originally developed for students who are deaf-blind, the program consists of a curriculum and 14 basic instructional strategies.	Limited research, conducted several years ago demonstrates some effectiveness (Siegel-Causey & Guess, 1989; Stillman & Battle, 1984); lack of recent research raises questions regarding validity.

Behaviorally-Based Interventions

Program	Purpose	Authors	Method	Research
Discrete Trial Training	Train specific skills as identified through analysis of deficits in child's functioning.	Many researchers have used applied behavior analysis and discrete trial training to teach skills; Lovaas (1987) suggested that his particular version of discrete trial training could lead to a recovery from autism. Maurice (1993; 1996) perpetuates the idea.	Discrete trial training consists of giving a command, waiting for a response, consequating the response, and recording data during an intertrial interval; variations in the procedures are advocated by different authors who modify prompts used, consequences applied, trial presentation (massed vs. distributed), and individual vs. collective implementation, among other things.	There is copious empirical evidence supporting the use of applied behavioral analysis and discrete trial training for developing skills; the use of the Lovaas version has not been replicated as valid for promoting autistic recovery (Gresham & MacMillan, 1997).
Picture Exchange Communication System (PECS)	Functional non-verbal communication system based on initiation of communicative interactions.	Bondy & Frost, 1994; Frost & Bondy, 1994	Behaviorally based techniques of shaping, physical prompts, backward chaining, reinforcement, and fading are used to move through six phases of the program, from simple initiation to complex comments.	Replicated in numerous environments by different practitioners; support by Earles, Carlson, & Brock, (1998).

Relationship-Based Interventions

Program	Purpose	Authors	Method	Research
Gentle Teaching	Establish relationship through unconditional acceptance and positive experiences.	McGee, Menolascino, Hobbs, & Menousek, 1987; McGee & Gonzales, 1990	Adults engage with children in preferred activities; other activities modified for errorless learning so child will be successful. High levels of noncontingent positive and negative reinforcement are used; inappropriate behavior is ignored and redirected.	One study was conducted with 73 adults, most of whom were self-injurious; none were cured, but reduction of behavior was maintained during follow-up period; critics suggest the approach is ineffective (Mudford, 1995) and even harmful (Smith, 1996).
Options	Establish relationship through unconditional acceptance and promote child's unique interests and abilities. Unconditional acceptance is the ultimate goal and a cure is neither sought nor promised.	Kaufman, 1976; Kaufman, 1994; Options Institute, 1999	Spend all waking hours with the child, emulate his or her actions and build on interests as possible; approach is taught through training programs available from the Options Institute in Sheffield, MA.	No empirical research has been conducted; approach was popularized through the publication of Son-Rise and the subsequent TV movie entitled Son-Rise: A Miracle of Love. Validation is in the form of testimonials published by Kaufman.

Table 9.1 Synopsis of Intervention Approaches Categorized by Theoretical Perspective—(continued)

Relationship-Based Interventions—continued

Program	Purpose	Authors	Method	Research
Floor Time	Reestablish affective contact with primary caregivers and then foster warmth, intimacy, and pleasure in interactive relationships.	Greenspan, 1992a; Greenspan, 1992b; Wieder, 1996; Greenspan & Wieder, 1997; Greenspan & Wieder, 1998	Adult follows child's lead in activities, "plays dumb" and uses "creative obstructions" to entice the child to interact; emphasis is on building and lengthening "circles of communication" and on promoting growth on the Functional Emotional Assessment Scale.	Support is in the form of testimonials, case studies, and research conducted by the authors; Greenspan & Wieder (1997) conducted a retrospective review of charts of 200 children and reported that 58% had "very good outcomes," a term that was loosely defined; Degangi & Greenspan (1997) conducted a study on children who did not have autism.
Holding Therapy	Repair broken symbiotic bond with caregiver so that relationships can be formed.	Zaslow & Breger, 1969; Allan, 1977; Tinbergen & Tinbergen, 1983; Welch, 1988	Caregiver holds child closely and returns gaze and affection when child makes eye contact; even when not holding the child, caregiver must remain in close proximity with breaks of no longer than 2 hours; not commonly used in the U.S. because it is so invasive.	Little research has been conducted to validate the approach; Stades-Veth (1988) reports on a study conducted in Germany in which 13 of 104 participants were purportedly cured of autism.

Physiologically-Based Interventions

Program	Purpose	Authors	Method	Research
Sensory Integration	Reduces autism symptomology by changing individual's ability to perceive, process, and modulate sensory information.	Ayers, 1972, 1979; Fisher & Murray, 1991; Wilbarger & Wilbarger, 1991	Evaluate sensory needs and develop programming to increase or decrease stimulation as appropriate; sensory exercise (e.g., weight bearing, deep pressure, brushing) are used to adjust individual's sensory integration system.	Neuroscientific basis provides inherent plausibility, but validation consists of testimonials with little independent empirical research conducted to date.
Auditory Integration Training (AIT)	Reduces sound sensitivity to improve behavioral, social, and cognitive functioning.	Berard, 1982, 1993; Rimland & Edelson, 1994	Individuals use headphones to listen to sounds that have been modulated to eliminate certain frequencies; slowly, frequencies are reintroduced. A typical treatment consists of five, 2-hour sessions.	Popularized by Stehli (1991) who published a book chronicling her daughter's cure from autism through AIT. There is little research to support the effectiveness of AIT. Rimland & Edelson (1994) as well as Edelson et al. (1999) support its effectiveness, but theirs is clearly a minority view. Most others consider the treatment ineffective (Bettison, 1996; Gilberg, Johansson, Steffenburg, & Berlin, 1997).
Facilitated Communication	Overcomes individual's global apraxia to allow emergence of communication.	Crossley, 1988, 1992; Biklen, 1990, 1992, 1993	A trained facilitator supports the individual's arm/hand so that s/he can operate an augmentative communication device; over time, the facilitator fades the full physical support until only a light touch on the shoulder or mere proximity are required for the individual to operate the augmentative device.	No empirical evidence supports this approach; validity is discredited by numerous authors (Autism Society of America, 1992-93; Calculator, 1992; Mulick, Jacobson, & Kobe, 1993; Prior & Cummins, 1992; Rimland, 1992; Schopler, 1992; Simpson & Myles, 1995; Szempruch & Jacobson, 1993; Wheeler, Jacobson, Paglieri, & Schwartz, 1993).

EVALUATING INTERVENTION PROGRAMS

Never before have there been so many treatment and intervention programs promoted for use with individuals with autism, and the number of programs available continues to grow daily. The explosion in the number of programs is due in part to the increased awareness of and interest in autism and in part to the effort of entrepreneurs who see a wide open forum for marketing their products. Lack of understanding of the exact etiology of autism contributes to the confusion surrounding the efficacy of program options. Until there is more definite information regarding specific etiology of autism, interventions will be chosen based in theoretical preferences, analysis of research on program effectiveness, and faith in marketing promises. In piecing together treatments and interventions to create an appropriate program, teams of advocates (usually the IEP team) need to have a framework to guide the decision-making process. By incorporating a consistent set of guiding principles, teams can consider innovative approaches while making reasonable and informed decisions (Simpson, 1995). Prior to using any set of guiding principles to design an appropriate program, the team should collect all relevant information regarding the student's characteristics, the family's goals, and the facts about intervention or treatment programs being considered. Systematically, each option can be evaluated in relation to the student's characteristics and goals, and an appropriate program may be individually designed for that student (Campbell, Schopler, Cueva, & Hallin, 1996).

We recommend consideration of the following areas when evaluating interventions. The information presented in each area is not meant to be comprehensive, but rather is intended to serve as an initial criteria for evaluating interventions with regard to individual student needs.

Intervention Outcomes

The IEP team should consider whether the outcomes promised by the intervention match the student's IEP goals. This simply means that each child's individual needs as addressed in IEP goals must drive decision making about interventions. If the IEP team determines that the purported outcomes of the intervention match the IEP goals of the student, the team should next consider the likelihood that implementation of the program with a particular student will likely result in those outcomes. One means of doing this is to compare descriptions of students who have benefited from the program to the characteristics of the student for whom the program is being considered. Students who do not fit these descriptions may not demonstrate the same outcomes.

Potential Intervention Risk

Once the team of advocates has ensured that the outcomes promised by the option are appropriate and meaningful for the student, then the team should consider the potential for any negative outcomes; that is, the team considers whether or not there are any inherent risks in the intervention. The team needs to consider potential risk not only for the student, but also for family members and for school personnel. Risk may be related to physical health, behavior, or quality of life. Using one approach to the exclusion of other options might diminish a student's quality of life (Donnelly, 1996). If the quality of life for the student is diminished, a high likelihood exists that the family's quality of life will be similarly affected. Choosing to use interventions that exclude other approaches might also reduce teacher effectiveness and limit the student's education to the acquisition of useless splinter skills.

In addition to considering the potential negative effects for the student, family members, and school personnel, the team should also consider what would be lost if the intervention option fails. Teams may commit substantial time, energy, and financial resources to implementing an option. If the option fails to produce the desired result, what will the team have lost (Green, 1999)? Few entities have unlimited financial resources. High-cost options that fail can strain school system budgets, empty savings, and exhaust insurance coverage. Teams will want to consider less costly options that have the potential to produce the same or similar results. "Cost" should be considered not only in terms of financial resources needed, but in ethical terms as well. Consider the case of a student for whom 2 years in one-on-one programming does not result in meaningful benefit. Now the student is 2 years older and has lost out on many opportunities to socialize and develop relationships. Or consider the student who spends a majority of the school day receiving computerized instruction. The student enjoys working on the computer and demonstrates gains on targeted skills, but makes no progress in developing pleasurable relationships with others. Or consider a student for whom the exclusive focus of intervention is developing social relationships, and, as a result, he never learns basic functional skills. Intervention failure has implications not only for resources expended, but also for opportunities lost.

Evidence

One of the most contentious issues that a team of advocates should address is the availability of proof to substantiate the effectiveness of a treatment or intervention option. School systems are held accountable for their decisions and should use empirical evidence to defend their choices (Simpson & Myles, 1995). Empirical support can be obtained from professional literature, particularly from studies that replicate the findings of those who have developed innovative approaches. If researchers other than the originators of the program cannot duplicate the same favorable outcomes in other students, then the program has questionable validity and might be considered unsubstantiated.

However, we know that individuals with autism can be very different from one another, making it difficult to replicate findings and to predict the effects of a treatment or intervention under various conditions. Unfortunately families may be desperately seeking improvements in their children and relief for themselves (Lehr & Lehr, 1997) and therefore may be willing to try even unsubstantiated approaches. This willingness can result in hope being replaced by despair and the drain of personal and financial resources (Christopher & Christopher, 1989).

Teams of advocates should look for quantity, quality, and variety when considering available proof for substantiating a treatment or intervention option. The greater the quantity of supporting evidence available, the more the approach has been replicated. The team should also attend to who is doing the replication. A number of studies conducted by the originator or promoter of a program in the absence of support from other researchers do not meet the criteria of replication, because there is obviously a vested interest in promoting the program. Such is currently the case with Facilitated Communication (Crossley, 1988, 1992; Biklen, 1990, 1992, 1993), which to date has little replication data. If the program has never been replicated or uses flawed research methodology, then it is suspect. Likewise, if the approach uses predominantly personal testimonials or case studies as support, then there is less likelihood it will be an effective intervention in other situations. Approaches that are described and/or substantiated exclusively on the Internet are also suspect, because "the explosion of information on the Internet has suffered greatly by misrepresentation and inaccuracy" (Anderson & Romanczyk, 1999, p. 166). Finally, any approach that promises to be beneficial for all students, without regard to individual characteristics should be viewed suspiciously (Nickel, 1996).

Currently, most available proof supports the use of a structured educational program that has been individually tailored to the student's developmental abilities (Campbell et al., 1996; Freeman, 1997). The program should use systematic instructional practices and be provided in an intensive manner with specific programming for generalization (Powers, 1992; Quill, 1997). Parents should be involved in the programming, which should emphasize social and communication training (Fox et al., 1997; Powers, 1992). The strategies described in this book meet these criteria.

Considering Alternatives

Finally, a team considering intervention options should discuss how the selection of particular intervention options might affect the use of other approaches. Some program options require the exclusion of others. For example, we know of a situation in which a family insisted that their child's teachers use only Facilitated Communication for communication purposes. No other form of communication was allowed. This type of exclusionary practice is not only not natural (e.g., most individuals, even children with autism, use multiple forms of communication), but has potential for negative outcomes for the student if the exclusive practice does not produce desired outcomes. As discussed previously, such a situation may present a potentially unacceptable form of risk. Although few options specifically exclude the use of other programs, some can become exclusionary because of the amount of time required for implementation. For example, to decide to use 40 hours per week of any approach means that there is little time available for anything else. This becomes particularly critical when the 40 hours must be provided in an isolated setting (i.e., the student's home), denying the student access to peer interactions, and eliminating the opportunity to benefit from other program options. Any treatment, with specific or coincidental exclusions of other options, must be carefully considered.

Program Evaluation

If an intervention supports a student's IEP goals, presents manageable risk, has objective empirical evidence of effectiveness, and may be used in conjunction with other interventions, then the team may recommend its implementation as a part of the student's program. Prior to implementing the option, the team should decide how to measure the effectiveness of the program. Certain intervention options are easily monitored. Both discrete trial training and the use of individual work systems as in the TEACCH program (Mesibov, 1994; Schopler, Mesibov, & Hearsey, 1995) require the collection of specific data that can be analyzed to determine if progress is being made. In addition to data collected on the student's performance, objective data should be collected on how well

the intervention is being implemented. For example, discrete trial programming is provided in a systematic fashion that adheres to specific criteria. The person providing the discrete trial training should be observed to ensure that she or he is using the methodology accurately.

Unlike the options that have data collection as a component, some approaches are evaluated through subjective perceptions of improvement. For example, Floor Time (Greenspan & Wieder, 1997), Sensory Integration (Krueger, 1996), and Auditory Integration Training (Stehli, 1991) have been evaluated on the basis of whether or not an observer believes the student is improving in some area of functioning. There is a danger that these types of subjective impressions might be impacted by a "placebo effect" whereby improvements are seen only because they are expected (Lehr & Lehr, 1997). In this case, the team of advocates should discuss how the effects of an option can be evaluated in a more precise, less subjective fashion.

In addition to considering how to evaluate an intervention or treatment option, the team of advocates should determine who will conduct evaluations. Several members of the team may be given responsibility for portions of program evaluation, or consideration may be given to asking persons who are not on the team to conduct outside evaluations. Persons qualified to evaluate interventions must have knowledge of the student and the option and must not be biased in favor of the option; otherwise, the placebo effect is more apt to occur. For example, someone who is certified in sensory integration may be more likely to perceive that the student is benefiting from a brushing program because of a personal bias in favor of the approach. If the team articulates an objective method for evaluating an intervention's effectiveness, then there is less danger of observer bias.

Once the team has determined how to evaluate an intervention, and has decided who will be responsible for conducting evaluations, then they should discuss how often to evaluate. The length of time between progress checks is directly related to the ability to attribute any improvements to the intervention. If evaluation occurs every 4 months, improvements may be ascribed to simple student maturation or the influence of variables other than the implementation of the treatment or intervention. Infrequent evaluations also hinder the ability of the team to make timely modifications. The team should delineate clear outcome criteria prior to program implementation and use lack of progress toward those criteria to decide when to discontinue the program (Nickel, 1996). Additionally, the team may agree that the intervention option will be discontinued if only minimal progress is made within a 2-month period, or if the student or family suffers negative side effects. A program might be abandoned if improvements are temporary and disappear within a short period of time.

Probably the most critical factor in program evaluation is the ability to collect objective rather than subjective data to counteract the bias factor and invalid assumptions. Direct observation of target behaviors is recommended as the preferred objective evaluation method. Chapters 2 and 5 describe the process of selecting appropriate data collection techniques. Additional examples are presented in Table 9.2.

Implementation of an intervention should not become an end unto itself, but rather a means to achieve desirable outcomes for a student (Hanft & Feinberg, 1997). Table 9.3 provides a list of important questions for advocacy teams to consider before adopting an intervention program.

When teams carefully evaluate intervention options against the criteria described in this chapter, it is more likely they will choose appropriate programs for promoting attainment of student goals and objectives. Once a program is implemented, however, it must be monitored to ensure that the student continues to make progress toward IEP goals. Because autism constitutes a lifelong disability, an individual's needs will change over time (Campbell et al., 1996). The team must be sensitive to those changes and modify programs accordingly, utilizing agreed-on guidelines to facilitate ongoing discussions. The next section delineates reasons why programs may fail to benefit students. To enhance the likelihood that students will make progress toward IEP goals, teams should discuss strategies to circumvent these possible programming weaknesses.

WHY PROGRAMS FAIL

The process of giving careful consideration to a variety of intervention options will result in individually tailored programs. As you have learned, the best programming for students with autism consists of a structured educational program that is appropriately matched to the student's developmental disabilities and long-range expectations (Campbell et al., 1996; Freeman, 1997; Heflin & Simpson, 1998). The use of guidelines for discussing the multitude of intervention options available can facilitate agreement among IEP team members as to what constitutes an appropriate program. When agreement is not reached, the result is due process proceedings and hearing officers.

Table 9.2 Sample Data Collection Methods for Direct Observation

Objective	Intervention	Data Collection Method
Sherry will demonstrate appropriate non-verbal imitation by responding to a command to "do this" with 90 percent accuracy for 3 out of 5 days.	Discrete trial training	Restricted event recording
Michael will use his communication system to request items and/or activities at least 10 times per day for 3 out of 5 days.	PECS	Nonrestricted event recording
Lionel will participate in a group game during PE for 11 consecutive minutes.	Social stories	Duration recording

Table 9.3 Guidelines for Discussing Intervention Options

1. To guide consideration of the appropriateness of an intervention option for supporting a student's IEP goals, the team may ask:
   a. Have meaningful goals been written for the student?
   b. Do the goals promote independence and self-determination?
   c. Do the outcomes promoted by the option match the goals written for the student?
   d. Is the student similar to other individuals who have benefited from the program?
2. To guide consideration of the appropriateness of an intervention option based on the presence of potential risk, the team may ask:
   a. Are there any immediate or eventual health or behavioral risks for the student?
   b. Are there immediate risks for family members or school personnel?
   c. Will the option negatively impact the quality of life for the student, family, or school personnel?
   d. If the option fails, will the financial, time, and energy resources have been justified?
3. To guide consideration about how best to evaluate the effectiveness of an intervention option, a team may ask:
   a. What criteria will be used to objectively determine if an option is effective?
   b. Who will be responsible for conducting all necessary components of evaluation?
   c. How will bias in evaluation be controlled?
   d. How frequently will evaluation be conducted?
   e. What criteria will be used to decide if an option is to be continued or discontinued?
4. To guide consideration of determining the effectiveness of an intervention option, a team may ask:
   a. Are there a number of studies to support the effectiveness of the option?
   b. Are the studies of high quality?
   c. Is there empirical validation for the option or is all the support in the form of personal testimonials or case studies?
   d. Does the option promise the same benefits for all who participate?
5. To guide consideration of the potential value of an intervention option based on what other options would be excluded, a team may ask:
   a. Does this option require exclusive use or imply exclusivity based on intensity?
   b. What will be eliminated because of the excluded options or opportunities?
   c. Are less restrictive or less intensive alternatives available that may be just as effective?
   d. Are other options better researched than the one being considered?
   e. Does this option support the attainment of the functional needs of the student?

Increasingly, judges are asked to make programming decisions based on the most compelling legal arguments for a particular program. These decisions are often based on adherence to the letter of the law (lack of adherence is called a procedural violation) and not on evidence of an appropriate program. For example, it is not uncommon for a hearing officer or judge to tell the school district that it must provide whatever programming a parent requests because the district failed to give adequate notice of a meeting. It is less common but still possible for a hearing officer or judge to find that programming provided by the school district might be adequate and find against the parents because the parents never placed the student in the district's program. Analysis of hearing decisions and litigation outcomes reveal five issues that influenced due process decisions. These issues affected arguments presented by parents as well as school districts. To construct a carefully crafted program, advocates must guard against the following mistakes.

Lack of Defined a Program

Since the signing of P.L. 94-142 in 1975, decisions about how a student will be instructed have been left to the discretion of the schools (Boomer & Garrison-Harrell, 1995; Yell, 1998). The decision of how best to facilitate goal attainment is a decision regarding instructional methodology. Methodology controversies have been the basis of many disagreements between IEP team members when determining an appropriate education for students with autism. Program proponents argue that their methodology (e.g., Lovaas, TEACCH) is more effective than other methodologies and should therefore constitute the majority of, if not entire, program for students. Because of methodology controversies, the final regulations for P.L. 105-17 (Department of Education, 1999) support the specification of methodology in IEP documents. This is a dramatic change from previous insistence that methodologies not be written into the IEP. Regardless of whether or not an IEP team delineates methodology in the IEP, we recommend that teams specify a clearly defined program with appropriate intensity that emphasizes meaningful outcomes. If these factors are not defined, the program is likely to be judged inadequate, particularly by the courts.

A clearly defined program consists of carefully conceived and well described elements with the understanding that these elements have been used successfully with other children. Any advocate who refers to a proposed program as "pilot" or "new" is communicating that a tested model is not yet available. In these situations, due process decisions will favor the advocates who are proposing programs that have documented benefits (*Delaware County IU #25 v. Martin K.*, 1993; High Bridge Board of Education, 1995). Documented benefits are positive outcomes that are attributable to the program being provided. In pilot programs, the benefit is yet to be demonstrated.

Program intensity also influences outcomes. Programs may be found inadequate if they are not implemented with appropriate intensity. Ten hours of any treatment or intervention will probably be inferior when compared to 30 hours of another option (*Delaware Co. IU #25 v. Martin K.*, 1993). However, there is no magic number of hours of programming. The intensity of the programming provided must be balanced against the stamina and needs of the child. For example, to place a 3-year-old in a 40-hour-a-week program may be highly inappropriate if the child still requires naps and rest periods. Utilizing a 25-hour-a-week one-on-one program for teaching self-help skills may be inappropriate if the child's

socialization needs should take precedence. To create a clearly defined program, the team should specify appropriate intensity that will likely enable the student to make progress toward IEP goals without robbing the student of his or her childhood (Cohen, 1998).

Finally, a clearly defined program will emphasize meaningful outcomes for the student. The program developed by the IEP team should support student progress toward all goals. A program with an exclusive emphasis on teaching reading, for example, will fail to promote progress toward attainment of other, maybe more functional, skills (e.g., toileting). A program with a singular emphasis on socialization may ignore other priority needs, perhaps resulting in inappropriate programming (*Mark Hartmann v. Loudoun County Board of Education*, 1997). A well-defined program is one that links methodologies to student progress toward meaningful outcomes. Lack of a well-defined program may be insufficient to support goal attainment and may be indefensible if due process is requested.

Choosing Popular Rather Than Appropriate Options

A program for a student with autism runs a great risk of failing if the team of advocates incorporates options that are popular at the time rather than those that have been demonstrated to have beneficial outcomes as defined by the criteria described in the previous section. Nowhere is this more apparent than in the area of placement decisions. Although the federal law specifies that a full continuum of placement options be available and that placement decisions be individualized (Simpson & Sasso, 1992), some argue that it is morally wrong to educate students anywhere other than in the general education classroom (Wang & Walberg, 1988). The popular tide of inclusion may result in programming that is inadequate to meet some students' needs. Thus, it is incumbent on IEP teams to make placement decisions based on individual needs, rather than popular philosophy. In a recent court case, judges criticized full inclusion of a youth with autism, finding the placement detrimental to him and other students who were victim to his aggression. The court criticized the fact that he was not receiving intensive instruction in critical skills and decided that social benefit without academic progress was insufficient to justify placement in the general education classroom (*Mark Hartmann v. Loudoun County Board of Education,* 1997). This finding was supported by the Supreme Court when it refused to hear the case (Henry, 1998).

Implementing a popular option, such as full inclusion, without considering the student's unique needs may lead to program failure. The same is true of implementing the latest "cures" presented in the media. To avoid program failure, IEP teams should evaluate options not based on their popularity, but on merits revealed through careful analysis using the guidelines recommended in the preceding section. Implementing treatments and interventions with demonstrated benefit, rather than popular acceptance, can further a program's success.

Teaching Dependency

An appropriate program for students with autism should advance independent functioning and self-determination (Freeman, 1997; Hart, 1995). Unfortunately, programs often unwittingly promote the opposite when students are routinely given personal assistants or "shadows." Although one-on-one assistants are assigned to facilitate student engagement in programming, students may become overly dependent on this adult assistance. For example, a paraprofessional may be assigned to help a student respond to teacher directions or peer initiations. However, what the student may learn is not to line up when the teacher gives the direction or to say "Hi" when a peer gives a greeting, but to line up or say "Hi" when the assistant provides a prompt.

Unfortunately, the decision to provide an assistant is not always made with consideration of how the assistant's presence will be faded. Instead of a strategy to promote participation and inde-

pendence, the one-on-one assistant may become a permanent feature. Additionally, the provision of a shadow to promote interaction may actually be a deterrent to acceptance by peers (Giangreco, Edelman, Luiselli, & MacFarland, 1997) and may result in teachers viewing the assistant as the person primarily responsible for the student's learning (Marks, Schrader, & Levine, 1999). Programs fail when the price of participation is increased dependence on another. Program success will most likely be enhanced through systematic instruction in skills that promote independence without the need of a one-on-one aide.

One-Size-Fits-All Mentality

Programs may also fail when they apply identical services to all students with autism. By creating an "autism program," a school district is suggesting that all students with autism will need the same type of services. In designing a single program to meet the needs of a heterogeneous group of students, school districts may be opening themselves up to allegations of taking a "cookie cutter approach" (Board of Education of the Ann Arbor Public Schools, 1996; Independent School District No. 318, 1996), a position that is indefensible in due process proceedings.

Often the one-size-fits-all mentality is evident in the number of hours that programming is offered to students. Typically, districts offer young children a half-day program and older children a full-day program. These standard options may be inappropriate for students with autism. A young child with autism may benefit from a full-day program, whereas an older student may benefit from a half-day program in academics and a half-day program in community-based instruction. Furthermore, the length of the standard school year may not meet the needs of individual students. Students with autism may need a longer school year and may even need services during breaks of 2 weeks (*Eric S. v. Duncanville Independent School District,* 1984–85). For other students with autism, breaks from school programming may not inhibit progress toward IEP goals, so extended-year serv-

Table 9.4 Criteria for Evaluating the Need for Extended-Year Services

Factors to be considered are:

- The degree of the individual's impairment
- Whether EYS is extraordinary to the child's condition
- The ability of the child to interact with others
- The child's rate of progress
- Past regression/recoupment
- Professional opinion predicting the student's progress and intended progress.

ices (EYS) would be deemed unnecessary (*Cordrey v. Euckert*, 1990). Factors used for considering the appropriateness of EYS for students with autism are taken from the Tenth Circuit Court of Appeals decision in *Johnson v. Independent School District No. 4 of Bixby* (1990) and are presented in Table 9.4.

Finally, the one-size-fits-all mentality tends to ignore the individual learning characteristics of students with autism. Some students with autism may be auditory learners and may benefit from verbal prompting. Others may be visual learners and benefit more from visually cued instruction. Characteristics that must be considered when developing an individually tailored program include the student's responses to sensory input. Some students will need higher levels of stimulation, whereas others may respond better in carefully modulated environments. Programs may fail when they ignore unique student needs, appropriate program duration, and individual learning characteristics. To enhance success, programs should address unique needs and learning characteristics and consist of school days and school years that are appropriate in length.

Lack of Documentation

Programs may fail when school personnel are unable to demonstrate a relationship between program components and student outcomes. To support a program's effectiveness, data must be collected demonstrating that it is the implementation of the program, not other factors, that re-

sulted in progress toward IEP goals. Typically, school personnel conduct pre-testing and post-testing of special education students at the beginning and end of the school year to demonstrate such a relationship. Unfortunately, it is difficult to conclusively correlate methodologies to developmental or skill gains when evaluations occur 9 months apart. Fortunately, programs such as discrete trial training and TEACCH utilize frequent data collection, making it relatively simple to correlate instructional gains to methodology. Failure to incorporate ongoing data collection and analysis may result in program failure. The reader is referred to Chapters 2 through 8 in this book or chapters in Alberto and Troutman (1999) regarding procedures for collecting data and using the data collected to make programming decisions.

In summary, the likelihood that a program will be successful depends on carefully defined meaningful outcomes, efficacious methodologies used to promote the outcomes, and appropriate program intensity. Furthermore, treatments and interventions should be chosen based on their effectiveness, not their popularity. Because the use of one-on-one aides can result in increased dependency, alternate strategies should be considered so that students progress toward independence and self-determination. It is best not to create an "autism program" that might deny students' unique needs. Instead, programming must be individually tailored for each student in terms of length of school day, length of school year, and individual learning characteristics. Finally, frequent and ongoing data collection must be used to support claims that the treatments and interventions being used in the program are responsible for promoting the attainment of IEP goals.

A FAMILY'S SEARCH FOR AN EFFECTIVE PROGRAM

In Chapter 1 you met Cheryl, who shared her experiences as a parent of Jamie, a child with autism. We now continue with Cheryl's story and follow her exploration of interventions for Jamie. As you will see, Cheryl clearly describes the confusion and uncertainty she and her husband felt in their search for the "correct" treatment for Jamie: the treatment that would "cure" his autism. Once Jamie entered public school, Jamie's IEP team managed to avoid many of the programmatic mistakes described in this chapter and established an effective educational program. As we discussed earlier, an effective program is one that is flexibly responsible to the student's changing needs. Cheryl's story clearly describes the importance of this concept. Once again, we appreciate Cheryl's story because it provides us the opportunity to "walk in her shoes," an experience that no one but a parent of a child with autism could possibly describe.

Cheryl's Story—Part II

One day I was wandering among the shelves at our public library. I often did this even though everything I found on autism discouraged me even more. I found reading about autism perversely satisfying because I could bury myself even further in my personal misfortune. This time I came upon a book title I had never seen before. It was *Let Me Hear Your Voice: A Family's Triumph Over Autism* by Catherine Maurice. I was initially skeptical. "Triumph" and "autism" were not two words that went together in real life. Yet I knew the reputation of Bernard Rimland, the founder of the Autism Society of America and the Autism Research Institute, who wrote the book's foreword. There must be something of value in this book. It related the experiences of the mother of two children with autism. Both had made dramatic progress in a home-based program of intensive early behavioral intervention, or applied behavioral analysis (ABA). They had functionally "recovered" from autism and were growing up as normal schoolchildren. She related the

work of O. Ivar Lovaas at the University of California–Los Angeles, whose research included providing young children with autism a program of 40 hours a week of intensive behavioral therapy. Nearly half of the UCLA group (47 percent) was indistinguishable from normally developing peers by the time they were in first grade. Those who did not respond to that degree still showed improvement in social, communication, and cognitive skills. I showed the book to Rick, and we stayed up late one night talking. He got the journal articles cited in it and we read them. Again, we stayed up late into the night talking. We agreed that Jamie must have a chance to get intensive behavioral therapy. If we didn't act on this, we would never know how much it might have helped, and we would have to live with the consequences. At worst, if we did act and it helped only a little, we would know that we had given Jamie our best shot and would be better able to live with his autism. At best, Jamie might respond like the 47 percent in the UCLA study. We, of course, would hope for the best.

My spirits soared. I didn't tell anyone, even Rick, that in my imagination, I was being given the chance to "do over" whatever I had done "wrong" when I was pregnant. I somehow felt that I could give Jamie another chance to get the piece of prenatal development he had missed. I must have been experiencing the "bargaining" emotional response to grief or loss: "If we just do this (behavioral therapy), Jamie will be fine." I was able to use this emotional response to get into action. I had hope. There was something I could *do* for Jamie.

I contacted the UCLA Clinic for the Behavior of Children and requested an information packet and application for their program of home workshops.

They had a 1-year waiting list, but we could complete an application and begin waiting. The application process required that we obtain a formal diagnosis of pervasive developmental disorder (PDD) or autism for Jamie, which we eventually obtained at the University of Texas Developmental Clinic in Houston. Earlier in January I had taken Jamie to a pediatric neurologist who would not give an autism or PDD diagnosis. Because Jamie was only 17 months old, the neurologist would not even say that Jamie's delays *could* be caused by a pervasive developmental disorder. I was happy with this doctor's opinion for a short time, but because I lived with Jamie, I had little doubt that he would eventually be diagnosed with something related to autism.

During the half-day evaluation, Jamie was given a battery of tests, including the *Bayley Scales of Infant Development* and the *Vineland.* We were debriefed that afternoon. Jamie's diagnosis *was* pervasive developmental disorder, and they supported our idea of applying to the Lovaas Clinic for intervention. We could get started and return in a year for a follow-up evaluation. We received a complete written report late, and while I was prepared for it, Jamie's score of 57 on the *Bayley* dealt me yet another blow. That number was Jamie's IQ, and back then I believed that the IQ score was terribly significant. We *had* to change it. We couldn't just spend the next year waiting for UCLA to come. We had to start immediately. The research pointed to a brief window of opportunity during the early childhood years, and we didn't want to miss any of it. We ordered the Lovaas book *Teaching Developmentally Disabled Children (The Me Book)* and tried to follow it like a recipe. It was hard to do. It was hard to picture exactly what all of the

instructions meant in concrete terms. For example, the book recommended that I begin by teaching Jamie to sit down when told to do so. He was too small even for a preschool-size chair, so I set his booster seat on the floor for him. The next task was more daunting. He was supposed to look at me when I gave the instruction "Look at me." I worked on these skills for as long as I could each day, but still couldn't figure out how we would ever work up to 40 hours a week of this kind of instruction. I needed to talk with somebody who had done it before. The Internet was still much too new and I had *no* computer skills, so I used my telephone every afternoon on the days when Jamie napped. I contacted the Autism Society of America and started receiving their newsletter, the *Advocate.* I happened to see a letter to the editor from a couple in South Carolina who wrote about the success they were experiencing with their son in a home program. They lived in a small town, so I found their number through information, and eventually found myself talking to an actual mother of a child with autism. She was leading a home ABA program, guided by a replication site for the UCLA Young Autism Project. She answered my questions about "Sit down" and "Look at me," and described recent revisions in the original program. For example, "Look at me" was no longer the universally accepted way of starting to work with a child. Instead, a simple motor activity that would be easy to prompt hand-over-hand (e.g., dropping a block in a bucket) was recommended. She described several other activities, or drills, that beginners could do. Best of all, she gave me the telephone number of a mother in Texas whose son, now included in a first-grade classroom, had participated for several years in a UCLA home program.

I called the Texas woman that evening. She sent me all kinds of information, lists of UCLA Young Autism Project replication sites, and her personal account of day-to-day life with a child in a 30-hour-a-week program of behavioral therapy. Her son had made tremendous progress in every area, but still, at age 7, needed the help of an aide in order to succeed in a regular classroom. She described him as one of the "48th percent," meaning he was just shy of those fortunate 47 percent who had virtually recovered in the Lovaas study. She also gave me telephone numbers of a few more families in Texas, which led me to another woman from Texas whose little girl was just 2 months older than Jamie. This mother's experiences paralleled mine, and we soon became fast friends. She told me about a newer replication site in Madison, Wisconsin—the Wisconsin Early Autism Project—and we both got on their waiting list, which was only 4 months long.

During the months we were waiting for the visit from the Early Autism Project, we continued to work with Jamie. Well, that is a bit of an understatement. Jamie's program totally consumed me. When I wasn't working with him, I was watching someone else work with him (we worked with him for 10 to 15 hours per week). I thought about Jamie's therapy, Jamie's progress, and, more often than I'd like to admit now, obsessed over how much of a chance Jamie had to someday be "indistinguishable from his peers." I would go back time and time again and watch the video about the UCLA Young Autism Project that ended with interviews of three boys who were now living normal lives. Maybe someday Jamie would skateboard with a friend or talk about his college plans or kid around with his dad about the length of his hair. Maybe if we worked hard enough at Jamie's

therapy and did everything "right" (just like the UCLA Clinic), we might stem the tide of Jamie's autism. We were his only chance. It felt like an emergency, and only heroic measures would do.

We placed Katy in summer day camp so that I would be free to spend time working with Jamie and his trainers, whom we called therapists. Jamie sailed through the matching and receptive labeling ("point to the cow") drills and learned to do preschool puzzles. Non-verbal imitation (the trainer says "Do this," and Jamie imitates her action) required more effort for us and for Jamie. We performed the action, saying "Do this," then reached over and put Jamie through the action hand-over-hand (full prompting) for many, many repetitions. Actions involving objects such as hammering and putting blocks into a bucket were easiest. The objects acted as partial prompts, so Jamie was able to take them over for himself sooner. Even simple actions involving just his body (clapping hands, putting arms over the head) required many more hand-over-hand prompts. When Jamie had mastered a few non-verbal imitations, it was comparatively easy to teach him the receptive commands corresponding to them. (The trainer says "Clap your hands" or "Arms up," gradually dropping out the demonstration of the action.) Jamie was really good at repeating "ba" and even "ba-ba" or "ba-ba-ba," but we were unable to get him to repeat any other sounds during that first summer. Jamie's strengths seemed to be in receptive language, especially labeling; his weaker areas were non-verbal imitation and verbal imitation. Paying attention was always hard for Jamie. A lot of effort was required to capture and hold his attention during non-verbal imitation, and it was sometimes close to impossible to keep him with us during verbal imitation drills.

An average day for Jamie, during the year he was 2 years old, was packed with structured activity. He was typically engaged in one-to-one behavioral therapy with me or a therapist on his team for three 2-hour sessions. I tried to schedule a session with a therapist after school so that I could pick up Katy and give her some of the attention she wanted and needed so badly. In our family, the afternoon, evening, and bedtime routines called for two adults, so until Rick came home from work, I tried to make sure Jamie was "covered." Besides his home behavioral therapy program, Jamie participated in a number of outside activities. We took him to the Communications Disorders Clinic at Southwest Texas State University for speech/language therapy twice a week. ECI provided weekly therapeutic horseback riding, a parent–child program at our local gym for both typically developing children and children with developmental delays, a monthly visit with a physical therapist, and weekly home visits from our family consultant.

This schedule allowed for a minimum of unstructured time and virtually filled most of Jamie's waking hours. The home therapy program was made up of brief segments of structured teaching, divided up by short breaks that were just long enough for Jamie to take a couple of runs around the table or a few jumps on the bed. Jamie had a longer break of about 15 minutes every hour, when he could go outdoors with his therapist, take a walk, run around the house, or just have some "down" time. When Dad was at home, Jamie always played with him during these breaks. Dad's specialty is the rough-and-tumble play that Jamie craves. We often say that Jamie thinks his dad is "a ride." Jamie's activity level has always been high, and he has needed constant hands-on supervision.

He's never been a child who could sit and watch even his favorite videos on his own. A highly structured schedule was necessary from the beginning in order for Jamie to stay engaged and safe.

Jamie kept up his home therapy schedule 7 days a week, but on weekends he took more frequent outings for shopping or play. During Christmas vacation, we opted not to travel so that Jamie's structured program would not be disrupted, and on Christmas Day, one of his therapists, who didn't mind taking a break away from her own relatives, came over and did a session. The home behavioral therapy program was Jamie's (and our entire family's) way of life. Had it not been so positive, if Jamie had appeared to be distressed or unhappy, or if Jamie had not progressed, we could never have kept it up.

Our family has lived under a special kind of stress for more than 5 years now, since we first learned that Jamie was not developing normally. Perhaps the worst time for us was at the beginning when we had no idea that there was anything significant we could do for our child. After all, he had autism, and it seemed hopeless. The feeling of helplessness was terrible. Our daughter spent half of her first grade in the midst of our fear and grief and the other half in an atmosphere of frantic urgency. In a way it was good that Katy was not a child who could or would be overlooked. We had no choice but to find a way to give her all of the attention and energy we could possibly muster. It was obvious that nothing in this family could be taken for granted. Parenting these two children whom we loved so much was the greatest challenge either of us had ever faced. It was exhausting both physically and spiritually. Some evenings Rick looked at me and said, "I can't be dead. I still hurt." There have been many long nights, too. He has frequently greeted me in the morning with the question, "How many nights was that?"

We were fortunate that Jamie's needs did not thrust us into a financial emergency, as they well might have at an earlier time in our lives. Our health insurance did not cover any of the costs of behavioral therapy during the first year. Jamie's initial workshop with the people from the Early Autism Project, along with the consultant's airfare and lodging, cost around two thousand dollars, and our consultant returned from Wisconsin for a follow-up workshop every 12 weeks or so. Although we were able to split the cost of airfare and lodging with one or two other families in our area, these expenses added up. In addition, to implement the program we paid home therapists who worked a combined 30 to 40 hours a week. Jamie's program for the first 2 years was paid for with funds from the sale of land that I had inherited; that money is now long gone.

Eight months after Jamie's initial workshop, we returned to the UT Medical Center Developmental Clinic for a follow-up evaluation. Jamie's combined scores on the *Bayley* were over a full standard deviation above his initial scores. He had developed very little oral language due to his limited ability to echo, but his receptive language and cognitive skills were markedly improved. Our health insurance company, after reviewing Jamie's test results and consulting with the consultant from the Early Autism Project, agreed to pay a portion of Jamie's workshop fees during the next 2 years. The fact that we were able to present concrete data supporting the use of early behavioral intervention helped us make our case.

The concrete data that helped us acquire insurance coverage for Jamie's treatment were also helpful when we started preparing for Jamie's transition from Early Childhood Intervention to public school services. We wanted to continue working for 30 to 40 hours a week in individual ABA therapy, with support from the school district. A friend, Jo Webber, advised us to get to know the administrators of the special education program in our district as early as we could. I initiated a meeting with the district special education director more than a year before Jamie was actually scheduled to start to school. In fact, we met even before Jamie's initial workshop with the Wisconsin Early Autism Project. I introduced her to Jamie, we talked about early behavioral intervention, we exchanged reading material, and I invited her to see Jamie's program in our home. When we started having the Early Autism Project workshops, we notified the special education director so that she could encourage interested staff members to attend. By the time our first IEP meeting was scheduled, we had established a positive working relationship with our school district.

That first IEP meeting was a prime example of parents and educators having different goals for students with autism. Rick and I, as parents, wanted to convince the school district to provide the kind of intensive one-to-one home behavioral therapy that Jamie had been receiving. We felt that a school program would not be appropriate until Jamie had developed better communication skills, and that play and social skills ought to be introduced gradually by bringing one or two children into our home program for playtime. School district personnel, on the other hand, argued that Jamie should have opportunities for social interaction right from the start. They also took the position that a school program could provide him with an appropriate environment. They could not justify the considerable expense of providing a home program for Jamie. Yet they did agree that Jamie had shown a great deal of growth during the past year of intensive home therapy and could clearly see the issue from our point of view. By the end of the afternoon, it was clear that we would need to meet again in order to finish. We wondered if we might be setting a record for the longest IEP meeting in history.

Fortunately, Dr. Webber (who attended the meeting with us) helped us find a compromise. Jamie would attend school in the Primary Program for Children with Disabilities (PPCD) for 3 hours a day. He would receive individual behavioral therapy for 1 of those hours at school and participate in classroom and group activities as much as possible the rest of the time. In addition, the district would reimburse us for 2 hours a day of individual home therapy. Members of Jamie's home therapy team would continue to implement his program at home. Rick and I believed that this was a workable plan. We knew of parents who had "gone for broke" and settled for no less than 100 percent support from their school districts, but we felt that our time and energy would be better spent working together with Jamie than pursuing that goal. We have been able to maintain a good working relationship with the people who work with Jamie at school, as well as the district administrators, and the compromise we reached in the beginning helped.

Soon after Jamie started going to school, it became clear that it would be difficult to work with Jamie individually in the PPCD classroom because there were too many distractions for both Jamie and the teacher or aide working with him. The school was already filled to capacity, and there wasn't a single small, quiet space free of interruptions where Jamie could

work. His teacher was confined to working in the PPCD classroom with the other children, whose needs could not be ignored. So we all met for another IEP meeting, increased the number of hours provided by the district at home to 3, and decreased the time Jamie was to spend in the PPCD classroom.

As we worked together with Jamie's school teaching team, we learned that it was often most effective to address new and emerging cognitive and language skills in the home program. At school, Jamie had opportunities for socialization and generalization of skills learned at home. School helped Jamie to grow in flexibility and independence. I loved coming to school and catching him at recess playing with typical screaming, laughing children. His favorite "inclusion" activity was being pushed on the tire swing with two or three other children. To a casual observer, Jamie could have been just another kid on the playground, standing out more because of his red hair than his atypical behavior.

Jamie continued to make good progress in receptive and expressive language during most of the first 2 years we combined his home behavioral therapy with the PPCD school program. He was able to pronounce enough words for us to start teaching him to name things, and he began to use words to communicate. His articulation was difficult to understand and his speaking vocabulary was quite limited, but he could use words purposefully. He had a strong desire to communicate his wants. One day I was picking him up at the end of the school day, and he declared, "I want bus." The regular bus ride home would have taken nearly an hour, so we had not put him on the bus route. Nevertheless, I arranged a way for Jamie to ride a few blocks on the school bus to a nearby neighborhood stop where I picked him up every afternoon.

This was an exciting and promising time for us. We wished that Jamie's articulation and functional speech would improve, but we were increasingly confident that they would. We would just continue behavioral and speech therapy, and take every opportunity we could to encourage him to talk. I constantly asked him questions, wherever we were. When we were in the car, if I stopped to get fast food or snacks, he never got to just sit and eat. Every stop sign offered an opportunity. If the Frito resembled a letter of the alphabet (O, J, and U frequently appeared), I said, "What letter?" When he said the name, I let him eat it, and praised him profusely. He could identify sets of one, two, and three, so I held up a set of french fries, asking "How many?" The correct answer yielded the fries. During this time, we continued having home workshops with Wisconsin Early Autism Project consultants. With their help, we assessed Jamie's progress, worked on our teaching and behavioral therapy skills, and discussed strategies for surmounting roadblocks in the program.

The most persistent and frustrating roadblock was our inability to hold Jamie's attention. He didn't actively tantrum or run away; he just passively tuned out. We implemented a number of strategies that had worked with other children, such as interspersing difficult skills (like vocal imitation) with easy, fun ones, and collecting an endless storehouse of ideas for appealing reinforcers (both food and nonfood) because Jamie became satiated easily. Despite our tremendous efforts, Jamie's data notebook was full of notations of "N.A." (not attending).

Our other serious problem was Jamie's periodic, temporary loss of oral language skills. The first time

this happened, Jamie had developed laryngitis along with an upper respiratory and middle ear infection. He couldn't hear as well as usual, and it must have hurt to use his voice. He began whispering, then stopped talking altogether. After he got well, his speech gradually returned, but not without a lot of extra work. We retraced most of the vocal imitation steps we had used to help Jamie develop oral language in the first place (starting with "ba"). Jamie had frequent respiratory problems and ear infections, and loss of oral language, frighteningly, became a part of the pattern. I began to dread every sniffle and sneeze, afraid we would have to start over with speech yet again. Finally, during the Christmas vacation when Jamie was 4, he contracted another respiratory infection and, again, stopped talking. This time, retracing our steps was barely helping. We worked for the entire spring semester at home and in private speech therapy, and Jamie built up a limited repertoire of syllable imitations, but these faded out by the end of summer. He had two remaining words, "up" and "open." We set up every possible opportunity for him to use them, but we just couldn't help him hold onto them, and they, too, disappeared by fall. Jamie was now 5 years old and "non-verbal." I had honestly believed that with enough determination, I could find a way to keep this from happening, but I found that I was powerless to stop it.

Loss of speech was only part of the problem. Jamie was simply unable to pay attention to his behavioral drills, had become increasingly hyperactive, began to engage in pica (eating things that are not food, a dangerous and troubling behavior), and had increasing difficulty falling asleep and staying asleep almost every night. Jamie had never developed regular bowel habits, and alternated "holding in" of bowel movements with soiling and smearing at times when we could not directly supervise him (while we were driving the car or sleeping). In the middle of the night, we often woke up to a big cleanup job and a newly energized kid. When we weren't being awakened, we stayed "under siege," afraid of what might happen while we weren't watching. Rick and I had to alternate nights "on Jamie" so that we could count on one night of unbroken sleep for every disrupted night. We heard from friends in the autism community that their daughter's grandmother had made one-piece pajamas with a back zipper that their daughter couldn't remove, and enlisted this grandmother, who lived several states away, to make all of Jamie's pajamas, too. In addition, we secured the pajamas with 8 or 10 diaper pins every night to keep Jamie's arms from wiggling out. Exhausted and disheartened, we started taking Jamie to a pediatric neurologist for regular visits. Explaining that improved sleep would be his first treatment priority, he prescribed a drug called Clonidine, which helped Jamie's (and our) sleep. During the next several months, we tried other medications, hoping to see Jamie's hyperactivity and autistic behaviors decrease. Although the sleep situation was easier to live with now, the hyperactivity persisted. Small doses of Clonidine throughout the day helped him to settle down, but sometimes he could become impossibly sleepy or cranky instead of calmer. It was a hard time.

When our Wisconsin consultant came during this period of regression, she redesigned Jamie's program so that he was working only on tasks that required very little attention. We virtually started over from the beginning with simple imitation, receptive commands ("Touch your nose"), matching, and puzzles. It was terribly hard to go backwards. Jamie had to experience some success, and beginning skills were the only way. For awhile, I played the part of cheerleader for everyone, but, finally, I had to leave in the middle of one of Jamie's workshops so that everyone wouldn't see me burst into tears. He couldn't even do the matching activity he had done when he was barely 2 years old! Thank goodness for the wonderful people in Jamie's home therapy and school teams. While I was nearly immobilized with despair, they kept his program going and made sure he stayed engaged.

It was painfully clear that Jamie needed another way to communicate. Years earlier, before he was 3 years old, our family consultant had encouraged me to begin using the Picture Exchange Communication System (PECS). She wasn't able to convince me to try it. I was afraid that using an augmentative form of communication would inhibit Jamie's speech. I was afraid that if Jamie didn't need to talk, he wouldn't talk. A few months after Jamie began to lose his ability to speak, our Wisconsin consultant advised us to start Jamie on PECS. I had been reluctant to take this step until I was sure that the speech was not coming back any time soon. I was finally ready. Jamie was now 6 years old, no longer in the PPCD, but in an elementary school Alternative Learning Environment (ALE) classroom. He was starting his fifth year of autism intervention.

It felt good to be working on something new. It didn't take long for Jamie to learn to hand us a picture in exchange for a desired treat. However, we reached a roadblock when we increased the number of pictures in Jamie's PECS vocabulary too fast. We had not studied the PECS techniques for teaching picture discrimination thoroughly enough. To progress, Jamie needed more effective teaching. Nearly a year after being introduced to the program, I was able to attend a full-day PECS workshop. That day made a tremendous difference. I was able to show Jamie's therapy team and teachers how to help Jamie learn to choose the picture that represented what he really wanted. If he handed us a picture of a paper towel instead of ice cream, he got a paper towel. When we helped him correct his mistake, he could have a bite of ice cream. He began to realize that he would get exactly what he asked for, and his picture discrimination started improving. I was hopeful that, with enough practice, Jamie would be able to make spontaneous requests using PECS, thus initiating his own communication. We practiced picture discrimination with PECS at every opportunity. Jamie had a PECS book for home and a PECS book for school. We could see that acquiring spontaneous communication through PECS would require a tremendous amount of patience, effort, commitment, and discipline, but it seemed to be our only choice.

A few weeks after the PECS workshop, I attended still another workshop presented by Vincent Carbone and Patrick McGreevy. They described a model for language development based on the work of Mark Sundberg and James Partington. Advocating a behavioral classification of language, they approach language from the point of view of the child. How is she using the word? Is she labeling something that her teacher asked her to identify? Is she asking for something she wants? According to behavioral classification of language, a word is defined by its functional category, rather than by its form. In our more conventional ABA program, we were used to thinking of words in terms of their form. We said that Jamie had mastered the word "cookie"

receptively if he could point to a cookie in an array, and that he had mastered it expressively if he could say it. We probably thought that it was important to make sure that Jamie could identify a cookie and say "cookie" before he asked for one. We were overlooking the power of motivation. We should have provided him first with a way to ask for a cookie.

At the workshop, I learned how to do just that. The best thing of all for me was that I learned that the fact that Jamie was no longer speaking didn't mean that he had to remain stuck where he was in his ABA program. I was introduced to a set of teaching methods that were built on the basic techniques of applied behavior analysis. At the same time, they directly addressed the struggles we had experienced since Jamie had stopped making progress. These methods would be harder for us as teachers than our old familiar ones, but they could make learning easier for Jamie. First, we made our teaching as errorless as possible by prompting before a probable incorrect response. We used faster paced instruction, presenting tasks one after another in quick "spurts," mixing and varying tasks from different skill areas, and interspersing easy tasks with difficult tasks. We also began teaching Jamie to respond fluently (quickly and correctly), not just correctly. Our ABA program became a lot more relaxed and natural.

The way we reinforced Jamie for correct responses changed, too, providing many more opportunities for communication throughout the day. He learned, from the beginning, to ask for his reinforcers. Because Jamie could not echo speech sounds, we would use hand-over-hand prompting to teach him to sign requests ("mands") using American Sign Language. Up to this point, I had simply refused to consider trying to teach Jamie to sign. I was sure that sign language would be too difficult for Jamie because his imitation skills, especially fine motor, were so weak.

We chose something highly motivating to teach Jamie for his first mand (a request or demand): vanilla ice cream. We modeled the sign for ice cream, reached over and got Jamie to form the sign with hand-over-hand prompting, simultaneously pronouncing "ice cream," and immediately rewarded him with a bite. It didn't take long for him to make the connection, and he began to roughly approximate the "ice cream" sign on his own. After that, he quickly acquired an accurate sign for candy. He was using language to get something he wanted. This was infinitely more exciting to Jamie than trying to learn to sign labels for household objects or pictures of animals. This wasn't a drill. This was communication.

With assistance from Dr. McGreevy and others, we have planned Jamie's program. Currently he is still a beginning learner, and his program will concentrate on manding and motor imitation. It will also include activities to encourage him to develop an echoic (that is, the ability to do vocal imitation). For motor imitation, we will teach Jamie the fine motor skills that he will need for future signs. When he is ready to learn a new sign, he will have had plenty of practice in the necessary motor skills. Right now, all of Jamie's signs will be mands. Our goal is to eventually give him hundreds of opportunities to mand each day. He will move to tacting (labeling) after he has acquired a strong base of 20 to 30 mands. Other functions of language will come later in the program, but we don't want to make the mistake of expanding to tact and other functions too soon. Manding is where the motivation is, and we have to keep Jamie motivated.

For months, I had believed that we should accept Jamie's rough approximations of signs because he was attempting to communicate. I was so afraid that he would be turned off and stop trying that I avoided shaping them up. It was time to let go of that fear, a holdover from the time Jamie stopped speaking. Dr. McGreevy emphasized that our goal is for Jamie to learn to sign so that the signing community can understand him. We can't be the only ones who know what he's saying. Because careful shaping of Jamie's signs will help him get what he wants, it won't discourage him. I find that I am more optimistic about Jamie's future learning. We still have much that we can do. Moreover, I am again gaining confidence in my teaching skills. (The experience of standing by helplessly and watching Jamie regress took its toll.) That confidence is important right now because I am in the process of passing along these skills to people (including Jamie's teacher and his dad) who weren't able to receive instruction directly from Dr. McGreevy.

We are fortunate that our school district is working closely with us on Jamie's signing program. Jamie's teacher and I plan the signs to be used in the classroom and at home, and we practice our teaching techniques to ensure consistency. Jamie now attends a full day of school, and receives an hour of individual therapy at school, along with one-to-one instruction throughout the day with his teacher, paraprofessionals, speech therapist, and occupational therapist. We still provide 8 to 12 hours a week of ABA in our home program.

When he arrives at school, Jamie selects his name, takes it off the chart, and puts it up to indicate that he has arrived. Jamie's name card displays his picture and is bordered in red. Every child in the class has a special color, and Jamie's is red. His towel and wash-cloth, cup and toothbrush, and storage container are all red. His individual picture schedule and the hook where he hangs up his backpack are also bordered in red. This color-coding is one of the visual supports that help the children throughout the day. He checks his schedule, then joins in an inclusive play period with volunteers from regular third- and fourth-grade classes. Later all five of the children in Jamie's class participate in physical education with typically developing kinder-gartners and first-graders. When we're out in the community with Jamie, kids from school often come up to say "hello," proudly telling their parents, "That's Jamie! He goes to my school." It's amazing to me that so many people whom I've never met know Jamie.

Breakfast and lunch times are full of opportunities for communication, socialization, and self-help skills and for trying new foods. Jamie tolerates a very narrow range of foods. Even though I now send most of Jamie's food with him (he is on a gluten-free, casein-free diet this year), he is often willing to eat a greater variety at school than at home. Every child must help as much as possible with mealtime cleanup. After breakfast, students work on hand and face washing, teeth brushing, and hair brushing. Toilet training is a main goal for all students, and I am pleased (and relieved) that Jamie has made so much progress in this area during the past 2 years. It's a true collaborative effort, testing everyone's patience and perseverance at home and at school. I have noticed that, just as he will try more foods at school than at home, Jamie is willing to be more independent in self-help skills at school than he is at home.

I find that picking up Jamie at the end of the school day helps prepare me for the afternoon and evening ahead. The school does more than just provide a learning environment for Jamie. It provides us with a group of people who, like an extended family, share our concerns. They lighten the burden of raising this enigmatic little boy, approaching the task with more patience and good humor than I can often muster. Their patience extends not just to Jamie, but also to me and Rick. They have supported, and continue to support, us through everything we try—changes in teaching methods and ways of communi-cating (like errorless teaching and sign language), changes in diet (no wheat, no milk, high fiber), and changes in medication (accompanied by Jamie's sometimes unpredictable reactions to them). They have been remarkably flexible, yet still able to maintain the secure and predictable environment so necessary for Jamie and all of his classmates. During the past 6 months, they have seen us through endless problems with Jamie's ears. When they were really hurting, despite the maximum allotted doses of children's ibuprofen, he went through a round of biting (probably as a way to communicate that he was in pain). After having surgery to remove his old ear tubes, persistent problems with healing have made it necessary for him to undergo uncomfortable weekly procedures at the doctor's office. Now we are trying to help Jamie through a different, but related problem—extreme anxiety. Some mornings he begins trembling and hyperventilating even before he gets out of bed. Our best guess is that the anxiety was somehow triggered by the painful medical experiences he has recently undergone. He seems to be asking, "What will they do to me next?"

Often he resists going inside even familiar places. I try to reassure him, repeating, "It's okay; no ears," over and over all the way in. The anxiousness is widespread and generalized, so we have our work cut out for us. When anyone asks Rick "How's your family?," he is always tempted to reply "Oh, we're about the same—lurching from one disaster to the next." Thank goodness for the people who help us make it through these disasters and to lurch from one to another a little less painfully and a little more gracefully.

SUMMARY

Evidence is overwhelming that professionals, parents, and other advocates who are involved in the lives of children and youth with autism have the potential to make enormous positive changes. Indeed, implementation of appropriate interventions at appropriate times in a child's life can result in amelioration of many overt characteristics associated with autism, along with significant improvement in the quality of life for these individuals and their families. However, strident debate and disagreement remain regarding which interventions hold the most promise and have the most efficacy. This problem of methodology choice and judgment is exacerbated by an ever-increasing number of available options, many of which offer undocumented claims of extraordinary benefit.

Related to these controversies, we offered in this chapter information and guidelines that may form the foundation for a solution. Guidelines for evaluating the efficacy, utility, and appropriateness of various treatments and interventions were given, along with a discussion of legal precedents aimed at addressing some of the issues related to developing appropriate programs for students with autism.

KEY POINTS

1. A lack of agreement exists regarding which treatments are best for students with autism

and related disorders, and this results in confusion and conflict among advocates.

2. In general, behaviorally-based approaches provide the strongest evidence of effectiveness.

3. In designing appropriate programs, teams of advocates need to have a framework to guide the decision-making process.

4. The decision-making framework should include questions about outcomes, potential risk, evaluation, evidence, and alternative interventions.

5. Programs fail for many reasons, including lack of a defined program, choosing popular rather than appropriate options, teaching dependency, using a "one-size-fits-all" approach, and lack of documentation.

REFERENCES

Alberto, P.A., & Troutman, A.C. (1999). *Applied behavior analysis for teachers* (5th ed.). Upper Saddle River, NJ: Merrill/Prentice Hall.

Allan, J.A.B. (1977). Some uses of "holding" with autistic children. *Special Education in Canada, 51*, 11–15.

An open letter to families considering intensive behavioral therapy for their child with autism. (1999). *The Communicator, 10*(1), 4–8.

Anderson, S.R., & Romanczyk, R.G. (1999). Early intervention for young children with autism: Continuum-based behavioral models. *Journal of the Association for Persons with Severe Handicaps, 24*, 162–173.

Autism Society of America. (1992–93, Winter). Facilitated communication under the microscope. *Advocate*, 19–20.

Ayers, J. (1972). *Sensory integration and learning disorders.* Los Angeles: Western Psychological.

Ayers, J. (1979). *Sensory integration and the child.* Los Angeles: Western Psychological.

Berard, G. (1993). *Hearing equals behavior* (translation, original 1982). New Canaan, CT: Keats.

Bettison, S. (1996). The long-term effects of auditory training on children with autism. *Journal of Autism and Developmental Disorders, 26*, 179–197.

Biklen, D. (1990). Communication unbound: Autism and praxis. *Harvard Educational Review, 60*, 291–314.

Biklen, D. (1992). Typing to talk: Facilitated communication. *American Journal of Speech and Language Pathology, 1*(2), 15–17.

Biklen, D. (1993). *Communication unbound: How facilitated communication is challenging traditional views of autism and ability/disability.* New York: Teachers College Press.

Board of Education of the Ann Arbor Public Schools. (1996). 24 IDELR 621.

Bondy, A., & Frost, L. (1994). The picture exchange communication system. *Focus on Autistic Behavior, 9*(3), 1–19.

Boomer, L.W., & Garrison-Harrell, L. (1995). Legal issues concerning children with autism and pervasive developmental disabilities. *Behavioral Disorders, 21,* 53–61.

Boucher, J., & Lewis, V. (1989). Memory impairments and communication in relatively able autistic children. *Journal of Child Psychology and Psychiatry, 30,* 90–122.

Calculator, S.N. (1992). Perhaps the emperor has clothes after all: A response to Biklen. *American Journal of Speech and Language Pathology, 1*(2), 18–20.

Campbell, M., Schopler, E., Cueva, J., & Hallin, A. (1996). Treatment of autistic disorder. *Journal of the American Academy of Child and Adolescent Psychiatry, 35,* 134–143.

Christopher, W., & Christopher, B. (1989). *Mixed blessings.* Nashville, TN: Abingdon Press.

Cohen, D.J., & Volkmar, F.R. (1997). Preface. In D.J. Cohen & F.R. Volkmar (Eds.), *Handbook of autism and pervasive developmental disorders* (2nd ed., pp. xv–xxi). New York: John Wiley & Sons.

Cohen, S. (1998). *Targeting autism: What we know, don't know, and can do to help young children with autism and related disorders.* Berkeley, CA: University of California Press.

Cordrey v. Euckert, 917 F. 2d. 1460 (6th Cir. 1990).

Crossley, R. (1988, October). *Unexpected communication attainments by persons diagnosed as autistic and intellectually impaired.* Paper presented at the International Society of Augmentative and Alternative Communication, Los Angeles, CA.

Crossley, R. (1992). Who said that? In DEAL Communication Centre (Ed.), *Facilitated communication training* (pp. 42–54). Melbourne, Australia: DEAL Communication Centre.

Dalrymple, N. (1995). Environmental supports to develop flexibility and independence. In K.A. Quill (Ed.), *Teaching children with autism: Strategies to enhance socialization and communication* (pp. 243–264). Albany, NY: Delmar Publishers.

De Gangi, G.A. & Greenspan, S.I. (1997). The effectiveness of short-term interventions in treatment of inattention and irritability in toddlers. *Journal of Developmental and Learning Disorders, 1,* 277-278.

Delaware Co. IU #25 v. Martin K., 831 F. Supp. 1206, 1211 (E.D. Pa. 1993).

Department of Education. (1999). 34 CFR Parts 300 and 303. *Federal Register, 64,* 12406–12535.

Donnelly, J.A. (1996, July–September). The pros and cons of discrete trial training: Is the "Lovaas" behavior modification method appropriate for my student? *Autism Update, 20.*

Earles, T., Carlson, J., & Bock, S. (1998). Instructional strategies to facilitate successful learning outcomes for students with autism. In R. Simpson & B. Myles (Eds.), *Educating children and youth with autism: Strategies for effective practices* (pp. 55–111). Austin, TX: Pro-Ed.

Eric S. v. Duncanville Independent School District. (1984–85). EHLR 506:281.

Fisher, A., & Murray, E. (1991). Introduction to sensory integration theory. In A. Fisher, E. Murray, & A. Bondy (Eds.), *Sensory integration theory and practice* (pp. 3–27). Philadelphia: Davis.

Fox, L., Dunlap, G., & Philbrick, L.A. (1997). Providing individual supports to young children with autism and their families. *Journal of Early Intervention, 21,* 1–14.

Freeman, B.J. (1993). Questions to ask regarding specific treatment. *The Advocate, 25*(2), 19.

Freeman, B.J. (1997). Guidelines for evaluation intervention programs for children with autism. *Journal of Autism and Developmental Disorders, 27,* 641–651.

Frost, L.A., & Bondy, A. (1994). *The picture exchange communication system training manual.* Cherry Hill, NJ: Pyramid Educational Consultants.

Giangreco, M.F., Edelman, S.W., Luiselli, T.E., & MacFarland, S.Z.C. (1997). Helping or hovering? Effects of instructional assistant proximity on students with disabilities. *Exceptional Children, 64,* 7–18.

Gillberg, C. (1992). The Emmanuel Miller Memorial Lecture 1991. Autism and autistic-like conditions: Subclasses among disorders of empathy. *Journal of Child Psychology and Psychiatry, 33,* 813-842.

Gillberg, C., Johansson, M., Steffenburg, S., & Berlin, O. (1997). Auditory integration training in children with autism. *Autism: The International Journal of Research and Practice, 1,* 97-100.

Grandin, T. (1995). *Thinking in pictures.* New York: Doubleday.

Gray, C. (1995). Teaching children with autism to "read" social situations. In K.A. Quill (Ed.), *Teaching children with autism: Strategies to enhance socialization and* communication (pp. 219–241). Albany, NY: Delmar Publishers.

Gray, C., & Garand, J. (1993). Social stories: Improving responses of students with autism with accurate social information. *Focus on Autistic Behavior, 8,* 1–10.

Green, G. (1999). Science, pseudoscience and antiscience: What's this got to do with my kid? *Science in Autism Treatment, 1*(1), 5–7.

Greenspan, S.I. (1992a). Reconsidering the diagnosis and treatment of very young children with autistic spectrum or pervasive developmental disorder. *Zero to Three, 13*(2), 1–9.

Greenspan, S.I. (1992b). *Infancy and early childhood: The practice of clinical assessment and intervention with emotional and developmental challenges.* Madison, CT: International Universities Press.

Greenspan, S.I., & Wieder, S. (1997). Developmental patterns and outcomes in infants and children with disorders in relating and communicating: A chart review of 200 cases of children with autistic spectrum diagnoses. *Journal of Developmental and Learning Disorders, 1,* 87–141.

Greenspan, S.I., & Wieder, S. (1998). The child with special needs: *Encouraging intellectual and emotional growth.* Reading, MA: Addison-Wesley.

Gresham, F.M., & MacMillan, D.L. (1997). Autistic recovery? An analysis and critique of the empirical evidence on the Early Intervention Project. *Behavioral Disorders, 22,* 185–201.

Hagiwara, T., & Myles, B.S. (1999). A multimedia social story intervention: Teaching skills to children with autism. *Focus on Autism and Other Developmental Disabilities, 14,* 82–95.

Hanft, B.E., & Feinberg, E. (1997). Toward the development of a framework for determining the frequency and intensity of early intervention services. *Infants and Young Children, 10,* 27–37.

Hart, C. (1995). Teaching children with autism. What parents want. In K.A. Quill (Ed.), *Teaching children with autism: Strategies to enhance communication and socialization* (pp. 53–69). Albany, NY: Delmar Publishers.

Heflin, L.J., & Simpson, R.L. (1998). Interventions for children and youth with autism: Prudent choices in a world of exaggerated claims and empty promises. Part II: Legal/policy analysis and recommendations for selecting interventions and treatments. *Focus on Autism and Other Developmental Disabilities, 13,* 212–220.

Henry, T. (1998, March 11). Boy with autism gets hard lesson in court. *USA Today,* pp. 1D–2D.

Hermelin, B., & O'Conner, N. (1970). *Psychological experiments with autistic children.* London: Pergamon.

High Bridge Board of Education. (1995). 24 IDELR 589.

Hodgdon, L. (1995). *Visual strategies for improving communication.* Troy, MI: QuirkRoberts.

Independent School District No. 318 (1996), 24 IDELR 1096.

Izeman, S. (1996, Winter). Points to ponder. *Coalition Quarterly: Early Childhood Bulletin,* pp. 1–2.

Johnson v. Independent School District No. 4 of Bixby, 921 F. 2d. 1022 (10th Cir. 1990).

Kaufman, B.N. (1976). *Son-rise.* New York: Harper & Row.

Kaufman, B.N. (1994). *Son-rise: The miracle continues.* Tiburon, CA: H.J. Kramer.

Klin, A., & Cohen, D.J. (1997). Ethical issues in research and treatment. In D.J. Cohen & F.R. Volkmar (Eds.), *Handbook of autism and pervasive developmental disorders* (2nd ed., pp. 828–841). New York: John Wiley & Sons.

Krueger, S. (1996, October 17). OT makes the difference for a sensory defensive client. *OT Work,* 18-19.

Kuttler, S., Myles, B.S., & Carlson, J.K. (1998). The use of social stories to reduce precursors to tantrum behavior in a student with autism. *Focus on Autism and Other Developmental Disabilities, 13,* 176–182.

Lehr, S., & Lehr, B. (1997, November). *Scientists and parents of children with autism: What do we know? How do we judge what is right?* Draft paper distributed at the Autism National Committee and Greater Georgia ASA Conference, Decatur, GA.

Logan, K.R., Bakeman, R., & Keefe, E.G. (1997). Effects of instructional variables on engaged behavior of students with disabilities in general education classrooms. *Exceptional Children, 63,* 481–497.

Lovaas, O.I. (1987). Behavioral treatment and normal educational and intellectual functioning in young autistic children. *Journal of Consulting and Clinical Psychology, 55,* 3–9.

MacDuff, G., Krantz, P., & McClannahan, L. (1993). Teaching children with autism to use pictographic activity schedules: Maintenance and generalization of complex response chains. *Journal of Applied Behavior Analysis, 26,* 89–97.

MacFarland, S.Z.C. (1995). Teaching strategies of the van Dijk curricular approach. *Journal of Visual Impairment and Blindness, 89,* 222–228.

Mark Hartmann v. Loudoun County Board of Education (1997). [On-line]. Available: http://lw.bna.com/lw/19970722/962809.html

Marks, S.U., Schrader, C., & Levine, M. (1999). Paraeducator experiences in inclusive settings: Helping, hovering, or holding their own? *Exceptional Children, 65,* 315–328.

Maurice, C. (1993). *Let me hear your voice: A family's triumph over autism.* New York: Ballantine.

Maurice, C. (Ed.). (1996). *Behavioral interventions for young children with autism: A manual for parents and professionals.* Austin, TX: Pro-Ed.

McGee, J.J., & Gonzalez, L. (1990). Gentle teaching and the practice of human interdependence: A preliminary group study of 15 persons with severe behavioral disorders and their caregivers. In A.C. Repp & N.N. Singh (Eds.), *Perspectives on the use of nonaversive and aversive interventions for persons with developmental disabilities* (pp. 237–254). Sycamore, IL: Sycamore.

McGee, J.J., Menolascino, F.J., Hobbs, D.C., & Menousek, P.E. (1987). *Gentle teaching: A nonaversive approach to helping persons with mental retardation.* New York: Human Sciences Press.

Mesibov, G.B. (1994). A comprehensive program for serving people with autism and their families: The TEACCH model. In J.L. Matson (Ed.), *Autism in children and adults: Etiology, assessment and intervention* (pp. 85–97). Belmont, CA: Brooks/Cole.

Mirenda, P., & Santogrossi, J. (1985). A prompt-free strategy to teach pictorial communication system use. *Augmentative and Alternative Communication, 1,* 143–150.

Mudford, O.C. (1995). Review of the gentle teaching data. *American Journal on Mental Retardation, 99,* 345-355.

Mulick, J.A., Jacobson, J.W., & Kobe, F.H. (1993). Anguished silence and helping hands: Autism and facilitated communication. *Skeptical Inquirer, 17* (3), 270–280.

Nickel, R.E. (1996). Controversial therapies for young children with developmental disabilities. *Infants and Young Children, 8*(4), 29–40.

Options Institute (1999). Autism Treatment Center of America: Son-Rise program. Available from: http://sonrise@option.org.

Powers, M.D. (1992). Early intervention for children with autism. In D. Berkell (Ed.), *Autism: Identification, education and treatment* (pp. 225–252). Hillsdale, NJ: Erlbaum.

Prior, M., & Cummins, R. (1992). Questions about facilitated communication. *Journal of Autism and Developmental Disorders, 22,* 331–338.

Quill, K. (1997). Instructional considerations for young children with autism: The rationale for visually cued instruction. *Journal of Autism and Developmental Disorders, 27,* 697–714.

Ricks, D.M., & Wing, L. (1976). Language, communication, and the use of symbols in normal and autistic children. In J.K. Wing (Ed.), *Early childhood autism: Clinical, social, and educational aspects.* Oxford : Pergamon.

Rimland, B. (1992). A facilitated communication "horror story." *Autism Research Review, 6*(1), 1, 7.

Rimland, B., & Edelson, S. (1994). The effects of auditory integration training on autism. *American Journal of Speech-Language Pathology, 3,* 16–24.

Schopler, E. (1992). Facilitated communication—hope or hype? *Autism Society of North Carolina, 8*(3), 6.

Schopler, E., Mesibov, G.B., & Hearsey, K. (1995). Structured teaching in the TEACCH system. In E. Schopler & G.B. Mesibov (Eds.), *Learning and cognition in autism* (pp. 243–268). New York: Plenum Press.

Siegel-Causey, E., & Guess, D. (1989). *Enhancing nonsymbolic communication interactions among learners with severe disabilities.* Baltimore, MD: Paul H. Brookes.

Sigman, M. & Ungerer, J.A. (1984). Attachment behaviors in autistic children. *Journal of Autism and Developmental Disorders, 14,* 231-244.

Simpson, R.L. (1995). Children and youth with autism in an age of reform: A perspective on current issues. *Behavioral Disorders, 21,* 7–20.

Simpson, R.L., & Myles, B.S. (1995). Effectiveness of facilitated communication with children and youth with autism. *Journal of Special Education, 28,* 424–439.

Simpson, R.L., & Sasso, G.M. (1992). Full inclusion of students with autism in general education settings: Values versus science. *Focus on Autistic Behavior, 7* (3), 1–13.

Smith, T. (1996). Are other treatments effective? In C. Maurice (Ed.), *Behavioral Intervention for Young Children with Autism: A Manual for Parents and Professionals.* Austin, TX: Pro-Ed.

Stades-Veth, J. (1988). Autism broken symbiosis: Persistent avoidance of eye contact with the mother. Causes, consequences, prevention, and cure of autistic form behavior in babies through "mother-child holding." (ERIC Document Reproduction Service No. Ed. 294-344).

Stehli, A. (1991). *The Sound of a Miracle: A child's triumph over autism.* New York: Doubleday.

Stillman, R.D., & Battle, C.W. (1984). Developing prelanguage communication in the severely handicapped: An interpretation of the van Dijk method. *Seminars in Speech and Language, 5,* 159–170.

Swaggart, B., Gagnon, E., Bock, S.J., Earles, T., Quinn, C., Myles, B.S., & Simpson, R. (1995). Using social stories to teach social and behavioral skills to children with autism. *Focus on Autistic Behavior, 10,* 1–14.

Szempruch, J., & Jacobson, J.W. (1993). Evaluating facilitated communication of people with developmental disabilities. *Research in Developmental Disabilities, 14,* 253–264.

Tinbergen, N., & Tinbergen, E. A. (1983). *"Autistic" children: New hope for a cure.* London: Allen and Unwin.

Trachtman, P. (1994, September). NIH looks at the implausible and the inexplicable. *Smithsonian*, 110–123.

van Dijk, J. (1967). The non-verbal deaf-blind child and his world: His outgrowth toward the world of symbols. *Proceedings of the Jaarverslag Instituut voor Doven, 1964–1967* (pp. 73–110). Sint Michielsgestgel, The Netherlands: Instituut voor Doven.

van Dijk, J. (1986). An educational curriculum for deaf-blind multihandicapped persons. In D. Ellis (Ed.), *Sensory impairments in mentally handicapped people* (pp. 374–382). London: Croom-Helm.

Wang, M.C., & Walberg, H.J. (1988). Four fallacies of segregationism. *Exceptional Children, 55,* 128–137.

Welch, M.G. (1988). Mother-child holding therapy and autism. *Pennsylvania Medicine, 91* (10), 33–38.

Wheeler, D., Jacobson, J., Paglieri, R., & Schwartz, A. (1993). An experimental assessment of facilitated communication. *Mental Retardation, 31,* 49–60.

Wieder, S. (1996). Integrated treatment approaches for young children with multisystem developmental disorder. *Infants and Young Children, 8* (3), 24–34.

Wilbarger, P., & Wilbarger, J. (1991). *Sensory defensiveness in children ages 2–12: An intervention guide for parents and other caretakers.* Denver, CO: Avanti Educational Programs.

Wimmer, H., & Perner, J. (1983). Beliefs about beliefs: Representation and constraining function of wrong beliefs in young children's understanding of deception. *Cognition, 13,* 103-128.

Wolfberg, P., & Schuler, A. (1993). Integrated play groups: A model for promoting the social and cognitive dimensions of play. *Journal of Autism and Developmental Disorders, 23,* 1–23.

Yell, M. (1998). *The law and special education.* Upper Saddle River, NJ: Merrill/Prentice Hall.

Zaslow, R.W., & Breger, L. (1969). A theory and treatment for autism. In L. Breger (Ed.), *Clinical Cognitive Psychology* (pp. 246–289). Englewood Cliffs, NJ: Prentice Hall.

Index